Understanding American Jewry

Understanding American Jewry

Edited by
Marshall Sklare

Center for Modern Jewish Studies
Brandeis University

Transaction Books
New Brunswick (U.S.A.) and London (U.K.)

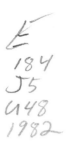

Library of Congress Catalog Number: 81-14795
ISBN: 0-87855-454-8 (Cloth)
Printed in the United States of America

Library of Congress Cataloging in Publication Data

Main entry under title:

Understanding American Jewry.

    Papers delivered at the Planning Conference for a Center for Modern Jewish Studies which took place on the Brandeis campus on Oct. 21-24, 1979.
    Includes bibliographical references and index.
    1. Jews — United States — Research — Congresses. 2. Judaism — United States — Research — Congresses. 3. Brandeis University. Center for Modern Jewish Studies — Congresses. 4. United States — Ethnic relations — Research — Congresses. I. Sklare, Marshall, 1921- . II. Brandeis University. Center for Modern Jewish Studies. III. Planning Conference for a Center for Modern Jewish Studies (1979 : Brandeis University)
E184.J5U48   973'.04924072   81-14795
ISBN 0-87855-454-8   AACR2

Contents

List of Participants

Planning Conference for a Center for Modern Jewish Studies*

Herbert Bienstock
    Regional Commissioner of Labor Statistics, Bureau of Labor Statistics, U.S. Department of Labor

Saul Cohen
    President, Queens College of the City University of New York

Lucy Dawidowicz
    Author and Historian, New York, N.Y.

Daniel J. Elazar
    Chairman, Center for Jewish Community Studies; Professor of Political Science, Bar-Ilan University and Temple University

Eli N. Evans
    President, Charles H. Revson Foundation

Roy E. Feldman
    Senior Research Associate, Regional Institute on Employment Policy, Boston University

Marvin Fox
    Director, Philip W. Lown School of Near Eastern and Judaic Studies; Chairman, Department of Near Eastern and Judaic Studies; Professor of Jewish Philosophy, Brandeis University

Calvin Goldscheider
    Chairman, Department of Demography and Associate Professor of Sociology and Demography, Hebrew University

Sidney Goldstein
    Professor of Sociology, Brown University; Director, Population Studies and Training Center, Brown University

Benjamin Halpern
> Professor of Near Eastern Studies, Brandeis University

Simon Herman
> Professor of Psychology, Institute of Contemporary Jewry and Department of Psychology, Hebrew University

Harold S. Himmelfarb
> Associate Professor of Sociology, Ohio State University

Leon A. Jick
> Associate Professor of American Jewish Studies, Brandeis University

Nathan Kaganoff
> Librarian-Editor, American Jewish Historical Society

Sheila Kamerman
> Associate Professor of Social Policy, Columbia University School of Social Work

Drora Kass
> Psychologist, New York, N.Y.

Samuel Z. Klausner
> Professor of Sociology, University of Pennsylvania; Director, Center for Research on the Acts of Man

Neal Kozodoy
> Executive Editor, *Commentary*

Charles S. Liebman
> Professor of Political Studies, Bar-Ilan University

Seymour M. Lipset
> Professor of Political Science and Sociology, Stanford University

Bruce Phillips
> Research Director, Planning and Budget Department, Jewish Federation Council of Greater Los Angeles

Earl Raab
> Director, Jewish Community Relations Council, San Francisco

Bernard Reisman
> Director, Hornstein Program for Jewish Communal Service; Associate Professor of American Jewish Communal Studies, Brandeis University

David Resnick
>Acting Dean of the Seminary College of Jewish Studies; Assistant Professor of Education, Jewish Theological Seminary of America

Charles Silberman
>Author, New York, N.Y.

Ira Silverman
>Director of Special Programs, American Jewish Committee

Marshall Sklare
>Professor of Contemporary Jewish Studies and Sociology, Brandeis University

Chaim I. Waxman
>Associate Professor and Chairman, Department of Sociology, University College, Rutgers University

Stephen J. Whitfield
>Associate Professor of American Studies, Brandeis University

Jonathan Woocher
>Assistant Professor of Jewish Communal Service, Brandeis University

Note

*Titles are current as of the date of the Conference (October 21–24, 1979).

Preface

The last two decades have seen the rapid growth of Jewish studies at American universities. In some cases this growth has resulted in the development of departments of Jewish studies, though in most cases what has been established are interdepartmental programs. There are of course more than a few campuses which have not taken part in this development, or where only one or two appointments have been made to teach that vast array of subjects collectively known as "Jewish studies."

It was natural that as a result of the growth of Jewish studies programs thought would eventually be given to the establishment of research centers which would organize projects and programs beyond the resources of a single faculty member. In the past several decades centers related in one way or another to the contemporary world have proliferated at research-oriented universities. These research institutes were sometimes organized on an area-wide basis and included Russian and East European research centers, Southeast Asian research centers, and Latin American research centers. Research centers specifically American in orientation generally focused on subject or problem areas: the family, aging, crime, poverty, juvenile delinquency, demography. It was to be expected that at some point concerned individuals would begin thinking about a research center on contemporary Jewish studies.

The need for a center on contemporary Jewish studies, and more specifically on American-Jewish studies, was reinforced by the absence of such facilities. American-Jewish organizations had not succeeded in maintaining research divisions over a continuous period of years. Even the most research-minded Jewish organizations generally have only a very small in-house staff. They contract out investigations of a substantial character. While such research may occasionally be more than service-oriented, most Jewish organizations have not moved in the direction of conducting basic research. The rare organizations specifically established to promote research are generally not strong agencies and have not succeeded in fulfilling the ambitions of their founders. None of the Hebrew colleges have sponsored research institutes in the field of contemporary Jewish studies. The same has been true for rabbinical seminaries despite their expansion into new activities and projects.

The most widely known research institution in the field of contemporary Jewish studies is located in Jerusalem: the Institute of Contemporary Jewry of the Hebrew University. The Institute sponsors a variety of research programs but does relatively little in the field of American-Jewish studies. It concentrates its attention on diaspora communities small in size and weak in scholarly resources. The work of the Institute is supplemented by another agency with headquarters in Jerusalem: the Center for Jewish Community Studies. The Center engages mainly in contract research.

At various points in its brief history, faculty members and administrative officials of Brandeis University have given thought to the establishment of a research facility in the area of contemporary Jewish studies. The history of Jewish studies at Brandeis has some singular features. The Department of Near Eastern and Judaic Studies came into being soon after the university was opened. Thus Jewish studies at Brandeis established its identity and importance from the earliest days of the university. Jewish studies at Brandeis is organized in the form of a department with its own roster of faculty. The department seeks to include instruction and research from earliest antiquity to the contemporary period. And since the university sponsors a training program for Jewish communal service (the Hornstein Program in Jewish Communal Service) this facility has had an obvious interest in contemporary Jewish studies.

In 1978 university officials met with the Charles H. Revson Foundation to discuss the possibility of a grant for a center for contemporary Jewish studies. The Foundation was interested but felt that a conference should be convoked to assess the state of the field and the feasibility of such a center. A generous grant from the Foundation enabled us to hold a conference entitled Planning Conference for a Center for Modern Jewish Studies, which took place on the Brandeis campus on October 21–24, 1979.

Understanding American Jewry consists of the papers delivered at that conference.* As director of the conference the most difficult part of my task was limiting the agenda to a manageable number of topics. The majority of the papers were to be devoted to substantive areas on which a center might do research. Thus the number of possible subjects far exceeded what might profitably be discussed at a single conference. Seven topics survived the scrutiny of my associates and myself: (1) demography; (2) Jewish identity; (3) religion and religious life; (4) Jewish education; (5) the family; (6) the Jewish community; and (7) anti-Semitism and intergroup relations. In addition, a paper was commissioned on the subject of recent immigration to the United States, especially immigration of Jews from the Soviet Union and from Israel.

We were fortunate to find able scholars for each of these topics. In the case of the family two papers were commissioned — one from a researcher who had worked chiefly in the area of the family in Western society, and the second from a researcher whose primary area of interest was in the Jewish family. Each author of a substantive paper was asked to review the relevant literature, assess the state of research in the field, formulate research needs, and provide suggestions for specific projects.

It was apparent to us that the type of research center we had in mind would have to build relationships with the Jewish community, and more specifically with the agencies and institutions which play a vital role in that community. As a result two further papers were commissioned. One paper deals with the research needs of national Jewish agencies and the other with those of local agencies. I presented a paper on quite a different topic: the preparation of a sociology of American Jewry.

Not every conference has a happy ending. It is a pleasure to record the fact that the Planning Conference for a Center for Modern Jewish Studies had a positive result. The Revson Foundation was encouraged by the papers prepared for the conference and by the discussion which took place. Brandeis University's proposal for a grant was acted upon favorably and the Center for Modern Jewish Studies formally came into existence in July 1980. Its name is ambitious — for the immediate future the Center will concentrate on selected topics in American Jewish studies with special emphasis on the contemporary period. On a longer range we hope to expand the scope of the Center and deal with other aspects of modern Jewish studies.

In addition to research the Center recognizes the need to train graduate students and thus to supply in the years ahead a cadre of individuals qualified to teach and do research in the field of contemporary Jewish studies. The teaching activities of Center staff will also serve to enrich undergraduate offerings at Brandeis in contemporary Jewish studies. Finally the Center looks forward to collaborative efforts with other agencies. It welcomes the establishment of institutions with related objectives at other universities both in the United States and abroad.

It is a pleasure to record the thanks of the university, as well as my own gratitude, to the Revson Foundation, and particularly to its president, Eli Evans. His interest was manifest from the start and his encouragement gave us the drive to forge ahead. It should be noted that this book was made possible by funds granted by the Charles H. Revson Foundation. The statements made and views expressed, however, are solely the responsibility of the authors.

Brandeis President Marver H. Bernstein also provided much encouragement. His support for the development of the Center was a crucial ingredient in its establishment. President Bernstein has a long and distinguished record of participation in Jewish communal activity. I am grateful that President Bernstein's interest has been supported by the dean of faculty at Brandeis, Jack S. Goldstein. Dean Goldstein has made important contributions to our effort to establish this new facility. Abram L. Sachar, chancellor emeritus of Brandeis University, has expressed a deep interest in this endeavor and has offered us every encouragement.

The Center owes a considerable debt of gratitude to Professor Marvin Fox who serves as director of the University's Lown School of Near Eastern and Judaic Studies. Professor Fox manifested his interest and concern with the field of contemporary Jewish studies on numerous occasions when we were engaged in planning the Center. While an authority in medieval Jewish philosophy, Professor Fox has a strong belief in the unity of all Jewish studies. He is blessed with the ability to understand needs in fields of study quite different from the one in which he specializes.

I should also like to record my gratitude to Anne Meixsell, Gerald Showstack, and Nancy Leathers for their help in assuring the success of the conference.

Marshall Sklare

Note

*Samuel Z. Klausner presented a paper on the genesis and organization of research centers. However, because the paper was not in the field of contemporary Jewish studies we concluded that it would be more appropriate to publish it elsewhere.

1.

Demography of Jewish Americans: Research Findings, Issues, and Challenges

Calvin Goldscheider

Social scientists have long recognized the centrality of population processes for understanding the evolution of the American Jewish community and the changing levels of integration of Jewish Americans. The major features of American Jewish demography are well known, but neither the demographers who have analyzed those patterns nor the social scientists who have used information on population processes have been satisfied with the quality of demographic data or the depth of demographic analyses. This chapter reviews and summarizes what is generally known about the demography of Jewish Americans, with particular attention to the limitations of available research. A concluding section focuses on a series of research suggestions and priorities that emerge from the critical review of what is known about the demography of the American Jewish community.

Demography of American Jews: Scope and Analytic Issues

The analysis of American Jewish demographic patterns involves a number of central themes, some of which are common to a general demographic analysis of total societies while others are unique to the demography of minority groups. It is important to spell out the scope and focus of our review and evaluation. First, a systematic examination of the demography of American Jews involves an analysis of the entire range of population elements and processes. The study of population size, growth, distribution, structure, and composition[1] is integral to demographic analysis regardless of the unit of analysis. This is also true for the population processes of mortality, fertility, and migration. For the Jewish population as for other subgroup analyses, an additional process of "entering" and "exiting" must be examined: in- and out-marriages. The study of losses and gains through intermarriage is a central feature of the demography of

1

minority groups. Minority populations increase in size through births, immigration, and in-marriages; they decrease in size through deaths, emigration, and out-marriages. Population changes and variations are products of these exiting and entering processes. At the local level, immigration and emigration are of particular significance. Because of the importance of the timing and extent of marriage for reproduction and childbearing, demographic analysis also treats issues of nuptiality and dissolution (divorce and separation).

A second feature of minority group demography is the need to select among a wider range of comparisons for analysis. The population processes of a minority group may be compared to the majority population and/or to other minority/ethnic groups. One of the central analytic questions in the demography of minority groups is whether demographic differences between majority and minority populations are reflections of the particular matrix of socioeconomic characteristics differentiating these populations or whether particular features of the ethnic group influence demographic processes. These features may relate to cultural or structural differences or to the fact of minority group status per se. The centrality of this issue requires that comparisons be made between minority and majority populations, controlling for socioeconomic and related characteristics. A further comparison in the demography of American Jews involves Jews in other countries. Such comparisons clarify the uniqueness of the American Jewish condition or the differences between Jews in situations of a minority and those in a society where Jews are a majority.

Another important type of sociological and demographic analysis associated with the study of minority subpopulations relates to the question of residential clustering. There is a series of complex issues associated with residential segregation and integration of minority groups and the implications of the changing population concentration, dispersal, and density of subgroups within society. For the Jewish population, residential segregation and integration are tied in to the intensity of Jewish identification and related issues of Jewish community organization.

Although minority subgroups tend to be smaller and relatively more homogeneous units of analysis than total societies, there remains sufficient subgroup variation within ethnic groups to allow for detailed investigation. The analysis of variation within the Jewish group provides clues to the direction of change in which the Jewish group as a whole may be moving. The examination of subgroups in the forefront of change (the more educated, the young, or the elite) is one basis for projecting the future direction of the total community. This is particularly important when trend data or longitudinal analyses are lacking.

Finally, the implications of demographic patterns for minority and majority populations may vary. Rates of growth, distribution, composition and levels of mortality, fertility, and migration may have different consequences for minority populations. Zero population growth has a set of consequences for a total society, for example, that cannot be uniformly applied to every subpopulation. Policies to control, regulate, or channel population growth and processes applied to total nations do not necessarily fit the goals, needs, and aspirations of selected ethnic segments. There are a variety of socio-politico-economic consequences of differential population growth of majority and minority/ethnic populations. Minority populations that are rapidly increasing in size within a society whose rate of demographic growth is stable are as problematic as minority populations that are declining or stable while the total population is expanding rapidly.

The heart of the demographic argument is that there have been and continue to be revolutionary changes, subtle but of profound importance, in the size, growth, composition, and distribution of the American Jewish population and in the demographic processes shaping these patterns. These demographic changes are critical for understanding modern American Jewish life, primarily because they reflect and have implications for the quality of Jewish life in America — and the quality of Jewish life is the key to Jewish survival. Population size is a necessary but not sufficient condition for survival; the immediate Jewish future in America is tied to questions of quantity only indirectly. However, since demographic patterns are consequences and determinants of Jewish life in America, the analysis of American Jewish demography provides a context within which Jewish quality can be evaluated.

The less disputed meaning of demographic patterns and their clearer documentation and trend must be balanced by the fact that some demographic changes are subtle and it is often difficult to appreciate their long-term implications and repercussions. While a decline in financial support for Jewish organizations may be immediately appreciated, declining birth rates, changing marriage patterns, and increasing population age take a longer time to be documented and absorbed as social facts. Of primary importance, the demographic processes that affect population size, composition, and distribution are extraordinarily difficult to reverse unless some of the basic values, attitudes, and social processes change. Jewish demographic processes are integral to the social conditions of American Jewish life, not marginal or independent of social structure. To change, redirect, or channel population trends, the societal context must also be altered. Jewish demographic patterns fit the pattern of American Jewish life and may be viewed as the price paid by American Jews for their level of commitment to Jewish survival. To reverse demographic patterns, some major commitments of American Jewry have to be reordered in priority.

Population structure has an internal set of dynamics as well. Past patterns of immigration and fertility, for example, have an impact on current and future age structure. The number of births in the 1970s will have effects on marriage and reproduction around the turn of the century and on patterns of aging well into the twenty-first century. Issues of quantitative and qualitative Jewish survival must be considered not only in a national American Jewish context but also in the local Jewish community system where size and quality are more obviously correlated. Within this context, demographic variation and heterogeneity dominate; population size and processes vary among Jewish communities in the United States. Differentiation among them is related to the density of Jewish settlement, the demographic and social composition of local areas, the degree of local population dispersal, generational composition, and the broader socioeconomic opportunities of areas that retain population and encourage immigration or lose population through out-migration.

Sources of Demographic Data on the American Jewish Population

To evaluate the demographic patterns of Jewish Americans, assess research issues, and identify research priorities, a brief review of the sources of demographic data for studying American Jews will be presented. More specific data problems will be reviewed in the discussion of particular demographic processes (for earlier reviews of data on religion see Good, 1959; Landis, 1959; Goldstein, 1971; Engelman, 1947).

Traditional sources of demographic data are largely unavailable for studying the size, growth, distribution, composition, and characteristics of the American Jewish population or for the analysis of the demographic processes of fertility, mortality, and migration. These sources include regular decennial censuses and a continuous system of birth and death registration. In the United States these sources have never included a question on religious preference or affiliation. Indirect and useful data from American censuses may be obtained for the Jewish population through an analysis of those reporting Yiddish as their mother tongue and data on the Russian-born and ethnic populations that reflect segments (and in earlier periods the overwhelming majority) of the American Jewish population. Analysis of these data has been restricted to the selected tabular material published by the Census Bureau. As the proportion of second and third generations in the American Jewish population increases, the value of these indirect data decreases (see particularly Goldberg, 1945–46, 1948, 1962; Rosenthal, 1975).

The utility of annual birth and death records is more limited. In addition to the absence of information by religion, analysis of these data requires detailed information on population size, structure, and distribution obtained from census-type data unavailable for the Jewish population. Birth and death records may be useful in local communities when supplementary sources of information on Jewish births (from hospital records) and deaths (from funeral directors and/or Jewish cemeteries) are available. This would require problematic individual record-matching. Birth and death records may also be allocated to small subareas (e.g. census tracts) where there is a high proportion of Jewish population concentration. Since an analysis of annual birth and death rates requires two sets of problematic data for American Jews, only limited attempts to exploit these data have been made.

Annual marriage and divorce statistics in the United States do not contain data on religious affiliation (except for the marriage records of Iowa and Indiana). Government statistics on immigration have included information on Jews (Hebrews) for 1881–1943, but except for selected characteristics (numbers, age, sex, previous occupation, and country of origin), details are not available (Lestschinsky, 1960; Hersch, 1949).

To obtain intercensal population estimates and identify continual changes in socioeconomic and labor force characteristics, fertility, geographic mobility, and migration of the American population, the U.S. government carries out a series of annual surveys. The Current Population Survey included a question on religion only once (in 1957) and provided national data on the socioeconomic and geographic characteristics of the Jewish population as well as information on fertility and intermarriage. These data have been fully exploited and represent a unique and important data source in American Jewish demography (Glick, 1960; Goldstein, 1969; Mueller and Lane, 1972; U.S. Bureau of the Census, 1958).

A final source of data of limited utility has been the federally sponsored Censuses of Religious Bodies. These were limited to reports from organizations and community institutions rather than individuals. The last such census was conducted in 1936 and, owing to its limited usefulness for government or community planning, has been discontinued (Engelman, 1947).

All official data sources have limitations for in-depth research, even for the American population as a whole, since the amount of socioeconomic data included is minimal. Detailed national sample surveys have been undertaken, particularly on fertility and related patterns. Owing to the small proportion of Jews in the total American population, representative samples include only a small number of Jews for analysis. Not only are details unavailable, but high rates of sampling errors characterize these sources for the study of American Jewish demography (see the review in Goldscheider, 1967, 1971; and detailed discussion below).

Given the limitations of official data sources and general sample surveys for the analysis of Jewish demographic patterns, an increasing number of local Jewish community surveys have been undertaken. These surveys provide basic demographic information on the structure and composition of the Jewish population and often include questions on fertility and migration. In most cases these surveys have been sponsored by local Jewish Federations and have been useful for planning purposes. Often data details have not been published, and only simple cross-tabulations have been prepared. The major limitations of these Jewish surveys relate to the degree to which scientific sampling criteria are used and whether nonaffiliated segments of the Jewish population are included. These surveys are extremely uneven in quality. Often intercommunity comparisons are problematic as are comparisons to the general American population.

The only national data source for the study of Jewish demographic patterns is the National Jewish Population Study (NJPS) carried out 1970–71. This was the first attempt to design a national sample of American Jews (Lazerwitz, 1973a, 1978; Massarik, 1973; Massarik and Chenkin, 1973). Details from this study have not been published, but it should provide a major data source in the analysis of American Jewish demographic patterns.

In addition to the specific limitations of data sources noted above and those discussed in our review of demographic processes, three general data-related problems should be noted.

First, the data available from local Jewish community surveys have often been prepared for local planning purposes rather than for scientific analysis. The secondary use of these materials for reviews and comparisons among Jewish communities has been limited to these published reports. There is a need to more fully exploit these data for the comparative analysis of Jewish communities and prepare more detailed, comparable data tabulations. More consistent and comparable data collection and preparation should be encouraged in future studies. The lack of full data exploitation is not limited to local Jewish community studies. More systematic detailed analysis is needed of U.S. census materials, particularly past censuses focusing on those reporting Yiddish as their mother tongue and similar data for the 1970 census. Given the limited data available and the high cost and problems associated with collecting new data, efforts should be made to exploit data already collected.

Second, because much of what is known about Jewish demographic patterns is based on local Jewish surveys designed to meet local community needs, selected areas of demographic inquiry have been neglected. Questions regarding emigration, details on selected sectors of the Jewish population (e.g. the young, nonmarried, elites, and the intermarried), or on selected subcommunities (e.g. Hasidic Jews or Israelis) have not been addressed systematically. Often available data have determined the analytic questions social scientists ask rather than the other way around. Some issues may be clarified when the results of the NJPS are published and evaluated. But even these data have limitations for the analysis of Jewish population dynamics.

Third, despite the potential of the NJPS, its value will remain limited if it is not part of a continuing series of studies conducted on a regular basis in coming decades (cf. Goldstein, 1973a). The American Jewish community is constantly changing, reflecting in part changes in American society and in part factors unique to the Jewish community. Already some of the data collected in 1970 are outdated — even before they are published. There has never been a reliable source of continuous systematic data to evaluate the changing demographic patterns of American Jews. Nor have there been longitudinal studies to follow dynamic population processes over the life cycle. Rarely have there been repeat surveys of Jewish communities to systematically analyze data on structural and compositional population changes. As new issues emerge and old issues remain unexplored there will be need for the continuous search for new data sources and ways to exploit those now available.

Analysis of the demography of Jewish Americans is based on a series of bits and pieces from national and local Jewish community studies of varying degrees of quality, for different periods of time, and for limited demographic issues. Population growth and distribution data for Jews are based on cumulative estimates that have an unknown range of error (Schmelz, 1969). General sample surveys include demographic details for analysis and allow comparisons between Jews and other ethnic populations, but the number of Jewish respondents is small. Jewish sample surveys include a larger number of Jewish cases but usually do not include comparative data on non-Jewish population, often details on specific issues (e.g. fertility or migration) are not included, and issues of sample design, particularly full coverage of the Jewish population, remain problematic. Social scientists have attempted to use these data sources in supplementary and complementary ways and have pieced together the advantages of each of these sources to provide a basis for evaluating American Jewish demographic patterns. Relative to other areas of scientific inquiry about modern American Jews, demographic patterns are among the most consistently reported and best documented.

Jewish Population Size and Growth

The absence of reliable national data on Jewish population size and growth, historically and in the contemporary period, prevents a clear assessment of this basic demographic issue. For estimates, we must rely on data put together from various local communities and from estimates and guesses from a variety of sources. These have been published regularly in the *American Jewish Year Book* (see the review by Goldstein, 1971). Only the highlights of these well-known data will be reviewed.

Starting with an estimated Jewish population of 1,200 in 1790, Jewish population growth increased to about 50,000 by 1848 and to slightly less than a quarter of a million before the mass migrations from Eastern Europe. Reflecting high rates of immigration and natural increase, the Jewish population in the United States increased to over one million by the turn of the twentieth century and to over four million by the mid-1920s. Jewish population growth during this period was greater than for the American population as a whole and hence the proportion of Jews to the total U.S. population increased from one-tenth of one percent in 1840 to 3.6 percent in 1927. By 1950, the American Jewish population was estimated at five million — a one hundred-fold increase in a century.

The American Jewish population "explosion" ended in the mid-1930s as the level of Jewish immigration from Eastern Europe declined substantially with quota restrictions a decade earlier and fertility levels of second-generation Jews plummeted to replacement levels during the economic depression. It is likely that the Jewish population of the United States has not yet attained the six-million mark. Estimates of Jewish population size from the NJPS of 1970–71 are around 5,775,000, with a margin of error of almost a quarter of a million on either side.

Since the mid-1930s the Jewish population has grown slowly and during the last decade — taking into account the whole range of demographic processes affecting growth (mortality, fertility, immigration, emigration, and net losses due to out-marriages) — the Jewish population hovers at zero population growth or perhaps slightly below. Because Jewish population growth has been slower than that of American society as a whole, the proportion of Jews in America has declined to less than 2.7 percent according to *American Jewish Year Book* estimates in 1979. This is the lowest proportion since the first decade of the twentieth century.

The decline in the proportion of Jews and the attainment of zero population growth has concerned some American Jewish community leaders. Fears about the vanishing of American Jewry, the political significance of declining numbers, and the absence of vitality and growth in the Jewish community have been repeatedly expressed. The issue of Jewish demographic vitality has called into question broader issues of Jewish survival in modern society. While these broader issues are important to raise and the connections between demographic processes and the quality of American Jewish life are strong, much of the concern seems misplaced. American Jews have never constituted a large segment of the U.S. population nor have their political or economic powers been functions of population size. America has become the world Jewish demographic center as a result of the combined impact of population growth through mass immigration from Eastern Europe between 1880 and the 1920s and the destruction of European Jewry in World War II. It is not likely that this population cen-

trality will be overtaken by any other Jewish community in the world —
including Israel — for the rest of this century.

American Jewry is not about to die or vanish either demographically or
sociologically. The American Jewish population may be experiencing some
small decline in size, but it is changing in composition, characteristics, and
distribution. Concerns about quantitative survival nationally are much less
real than problems of growth, size, and structure of local Jewish communities. The future of American Jewish life is less tied to the question of its
demographic survival than to which subsections or segments of the Jewish
community will survive and what will be the quality of Jewish life for most
American Jews (for a more elaborate discussion of this issue see Goldscheider, 1978). The demography of American Jews is an integral part of
the social, political, cultural, and economic processes of the American Jewish community. This is not only because Jewish demographic processes are
reflective of Jewish social life, but demographic processes and structure
have implications for Jewish communities and Jewish identification.

Jewish Immigration to the United States

Much has been written about Jewish immigration to the United States
and indeed immigration has shaped American Jewish social and demographic history. While the number of Jewish immigrants has been somewhat differently reported in various sources (cf. Hersch, 1949;
Lestschinsky, 1960; *American Jewish Year Book*, 1977), there is consensus on the following major themes:

Between 1820 and 1870 an estimated 50,000 German Jews immigrated
to America. Their socioeconomic background is difficult to determine from
existing data but most probably they came from the commercial classes,
since both the proportion of professionals and artisans among German
Jewry was small (Lestschinsky, 1960). Their socioeconomic background,
social mobility, geographic dispersion, and prior exposure to secularization
resulted in rapid integration in American society. By the second generation
German Jews had moved further away from traditional Judaism, significant proportions were intermarrying, and rapid assimilation seems to have
occurred. Many of the second and subsequent generations of German Jews
fully assimilated to American society, although the extent and nature of
these changes have not been clearly documented. As German Jews in
America faced the growing number of Eastern European migrants, their
importance (at least demographically) diminished. For a variety of reasons
associated with the attitudes of American society toward the growing number of Jewish immigrants at the turn of the century and their impact on the
American Jewish community, Jews of German origin in America slowly
changed, and in some ways became more "Jewish" than they had been
(Glazer, 1960).

Beginning in the 1870s and increasingly after 1881, a mass migration of Eastern European Jews took place. Between 1881 and 1924 approximately 2.5 million Jews from Eastern Europe immigrated to the United States. Immigration and natural increase enlarged the American Jewish population from less than a quarter of a million in 1880 to over 4 million in the mid-1920s. While mass immigration did not begin until 1881, estimates of Eastern European Jewish immigration suggest that approximately 100,000 Eastern European Jews immigrated to the United States before then — 70,000 during 1871–80 and 30,000 during 1820–70 (Lestschinsky, 1960).

The overwhelming majority of Eastern European Jewish immigrants remained permanently in the United States. Sex ratio data, the proportion of children, and data on families all point in this direction. Direct estimates indicate that of the more than one million Jewish immigrants in 1908–25 only 52,000 emigrated from the United States — about 5 percent. This compares to 40 percent of the Poles and 50 percent of the Russians who were not Jewish who emigrated and to 56 percent of the Italian immigrants who returned to Italy. Even one-sixth of the French and English immigrants returned — three times as high as Jewish return migration (Lestschinsky, 1960, table 5). Jewish immigrants were exceptional in their permanent settlement in America relative to other immigrants.

The mass immigration of Eastern European Jews to America converted the American Jewish community from an insignificant minority too small to establish anything more complex than localized Jewish communal life to a national American subcommunity (Goldstein and Goldscheider, 1968). By the end of this mass immigration, the German and Sephardic Jews no longer constituted the dominant Jewish communities in America but were submerged by the overwhelming numbers of East European immigrants.

The demographic dominance of Eastern European Jews has had implications for the internal changes associated with Jewish American integration. The transition from an immigrant subsociety to an Americanized second-, third-, and fourth-generation American ethnic group has been the master theme in the sociology and demography of American Jews. In the 1970s, approximately 80 percent of the Jewish population was native born and half of those were at least third-generation Jews. Generational status is a key axis along which vary the range of demographic and social processes of American Jews and the character of American Jewish communities. Generational changes in residential location, family structure and size, intermarriage, social class (education, occupation, and income), religious identification, and measures of Jewish religiosity and commitment have been analyzed for various Jewish communities. Variations and changes by distance from the immigrant generation provide the most important clues about processes of Jewish American assimilation and acculturation.

While the U.S. immigrant quota legislation ended mass immigration from Eastern Europe in the mid-1920s, Jewish immigration did not cease entirely. Between 1925 and World War II almost a quarter of a million Jews arrived, many of them refugees and escapees from Central Europe. From a demographic and sociostructural point of view these immigrants not only contributed to the population growth of American Jewry but were in occupations quite different from those of immigrant masses from Eastern Europe.

Between 1944 and 1959 about 192,000 Jewish immigrants entered the United States and an additional 129,000 immigrated between 1959 and 1975. Altogether, from World War II to 1975 over 320,000 Jews immigrated to the United States. These immigrants confronted a well-established Jewish community that had already numbered over 4 million by the mid-1920s and had developed communal organizations and social institutions. On the one hand mass Jewish migration and subsequent generational patterns define the character of the American Jewish community. On the other hand the continuous immigration stream after the 1920s cannot be dismissed either demographically or sociologically.

It is not clear what proportion of these recent immigrants follows the generational model of change characteristic of Eastern European immigrants. Some were affected by social changes characteristic of particular periods shaped by the character of the children and grandchildren of Eastern European immigrants. Others may have remained outside the boundaries of these generational changes, particularly the Hasidic, Israeli Americans, and the select number of orthodox German immigrants.

From the mid-1950s until the mid-1970s Jewish immigration to the United States averaged 8,000 annually. This may be a conservative estimate based on immigrants assisted by HIAS and an estimate of assisted to nonassisted immigrants of an earlier period (Goldstein, 1973a). Several tens of thousands of former Israeli residents have settled in the United States in recent decades. Some initially came as students and some have stayed illegally. Many have neither been recorded in official immigration statistics nor have they been assisted by American or international immigration organizations. There has been a significant increase in Soviet Jewish immigration in the last several years. In 1973, for example, only 1,449 Soviet Jews immigrated to America (about 15 percent of the estimated total Jewish immigration to the United States). In 1974, the number of Soviet Jewish immigrants doubled to 3,490 (almost 30 percent of estimated Jewish immigration to America) and increased to 5,250 in 1975 (Edelman, 1977). Data for the last several years are not readily available; it is safe to assume that there has been a significant increase in the number of Soviet Jewish immigrants to the United States as the number leaving the Soviet Union increases and the proportion of those receiving exit visas who immigrate to Israel decreases.

One of the immediate consequences of this recent Jewish immigration — and indeed the immigration of Jews to the United States since the 1960s — has been to change the balance of demographic processes in the American Jewish community. In a crude and preliminary attempt to assess the demographic importance of recent Jewish immigration to the United States, a series of estimates of births, deaths, and net immigration were prepared for the period 1967–69 (see Appendix). These estimates reveal that Jewish immigration to the United States may have more than balanced the negative growth resulting from the excess of deaths over births. Whether net Jewish immigration also compensates for losses due to Jewish out-marriages is difficult to assess until more complete data are available. The significance of recent Jewish immigration for the demography of American Jews has been underestimated. There is a need for specific research to focus on long-term demographic and sociological consequences of both Israeli and Soviet immigration.

Emigration of Jews from America

To complete the picture of the role of migration in shaping Jewish population changes in the United States, we should note not only Jewish immigration to America but Jewish emigration from America. Earlier research on the emigration (or return migration) of Eastern European Jews who came to America reveals the very low proportions of Jewish return migration. This is not surprising given the general integration of Jews in America, their social mobility, the socioeconomic opportunity structure of American society, ideological and normative characteristics of America as the haven for those who have been religiously and politically oppressed, the relative absence of institutional anti-Semitism, and for most Jewish immigrants, the lack of viable alternatives in terms of returning to Eastern or Central Europe.

The only major country representing an alternative to American society has been Israel. Studies of American Jewish immigration to Israel (*aliya*) indicate the very small number of Jews from the United States settling in Israel. Up to the end of the 1950s the numbers of American immigrants to Palestine and Israel were very small — around 200 per year for 1919–48 and 400 per year for 1948–60. Beginning in the 1960s and increasingly between 1967 and 1973 several thousand Jews from the United States immigrated to Israel annually (for details see Goldscheider, 1974). These figures only relate to Americans who arrived in Israel as either immigrants or temporary residents (defined formally after 1969 as "potential immigrants"). Estimates of return migration to the United States indicate that after about three years 30–40 percent return. Since 1971 when the number of American immigrants was at a peak of 7,364 (1,049 immigrants and

6,315 potential immigrants), annual levels have declined. In 1977, 2,571 American Jews immigrated to Israel — 279 immigrants and 2,292 potential immigrants (Israel, *Statistical Abstract*, 1978).

The level of American *aliya* to Israel relative to the population size of American Jewry has been minuscule. However, given the delicate balance of factors affecting American Jewish population growth, even the emigration of small numbers may have demographic significance. Barring unforeseen and unpredictable circumstances, no mass *aliya* of Jewish Americans can be expected to occur in the near future. This is because alongside the near universal American Jewish concern for Israel lies the almost unanimous Jewish commitment to America.

In addition to the question of the number of Jewish emigrants from America to Israel is the selectivity of that immigration. Research has shown that American immigrants to Israel are younger than the American Jewish population as a whole, more likely to have had extensive Jewish education, and are more identified as committed Jews along a variety of dimensions (religious institutional identification, self-definition, Jewish education, ritual observances, and Jewish organizational membership). From the point of view of the American Jewish population this selectivity, however small in number, may dilute selected Jewish communities of the more committed younger American Jews and potential Jewish leadership. On the other hand, American *aliya* might also strengthen and reinforce the interdependence between the American Jewish community and Israeli society. A continuous monitoring of these patterns seems justified in terms of the demographic and sociological interdependence of these two major Jewish communities.

Population Distribution: Regional Patterns

Of greater importance than issues of national Jewish population size and growth are changes in its distribution. The pattern of Jewish immigration and settlement resulted in a high Jewish population concentration in the American Northeast and a sharply reduced level of concentration in the South. In 1930, *American Jewish Year Book* estimates show that 68 percent of the Jewish population was concentrated in the Northeast and 60 percent was in the Middle Atlantic states. Less than 20 percent were in the North Central region and only 4.6 percent were in the West. Particularly affected by immigration and settlement were areas in the South that contained only 7.6 percent of the American Jewish population, a decline of almost 50 percent from 1900.

These patterns began to change as second- and third-generation Jews (and some first-generation Jews as well) moved away from traditional areas of Jewish population concentration. Between 1930 and 1968 the pro-

Table 1.1
Estimates of Regional Distribution of the American Jewish Population,
1968 and 1978

Region	1968		1978	
	Jewish	Total U.S.	Jewish	Total U.S.
Northeast	64.0	24.2	58.7	22.8
New England	6.8	5.7	6.7	5.7
Middle Atlantic	57.1	18.5	52.0	17.1
North Central	12.5	27.8	12.2	26.8
East North Central	10.2	19.8	9.9	19.0
West North Central	2.3	8.0	2.3	7.8
South	10.3	31.2	15.2	32.3
South Atlantic	8.1	15.0	12.8	15.9
East South Central	0.7	6.6	0.7	6.4
West South Central	1.5	9.6	1.7	10.0
West	13.2	16.8	13.9	18.1
Mountain	0.9	4.0	1.5	4.6
Pacific	12.2	12.8	12.4	13.5
Total United States				
Percent	100.0	100.0	100.0	100.0
Number (in 1,000s)	5,869	199,861	5,781	216,332

Source: *American Jewish Year Book* estimates, vol. 70 (1969); vol. 79 (1979).

portion of Jews living in the Northeast and North Central regions declined
(as did the general American population) and increased sharply in the
West and South (Goldstein, 1971).

Recent estimates presented in Table 1.1 show that these regional patterns have continued over the last decade. In 1978, 59 percent of the American Jewish population lived in the Northeast, a decline of 8.3 percent from
1968. This represents a greater decline than for the American population
as a whole (5.8 percent for the decade). Smaller declines may be noted for
the North Central region. In the Southern states, Jewish population has
increased from 10 percent of the total Jewish population to more than 15
percent, an increase of almost 50 percent compared to an increase of only
3.4 percent for the total population. The increasing Jewish concentration in
the West has continued but at a much slower pace relative to the earlier
period and slower than the American population as a whole. (These data
are based on estimates of population prepared by the *American Jewish
Year Book* and may understate the amount of changes occurring.)

Regional growth patterns reflect the geographic mobility and interstate migration patterns of American Jews. These patterns may be assumed to characterize younger third- and fourth-generation Jews more than older Jews. Such selective migration has an impact on areas of traditional Jewish concentration not only in terms of reducing population size but in the resultant age composition of these communities. The changing redistribution of the Jewish population by region may also imply migration to areas of lower Jewish population density. Changes in the density of Jewish population and the specific impact of migration are major demographic processes that have not received sufficient research attention.

A recent study of the geographic distribution and change of the American Jewish population (1952–71, by counties) shows some important details on changing Jewish population concentration (Newman and Halvorson, 1979). First, out of over 3,000 counties included in the analysis of the continental United States, Jews are concentrated in only 504. For the rest of the counties, there were either no Jews or less than 100. Jews are far less dispersed than eight Protestant denominations included in the study, despite the fact that several of them are markedly smaller in total numbers. Second, much of the highest Jewish growth during 1952–71 occurred outside of the traditional counties of Jewish population concentration. A total of 77 counties containing Jews were added in that period. A large part of this pattern reflects suburbanization within metropolitan areas and regional declines. Third, in both 1952 and 1971, the Jewish population was far more concentrated than the total population but was becoming more dispersed over time. The extent to which young Jews have recently moved to nonmetropolitan areas of the United States and small towns is largely unknown. Since *American Jewish Year Book* estimates are based on reports from organized Jewish communities, they are not likely to cover these segments of American Jewry.

Jewish Population Density and Migration

The disproportionate concentration of Jews in particular metropolitan areas is a well-known feature of American Jewish demography. The differential impact of population concentration and dispersal on local institutions and organizations has been noted in a variety of studies (Goldstein, 1971). In terms of the vitality of local Jewish communities, migration and population redistribution are of greater significance perhaps than any other single demographic factor. The dispersal of Jews within metropolitan areas and in new communities throughout the United States is of critical importance since there are clear implications of differential Jewish density levels for Jewish survival — demographically and sociologically. Migration and population dispersal have increased among third- and fourth-generation Jews, particularly those highly educated and in professional and salaried occupations. Changes in the occupational structure of Jews, in the labor market, and the educational level of young Jewish men and women may result in greater future mobility. There are indications that the migration of Jewish Americans is greater than for the total American population and that rates have increased in the last decade among third- and fourth-generation Jews (Goldstein, 1971, 1979b).

The nonrootedness of the young generations and the movement away from centers of Jewish concentration — regionally and within metropolitan areas — are among the major determinants of lower levels of Jewish commitment. To be sure, the willingness to move to areas of low Jewish population density already implies lower levels of Jewish commitment. Nevertheless, areas of low Jewish population density have had in the past important consequences for Jewish identity, Jewish community participation, intermarriage, and lower rates of Jewish continuity. Although the major centers of Jewish concentration are likely to remain and new centers of high Jewish density will emerge, it is likely that significant proportions of fourth-generation Jews will be living in areas of lower Jewish concentration. Their mobility and residential environment imply a weakening of Jewish community ties and a challenge to Jewish continuity in these areas.

Jewish communities and subcommunities are undergoing significant structural changes in age composition because of a combination of selective out-migration and low fertility rates. Neighborhoods of major centers of Jewish concentration have become heavily weighted toward the older segments of the age pyramid as have new retirement centers around the country. These areas have little potential for Jewish population renewal except through selective immigration. Yet it seems less likely that fourth-generation Jews will move to areas of Jewish concentration as they age and retire, given their pattern of residential integration throughout their life cycle. In short, a variety of areas of both low Jewish density and high density with an older population will decline in the next generation and then disappear. Jewish demographic survival is likely to be most pronounced in the large metropolitan centers of Jewish concentration — old and new.

The importance of migration for understanding the Jewish community rests with several important considerations. First, migration has an impact on the size and composition of areas of origin and destination. Second, migration in the recent period seems to be away from areas of heavy Jewish concentration. In turn, the degree of Jewish population dispersal affects the quality and intensity of Jewish identification. Third, the migrant and the repeat migrant tend to be less attached to local Jewish communities and institutions. Finally, migration patterns may affect relationships between members of extended families in a variety of ways. While geographic mobility does not necessarily eliminate extended family ties, it tends to alter their quality and intensity. These issues are central to an understanding of the demography of American Jews and have not been systematically investigated.

National migration data for the Jewish population are not available from any official source and only preliminary reports have been available to date from the NJPS. Local community studies have provided some insight into the amount of residential mobility within selected metropolitan areas (Goldstein, 1971, 1973a), but these have limited value for gauging out-migration. Indicative of the high rates of mobility, preliminary data from the NJPS found that only 62 percent of the Jewish population aged 20 and over in 1970 were still living in the same city in which they resided in 1965. The rates of mobility are even higher among young Jews: of those 25–39, over half changed their city of residence at least once in 1965–70 and over 20 percent lived in a different state. Even among the elderly aged 65 and over, 30 percent had moved within a five-year period (reported in Goldstein, 1979b).

In one state, data show very high absolute rates of Jewish out-migration and higher rates relative to other religious and ethnic subgroups. Over 70 percent of the Jewish children of couples interviewed in Rhode Island (1967–69) migrated out of the state compared to less than half of the Protestant and about one-third of the Catholic children. Among Jewish fathers with some college education the proportion of children migrating out of the state was even higher. Even controlling for educational level, out-migration is higher among Jews (Kobrin and Goldscheider, 1978). While out-migration from one area implies immigration to other areas, the long-term consequences of such geographic mobility for patterns of social and cultural life — in neighborhoods, communities, states, and regions — requires research attention. While migration may have limited implications for mortality and fertility at the individual level, migration selectivity has important consequences for levels of mortality and fertility of specific areas and, in turn, for population growth and structure.

Jewish Mortality Patterns

Heavy reliance on official death records for the study of mortality trends and differentials and the absence in the United States of any information on religious affiliation on these records have been major barriers to the analysis of Jewish mortality. In the absence of official death statistics, demographers have developed techniques for estimating mortality from sample surveys or censuses. While these techniques have been applied in historical demographic research and in developing countries, no attempt has been made to use them for estimating national mortality rates for Jews. Nor have there been follow-back surveys of the families of deceased persons to obtain information on socioeconomic and demographic characteristics. No national estimates are available to analyze the mortality patterns of Jewish Americans.

Several post–World War II studies of Jewish mortality have used local community data sources to estimate mortality levels and have examined selected demographic variation (primarily age, sex, and cause of death) in mortality. These data on Jewish deaths have been based on the records of funeral directors who handle a significant proportion of Jewish deaths and Jewish cemeteries. These records appear to cover most of all Jewish deaths in a community in a given period, although there are few independent checks of coverage. To estimate rates of mortality, these data must be used in conjunction with a base population. Such data are themselves estimates and are often lacking, particularly by age and sex. The small numbers of annual Jewish deaths in any year, even where these are related to local population estimates, preclude detailed analyses of cause of death or socioeconomic characteristics. Whether the patterns of mortality estimated for several select communities are indicative of national levels and whether significant shifts in Jewish American mortality have occurred in the last decade remain open questions.

Despite these limitations, a fairly consistent but general picture of Jewish mortality levels emerges from these community studies. Estimated Jewish mortality levels are low, particularly for infant and child mortality, when compared to the total White population. This appears to characterize males more than females. Age-specific mortality rates and life table measures based on these rates tend to be similar for Jews and the total American population among the older ages and often slightly higher among Jews. It seems reasonable to conclude that mortality differences between Jews and the total American population are small and do not account for population growth differences by religion. (These studies are reviewed in Goldstein and Goldscheider, 1968; Goldstein, 1971. See also Gorwitz, 1962; Seidman, et al., 1962; Liberson, 1956; Fauman and Mayer, 1969; Schmelz, 1971.)

While this conclusion applies to the post–World War II period, data for the late nineteenth and early twentieth centuries show significantly lower Jewish mortality levels than for the general American population. Estimates of infant and early childhood mortality, for example, reveal that for the period beginning in 1885 through 1915, Jewish rates were about 50 percent lower than for the total American population (Billings, 1890; Woodbury, 1926; Liberson, 1956; Schmelz, 1971 who reviews these and comparative Jewish rates for the last 150 years in a variety of countries). This pattern of lower infant and childhood mortality among Jews characterizes recent studies as well, although differences between Jews and the total population have narrowed. There is some evidence (cited by Schmelz,

1971) that the lower infant and childhood mortality among Jews compared to other immigrant Americans or American-born Whites at the turn of the century characterized both high- and low-income categories. The greater care of children by Jewish mothers, the high proportion of breast-feeding, and the low proportion of Jewish mothers who worked in factories have been cited as part of the explanation of low infant mortality during this period. The infant mortality difference between Jews and others has probably narrowed in recent decades.

Since mortality variation and levels are significantly affected by age structure, it is likely that mortality variations among Jewish communities in the United States are largely reflections of the differential age composition of these communities. However, a sufficient number of community comparisons is lacking for any definite conclusions. Other sources of mortality variations among Jews, particularly socioeconomic, residential (urban, suburban, or regional), and by marital status have not been systematically analyzed. Comparisons between the mortality of Jewish and total White populations have rarely been made controlling for various socioeconomic characteristics. Hence explanations of mortality differences have been problematic. Genetic selection, higher socioeconomic status, or particular Jewish factors have been invoked to account for mortality differences between Jews and non-Jews (Goldstein and Goldscheider, 1968).

Given the social and economic characteristics of the American Jewish population and judging by what is known about general differential mortality in the United States, we can infer that there are few major differentials in mortality among Jews except age and sex. This inference seems reasonable for the contemporary period but is not likely to have characterized the Jewish population at the turn of the century when immigration was high and socioeconomic and demographic conditions among Jews were more heterogeneous. Data on sex differentials in mortality among Jews indicate the greater longevity of Jewish women, parallel to patterns of the general American population. This pattern has resulted in a high proportion of widows among the older population. While Jews may not be exceptional in this regard, the low proportion of males to females among the elderly has a variety of consequences for family structure, household and living arrangements, as well as for Jewish and general community services. The implications of sex differential mortality among Jews for these and related issues have never been studied systematically.

Perhaps because mortality rates among Jews are relatively low and not very different from those of other White Americans, and because deaths are heavily concentrated among the aged — disengaged from major work, family, and community commitments — and contribute little to the population growth differentials between the Jewish and total American populations, mortality issues have never been high in the list of research priorities.

Data constraints have been discouraging even to the most persistent and ingenious demographers. Nevertheless, there remains a series of basic demographic and sociological questions associated with Jewish mortality that merit investigation. These questions cover a wide range of topics from historical trends in national Jewish mortality rates to socioeconomic and demographic differentials in Jewish mortality; from the consequences of mortality for American Jewish social structure to the role, if any, of specific Jewish values and practices associated with death and dying. The whole area of research on the relationship between morbidity and mortality has been neglected.

Over a decade ago, a detailed review of Jewish mortality research in America concluded that "identification as a Jew continues to affect the life chances of individuals" (Goldstein and Goldscheider, 1968, p. 151). Then as now, documentation of this generalization is problematic and the analysis of specific reasons underlying Jewish mortality trends and variations must remain speculative until more systematic and comprehensive research is undertaken.

Trends and Differentials in American Jewish Fertility

In contrast to the paucity of data on Jewish mortality patterns, a wide range of data sources and research studies has been available to analyze Jewish fertility patterns in the United States in detail. Although each data source has limitations, taken together the data have been remarkably cumulative and allow for a more comprehensive analysis of trends and differentials in Jewish fertility. Because we know more about Jewish fertility patterns in America, the analytic questions raised have become more sophisticated and the issues more complex. This in turn demands even more systematic and detailed research. The investigation of fertility generally involves more complex theoretical and methodological problems than mortality analysis. While mortality levels in contemporary America remain low with only small annual fluctuations, and mortality differentials have narrowed and declined in importance, such is not the case for fertility. Fertility fluctuations over the last several decades have been substantial and responsive to economic depressions, recessions, war and postwar social changes, and the revolutions in women's role and in sexual norms. Annual birth rates have varied much more than cohort rates or family size. Population growth and structure are much more affected by fertility than mortality. These characteristics of American fertility are no less true for Jews.

While mortality risks are higher for some ages than others and vary by sex, childbearing is biologically circumscribed to fecund women in the reproduction ages and sociologically to married women. Hence population compositional changes (for example in the number of women of reproductive ages) or changes in marriage patterns (the proportions married or ages at marriage) have important effects on annual birth rates, reproduction and population replacement, and often on family size as well. Changes in the timing of births and the tempo of childbearing and family formation are also important for an understanding of fertility trends and differentials.

The centrality of fertility for population growth and the relationship between family structure and fertility have made the study of fertility in general, and Jewish fertility in particular, of major analytic concern for sociologists and demographers. An analysis of the demographic vitality of the American Jewish community or changes in the Jewish family has at its core issues associated with fertility variation and change.

To place in perspective the highlights of what we know about Jewish fertility, a brief review of data sources and their limitations is necessary. This provides the basis for assessing major trends and differentials in Jewish fertility and evaluating what types of further research should be carried out. While some of this review duplicates the discussion of data sources on American Jewish demography presented earlier, studies of Jewish fertility have been more extensive and detailed and merit separate treatment.

Data Sources on Jewish Fertility

There are four main categories of data sources for the study of Jewish fertility, nationally and in local communities (see reviews in Goldscheider, 1967; Goldscheider, 1971; Goldstein, 1971, 1973a, 1979a).

Official Government Statistics. Data on religious affiliation or preference have never been included in American decennial censuses. Indirect estimates of Jewish fertility from censuses have been made from mother-tongue data (those declaring Yiddish as mother tongue) or for the Russian-born and Russian-origin population (on the assumption that a substantial proportion are Jews). For earlier periods these data provide a reasonable basis for evaluating national Jewish fertility levels but their utility for the postwar contemporary period is limited (Goldberg, 1948, 1962; Rosenthal, 1975). In the past, analysis of these data has been limited to published data. Recent advances in computer technology and the growing availability of selected census tapes for specific minority groups may allow for a more detailed historical reevaluation of these data. In the 1970 United States Census, mother-tongue data including Yiddish were collected, as were data on fertility. While these data are now available on special computer tapes, they have not been exploited. While providing only a partial picture of national Jewish fertility, they remain useful for comparisons between Jews and others.

The major government statistics relating directly to Jewish fertility are contained in the Current Population Survey of 1957 — a sample survey covering 35,000 American households and about 1,000 Jewish households. This unique data source inquired about religious preference for the first (and up to now the only) time as well as socioeconomic and fertility patterns. These data have been exploited fully (Goldstein, 1969; Glick, 1960; Rosenthal, 1961). Although fertility levels by religion can be examined with these data, no analysis of fertility differentials or trends is possible. Only one state census has included a question on religion and fertility (the Rhode Island Census of 1905). Only crude data were published (Goldscheider, 1967) but the original records are available and may be useful for some historical-demographic research.

Another major source of official statistics basic to demographic analyses of births and fertility are birth records, but again no data on religious affiliation are collected. A new series of national fertility surveys under the title National Survey of Family Growth has been undertaken by the National Center for Health Statistics beginning in 1973–74. Religious affiliation, along with details on births and socioeconomic background materials, is included. The number of Jews included will be about 125 cases and therefore will be limited (Goldstein, 1978).

A previous set of surveys, also carried out by the National Center for Health Statistics in 1967, 1968, and 1969 included data on the religion of mothers and fathers. These data based on samples of births and follow-back questionnaires provide a unique data source for national estimates of current Jewish birth and reproduction rates in conjunction with selected demographic and socioeconomic characteristics. A thorough analysis of these data along with a discussion of their limitations has been published (Goldstein, 1979a). These data based on current births are limited to a small number of those currently identified as Jews (167 cases). No population base data by religion are available to compute rates, and major categories of women are omitted (childless couples, mothers of children born out of wedlock, births before 1967). As a view of "period" birth rates and as a supplement to what is known about trends and differentials in Jewish fertility, these data are useful.

General Fertility Surveys. Given the limitations of official statistics for the detailed examination of fertility and fertility-related issues (e.g. timing and tempo of childbearing, contraceptive usage, family planning and fertility norms, preferences, and attitudes), major sample surveys of American fertility have been undertaken. These surveys have included over the last several decades questions on religious affiliation, preferences, and religiosity. Starting from clinical studies in the 1920s to the classic Indianapolis study, the Growth of American Family Studies, the Princeton Studies of the 1950s and 1960s, and the latest national fertility surveys in the 1970s, data on Jewish (compared to Protestant and Catholic) fertility and family planning have been published. These studies have provided rich details on fertility behavior and attitudes, contraceptive practices, and family planning, and present a comprehensive view of these patterns (trends and variations) for the American population. However, because Jews represent less than 3 percent of the American population, the number of Jewish respondents has always been small — seldom more than one hundred cases. As a result, detailed analyses of these data are restricted. Nevertheless, they represent an important comparative basis for examining Jewish fertility patterns. These studies have been reviewed in several publications (Goldscheider, 1967, 1971; Goldstein and Goldscheider, 1968; Goldstein, 1971, 1979a) and provide confirmatory evidence that supplements other official and Jewish community data sources. Other general surveys, based on the total population, have included questions on religion and fertility but again, the small number of cases for Jewish women in the reproductive period precludes detailed analysis. Gallup and NORC polls are therefore of minimum utility for an analysis of Jewish fertility (cf. Goldstein, 1979a on combined NORC data, Table 2).

Jewish Community Surveys. The most detailed and comprehensive data on Jewish fertility trends and differentials have been derived from general sample surveys of Jewish communities. The quality of these data vary enormously in terms of sample design and coverage and in terms of details available on fertility trends and variations among Jews. These data tend to be limited to the Jewish population and comparisons with other ethnic-religious groups have been limited (for an exception see Lazerwitz, 1973b). Nor have details on fertility been included beyond family-size patterns, birth intervals, and fertility expectations (for younger women). The most comprehensive use of these surveys has been for an analysis of cohort fertility trends and a variety of socioeconomic and religious differentials (Goldscheider, 1965a, b, c, 1966, 1967, 1971; Goldstein, 1971, 1973b, 1979a). The degree to which patterns analyzed for local communities characterize national trends remains an open question. Details on Jewish fertility from the NJPS have not been analyzed. This latter source should provide valuable evidence on trends and differentials in Jewish fertility at the national level.

Each of these data sources has limitations and analysis based solely on any one of them is problematic. Nevertheless, picking up the various pieces of evidence from these studies, a remarkably consistent picture of Jewish fertility emerges. There continue to be gaps in our knowledge about Jewish fertility trends and differentials that will require new research efforts based on new data sets and reanalyses of data sources now available. The substantive review of American Jewish fertility will focus on four major themes: (1) the trend and level of Jewish fertility; (2) explanations of Jewish/non-Jewish differences in fertility; (3) socioeconomic and religious variations in Jewish fertility; (4) areas of neglected research associated with Jewish fertility. A related theme on changes in family structure will be reviewed in a separate section.

Levels and Trends in Jewish Fertility

Since the end of the nineteenth century research in the United States has pointed to the unmistakable conclusion that Jews have lower fertility than the American population as a whole or other ethnic groups. The major fertility and community studies available as well as data from official government statistics have consistently confirmed this observation for a wide range of fertility and related measures. Indicators of fertility norms, desires, and expectations, family size, annual birth and reproduction rates, contraceptive knowledge and practices, family planning, and the timing of reproduction all point in the same direction: Jewish couples want, plan, and have small families. Fertility among Jews is low in terms of absolute levels as well as relative to other ethnic-religious groups in America.

Low Jewish fertility is not a new American pattern. As far as can be discerned from the available data, particularly by marriage cohort, fluctuations around replacement level fertility have characterized Jewish marriage cohorts as early as the mid-1920s. Marriage cohort data in one study (Goldscheider, 1966) reveal that average Jewish family size of those marrying before 1910 was 3.5 children declining to 2 children for the cohorts between 1925 and 1944. Postwar marriage cohorts, as was true for other American couples, experienced an increase in family size to around 2.3 children. The decline and postwar increase are indicated not only by average family size but by specific parity data as well.

The decline in fertility inferred from these cross-sectional data parallel similar inferences from census data on Polish and Russian women who reported Yiddish as their mother tongue in the 1940 U.S. Census (Goldberg, 1948). These data suggest that the decline in fertility for Jews was greater than for the total population. Similarly, the post–World War II increase seems to have been less than that characterizing the White population as a whole.

Similar prewar declines and postwar increases were reported when family size was examined by generational and age-generational groupings. The increase in family size among third-generation Jews may have been followed by a subsequent downturn, particularly for marriage cohorts of the 1960s and 1970s. This would parallel what has happened in the American population in general. Some limited period data on annual births of Jews in 1967–69 point in that direction. It is unclear whether these period rates will reflect eventual family size or whether changes in the timing and tempo of childbearing have pushed these annual rates to unprecedented low levels (cf. Goldstein, 1979a).

Examination of the fertility of married couples may differ from that of the total Jewish population when there are significant proportions of non-married or delays in marriage and childbearing. Cohort patterns (births to women who marry or are born during a particular period) may differ from a cross-sectional view of annual birth rates. Both perspectives are necessary for a full examination of fertility levels. The examination of family size changes among different cohorts of women as they pass through their childbearing cycle is essential for a view of completed family size and analysis of the dynamics of family formation. Cohort data of this type have not been available for recent marriage cohorts among Jews.

Another view examines annual birth rates or other period measures that relate to family formation and childbearing at particular periods, irrespective of the ages or cohorts of women giving birth or their previous childbearing experience. Examining births in a given year, for example, related to births occurring to women in a variety of childbearing stages and from various marriage cohorts. Included in an annual rate of fertility are women completing their childbearing as well as those just beginning and those in the middle stages. Average family size among ever-married Jewish women may remain relatively stable while annual Jewish birth rates fluctuate greatly.

Jewish women marrying in the 1920s and 1930s had by the end of their childbearing period around two children. However, births occurring during those years were not only to women marrying during these years but to women who had been married for longer durations — older marriage cohorts whose fertility was higher. Most of those marrying in the 1920s and 1930s were second-generation Jews whose family of orientation was relatively large. The economic depression of the 1930s and the war years were periods of general low fertility in America and were viewed as transitory. In the immediate postwar period of the 1940s and 1950s a "baby boom" occurred among Jews as among the general American population. Although the baby boom reflected in part changes in the timing of childbearing and the making up of postponed births and delayed marriages, the normative experience of this period was childbearing and early family formation. There is some evidence that small increases in Jewish family size characterized the immediate post–World War II cohorts. Yet it was not until the 1960s that both families of orientation and procreation were small in size; almost all Jewish women giving birth during this period were characterized by relatively small families, efficient contraceptive usage, and the planning of the number and spacing of all births.

During the 1960s and 1970s some delayed marriage and nonmarriage began to emerge on the American Jewish scene. These marriage and family formation changes may have been accompanied by changes in the timing of childbearing among married women. If the proportion of married women declines significantly and delayed childbearing within marriage takes place, a family size of 2-3 children will not necessarily imply *annual* population replacement rates. While the long-run trend in Jewish fertility among married couples is toward the two-child family, annual fertility rates during the 1960s and early 1970s may have been distorted by timing and marriage changes.

Further accentuating this pattern of the changing tempo of childbearing for the Jewish population during this latter period (rather than average family size for ever-married women) is the fact that the number of Jewish women of childbearing age may have been significantly lower in the 1960s. Most Jewish women marrying in the 1960s were born in the late 1930s and early 1940s. The number of Jewish babies born during that period was probably significantly lower than in the previous period or the subsequent post–World War II boom. Hence fewer Jewish women were around to have children. A substantial part of the explanation of very low annual Jewish birth rates in the last decade may lie in these combined changes in the timing of family formation and childbearing and in the number of Jewish persons entering the childbearing period. Nevertheless, replacement levels for those who marry is not synonymous with replacement levels for the population as a whole, particularly if a growing proportion of women do not marry or delay marriage.

Community planning, educational enrollments, and the general presence of children in communities are based not on a cohort view of childbearing but on the number of children born in particular periods. Delayed childbearing through nonmarriage, postponed marriage, and divorce, as well as timing changes within marriage, combined with the changing numbers of persons reaching the childbearing ages must be considered in evaluating changing period rates of reproduction. Add to these processes the general low replacement level fertility of Jews and the ability of Jewish couples to plan total family size and the spacing of all children and the results are clear: an impressive and conspicuous reduction in the number of Jewish children born in the last decade.

When family size is low and marriage patterns, cohort age structure, and the timing of family formation and childbearing are all changing to push marital fertility rates below population replacement, a small minority group cannot sustain losses due to emigration or out-marriage. Small population declines become problems when additional sociodemographic processes exaggerate that decline. For Jews in America, as will be discussed in a subsequent section, rates of intermarriage increased precisely during the 1960s and early 1970s. Young Jews marrying in this latter period were largely third- or fourth-generation Americans, characterized by significantly less Jewish commitment. Even minimum net losses through out-marriage combined with these annual patterns of below replacement fertility raises the specter of the declining American Jewish population. Research has shown that average family size among Jewish women remains around two children, with little preference for childless or one-child families. Further research must attempt to more systematically document both cohort and period rates of fertility, particularly for younger, recently married Jewish couples.

Explanations of Jewish Fertility

The low absolute and relative levels of Jewish fertility are consistent with the general socioeconomic and residential characteristics of Jews in the United States. The concentration of American Jews in particular statuses and residential locations associated with low fertility supports this observation. The high level of educational attainment among Jews, their concentration in professional and managerial occupations, their high incomes, and the unique urban-metropolitan distribution of Jews have been well documented. These characteristics individually and in combination have been associated with low fertility. Since fertility levels reflect these status and residential categories, the "uniqueness" of Jewish fertility, particularly its low level, reflects the unique socioeconomic and ecological characteristics of the Jewish population.

Jewish fertility levels are integral to the socioeconomic and urban-metropolitan characteristics of the Jewish population. Several pieces of evidence, however, suggest that such an explanation is incomplete. First, Jewish fertility tends to be lower than Protestant and Catholic fertility of similar socioeconomic and residential characteristics. A variety of national and local community studies have shown that fertility differences between Jews and non-Jews remain after the socioeconomic and residential variations have been controlled. Second, the "characteristics" explanation of Jewish fertility would have to assume that Jews in other Western countries have had for the last century the same matrix of characteristics as Jews in the United States or those associated with lower fertility. It would similarly have to be assumed that Jews in the United States for the last century have had these same social and economic characteristics. Empirical evidence shows the very opposite; contemporary Jews do not have the same matrix of characteristics that characterized prior generations. We not only have to explain why Jews are concentrated in particular status and residential categories in order to account for low Jewish fertility, but we must consider other factors particular to the Jewish group — historically and comparatively — to explain the lower Jewish fertility levels compared to non-Jews of similar status and residential characteristics.

There is no clear consensus among social scientists as to what these additional factors might be. Some have argued that social mobility factors are operating (Rosenthal, 1961). Low fertility has been associated with the

rise of Jews into the middle class. Even before attaining middle-class status, it is argued that Jews had a middle class "mentality" and psychologically shared middle-class values including small family size. Some have
argued that low fertility relates to the changing role and status of Jewish
women and their changing self-conception (Sklare, 1971). Others have attempted to relate low fertility to broader patterns of assimilation and accu-
luration and have argued for a more comprehensive theory related to the
changing nature of Jewish social structure and culture. This approach
places particular emphasis on the changing role of minority group status
and the associated feelings of discrimination and insecurity that may be
associated with low fertility. While not neglecting social characteristics,
social mobility, and changing roles and statuses of Jewish women, this view
suggests that the "uniqueness" of Jewish fertility relates to the particular
position of Jews in the social structure.

The combination of minority group status and the interpretation of related values and statuses within that framework helps to account not only
for the unique American Jewish patterns but relates as well to other American minority groups (e.g. Japanese- and Chinese-Americans) and to com-
parative-historical research of Jews (and other minorities). There has
never been a systematic test of the role of minority group status in accounting for Jewish fertility levels or alternative theories explaining Jewish fertility. To do so would require research focused on this issue (Goldscheider,
1967, 1971).

Differentials in Jewish Fertility

Given the pattern of low fertility levels and norms among American
Jews, it is instructive to ask whether there are any subgroups within the
American Jewish population that have larger family size patterns. The issue of differentials in Jewish fertility is hampered by the absence of detailed data from most data sources noted above. The analysis of the NJPS
data when published should help clarify some of these differentials.

On the basis of the evidence now available it is reasonable to argue that
there are few major differentiators in the fertility of contemporary American Jews. The American Jewish population has become more homogeneous in terms of major socioeconomic characteristics than in the past. In
the last several decades there have been processes of diffusion in terms of
family planning and overall American norms of small family size such that
most segments of the Jewish community have been exposed to and adopted
these norms. For the American population as a whole, fertility differentials
have converged over the last decade. Traditional variables associated with
higher fertility in America — rural residence, poverty, contraceptive ignorance, low education, farm and blue-collar occupations — are nonexistent
among Jewish men and women of childbearing age.

Some variations in Jewish fertility in America continue to characterize contemporary Jewish couples. Looking first at the variation by socioeconomic status (education, occupation, and income), available research suggests that the traditional inverse relationship between socioeconomic status and fertility only characterized foreign-born, first-generation American Jews. For second- and third-generation Jewish couples, socioeconomic variations in fertility were unclear with some indication of a positive relationship — higher-status Jews had somewhat larger families than lower-status Jews. There is clear evidence of convergence and greater homogeneity in the fertility patterns of Jewish couples. The contraction of socioeconomic differentials has been viewed as further evidence of the widespread rationality with which the majority of contemporary Jews plan their families, the absence of rapid upward mobility characteristic of earlier generations, and the greater homogeneity of contemporary Jewish social structure. The lack of wide class distinctions among third-generation Jews may account for the absence of striking fertility differences within the Jewish population (Goldscheider, 1967; Goldstein and Goldscheider, 1968; Goldstein, 1973b, 1979a).

Traditional Judaism has emphasized large family size and limited the permissibility of mechanical contraception to reasons of health (broadly defined). If judged by the low levels of fertility and efficient use of contraception for family planning among American Jews, these traditional norms have been largely ignored. Until recently, there has been no reason to postulate that the religious elite of the American Jewish community have viewed issues of family size or planning as high priority. Scattered evidence indicates that American Jews are not aware of these norms or prohibitions. Nor is there any clear fertility ideology or theology in Reform or Conservative Judaism that has been clearly conveyed to those identifying with these denominations.

Research carried out in the 1960s suggests that the relationship between religiosity, defined in a variety of ways, and Jewish fertility is complex. For the older foreign-born generation, there seems to be a positive relationship — the higher the religiosity, the larger the family size. This pattern did not characterize younger, American-born generations. Detailed evidence reveals that family size differences among those identifying with various religious divisions within Judaism disappear when socioeconomic status was controlled (cf. Goldscheider, 1965a; Lazerwitz, 1973b; Ritterband and Cohen, 1979). These studies concluded that religious identity and identification have little relationship to Jewish fertility that cannot be accounted for by social class factors. The secular nature of religion for modern Jews implies that Judaism as a religion plays a minor role in determining their fertility.

Studies have not focused on self-segregated religious subcommunities of Jews in selected metropolitan areas of the United States. Impressionistic evidence suggests, for example, that among this segment of committed American Jewry, higher fertility values, ideals, and behavior prevail. In part, these traditional Jewish communities have rejected in a variety of ways the integrationist ideology of the vast majority of American Jews. In their emphasis on traditional roles for women, family and spiritual central-ity, and general resistance to acculturation, large-family values and behavior have been retained and supported. These groups have probably contributed a disproportionate share of children to the American Jewish community.

This impressionistic evidence relates to the small but conspicuous Has-idic sects and more fundamentalistic (less modern, integrated) orthodox subcommunities. Growing Jewish public concern with low or declining rates of American Jewish population growth may have an effect for se-lected committed segments of American Jewry in the direction of some-what larger family size. An increase in family size among those whose religious orientation has moved toward greater self-segregation and funda-mentalism would represent a significant shift in American Jewish fertility patterns. Research on these subcommunities should be carried out to iden-tify the extent and direction of this phenomenon and its implications for understanding future fertility patterns among Jews.

Another source of fertility variation within the American Jewish popula-tion, related to the issue of religiosity, is the difference between the family size of couples where the husband and wife are Jewish compared to inter-married couples. Parallel to general findings on intermarriage between Protestants and Catholics, several studies have shown that Jewish inter-marriage results in lowered fertility. Intermarried couples have fewer chil-dren and higher childless rates than homogenously married Jewish couples (Goldstein and Goldscheider, 1968; Goldstein, 1979a). Fertility differ-ences between the intermarried and nonintermarried seem to be narrower among younger couples and may provide some indication of the greater ac-ceptability of intermarried couples within the Jewish community. We shall return to this theme in our review of intermarriage.

One final issue in the analysis of variation in Jewish fertility relates to place of residence. Fertility levels tend to be somewhat higher in suburban than in urban areas and highest in rural areas. Since the number of Jews in rural areas is very small, the issue remains whether suburbanization has an effect on Jewish fertility. Some have speculated on the basis of Protestant-Catholic patterns that there is a convergence in fertility among religious groups in the suburbs (Zimmer and Goldscheider, 1966). Others have argued the case for Jews without empirical evidence (Rosenthal, 1961). Some evidence is available indicating that suburban Jewish family size is larger than among Jews residing in urban areas and birth intervals are longer as well (Goldstein and Goldscheider, 1968).

It is unclear whether the relatively higher fertility of suburban Jews is a reflection of the impact of suburban residence and the equalizing-acculturating effects of the suburbs or whether there is a selective migration to the suburbs of those who want larger families. Some evidence from the Providence study suggests that the majority of suburban residents moved there after their first child was born. The implication is that for many reasons suburban areas are attractive to people with families and this probably accounts for their slightly larger family sizes. More recent detailed research should pursue this relationship further. Data from the NJPS should prove valuable in analyzing this and other differentials reviewed above. However, in order to analyze these patterns fully, a longitudinal research design is necessary.

Neglected Areas of Research in Jewish Fertility

In the review of trends and differentials in Jewish fertility and the issues associated with the explanation of Jewish fertility, we have noted the limitations of previous research. Many of the findings reviewed have been based on inadequate and incomplete evidence or data sources that have serious methodological problems. We also noted the need for research on the fertility of more recently married cohorts and the desirability of longitudinal research designs to identify family formation dynamics.

One area of research that has been neglected relates to the consequences of low Jewish fertility. While assessments of the implications of fertility patterns for Jewish population growth have been made within the limitations of available data, other consequences have not been studied. Three such areas should be investigated. First, what are the consequences of Jewish fertility patterns for the educational attainment of children, occupational-career patterns, income, and general socioeconomic status? More generally, what implications does low Jewish fertility have for leisure activities, career patterns for women, and general lifestyles? While socioeconomic and related issues have been viewed as determinants of fertility, almost no research has focused on these patterns as consequences.

A second neglected area of fertility consequences relates to the issue of Jewish identification and religiosity. Some evidence suggests that childless couples are less likely to be formally affiliated with the Jewish community in terms of self-identification, synagogue or temple membership, or in terms of a broad range of Jewish communal organizations. Jewish ritual observances that have become defined as child- or family-oriented are less likely to characterize childless couples (Goldscheider, 1973). It has been suggested that having children and socializing them into the minority subculture often involves parents in roles and decisions which relate them to the Jewish community and develop or enhance parental Jewish identification (Sklare and Greenblum, 1967). A more thorough investigation of the implications of fertility (not only childless but one- and two-child families) for Jewish identification and affiliation of both parents and children over the life cycle is required. A related issue focuses on the macro level: What are the implications of low fertility for the structure of the Jewish community, for community organizations, and community services?

The research issues involved in examining the consequences of Jewish fertility are complex and new research designs must be developed to cope with these issues. It is analytically important to treat the relationship between social structure and fertility as a two-way process where fertility is both a consequence and a determinant of social patterns at the individual and community levels. The consequences of low Jewish fertility go beyond the demographic issues of population growth and structure. Jewish fertility patterns have indirect effects on Jewish institutions and families through their consequences on population dynamics. They may also have direct consequences on socioeconomic, family, religious, and communal institutional patterns.

Jewish Family Structure

The family functions to maintain group continuity and is one of the basic units of socialization and cultural transmission for the next generation. Demographic and cultural continuities have been primarily located in the family. This is no less true for the Jewish subgroup than for total societies. Because of the interdependence of family and other aspects of society, it is not unexpected that as broader societal changes unfold, family patterns will be altered as well. Several demographic aspects of Jewish family structure will be reviewed below. These include the extent of marriage and non-marriage, the timing of marriage (particularly age at marriage), the duration of marriage (divorce, separation, and remarriage), and demographic aspects of extended family patterns (particularly household structure). Research on the size of families and mate selection (specifically intermarriage) are reviewed in separate sections of this paper.

Despite the centrality of family patterns for demographic and sociological analysis, few detailed studies are available. Some limited information may be obtained from the 1957 Current Population Survey data and from Jewish community studies and preliminary data published from the NJPS. More recent changes based on impressionistic observations require careful and detailed research focused on Jewish family structure.

American Jews have been until recently remarkably successful in maintaining patterns of family stability and cohesion. The family has remained central in the lives of Jews despite social and geographic mobility and general acculturation and integration. The persistence of almost universal but somewhat later ages at marriage, low divorce rates, and nuclear family structure has indeed been exceptional considering the radical social transformations of American Jews in the last century (Goldstein and Goldscheider, 1968).

Data from the 1957 CPS survey show the very high proportion of Jewish men and women who ever marry: among those aged 35–44 only 5 percent of Jewish men and 8 percent of Jewish women were single or never married. These findings have been repeatedly observed in various community studies (Goldstein, 1971). Divorce rates seem to be lower for Jews than for the total American population (Goldberg, 1968). Consistent with their higher levels of education, age at marriage tends to be higher among Jews than for the total American population (Goldscheider and Goldstein, 1967; Goldstein, 1971; Kobrin and Goldscheider, 1978).

Marriage cohort data reveal that later age at marriage has characterized Jewish women since at least 1920. Average age at marriage seems to have increased from 19 to 23 years up to World War II cohorts and declined subsequently for cohorts marrying in the 1950s and early 1960s. These patterns follow the general American population, but at higher average ages. Thus while higher education may have been a factor in the delayed marriage of women in the pre–World War II period, other factors (such as the greater separation of marriage from early childbearing due to the use of efficient contraception) must be operating in the post–World War II period. Although data are not available for the analysis of changes in the last decade, it is likely that delayed marriage among selected segments of the Jewish population has occurred. This may be related to greater separation of sexual activity from marriage and revolutionary changes in the role and status of women during this period.

While marriage and family-building patterns emerging primarily from Jewish community studies are fairly consistent, several methodological and theoretical issues remain. First, since available data are cross-sectional and marriage and divorce records do not contain information on religion, the dynamics associated with family changes and family formation must be inferred. More serious are possible biases associated with the sampling design of Jewish community surveys. These surveys have relied heavily on Jewish community master lists. These have been biased toward family units and may not have included younger (or older) single persons. Some scattered evidence pointing to lack of formal Jewish community affiliation among this group would further bias samples focused on the more affiliated. Finally, it is not clear whether marriage patterns (the extent or timing) and divorce levels are exceptional for Jews compared to the total population when the unique socioeconomic and residential characteristics of Jews are controlled. As in the explanation of Jewish fertility, it is not clear whether specific Jewish values or particular features of Jewish social structure account for these marriage and family patterns or whether they reflect the social characteristics of the Jewish population.

Patterns of household formation and structure, particularly the degree of family extension, have never been studied systematically for Jewish Americans. Community surveys have revealed the small size of Jewish households, mainly reflecting low Jewish fertility. Following the general American pattern, nuclear family structure predominates among Jews (Goldstein, 1971). Recent research on the American population has pointed to changing patterns of household structure, particularly the significant growth of single-person household units (Kobrin, 1976; Kobrin and Goldscheider, 1979). This view examines the proportion of all nuclear households and the household structure of nonnuclear family members. Research focused on the living arrangements of both the older and younger adult ages has pointed to growing proportions who select the alternative of living alone rather than either the nuclear or extended residential arrangement. Preliminary evidence from the NJPS shows that 30 percent of household heads under age 30 live alone or outside the nuclear or extended family pattern (Massarik and Chenkin, 1973).

The review up to this point has emphasized the research available and its limitations up to the 1960s. Recent changes over the last fifteen years that may alter this general picture have not been systematically studied. While there are some clues to these changes from the NJPS for the youngest marriage cohort — particularly the increasing levels of single-person household, delayed marriage, and higher divorce rates — these data may not have fully tapped changes in the last decade (Massarik and Chenkin, 1973).

A variety of indirect indicators suggests that a series of revolutionary family changes are unfolding among selected segments of fourth-generation Jews. For the first time in recent American Jewish history significant proportions of men and women aged 20–35 are not marrying. The increasing proportions of the never married adds to the growing number of nonmarried, divorced, and separated Jewish men and women. These groups represent a new phenomenon in American Jewish life and are a challenge to institutional, organizational, and community structures that have in the past focused almost exclusively on the family as the unit of greatest significance.

The increasing proportion of nonmarriage, delayed marriage, and divorce among Jews has obvious implications for fertility and reproduction patterns, family values, as well as demographic and sociocultural continuity. The implications of these patterns of family and marriage are unmistakable even if they are only temporary responses to social and economic conditions, reflections of peculiar demographic limitations associated with

the availability of Jewish mates in particular locations, statuses, or age categories, or are more deeply related to changes in marriage and family values, women's roles, and sexual behavior characterizing America of the
1970s. If these impressions of changes in nonmarriage and higher divorce
rates are accurate, patterns of low fertility and high intermarriage rates
will be further exacerbated among Jews. Changes in marriage and family
behavior and norms have a direct impact on the timing of marriage, decisions not to marry, processes of separation, divorce, and remarriage, number and timing of births, the relationship of children to their families of
orientation and extended family networks, and mate selection.

The sexual revolution, changes in women's roles and, in turn, changes in
marriage and family patterns have special significance for Jews because of
their tradition of family cohesiveness and unity, endogamy, and universal
marriage patterns. Changes in Jewish fertility have been less in the direction of zero and one-child families and more in the direction of almost universal two- to three-child families among those married. However, when
fewer Jews are getting married, some are marrying at later ages, and still
others deciding to have no children because of career patterns for women,
then two- to three-child families are insufficient to attain overall population replacement levels. Changes in marriage and the timing of childbearing may not have the effect of reducing marital fertility in the long run but
may reduce current birth rates below replacement levels and place the burden of population replacement on a smaller group of married women.

Jews have tended in the past to be in the forefront of major sociodemographic revolutions. American Jews are located in social statuses and geographic locations most responsive to changes in marriage and the family.
The high proportion of Jews with college and graduate-level educations,
their disproportionate concentration in select metropolitan centers, and
their middle-class backgrounds and values place them in the avant-garde
of social change. For Jews, the decline of the family may imply additional
strains on Jewish social, cultural, and demographic continuity in America.
When added to the empirical results of increasing rates of intermarriage
and low levels of fertility, changes in marriage and the family are clearly in
the direction away from Jewish demographic vitality in America.

Demographic Aspects of Jewish Intermarriage

Much more so than fertility levels or changes in marriage patterns, intermarriage between Jews and non-Jews has called into question the possibility of quantitative and qualitative survival of a small ethnic-religious
minority group in an open society. No other issue symbolizes more clearly
the conflict between universalism and particularism, between the American melting pot and sociocultural universalism and pluralism, between as-

similation and ethnic continuity in American society. The unresolved dilemma for American Jewry revolves around traditional values of family cohesion, Jewish continuity and endogamy, on the one hand, and the consistency between out-marriages and the structural-cultural features of American Jewish life, on the other.

Until the 1960s, the Jewish group in America had been accurately described as the classic illustration of voluntary group endogamy. Social scientists hardly had a basis for questioning Jewish group continuity when intermarriage rates were low, Jewish marriage rates high, and family patterns among Jews strong and cohesive. Demographic survival issues were rarely raised when intermarriage was a marginal feature of American Jewish life, even when Jewish fertility patterns fluctuated around replacement levels.

Evidence of increasing levels of Jewish out-marriage began to accumulate in the early 1960s and intermarriage and conversion have become more prominent features of the American Jewish situation. In the 1960s and 1970s the demographic concerns of numerical losses through Jewish intermarriages were heightened since American Jewish population size was relatively small, dispersion more pronounced, growth through immigration small, and natural increase low. Intermarriage rates indicating significant losses among the young pose a particular demographic threat to a small minority reproducing at replacement levels. The concern of the American Jewish community about population reduction through intermarriage was not directed to macrodemographic issues that have rarely been fully understood or well documented statistically. Rather Jewish intermarriage has come to symbolize significant shifts in Jewish family life and group continuity.

Jewish intermarriage in contemporary American society does not appear to be the result of a specific desire to assimilate or a consequence of particular intermarriage norms. It is the direct result of the structure of American Jewish life and general values shared by American Jews. It is the structural integration of American Jews that results in higher rates of intermarriage among the fourth generation. These structural features include greater residential integration of Jewish and non-Jewish neighborhoods, social interaction between Jews and non-Jews, and public school and college attendance where Jews are a minority in a middle-class environment. A set of ideological commitments and value patterns reinforces these structural features. Conducive to high rates of intermarriage are egalitarian beliefs, emphasis on liberalism, faith in minority group integration, rejection of ethnocentrism, and commitment to universalism (Sklare, 1971). These structural features and cultural values have come to characterize the Jewish ethnic group in America.

Intermarriage (and its sociodemographic consequences) can no longer be treated as marginal when it is the result of a deep-rooted sociopolitical ideology and value structure and a function of lifestyle, residential pattern, and educational and occupational structure. It cannot be ignored within the Jewish community when few Jewish families have not experienced intermarriage directly or through friends and neighbors. The intermarriage issue has become central to the internal struggles of American Jewry. For those who view intermarriage as a threat to Jewish demographic continuity in America, the ultimate choice appears to be between changing the social structure and value orientations of the American Jewish community or to accommodate and accept the intermarried. There are no indications that the first alternative has been or will be selected by the majority of American Jews.

Data sources on Jewish intermarriage have been limited for comprehensive demographic analysis. Although some data on religion are available on the marriage records of two states (Iowa and Indiana) and from the 1957 Current Population Survey, these have limited value for any extensive analysis of Jewish intermarriage rates (Rosenthal, 1963, 1975; Glick, 1960; Goldstein, 1973b).[2] The major source for an analysis of trends and differentials in intermarriage are Jewish community surveys. While allowing for the inclusion of details on the background characteristics of intermarried couples, these surveys have limitations in terms of full coverage of marginal Jewish households and the nonaffiliated.

A brief overview of findings on changes and variations in Jewish intermarriage in the United States reveals the following patterns. Jewish endogamy is high and intermarriage rates are low relative to large American ethnic-religious groups. However, given the specific demographic characteristics of American Jewry, the level of intermarriage probably represents a diminution in the size of the American Jewish population. No evaluation of the demography of American Jews can ignore the centrality of Jewish intermarriage in absolute and relative Jewish population changes.

The general pattern of low rates of intermarriage based on a cross-section of the Jewish community obscures the effects of age and generation and confuses cumulative and current rates. The separation of period and cohort perspectives is no less required in the analysis of intermarriage than in fertility studies. An examination of intermarriage rates by age and generation as well as general levels of intermarriage between different periods reveals a pattern of increase in Jewish intermarriage. Some scattered evidence and impressions suggest that disproportionate shifts in the rate of intermarriage have occurred in the 1960s and 1970s among young Jews of third and fourth generations.

Systematic evaluation of the quantitative significance of changing intermarriage trends is incomplete since the level of conversion to Judaism is not well documented. Nor do we know the eventual Jewish commitment by children of intermarried couples. The general impression from selected community studies including the NJPS is that the level of conversion to Judaism has increased, and some significant proportion of the children of intermarried couples are being raised as Jews. Although it is impossible to be precise, there is no question that current rates of Jewish intermarriage affect the size of the American Jewish population and have longer-term demographic significance for the size of generations yet unborn. It is also clear that not all Jewish intermarriages imply the loss to the Jewish community of the Jewish partner, the non-Jewish spouse, or the couple's children. On the contrary, for some select proportion of intermarried couples, the Jewish community gains rather than loses members through conversion and the Jewish socialization of the children of intermarried couples. Some data show a tendency among those who intermarry and remain within the Jewish community to be more religious and committed as compared to Jews endogamously married.

In addition to the question of changing intermarriage rates and their demographic implications are issues relating to differential levels of intermarriage among American Jewish communities and subgroups within the Jewish community. The level of Jewish intermarriage varies considerably between communities and reflects in part social compositional variations. Communities and subcommunities (suburbs, for example) vary in the rate of intermarriage simply because of variation in the size of the Jewish population and in generational and socioeconomic characteristics as well as related factors such as religiosity. It is not clear whether communities with higher intermarriage rates foreshadow what will come to characterize the American Jewish population in the future or whether because of their size or composition these communities are exceptional. The size of the Jewish community and the implied density of Jewish residential patterns appear to be important factors in intermarriage rates.

There are some indications emerging from the literature that sociological differences between the intermarried and nonintermarried have diminished among recent cohorts. Analysis of changing patterns of age at marriage, fertility, socioeconomic status, and sex differentials suggests some convergence of the intermarried and nonintermarried in these characteristics. These tentative findings fit in with the notion that intermarriage is no longer a marginal or deviant phenomenon in American Jewish life. There appears to be much less selectivity in intermarriage among contemporary Jews and the intermarried may become in terms of their characteristics and subsequent behavior not significantly different from those in endogamous marriages. The social background characteristics of Jewish and non-Jewish partners to the intermarriage tend to be similar among recently intermarried couples as compared to intermarried couples of previous generations.

Two social characteristics are related to intermarriage: Jewish residential segregation and Jewish education. An empirical relationship has been reported in a variety of studies between the character of residential neighborhoods and intermarriage rates. Jews living in areas of greater Jewish population concentration are more likely to be endogamous than Jews living in areas of low Jewish population densities. This may reflect the fact that contact and interaction between Jews and non-Jews are integral processes determining levels of intermarriage. The more extensive and significant the interaction between Jews and non-Jews in school, neighborhoods, organizations, social and business activities, the greater the likelihood of intermarriage. It is not clear whether residence in areas of low Jewish population density is a determinant of high intermarriage rates or a consequence of selective migration patterns of intermarried couples.

A key finding of previous research has been that extensive and intensive Jewish education is generally correlated with endogamy. Again, the implications are less clear than a superficial examination might suggest. It is not obvious, for example, what is the relationship between Jewish education and residential segregation or that between Jewish education and a variety of dimensions of Jewish identity and commitment. Nor does this finding specify the amount or type of Jewish education that clearly results in endogamy. However, the finding at the most simple level indicates at a minimum that commitment to Jewish survival either through Jewish education or through processes reflected in Jewish education are conducive to Jewish endogamy and continuity. Jewish intermarriage rates therefore tend to be highest among those who stand at the least committed end of the Jewish continuum.

Data on the relationship between educational attainment and occupational status and intermarriage levels do not show clear patterns. Results from one community lead to the conclusion that Jewish intermarriage rates do not vary in a consistent way with current class position (Goldstein and Goldscheider, 1968). The same study noted that marriage instability is very much associated with intermarriage. It is nevertheless clear that a fuller examination of variation in intermarriage requires a dynamic, longitudinal research design to unravel the determinants and consequences over the life cycle. Such studies have never been undertaken (cf. the research by Sherrow reported in Schwartz, 1970).

A final point requires reemphasis: it is not the level of Jewish intermarriage per se that challenges the sociodemographic survival of Jews in America. Nor are the patterns of Jewish reproduction, migration, family, or age structure exceptional in their individual and separate levels and trends. Rather it is the specific demographic context within which intermarriage rates operate in America that is of paramount significance. The combination of low fertility, geographic dispersion, minimum potential sources of population renewal through immigration or further mortality reduction, declines in family cohesion, *and* relatively high intermarriage rates have resulted in issues associated with the demographic vitality of Jewish Americans. Given the limitations of available research on all the demographic factors related to Jewish population growth, it is not possible to assign relative weights to individual factors or fully assess the level of Jewish population growth (stability or decline).

Research Challenges and Priorities: Data Collection, Documentation, and Types of Analysis

The critical review of research on the demography of Jewish Americans reveals a reasonably solid foundation upon which to build future cumulative studies. While empirical evidence supporting specific generalizations on particular topics may be less than satisfactory from a methodological point of view, a considerable amount of research has been carried out on major aspects of American Jewish demography. Future research must build upon what is known and hypothesized rather than proceeding in a research vacuum. Undoubtedly, careful and systematic research will qualify and refine existing findings on American Jewish demography, correct previous errors, and contribute new insights and generalizations. Future research on the demography of American Jews must explore new unresearched topics suggested by previous studies and apply different methodological strategies in addressing particular analytic issues. There is also continuing need for reorganizing existing data sources, providing documentation of previously researched issues, and evaluating more systematically data now available.

The overview of past research presented here has pointed to the variety of substantive issues and research topics included in the demography of American Jews. For each of these topics there are a variety of data sources, many of them limited and unsatisfactory for an in-depth examination of major analytic issues. Therefore research challenges for future studies are also pluralistic: no single research design or methodological strategy can encompass the broad range of topics that require research attention in the future. In considering the types of research that should be pursued and the priorities associated with particular topics and activities, we begin with the premise that there are diverse methodological approaches for studying the range of demographic topics for the heterogeneous subgroups that encompass the American Jewish population.

Before considering specific demographic research activities of the proposed center of modern Jewish studies and discussing research priorities that emerge from our review of the demography of American Jews, two caveats must be considered. First, we shall avoid proposing an ideal, comprehensive survey design for an all-encompassing study of American Jewish demographic processes. Such a multipurpose design is neither desirable nor feasible at this stage, and there are other research activities of greater value. It is premature to consider grand research projects before exploring more modest but fruitful alternative research strategies. In-depth research on specific demographic topics using appropriate research designs is required rather than some overall project attempting to obtain information on a broad range of topics that inevitably fall short — for both methodological and design reasons. Sampling problems and financial issues must also be considered. Although any sample survey carried out by a new research center would incorporate selected demographic data, surveys designed to investigate demographic issues should focus on particular topics and research these in depth.

There is a need to specify research priorities among the variety of demographic issues. Some priorities emerge from the review of what we know about American Jewish demographic processes. There are also subjective elements involved in selecting among research priorities. The suggested research topics that will be outlined below seem to me to have the greatest priority. It is possible that a demographer with specific interests, as for example in model building, demographic history, or morbidity and epidemiology, would assign different priorities to future research topics. Four major activities are suggested for the proposed new center. These include: (1) documentation and organization of existing materials; (2) coordination and consultation; (3) initiation of research on continuous demographic changes; and (4) research on specific issues — evaluative and substantive.

Documentation

The first set of proposed activities relates to the organization and exploitation of existing research materials. This includes two specific tasks. First, the proposed center should obtain and organize all materials published on the demography of American Jews. This documentation should include all publications in the general literature pertaining to the Jewish group in America as well as the various Jewish community studies that have been carried out. This documentation function is essential for both teaching purposes and research. Second, there is a need to obtain unpublished data from various Jewish and general sources. Ideally, the original data files — cards, computer tapes — should be available for more detailed and uniform tabulations for intercommunity and historical comparisons. There is a wealth of data from Jewish community studies that has not been fully analyzed and has not been sufficiently organized for detailed comparisons. In addition to specific community studies the basic data file of the NJPS should be obtained. Most demographic comparisons have been limited to published materials and as a result are less than comprehensive.

Despite the limitations of general surveys for the analysis of Jewish demographic processes, some of these data — published and unpublished — are extremely valuable. The original data sets of the major fertility studies are readily available and should be on file at the proposed center. Gallup and Roper polls that contain information on Jews as well as the birth data obtained in the National Center for Health Statistics studies are additional data sources. Special U.S. census tapes may be ordered for specific subpopulations — those reporting Yiddish as their mother tongue, or the Israeli-born — that provide data on subsections of the American Jewish population. A systematic inventory of ongoing demographic projects should be made to uncover whether useful data on the Jews are included. Historical data from previous censuses should be obtained where possible. In short, one of the major functions of the proposed center should be the organization of existing materials and the exploitation of unpublished data sets. The center should include a comprehensive and continuous Jewish data bank as an integral part of its activities.

Coordination and Consultation

The proposed center should also serve for the coordination of future Jewish community studies and as a consultant to sample surveys of local Jewish areas. There is an urgent need to improve the quality of these surveys and tackle the complex methodological issues of sampling and coverage. This should be centrally coordinated to insure the highest-quality data collection under local sponsorship. Only through such coordination and consultation can minimum standards of quality and comparison be maintained. Although most of these surveys are carried out to meet local needs, the utility of these data could be improved with centralized consultation. Beyond consultation on methodological and design issues, standard tabulation formats might be organized to facilitate data analysis. The center should be the data depository of all future surveys.

Related to coordination of studies initiated in local areas, the center might become involved in initiating, jointly with local Jewish community agencies, research projects involving the collection of demographic data. This is particularly needed in areas where Jewish community studies have not been undertaken, in newer Jewish communities where recent population growth has been substantial, and in communities where surveys have been undertaken in the past but are now dated.

While this paper has focused exclusively on the demography of American Jews, some consideration might be given to broadening the focus to other countries. Rich data sources are available on the demography of Canadian Jewry, for example. The similarity of conditions in Canada and the United States argues strongly for the exploitation of official demographic data from Canada. Cooperation with Statistics Canada should be encouraged. Since the Institute of Contemporary Jewry at the Hebrew University in Jerusalem has a unit for the documentation of Jewish statistics and demography around the world, it would be unnecessary for the proposed center to duplicate their activities. There is a need to establish channels of communication and cooperation so that duplication is avoided.

Cooperation with the Central Bureau of Statistics in Israel should also be encouraged. Data are available on American Jews settling or visiting Israel. Census data sources and special studies of immigrant adjustment in Israel have contained data on American Jews. While the proposed center should not attempt to focus on the comparative demography of world Jewry, comparative materials on Jews in other countries — similar and different from American Jews — should be included in the center's activities. These comparative materials should be valuable in isolating the particularly American aspects of American Jewry as well as the commonalities of the Jewish demographic experience in a variety of national contexts.

Research on Continuous Demographic Changes

The research reviewed here has almost invariably been cross-sectional in design. To my knowledge, there has never been a study designed for an analysis of continuous demographic (or broader sociological) changes among American Jews that has been longitudinal in design. There are methodological and analytic limitations to cross-sectional studies, although these should be encouraged wherever possible. The dynamics of Jewish demographic change have been inferred from cross-sectional studies over a period of time (usually from different communities). We have reached the point in our studies of Jewish demographic changes where methodological and analytic issues require a new research emphasis. This demands a research design to tap the dynamics of changes as they unfold rather than retrospectively.

It was argued earlier that a grand survey design for uncovering demographic processes would not be proposed here. Nevertheless, the proposed center should consider the range of possibilities of longitudinal research that may find financial support outside the center. Such projects might be initiated with minimal funds to demonstrate feasibility and subsequently turn to government sources and private foundations for more substantial grants. Such projects might include repeat interviewing among a select subsample of the NJPS or the selection of a particular community (or communities) where pilot projects may be initiated. The specific focus of the pilot project will be determined by the sample design and substantive priorities discussed below. The objective would be to obtain information on early family formation stages and follow-up processes of fertility and migration. The goal would be to analyze these family-fertility-migration processes over time, and in relationship to measures of Jewish identification and commitment at macro and micro levels, rather than an analysis of population structure and composition for a specific community. Even a modest attempt in this direction should prove valuable. The involvement of students in the analysis of longitudinal changes should be a major research experience that would include all the various research issues and stages — research design, sampling problems, questionnaire construction, and data analyses. An ongoing project should allow for the inclusion of questions that may be related to changing demographic processes but not focused solely on demographic issues per se. Thus for both research and teaching purposes an ongoing longitudinal study of the Jews would be of enormous value.

Topics and Issues: Evaluative and Substantive

In the context of our review of previous research on the variety of major demographic processes we have noted specific research issues that require further investigation as well as neglected issues. It is unnecessary to repeat in this section the details of those suggestions or to list them all. Rather, several major themes in American Jewish demography appear to be of greater research priority. These are subdivided into two categories: those with higher and those with lower priority. Before turning to these topics, it is important to note the need for research designed to evaluate data sources now available.

Evaluation Research. One theme repeated throughout this chapter has been the methodological problems associated with the various data sources available for studying American Jewish demography. The heavy reliance on data collected for purposes other than scientific analysis requires caution in interpretation and analysis. The cumulative nature of much of the research available may support particular empirical generalizations and hypotheses. Cumulative findings based on limited data of poor quality may also reflect similar methodological biases and cumulative error.

Great reliance has been placed on *American Jewish Year Book* estimates of population size and distribution. These estimates have rarely been systematically challenged or evaluated and when they have, serious biases have been uncovered (Schmelz, 1969). All too rarely have Jewish community studies been evaluated in detail to include sampling error estimates, coverage biases, and related methodological issues. While the NJPS remains the best potential source for examining selected aspects of Jewish demography at the national level, no comprehensive methodological evaluation is available of this study. The heavy dependence on Jewish community studies for understanding Jewish demographic processes requires that evaluation research be carried out. It is likely that Jewish-sponsored research will remain the major source of demographic information on the Jews in the future as in the past. Given this situation and the uneven quality of these data so often noted in the literature, it is necessary to design studies to allow for the comprehensive methodological evaluation of this data source.

High-Priority Research Topics. Whether the research design is longitudinal or cross-sectional and whether the study area is local, comparative, or national, the following topics in the demography of American Jews should receive the highest research priority. Studies of family structure, formation, marriage, and fertility among recent cohorts should be carried out. No evidence is available on changes in the 1970s on these fundamental topics. The focus should be on young persons — married and unmarried — and should include attitudinal and behavioral data associated with these processes. Preferably these data should be collected as part of a longitudinal design to evaluate changes in these family and childbearing processes as they unfold. Such a study should begin ideally with a cohort of unmarried young persons and follow them over time to study processes of mate selection, child spacing, marriage attitudes, decisions to and timing of marrying, living arrangements, and marriage stability. Other topics listed below could be incorporated into such a study.

Since by their very design, longitudinal studies take time to uncover the processes of change, special studies ought to be encouraged on related topics of critical importance. These include divorce and remarriage patterns and reproductive behavior and attitudes among persons marrying in the last decade or so. A related area should focus on the changing status and role of Jewish men and women regarding marriage and reproduction as well as other areas of Jewish community life.

Another area of investigation relates to household structure and living arrangements of both younger and older segments of the American Jewish population. Research on social processes associated with living alone (or in nonnuclear and nonextended family units) should be designed. If American Jews follow the general pattern emerging in the United States (and there is no reason to assume that they do not), changes in household structure have been substantial in the last decades. These changes have not been investigated among Jews and may be of demographic and sociological importance at the individual and community levels. As the structure of the Jewish population becomes more heavily concentrated in the older ages, special studies of this group — particularly family and Jewish institutional issues — should be designed.

One of the most neglected topics in the demography of American Jews has been that of migration patterns and population dispersal. Because of the educational and occupational concentration of Jews, the changing structure of occupational opportunities, and changing levels of Jewish commitment, younger Jews may be migrating more than previous generations. These migration patterns involve more than just the process of mobility. They include moving away from traditional areas of Jewish population concentration. If Jews follow recent patterns of the American population as a whole, migration may imply moving to nonmetropolitan areas and small towns. The relationship between Jewish population density and commitment to Jewish communities (and Jewish identification) make this a central topic in evaluating the demography and sociology of American Jews. Since migration lessens ties to local community institutions and the integration of migrants in local communities requires time, the issue remains whether Jewish commitments of migrants are transferred to a more national level of identification or with international issues (such as Israel or a sense of peoplehood), or whether in the absence of local community integration, Jewish commitments decline generally. Population dispersal, residential integration, and migration patterns are complex research topics at both local and national levels and remain one of the critical research challenges of the highest priority.

The importance of intermarriage for the demographic future of the American Jewish population cannot be overstressed. Despite the centrality of the issue and the voluminous scientific, ideological, and popular literature that has dealt with it, fundamental research remains to be done. Research on Jewish intermarriage has been cross-sectional and retrospective in design. Hence we have not been able to fully analyze selection and change in Jewish intermarriage nor the dynamics associated with normative and structural shifts within the American Jewish community. Except for small, unrepresentative samples of limited utility, no social science research has focused systematically and comprehensively on the determinants and consequences of Jewish intermarriage.

Studies of Jewish intermarriage and its implications for the retention of Jewish identity (for Jewish and non-Jewish partners as well as for the children of intermarried couples) need to be carried out. Again, the preferable design should be longitudinal and prospective rather than cross-sectional and retrospective. Detailed research on the selectivity of intermarriage by socioeconomic background, religious commitment, Jewish education, residential patterns as well as dating and interaction between Jews and non-Jews should be systematically carried out.

One of the interesting related areas of investigation from a demographic point of view is the relationship between the availability of mates and marriage choices. One factor involved in lower rates of intermarriage in communities with large Jewish populations may be the larger "marriage market" of Jewish men and women. Overall population size and particularly the size of various cohorts of unmarried men and women set structural limits to endogamy. The choice of those faced with a "Jewish marriage squeeze" ranges from migration to another community where

Jewish marriage markets are larger, marriage out of the Jewish community, or nonmarriage (or delayed marriage).

Fluctuations in availability of Jewish mates at the local level may be affected by patterns of migration and indirectly by past patterns of childbearing (cohort and period fertility fluctuations). While we do not have any direct research on this issue, it seems reasonable to speculate that migration selectivity and period fertility fluctuations among Jews have had a structural impact on Jewish marriage markets in some communities. In turn, these structural demographic changes have had repercussions on intermarriage, patterns of nonmarriage, and changes in marriage timing.

Studies of the impact of intermarriage on present and future Jewish population need to be designed. Similarly, the structural demographic antecedents to intermarriage, particularly the role of marriage markets and squeezes need to be specified and analyzed. Intermarriage is one of the master themes in American Jewish life and has been described as the "quintessential dilemma" for American Jewry. Research on this issue is of highest priority.

National data on Jews do not allow for the systematic analysis of Jewish heterogeneity in terms of communities and specific subgroups. Local Jewish community studies are designed for overall planning purposes and for the description of the total population in these areas. Specific research is needed on particular subgroups and subcommunities to evaluate the range of Jewish heterogeneity. Demographic studies of segregated Jewish communities — such as Hasidic and segregated orthodox communities — are necessary. Since these Jewish communities are densely settled and relatively more organized, they are easier to study, although their social closure often limits research access. At the other end of the Jewish commitment continuum are Jewish subgroups residentially and socially integrated, where the levels of Jewish identification and continuity are low. As a supplement to national and local Jewish population studies, there is a need to select several major Jewish subgroup types and collect data on Jewish demographic processes. The research objective would not be to describe the population structure of total Jewish communities, but to select for analytic comparisons the range of subgroups within the Jewish community. This focused research strategy may be particularly useful given the more general sampling problems associated with covering the various segments of the Jewish community. Even when local Jewish community studies have made efforts to incorporate nonaffiliated and marginal subgroups, their numbers have been too small for detailed analysis. Research focused on specific Jewish subpopulations to maximize the comparative analysis of Jewish heterogeneity is a viable alternative to supplement in detail what is known about Jewish American demographic processes.

There are other Jewish subgroups that should be the focus of special analytic demographic studies. These include Jewish community leaders, religious personnel (rabbis, teachers in religious schools), academics, and members of particular occupational categories (e.g., physicians, lawyers). The study of the demographic patterns of the Jewish elite, however defined for research purposes, would include behavioral and attitudinal dimensions associated with reproduction, marriage, migration, and intermarriage. From a sampling point of view these subgroups would be more readily available and less problematic. Again, while not representing the broader cross-section of the Jewish community, they may represent significant patterns of variation and change, serving as a demographic barometer of the future of the American Jewish population. In part, the Jewish elite and influentials, directly and indirectly, by action or inaction, through personal behavior and attitude, shape the overall normative climate of the Jewish community's response to issues associated with key demographic processes.

The final topic of high research priority relates to recent Jewish immigration. If estimates over the last decade are accurate, well over 100,000 Jewish immigrants have settled in the United States. These have mainly come from the Soviet Union and Israel. Research on all aspects of immigration, settlement, and integration (or nonintegration) within the larger Jewish community is necessary. This should include more accurate data on the volume of immigration and selective characteristics of immigrants as well as their reproduction, migration, and marriage patterns.

Low-Priority Research Topics. Several areas of demographic research, focusing on specific demographic processes and requiring particular analytic techniques, will be included in this section. The lower priority assigned to these proposed projects is based either on the availability of previous research providing an approximation of the patterns, or the judgement that the issue is of less analytic importance for the demography of American Jews. Some research suggestions made in the review of specific demographic processes have not been included in this section. Other research suggestions unfeasible in the immediate future, although highly desirable — e.g. Jewish population growth rates for local areas, more reliable Jewish population distribution estimates — are also not included.

These topics of lower priority will be listed without elaboration. They are as follows: (1) Family planning practices among younger Jewish couples including contraception, abortion, sterilization, and sexual attitudes and behavior. (2) Health-related issues, particularly among the elderly, and their relationship to mortality variation and change. (3) Use of ecological techniques to obtain data on mortality (and birth) levels in selected areas of high Jewish population density, historically and for the contemporary period. (4) Jewish population projections for local areas and regions. (5) Studies of population attitudes and issues related to the feasibility of Jewish population policies. (6) Historical work on Jewish immigration selectivity and the marriage patterns of Jewish immigrants from Eastern and Western Europe. (7) Comparative demography of specific ethnic communities within the Jewish population (e.g. Jews of Sephardic origin, descendants of German Jews, Holocaust survivors and their children, Israeli-Americans).

The list of suggested research topics on the demography of American Jews represents a major challenge. Combined with proposals for a documentation unit, a continuous Jewish data bank, consultation and coordination functions, and the initiation of some longitudinal studies on the social demography of American Jews, these research priorities are of major importance in designing a center that will meet research and teaching goals of the highest standards.

Demographic studies and research are central in understanding the American Jewish community. They are too important to be left to the sole purview of the demographer. Demographic research gains enormously by the theory and analysis of other social scientists. In the past some demographic research has been carried out by sociologists who at times failed to appreciate elementary demographic techniques. Often research on demographic issues has been relegated to the statistical demographer who has failed to incorporate demographic data within a broader social scientific perspective. There is a need to involve sociologists, political scientists, historians, and psychologists in the analysis of demographic data on American Jews. The proposed facility should serve as a center of interdisciplinary research and training encouraging scholars and students to exchange ideas and research on the wide range of issues associated with the demography of Jewish Americans.

Appendix

An Illustrative Exercise of the Balance of Factors Influencing the Jewish Population Equation in America, 1967–69

To illustrate the relative importance of recent immigration in the population growth equation of the American Jewish community, a simple demographic exercise was prepared. The only estimates of the number of annual births among Jews nationally is from the national natality survey described earlier. These estimates for 1967–69 indicate an annual average of 55,162 Jewish births (Goldstein, 1979). Accepting the Jewish population size medium estimate from the NJPS of 5,775,000 and the crude death rate for the Providence Jewish community (1962–64) of 10.1 (Goldstein and Goldscheider, 1968) as an estimate of national Jewish death rates yields an estimated number of 58,328 annual Jewish deaths. From these estimates the excess of deaths over births annually is 3,166. Estimated Jewish immigration to the United States was 24,800 for 1967–69, averaging 8,267 annually (Diamond, 1977). Some estimate of Jewish emigration from the United States is provided by figures of the number of Jews arriving as immigrants and potential immigrants in Israel during 1967–69 (Goldscheider, 1974). A total of 2,268 American Jews arrived in Israel as "immigrants" and an additional 13,735 arrived as "potential immigrants" (1967–69). Not all American Jews who arrived remained in Israel. In a special longitudinal study of immigration to Israel, the Israeli Central Bureau of Statistics noted that after three years in Israel 16 percent of the North American immigrants arriving during 1969–70 left Israel and 34 percent of the potential immigrants returned (Israeli CBS, 1975, p. 56). Applying these proportions to the number of American Jews immigrating to Israel in 1967–69 indicates an estimate of 10,970 American Jews remaining in Israel after three years or an average annual net emigration from the United States of 3,657.

Putting all these estimates together suggests that for 1967–69 with a base Jewish population of 5,775,000, we add 165,486 births, subtract 174,984 deaths, add 24,800 immigrants, and subtract 10,970 emigrants. This results in a net estimated *loss* due to the excess of deaths over births of 9,498 for the three-year period, but a net estimated *gain* of 13,830 from the balance of immigration and emigration. This is a net growth of 4,332 Jewish Americans for the three-year period. This comes very close to zero population growth. The important point is that net Jewish immigration compensates demographically for losses due to the excess of births over deaths and pushes American Jewish population growth from decline (negative growth) to about zero growth.

This is just an illustrative exercise. There are reasons to argue, as discussed in this chapter, that the estimated annual Jewish birth rates in 1967–69 may have been low due to compositional and timing factors rather than family size per se. There is no way to determine whether the crude death rate for Providence is an accurate reflection of rates for the total Jewish population in the United States. And the immigration figures may be underestimates while the number of American Jews remaining in Israel is probably an overestimate. This demographic exercise suggests that the demographic role of Jewish immigration to the United States has been underestimated. If that immigration increases and Jewish emigration decreases (as has been the case in the last number of years), net Jewish immigration will be an increasingly significant part of the American Jewish demographic picture.

Net Jewish immigration to the United States does not change the number of Jews in the world, since one community's gain is another community's loss. There is reason to hypothesize that the probability of remaining

Jewish is somewhat higher in America than in the Soviet Union (one source of recent immigration). This requires careful monitoring. There are a series of demographic consequences to zero population growth, particularly in terms of aging and population structure and dynamics, that require further analysis. Without further evidence on the age structure of immigrants and their reproductive patterns, it is difficult to estimate these structural changes and their future implications.

Lack of adequate data on demographic losses due to intermarriage prevents any attempt to include that factor in calculations of annual population gains and losses. A crude and very limited attempt will be made to indicate that losses due to Jewish out-marriage are of much less demographic significance than has been commonly suggested. Data are not available to estimate crude annual marriage rates among Jews. For the purpose of illustration let us assume that the crude marriage rate for the American population in 1969 can be applied to the Jewish American population. In 1969 the rate of marriage was 10.6 per 1,000 for the American population and would imply 61,215 Jewish marriages assuming the Jewish population was 5,775,000 (given the structure of the American Jewish population, this is probably an overestimate). For the sake of argument we can estimate that 20 percent of these marriages involved a non-Jewish spouse or 12,242 marriages. These marriages involved 6,121 Jews who married non-Jews in 1969. Of these 6,121 Jews who married out, let us assume that half retained their Jewish identity. This would imply that 3,060 Jews could be considered a demographic loss to the American Jewish community. If we further assume that in half of the intermarriages the non-Jewish spouse identifies with the Jewish community either through formal conversion or through self-identification, the annual demographic loss through intermarriage would be of about 1,500 Jews. That figure is balanced by the net annual gain through other demographic processes estimated for 1969 at 1,444. These estimates are built on a series of very problematic assumptions, any one of which might be seriously in error. I would guess that the net loss to the American Jewish community due to intermarriage is higher than these data show. However, placing intermarriage in the annual population growth equation does not seriously alter the conclusion that American Jewish population growth is about zero, but not much lower. Population projections that do not take into account the range of demographic factors that influence growth and are based on naive straight-line extrapolations from the past lead to serious miscalculations and absurd conclusions. Dire predictions about the virtual extinction of the American Jewish population over the next century (and speculation about the vanishing American Jew) — a projection of a Jewish population size of 10,420 by the year 2076 — are seriously misleading and demographic nonsense (Bergman, 1977; Lieberman and Weinfeld, 1978).

Notes

1. Although population composition, particularly by education, occupation, and income, is often included by demographers, there is no theoretical justification for treating these as demographic variables beyond their availability in census materials (Goldscheider, 1971). Hence these will not be included in the present review. For a review of the socioeconomic composition of the American Jewish population see Goldstein (1971).
2. Since so much has been written about the 1957 study, it should be noted that less than 75 Jewish intermarried couples nationally were included in the sample. The number of cases in Iowa was less than 45 cases a year (1953–59), and less than 100 cases a year in Indiana (1960–63). A total of around 400 Jewish intermarriages of all ages and generations were included in the NJPS.

References

American Jewish Year Book (various issues).

Bergman, Elihu, "The American Jewish Population Erosion," *Midstream* (October 1977).

Billings, John S., "Vital Statistics of the Jews in the United States," *Census Bulletin* no. 19 (December 30, 1890).

Diamond, Jack, "Jewish Immigration to the United States, 1881–1976," *American Jewish Year Book* (1977).

Edelman, Joseph, "Soviet Jews in the United States: A Profile," *American Jewish Year Book* (1977), pp. 157–81.

Engelman, U.Z., "Jewish Statistics in the United States Census of Religious Bodies (1850–1936)," *Jewish Social Studies* 9 (1947), pp. 127–74.

Fauman, S. Joseph, and Mayer, A.J., "Jewish Mortality in the United States," *Human Biology* (September 1969), pp. 416–26.

Glazer, Nathan, "Social Characteristics of American Jews." In L. Finkelstein (ed.), *The Jews*, 3rd ed. (Philadelphia: Jewish Publication Society, 1960), pp. 1,694–1,738.

Glick, Paul, "Intermarriage and Fertility Patterns among Persons in Major Religious Groups," *Eugenics Quarterly* 7 (1960), pp. 31–38.

Goldberg, Nathan, "Occupational Patterns of American Jews," *Jewish Review* 3 (1945–46).

Goldberg, Nathan, "Jewish Population in America," *Jewish Review* 5 (1948), pp. 36–48.

Goldberg, Nathan, "Demographic Characteristics of American Jews." In Jacob Fried (ed), *Jews in the Modern World* (New York: Twayne, 1962), vol. 2.

Goldberg, Nathan, "The Jewish Attitude toward Divorce." In Jacob Fried (ed.), *Jews and Divorce* (New York: KTAV, 1968).

Goldscheider, Calvin, "Ideological Factors in Jewish Fertility Differentials," *Jewish Journal of Sociology* 7 (June 1965a), pp. 92–105.

Goldscheider, Calvin, "Nativity, Generation, and Jewish Fertility," *Sociological Analysis* 26 (Fall 1965b), pp. 137–47.

Goldscheider, Calvin, "Socioeconomic Status and Jewish Fertility," *Jewish Journal of Sociology* 7 (December 1965c), pp. 221–37.

Goldscheider, Calvin, "Trends in Jewish Fertility," *Sociology and Social Research* 50 (January 1966), pp. 173–86.

Goldscheider, Calvin, "Fertility of the Jews," *Demography* 4 (1967), pp. 196–209.

Goldscheider, Calvin, *Population, Modernization, and Social Structure* (Little, Brown, 1971).

Goldscheider, Calvin, "Childlessness and Religiosity: An Exploratory Analysis." In *Papers in Jewish Demography, 1969* (Jerusalem: Institute of Contemporary Jewry, The Hebrew University, 1973).

Goldscheider, Calvin, "American Aliya: Sociological and Demographic Perspectives." In M. Sklare (ed.), *The Jew in American Society* (New York: Behrman House, 1974), pp. 335–84.

Goldscheider, Calvin, "Demography and American Jewish Survival." In M. Himmelfarb and V. Baras (eds.), *Zero Population Growth: For Whom?* (Westport, Conn.: Greenwood, 1978), pp. 119–47.

Goldscheider, Calvin, and Goldstein, S. "Generational Changes in Jewish Family Structure," *Journal of Marriage and the Family* 29 (May 1967), pp. 267–76.

Goldstein, Sidney, "Socioeconomic Differentials among Religious Groups in the United States," *American Journal of Sociology* (May 1969), pp. 612–31.

Goldstein, Sidney, "American Jewry, 1970: A Demographic Profile," *American Jewish Year Book* (1971), pp. 3–88.

Goldstein, Sidney, "Sources of Statistics on Jewish Vital Events and Migration in the United States." In *Papers in Jewish Demography, 1970* (Jerusalem: Institute of Contemporary Jewry, The Hebrew University, 1973a).

Goldstein, Sidney, "Completed and Expected Fertility in an American Jewish Community." In *Papers in Jewish Demography, 1969* (Jerusalem: Institute of Contemporary Jewry, The Hebrew University, 1973b).

Goldstein, Sidney, "Jews in the United States: Perspectives from Demography." YIVO conference (May 1978).

Goldstein, Sidney, "Jewish Fertility in Contemporary America." In Paul Ritterband (ed.), *Modern Jewish Fertility* (Leiden: Brill, 1979a).

Goldstein, Sidney, "A Demographic View of the Jewish Community in the 1980's." A JWB Greater Northeast Convention paper (April 20, 1979b).

Goldstein, Sidney, and Goldscheider, Calvin, *Jewish Americans* (Englewood Cliffs, New Jersey, 1968).

Good, Dorothy, "Questions of Religion in the United States Census," *Population Index* 25 (1959), pp. 3–16.

Gorwitz, K., "Jewish Mortality in St. Louis and St. Louis County, 1955–1957." *Jewish Social Studies* (October 1962).

Hersch, Liebman, "Jewish Migrations during the Last Hundred Years." In *Jewish People: Past and Present* (New York: Central Yiddish Culture Organization, 1949).

Israeli Central Bureau of Statistics, *Statistical Year Book* (various issues).

Kobrin, Frances, "The Fall of Household Size and the Rise of the Primary Individual in the United States," *Demography* 13 (February 1976), pp. 127–38.

Kobrin, Frances, and Goldscheider, Calvin, *The Ethnic Factor in Family Structure and Mobility* (Cambridge, Mass.: Ballinger, 1978).

Kobrin, Frances, and Goldscheider, Calvin, "Primary Individuals and Family Extension." Paper presented at the Population Association of America Meetings (Philadelphia, April 1979).

Landis, Benson, "A Guide to the Literature on Statistics of Religious Affiliation with Reference to Related Social Studies," *Journal of the American Statistical Association* 54 (June 1959), pp. 335–57.

Lazerwitz, Bernard, "The National Jewish Population Study: Sample Design." In *Papers in Jewish Demography, 1970* (Jerusalem: Institute of Contemporary Jewry, The Hebrew University, 1973a).

Lazerwitz, Bernard, "Jewish Identification and Jewish Fertility in the Chicago Jewish Community." In *Papers in Jewish Demography, 1969* (Jerusalem: Institute of Contemporary Jewry, The Hebrew University, 1973b).

Lazerwitz, Bernard, "An Estimate of a Rare Population Group: The United States Jewish Population," *Demography* 15 (August 1978), pp. 389–94.

Lestschinsky, Jacob, "Jewish Migrations, 1840–1956." In L. Finkelstein (ed.), *The Jews*, 3rd ed. (Philadelphia: Jewish Publication Society, 1960), pp. 1,536–96.

Liberson, David, "Causes of Death among Jews in New York City in 1953," *Jewish Social Studies* 18 (April 1956).

Lieberman, Samuel, and Weinfeld, M., "Demographic Trends and Jewish Survival," *Midstream* (October 1978), pp. 9–19.

Massarik, Fred, "The United States National Jewish Population Study: A Note on Concept and Reality." In *Papers in Jewish Demography, 1970* (Jerusalem: Institute of Contemporary Jewry, The Hebrew University, 1973).

Massarik, Fred, and Chenkin, A., "United States National Jewish Population Survey: A First Report," *American Jewish Year Book* (1973), pp. 264–306.

Mueller, Samuel, and Lane, Angela, "Tabulations from the 1957 Current Population Survey on Religion," *Journal for the Scientific Study of Religion* 11 (March 1972), pp. 76–98.

Newman, William, and Halvorson, Peter, "American Jews: Patterns of Geographic Distribution and Change, 1952–1971," *Journal for the Scientific Study of Religion* 18 (June 1979), pp. 183–93.

Ritterband, Paul, and Cohen, S.M., "Religion, Religiosity, and Fertility Desires." In *Papers in Jewish Demography* (Jerusalem: Institute of Contemporary Jewry, The Hebrew University, 1979).

Rosenthal, Erich, "Jewish Fertility in the United States," *Eugenics Quarterly* 8 (December 1961), pp. 198–217.

Rosenthal, Erich, "The Equivalence of United States Census Data for Persons of Russian Stock or Descent with American Jews: An Evaluation," *Demography* 12 (May 1975), pp. 275–90.

Schmelz, U.O., "Evaluation of Jewish Population Estimates," *American Jewish Year Book* (1969), pp. 273–88.

Schmelz, U.O., *Infant and Early Childhood Mortality among Jews of the Diaspora* (Jerusalem: Institute of Contemporary Jewry, The Hebrew University, 1971).

Schwartz, Arnold, "Intermarriage in the United States," *American Jewish Year Book* (1970), pp. 101–21.

Seidman, H., et al., "Death Rates in New York City by Socioeconomic Class and Religious Group and by Country of Birth, 1949–1951," *Jewish Journal of Sociology* (December 1962).

Sklare, Marshall, and Greenblum, J., *Jewish Identity on the Suburban Frontier* (New York: Basic Books, 1967).

Sklare, Marshall, *America's Jews* (New York: Random House, 1971).

U.S. Bureau of the Census, "Religion Reported by the Civilian Population of the United States: March 1957," *Current Population Reports*, series P-20, no. 79 (February 2, 1958).

Woodbury, Robert, *Infant Mortality and Its Causes* (Baltimore, 1926).

Zimmer, Basil, and Goldscheider, C., "A Further Look at Catholic Fertility," *Demography* 3 (1966), pp. 462–69.

2.

Research on American Jewish Identity and Identification: Progress, Pitfalls, and Prospects

Harold S. Himmelfarb

The study of American Jewish identity and identification has been a principal interest in the study of American Jews from the beginning. With the earliest studies by Fishberg (1911) and Wirth (1928), we find discussion and analyses of distinctive Jewish behavior and the conditions under which it will be maintained or diminished. Wirth's study became a classic in urban sociology and along with others in the Chicago school, it encouraged the rapid development of that discipline. Unfortunately but understandably, it did not have the same impact on the study of American Jewish identification.[1] Although the study of Jewish identification has had early roots, knowledge in the area has not grown steadily over the years. It has not kept pace with the growth of the social sciences, and it has not even kept pace with the study of other areas of American Jewish life such as demography and intergroup relations.

In his first compilation of studies on American Jews, Marshall Sklare (1958, p. 435) remarked "that knowledge in other areas [of modern Jewish life] has accumulated at a faster rate than has been true for the study of group belongingness and Jewish identification." Although written over two decades ago, Sklare's statement is probably still true today. Nevertheless, we know more about Jewish identification than we have been able to document and we have been able to document more than most Jews are willing to accept (in the sense of believing that the implications of research findings necessitate changes in structure or action).

This chapter will outline the unsteady progress in this area and some pitfalls encountered along the way. It will also suggest some directions for future research. This is not intended as a comprehensive review of the literature but as a description and analysis of major conceptual perspectives and methods used, findings which have resulted, and the implications of this past work for future research.[2]

56

Identity and Identification

It is useful to distinguish between studies of Jewish "identity" and "identification." *Jewish identification* is the process of thinking and acting in a manner that indicates involvement with and attachment to Jewish life. *Jewish identity* is one's sense of self with regard to being Jewish. Every person has numerous identities which vary in importance in different social contexts. Similarly one's sense of being a Jew as an important part of one's total self-concept or self-definition might vary in different social contexts. Operationally, identification studies seek to discover the extent to which the behavior and attitudes of Jews are oriented Jewishly. Identification studies ask questions about ritual observance, Jewish organizational involvement, attitudes toward Israel, intermarriage, and other matters related to Jewish life. Identity studies are concerned with what being Jewish means to individuals and the extent to which it is an important part of the way they view themselves in relation to others. These studies ask questions such as whether one considers oneself first a Jew and then an American or vice versa, the extent to which one is proud or embarrassed about being Jewish, the extent to which one is aware of being Jewish, and the extent to which one thinks such awareness affects his behavior and attitudes.

Simon Herman (1977, p. 28) has correctly remarked that currently "most studies of Jewish communities in the Diaspora . . . are at best studies of Jewish *identification*" rather than studies of Jewish *identity*, as they are typically called. However, a view of the area over time shows that most early studies *were* studies of Jewish identity and have gradually moved to studies of Jewish identification. This has been due to the historical circumstances of an early concern with immigrant adjustment and anti-Semitism and to a later concern with religiosity, ethnicity, and the preservation of Jewish distinctiveness. Or to use the theme on which Liebman (1973) expounds so well, the concern of early studies with identity was a concern for integration, the concern of later studies with identification has been a concern for survival. There are disciplinary reasons for this shift in emphasis too. The overwhelming number of studies in recent years have been conducted by sociologists (and a few political scientists) rather than psychologists. The former are much more likely to study the behavior of identification and the latter are much more likely to study the perception of identity. Whether this shift in focus has been beneficial is debatable and worthy of more discussion. For now, it will suffice to point out that there are two somewhat different phenomena that have been studied and that there has been a shift in concern from one to the other.

Conceptual Perspectives

The terminology of *conceptual* rather than *theoretical* perspectives is used here deliberately for two reasons. First, despite numerous attempts to categorize general, social, and psychological theories there remains quite a bit of overlap and ambiguity in the various categorical schemes. Second, work on Jewish identification has not flowed out of any major theoretical schools. What we have are certain concerns which have been analyzed with various concepts borrowed from major theoretical schools, intentionally and unintentionally.

Minority-Group Perspective

From the questions posed by Wirth's *The Ghetto* through the present, the most promiment question dealt with in Jewish identification has been how fast and in what ways Jews are assimilating. This question has been approached from two different angles: (1) To what extent do Jews feel accepted as Americans (the minority-group perspective)? (2) To what extent do Jews maintain distinctively Jewish behavior and attitudes (the acculturation perspective)? The first question was the predominant concern of early social scientists in this field. They were concerned with the adjustment of Jews to their minority group status. This was not simply a question of interest for those concerned with discrimination and anti-Semitism (although it was related), but the ways in which persons coped with minority status was seen as critical to their Jewish identities.

Reference Group Theory. The major theory for understanding the issues of minority status and identity was role theory, especially as applied in the notion of reference groups. Based on the work of Charles Cooley (1922) and George Herbert Mead (1934) and advanced by Robert E. Park (1950, 1955), early psychologists and sociologists viewed the process of socialization as one where the child increasingly internalizes the values, attitudes, and norms of others as his own. This occurs through interaction with "significant others," who are initially the child's caretakers, in most cases, parents. The child's perspective on what he sees and encounters in his environment is largely determined by how these significant others respond to those stimuli. Just as the child internalizes others' views toward objects, he also internalizes their views toward himself as an object. One's view of himself or his identity is shaped by his perception of the view of others toward the self.

As a child grows older and begins to participate in games and play roles, he learns the views of "generalized" others — friends, neighbors, the community. All these people have some impact upon the child's view of the world and of himself. As Park (1937, p. xvii) states: "The conception which each individual inevitably forms of himself is determined by the role which fate assigns to him in some society, and upon the opinion and attitude which persons in that society form of him — depends, in short, upon his social status." That status might be that of a minority group member. Each person encounters many groups in society and the extent to which they might influence his self-perception depends upon whether they become "significant others" or "reference groups."

Hyman (1942) first introduced the concept of reference groups to denote those with whom one compares himself to assess his own social position. The term has developed over time to also include groups which help set and maintain standards for an individual. It becomes a source of values which are internalized (Kelley, 1952). In short, it is a group with which the individual identifies. Whether it is a comparison reference group or a normative reference group, it might not be a membership group. Individuals might identify or compare themselves with those in a group to which they belong or with those in another group, perhaps with those in a group to which they aspire to belong. For minority group members, the important question became whether the minority or majority group was accepted as the most important reference group.

Wirth's *The Ghetto* describes the personal struggle of immigrant Jews to move out of a membership group which they no longer valued into a new membership group in which they were not completely accepted. This psychological struggle was amplified in the work of Stonequist entitled *The Marginal Man*, a term borrowed from Park (1928). According to Stonequist, "The individual who through migration, education, marriage or some other influence leaves one social group or culture without making a satisfactory adjustment to another, finds himself on the margin of each but a member of neither. He is a 'marginal man.'" For Stonequist the Jew was an example par excellence of such a man.

Studies of this phenomenon often discuss three alternative adjustments an individual can make to marginal status: an *ingroup reaction* (supportive of the minority group and rejecting the majority); an *intermediary reaction* (accommodating to both groups); an *outgroup reaction* (identifying with the majority and rejecting the minority).[3] It seems clear from the tone of most of these studies that the intermediary role was preferred by the individual Jew because it would minimize internal psychological conflict.[4] Some scholars like Wirth felt that it would only be a matter of time until identification with (or assimilation into) the majority group would be so far along that internal conflicts of this sort would be minimal. This was the predominant feeling of social scientists until the 1950s about the process of ethnic group assimilation generally. It became known as the "melting-pot theory," and over time took on numerous modifications (see Berkson, 1920; Glazer and Moynihan, 1963; Gordon, 1964).

Field Theory. Kurt Lewin (1948), the eminent social psychologist, was also interested in the three possible reactions of individuals to minority status. He spoke of Jews who "overemphasize their Jewishness, those who behave normally, and those who hide or underemphasize their Jewishness" (p. 182). For Lewin it was important for the individual to strike a balance between the two (as implied in the term *normal*) mainly because Lewin was much less confident than others that Jews could ever completely assimilate due to anti-Semitism. He arrived at this position from his own theoretical perspective. Trained in gestalt psychology from which "balance theory" is an outgrowth, Kurt Lewin broke new ground by focusing on individual motivations rather than perceptions. He became the founder of what is commonly known as "field theory" in social psychology, which emphasized the power of positive and negative forces in motivating individuals.

From Lewin's viewpoint attraction to the majority group in society was likely to be so positive that the minority group member who encountered problems in entering the majority would be likely to see his minority status as an impediment to the attainment of his goals. Minority group membership would become a negative force. In some cases it would become so negative that it would turn to self-hatred. A minority child unaware of the barriers to attaining full acceptance into the majority society was likely to have more psychological conflict when such barriers were encountered than those prepared for them. He would become a "marginal" person, an "eternal adolescent," not sure of his status in either group. Lewin's (1948, p. 183) solution, specifically for Jewish children, was that they needed to be well grounded in their own culture: "Such an early build-up of a clear and positive feeling of belongingness to the Jewish group is one of the few effective things that Jewish parents can do for the later happiness of their children."

To "softpedal" the problem of minority status, Lewin argued, "will in all likelihood make for greater difficulties in adjustment later on" (1948, p. 183). Lewin believed that identification with the Jewish group should not be based on a particular ideological stance (religious or nationalistic) but on an "interdependence of fate," which stressed mutual aid and a sense of responsibility of one Jew for other Jews. Lewin's ideas became very popular within the Jewish community and were used as arguments supporting programs such as Jewish centers which would foster group belongingness. Preservation of the Jewish group as protection against anti-Semitism is still a primary motive for Jewish identification generally and for support for Israel specifically among many Jews today. It seems to be a less compelling rationale for younger Jews who have not experienced much anti-Semitism.

Rothman (1965) reviewed the literature in the area of group identification and outgroup orientation. He pointed out that from Lewin's work one could conclude that strong ingroup identification by minority group members allows for sufficient personal security to enable them to desire to establish relationships with members of other groups. There are those who would argue ingroup identification would have just the opposite effect (Bettelheim, 1951; Dodson, 1955). A third view suggests that ingroup identification has no relationship with one's outlook on other groups (Fishman, 1955; Hill, 1946). Rothman's data support this third view. So do more recent studies by Zak (1973), E. Cohen (1977), and Herman (1977), which show little or no correlation between Jewish and American identity.

Psychoanalytic Theory. Another theoretical perspective or minority group identity as applied to Jews was articulated by Bruno Bettelheim who came to directly refute Lewin's theory. Writing from a psychoanalytic perspective, Bettelheim (1951) argued that it could be harmful to teach a child younger than seven or eight years old about group differences to protect him against anti-Semitism. First, young children do not understand concepts of group differences and the notion of ingroups and outgroups: "The younger child can know nothing about 'groups' — he knows only the private happiness he feels in belonging to his family and his small group" (p. 210).

Second, a discussion of group differences with young children will amplify the many insecurities and anxieties they already have as a consequence of childhood dependency and the necessity of repressing socially forbidden impulses. The child must feel secure within his family to be able to weather insecurities of later group identifications. Somewhat surprisingly, Bettelheim (1951, p. 217) calls for more positive motivations for Jewish identifications than anti-Semitism: "Communal emphasis on the cultivation of Judaism, not for its own sake, but only as an armor against prejudice, only further undermines the self-respect of the Jewish group as a whole and its individual members and serves to keep alive and feed anew insecurity, generation after generation."

Child Development. In contrast to Bettelheim's theoretical perspective, Marian Radke-Yarrow's (1958) review of child development studies shows that children develop a strong sense of group identification by the preschool and early school years. David Elkind's (1961) work with Jewish children agrees with Yarrow, but shows that the understanding of group differences in any manner approaching adult sophistication does not occur until ages 7–9, in accord with Bettelheim. Actually, it does not take on abstract qualities until ages 10–12.

Summary. Emphasis on the consequences of minority group status have been approached from several conceptual perspectives in psychology and social psychology: reference group theory, field theory, psychoanalytic theory, and child development. Research has been contradictory and inconclusive. There is no simple relationship between minority and majority group identity, if there is one at all. The development of group identity, while occuring early, is not very meaningful until middle to late childhood.

There has not been a great deal of research on identity in recent years. Many promising developments of earlier decades which were well grounded in basic theoretical perspectives have not continued to progress. The continuing efforts of Simon Herman (1970a, b, 1977) are a notable exception. There has been a major shift from the study of identity to that of identification. The historical circumstances of a largely native-born Jewish population and waning overt anti-Semitism have helped create the shift in concern. As Rothman (1965) pointed out, early studies showed that most Jews adopted an intermediate role between identifying with the ingroup and the outgroup rather than an overemphasis toward one or the other. Concern for marginality and self-hatred are only applicable to a few Jews. Most others are able to adapt to both the ingroup and the outgroup. Accordingly, scholars became more concerned with the nature of Jewish identification. They began to ask in what ways Jews maintained their Jewishness and in what ways they adopted majority habits. Finally, from a policy point of view the study of identity became less promising. Not only was there little evidence that Jewish identity affected other identities but there was little evidence that it affected Jewish identification. While it can be shown that those who have a greater sense of ingroup belonging are also more involved in Jewish life, it is not clear which is the cause and which the effect. With dissemination of Festinger's (1957) work on cognitive dissonance, there was new evidence to believe that behavior might affect attitudes rather than vice versa. During the 1960s there was a decline in attitude research generally (Eagly and Himmelfarb, 1978).

Acculturation Perspective

Research on identity to research on identification has been a shift to the second question outlined earlier — To what extent do Jews maintain distinctively Jewish behavior and attitudes? Although this question is usually handled under the rubric of "assimilation," it had been recognized many years ago that the complete merging of cultures into one, as implied by that term, is not characteristic of the American Jewish experience. Glazer (1950, p. 279) put it this way: "Jews show very little tendency to assimilate . . . . They do *acculturate* — that is, they drop traditional habits and speech, and become culturally indistinguishable from other Americans; yet the line that divides them from others remains sharper than that separating any other white group of immigrants."[5]

Socialization Approach. The concepts and theories used to study acculturation have relied on reference group theory as in the study of minority group status. The most common approach stems directly from it. This is the socialization approach to Jewish identification. Based on the theoretical premise that a person is most influenced by his "significant others" or reference groups, most sociological studies of Jewish identification within the last two decades try to assess the relative influence of various institutions and experiences upon a person's Jewish identification. Parents, spouse, friends, neighbors, Jewish and secular education have been looked at frequently. In addition certain demographic background characteristics such as generation American, age, sex, and social class have all been analyzed as indicators of the social milieu influencing identification. More will be said about findings on these variables later. Three psychological approaches to socialization studies have been hardly touched in the socialization approach to the study of Jewish identification:

Social Learning Theory. It emphasizes mechanisms of imitation, identification, and reinforcement (Goslin, 1969) and has been virtually ignored as it applies to religious socialization.[6] However, many of the learning mechanisms are implied in the reference group approach. That is, we assume that preference for one reference group over another is due to reinforcement or identification.

Developmental Studies. Although well entrenched in the socialization literature, developmental studies of religious socialization are rare. There are a few notable exceptions — the work of Radke-Yarrow (1958) and David Elkind (1961) on conceptions of group membership discussed above are two examples. Elkind studied children's conception of God, and found that they followed the general cognitive developmental stages outlined by Piaget. Lawrence Kohlberg's (1967, 1969) work on moral development also supports a Piagetian sequence of development.[7]

An interesting contrast to the cognitive development theorists is the recent contribution of Mortimer Ostow (1977). He presents a psychoanalytic approach to religious development which has many implications for timing the introduction of rituals, prayers, and biblical stories according to the child's psychosexual development. For example, during the preschool years where insecurities over separation from parents is acute, Ostow argues, the introduction of bedtime rituals such as a prayer before going to sleep is particularly welcome.

Theories of Social Influence and Attitude Change. With the exception of a recent contribution by Kelman (1977), the whole area of attitude change has been ignored in the study of Jewish identification. Kelman develops a model of social influence based on (1) importance of the induction, (2) the source of power of the influencing agent, and (3) the manner of achieving prepotency of the induced response. Responses to the influence can be (1) compliance, (2) identification, or (3) internalization. The desired response from Kelman's view is internalization which leads to an "authentic" identity. This identity is congruent with the individual's personality and is therefore flexible and changeable. Each individual develops his own unique form of Jewish identity. The fluidity of the context of identity in Kelman's model is in sharp contrast to Ostow's model which emphasizes the child's needs for constancy (rituals) and myths, as well as the necessity of presenting the adolescent with an ideal image that can be modeled.

Social influence theories could focus our attention on other factors as well: (1) types of appeal (emotional vs. rational, fear arousal, defensiveness), (2) credibility of the communicator, (3) amount of change advocated, and (4) the effects of social approval for advocated change, to name just a few (Cohen, 1964). This body of theory and research could be very useful in developing educational programs for promoting Jewish identification. An integration of developmental and social influence theories could move us far along in developing adequate theories of ethnic-religious socialization.

Structural Approach. Another approach to acculturation stems from the structural-functional school of sociology and anthropology. The structural approach has been dominant in the sociology of religion since Durkheim's work (1915). It has been a major perspective of sociologists generally. The basic premise of this perspective argues that humans organize their activities to fulfill certain functions but the structures they create affect consequent behavior. For individuals who enter a new society, or simply grow up in an existing society, prevailing conditions in that society will affect the way they structure their activities (Merton, 1957).

The structures analyzed from this perspective can be large or small. One level of focus has been societal conditions. Liebman's work (1973) is a good example. He argues that after emancipation in Western Europe Jews were considered (or chose to be considered) a religious rather than an ethnic group. In Eastern Europe Jews were considered a separate nationality or ethnic group. Liebman (1973, pp. 21–22) explains that:

> Where Jews chose the religious option, as in Western Europe, we find Reform Judaism, a high rate of intermarriage and assimilation, de-emphasis of the Hebrew language, anti-Zionism on the part of the leaders of the community, and an Orthodox religious group which favored secular education and participated in the social and political life of the country, but separated itself from the non-Orthodox Jews. In those countries where the communal option was chosen we find Jewish political parties, a demand for cultural separation, strong Zionist orientation among the masses, an absence of religious reform, low rates of intermarriage and assimilation, and a traditional Judaism which opposed secular education and did not encourage participation in

the social and political life of the country, but remained part of the total Jewish community vying for its leadership.

American Judaism, Liebman tells us, is mainly of Eastern European origin. Since America recognized the legitimacy of religious rather than ethnic institutions, Eastern Europeans set up religious structures and filled them with ethnic or communal content (p. 45).

Sharot (1976) has taken this kind of analysis further and has argued that over the centuries the extent to which Jews acculturated depended on whether the dominant religion was syncretic rather than insular, tolerant of pluralism or attempting to be monopolistic, and the extent to which Jews interacted with non-Jews. Acculturation was greater in syncretic, pluralistic, and socially interactive societies such as the United States.

Even established ethnic group theorists are beginning to refine their ideas regarding structural conditions. Milton Gordon, who formerly approached ethnic assimilation from a reference group perspective (1964), now writes about structural conditions too, such as economic and political structures of societies in which minorities are located, the diversity of groups in a society, the scarcity of available rewards, and prevailing ideologies (Gordon, 1975). Lipset (1963) has argued that Jewish identification can only be understood by systematic comparisons to the larger societies to which Jews belong. Comparative studies of structural conditions which until now have been only historical, would improve our knowledge if they took on more contemporary and empirical perspectives.

Structural explanations do not always focus on societal conditions. They have also focused on institutional arrangements within the Jewish community. The institutions of the Jewish community, while influenced by societal conditions, can have independent effects on Jewish life. Unique among contemporary analysts of Jewish identification is the work of Daniel Elazar (1976). While not the first to describe the organizational structure of the Jewish community (Karpf, 1938; Sklare, 1971; Maslow, 1974), Elazar is the only one who has developed a conceptual framework for discussing it. The overarching concepts in his work are drawn from political science notions of governance and make a useful perspective for describing the institutional network of the Jewish community and its leadership structure. Community power and influence, decision making and representativeness of leadership, are all issues which can influence individual and communal identification.

What remains to be done from a structural perspective is to focus even more microscopically. No one has yet focused on Jewish organizations individually using the conceptions of the formal organization literature in sociology and administrative science. Notions of administrative structures, staff recruitment, training, specialization and promotion, the use of technology to expedite organization, and analysis of the pervasive informal structure of formal organizations, to name just a few, can all be helpful perspectives for understanding organized Jewish life and its impact on Jewish identification.

Summary

Both the minority group and acculturation perspectives have drawn widely from existent social science concepts. The latter tends to be more sociological than the former, but both have drawn heavily on social psychology. Theoretical advancement in this field has not been systematic or continuous. We have jumped from one perspective to another. All of them need to be further developed and more explicitly applied to Jewish identification. After that, a synthesis of perspectives will be very much in order.

Methods

Here we shall consider matters of design, sampling, and measurement. Many issues in these areas are not peculiar to the study of Jewish identity and identification. In the interest of parsimony, I will limit the discussion to particularly relevant topics.

Study Design

The two most dominant types of study designs in the area of American Jewish identity and identification have been the community case study and the sample survey. Surveys are the most common type of design and are also frequently used in community case studies along with other methods. Each type of design has its benefits and limitations.

Community Case Studies. Case studies on American Jewish communities have been numerous, particularly if one includes historical community studies which often have information pertinent to Jewish identity and identification.[8] Community studies, because they use varied methods of data collection (in-depth interviews, written documents, field observations), often provide greater insight into the lifestyle and feelings of community members than is obtained in surveys. This is their greatest asset. The best example of this is the Lakeville studies (Sklare and Greenblum, 1967). On the other hand, community studies have usually been done on small or moderate-sized Jewish communities in the South or Midwest (Lavender, 1977; Kramer and Leventman, 1961), even though most Jews live in large urban areas in the Northeast. Studies often deal with Jews on either pole of Jewish identification. We have studies of new suburbs (Gans, 1958; Sklare and Greenblum, 1967) which typically contain a higher proportion of secular Jews than the general population, and studies of Hasidic (Poll, 1962; Rubin, 1972) or heavily Orthodox (Mayer, 1975) communities. In some cases we get studies of large town, Northeastern Jewish communities, but the focus is on older, less wealthy Jews who have been left behind in the transition of neighborhoods (Ginsberg, 1975). Focus on these nonmainstream groups has been very useful and helps us realize that Jews are indeed "a coat of many colors," as the title of Abraham Lavender's (1977) recent collection of such studies suggests. At issue in case studies is the idiosyncratic nature of the group under investigation. It would be helpful to examine similarities and differences in the findings of such case studies, and study a "typical" neighborhood in a fairly large Jewish community.

Three other design aspects of community studies ought to be mentioned. First, with the exception of the Lakeville studies, non-Jewish residents of Jewish communities have been ignored. If they are discussed, it is usually from the perspective of Jews interviewed for the study. Non-Jewish members of the community probably have some impact on the identity and identification of Jewish residents and ought also to be studied. Second, many community studies were done in the 1950s or earlier. It is time to go back and take a look at how the communities have changed since first studied. I know of two studies which have taken this perspective (Rothchild, 1975; Sklare, 1978).[9] They both make a point that I made earlier with regard to the changing concerns of those who study Jewish identification. During the 1950s, Jews in these communities were concerned with "integration" into the larger gentile community. Today, integration having been achieved (or having been too successful), the concern is with promoting Jewish identification and group "survival." Third, almost all case studies concentrate on residential communities. It would be helpful to have more case studies of Jewish organizations. Organizations also often have a community element about them. Heilman's (1976) recent work on a synagogue is exemplary for its uniqueness in this regard. David Schoem's (1979) recently completed ethnography of a Jewish afternoon school is also a notable example. We can use more case studies of organizations.[10]

Surveys. Survey research has been the dominant type of research design in the study of American Jews. Studies have often relied on small, purposively selected cross-sectional samples and analysis has been more descriptive than explanatory. In the last ten to fifteen years there has been increased use of data from large-scale representative samples of a longitudinal or semilongitudinal sort, analyzed with sophisticated multivariate and causal modeling techniques. Some of the more important developments in this regard have been the following:

Community Censuses. Now numbering well over a dozen, such surveys typically contain large representative samples of local Jewish communities. The data deal with demographic characteristics more than identification variables, and thus tell us more about the well-being of Jews as Americans than as Jews, but some yield useful information on identification too. The

Goldstein and Goldscheider (1968) survey of Providence is exemplary in this regard. Another interesting development is the movement into a second generation of such studies. The census data on the Boston Jewish community in 1965 can be compared to similar data collected in 1975 (Axelrod, 1967; Fowler, 1977; Cohen, 1978b, 1980), lending a longitudinal aspect to at least the aggregated data. Another type of design to emerge from a community census which has quasi-longitudinal aspects is represented by the work of Dashefsky and Shapiro (1974). From data collected in the Minneapolis-St. Paul Jewish community, Dashefsky and Shapiro analyzed factors leading to the Jewish identification of young adult males and their fathers. Unfortunately, they did not match the father-son samples exactly, blurring some of the generational comparisons.

The National Jewish Population Study (NJPS). This is a large representative sample of the American Jewish community and contains many questions on Jewish identification. The survey was taken in 1970–71 and the data is emerging in bits and pieces, most notably through the work of Bernard Lazerwitz. These data, while somewhat old now, still contain the most detailed national information available on Jewish identification. Within the next few years we will probably see a substantial increase in publications using this data source. The whole NJPS project needs to be reviewed carefully so that a similar type of study can be undertaken for the 1980s.

Surveys of College Students. Because there is such a high proportion of Jewish youth who attend college, several national samples of college graduates yield a significant number of Jewish students. These studies do not measure Jewish identification in detail, but they usually contain some questions about religious preference, religiosity, ethical values, and interfaith friendships and courtships related to Jewish identification. These data can be significant sources for comparative religion studies and also for studies of religious change, particularly where follow-up studies of the graduates were done. The only study of American Jewish identification I know of with longitudinal data, Caplovitz and Sherrow's (1977) study of apostates, comes from such a source.

Composite Samples. Survey research on ethnic groups are using composite samples with increasing frequency. Survey centers which take national samples of the population every year or two often ask questions pertinent to ethnic-religious identification. While a simple survey year might not contain sufficient numbers of Jews for detailed analysis, respectable numbers are often obtained by combining samples of several years. This type of study also allows for comparisons between several religious and ethnic groups. However, in analyzing factors related to ethnic identification, this type of data usually only contains information on demographic variables rather than socialization experiences likely to be more important.

(See S. Cohen, 1977, for an example of a study of Jewish identification using a composite sample as a data source.)

Experiments. Experimental designs in the study of Jewish identification are conspicuous by their absence. Since social psychologists have used laboratory experiments for studying anti-Semitism, it is surprising that they have not used them for at least studying identity or the attitudinal dimensions of identification. Natural experiments would be even more desirable. We have had studies of various types of experimental programs designed to increase Jewish identification such as camps, trips to Israel, weekend retreats, but few contain control groups or control sufficiently for factors other than the experimental treatment which might have caused positive outcomes. There is great need for controlled experimentation and evaluation in Jewish life.

Sampling

The entire field of contemporary American Jewish studies suffers from the absence of a question on religion in the U.S. census. While such a question would not yield information about Jewish identification, it would be a great help in locating Jews for other surveys. Without this information we have had to rely on data taken from inadequate samples. Random sampling is often too costly when Jews are such a small proportion of the population. The most common sample is usually taken from some organization list or combination of lists which contain Jewish names and addresses. These lists bias the sample toward affiliated Jews. This might not be a big bias in some small communities where affiliation rates are as high as 90 percent, but in large communities, where most Jews live, affiliation rates are much lower. Nationwide, only about half of all adults belong to a synagogue or Jewish organization (Bock, 1976). Thus the generalizability of many findings raises serious doubts.

Sampling problems have been somewhat overcome in recent years with some of the survey designs discussed above. Community censuses and the NJPS increased the efficiency of locating a Jewish respondent by first identifying geographic areas in which Jews are clustered and then sampling disproportionately according to estimated Jewish concentration. Typically, areas of Jewish concentration are determined by counting persons with "distinctive Jewish names" (Massarik, 1966).

One of the most innovative ideas for using distinctive Jewish names (DJNs) is found in a recent proposal by Ritterband and Cohen (1978). In designing a sampling method for the New York area Jewish population, they recommended random digit dialing of phone numbers within exchanges in which Jewish households are clustered. They hypothesize that about 90 percent of DJNs in a county may be clustered in one-quarter of the phone exchanges. By dialing numbers only within the "Jewish" quarter of phone exchanges rather than in all exchanges, great economy is achieved at the relatively minor cost of excluding 10 percent of the Jewish population from those to be sampled. If indeed the economy and accuracy of this method is as great as Ritterband and Cohen conjecture, it can be very useful.

Himmelfarb and Loar (1979a) asked whether sampling only individuals with DJNs would produce a sufficiently representative sample of the Jewish population. In comparing Jews in the NJPS sample with DJNs to all the other Jews in the NJPS sample, they found that the difference between the subsamples in both demographic background characteristics and Jewish identification measures were very small. They concluded that a DJN sample was adequately representative for studies of Jewish identification, particularly studies which were explanatory in nature and not primarily concerned with making accurate estimates of the distributions of population characteristics — although the groups were not very dissimilar in that regard either.

More research is needed to find low-cost methods of sampling Jews. It is possible that the DJN method is less biasing than the organization list, and perhaps the best alternative. The use of any sort of list (e.g. phone list) does create some biases, and we need to know what they are and how they might affect the results of our studies. Halvorson and Newman (1978, 1979) have recently developed a data archive for the United States which shows the concentration of various religious groups in 3,073 counties across the United States. These data could be used to develop stratified sampling procedures for Jewish concentrations of more than 100 persons and could be an alternative to name sampling.

Measurement[11]

When studying Jewish identity and identification scholars have disagreed about what behavior and attitudes ought to be considered. In a recent review of the literature, E. Cohen (1977) points out that the field of Jewish identity has used unidimensional, nondimensional, and multidimensional approaches. The same is true for Jewish identification.

Unidimensional Approaches. Unidimensional measures are often solely attitudinal and many researchers find such scales obscure and nonpredictive or simply insufficient as indicators of such a complex and diverse phenomenon. (For a recent attempt to use a unidimensional approach that reasonably approximates a broad definition of Jewish identification in the attitudinal sphere, see Dashefsky and Shapiro, 1974.)

Nondimensional Approaches. These approaches often use multiple criteria for measuring Jewishness but do not integrate these criteria into some theoretically meaningful constructs or dimensions. The preliminary reports of the NJPS published by the Council of Jewish Federations and Welfare Funds, 1974, are an extreme example of this approach.

Multidimensional Approaches. Most researchers today agree that Jewish identification is a multidimensional phenomenon. Yet there is little agreement as to how many dimensions there are. It has been argued that the debate in the sociology of religion over the number of dimensions of religiosity stems more from conceptual rather than empirical ambiguities. There have been problems of definition, such as measuring identity rather than identification, or measuring the motivations behind and the consequences of religious acts and beliefs. There have also been problems of classification which display (1) a lack of mutual exclusiveness and exhaustiveness of categories, (2) a mixture of temporally unrelated phenomena, and (3) the inclusion of phenomena at different levels of abstraction (Himmelfarb, 1975). Since these problems plague the religion field as a whole, it is not surprising that they also plague the field of Jewish identification.

Yet looking at multidimensional approaches, there is considerable consistency in specific dimensions that ought to be considered when measuring Jewish identification. A look at four recent schemes (Verbit, 1970; Lazerwitz, 1973, 1978; Himmelfarb, 1975; Bock, 1976) which have attempted to create fairly exhaustive typologies of Jewish or religious identification, shows the following commonalities in at least three of the schemes: (1) ritual behavior; (2) formal organizational participation; (3) informal social ties with other Jews (friends, neighbors, mates); (4) attitudes toward Israel; (5) doctrinal belief; (6) some intellectual dimension (having or seeking knowledge);[12] and (7) some measure of charity-giving.

Two attempts to conceptualize these measures warrant further consideration. Himmelfarb suggests that the various dimensions can be categorized by their objects of orientation (supernatural, communal, cultural, or interpersonal) and whether they are behavioral or ideational in character. These four orientations are also encompassed in Verbit's scheme. Bock argues that the ten dimensions of Jewish identification he measures can be divided into just two larger categories: public and private Jewishness.

Empirical proof of the independence of each of these dimensions of Jewish identification has been incomplete. Studies have relied on techniques which verify the internal consistency of scales, if that.[13] Few have attempted to verify the validity of their scales. The most rigorous testing of the validity and reliability of such scales is in Eli Cohen's work (1977), and his methodological approach could well be a model for further studies. However, some of the studies already mentioned present models of greater conceptual clarity.

A Short Index. How important is it that these multiple dimensions of Jewish identification are measured? The answer depends on the purposes of one's study and the amount of detail required regarding Jewish identification. Most studies using multiple dimensions show that each dimension has somewhat different antecedents and consequences (Goldstein and Goldscheider, 1968; Lazerwitz, 1973; Himmelfarb, 1974; Bock, 1976). There is also a tendency to form a single scale of identification from multiple dimensions to simplify analysis (Bock, 1976; Himmelfarb, 1977a; Lazerwitz, 1977a). No one has demonstrated that the combination of just a few indicators of different dimensions of Jewish identification (such as Kashrut observance, synagogue attendance, organizational membership, and charitable contributions — or some other combination of just a few measures) will yield a sufficiently sensitive scale to obviate the need for so many separate scales. More work is needed for the sake of efficiency and economy. A short index of Jewish identification could be useful for attaching to many different surveys (Jewish-sponsored and otherwise) designed for purposes other than Jewish identification.

The simplest and most efficient indicator of overall Jewish identification might well be denominational self-identification. On every dimension of Jewish identification there is a similar rank ordering of denomination with Jewish identification. Orthodox Jews score highest on each identification measure, Conservative Jews next, followed by Reform and nondenominational Jews respectively (Himmelfarb, 1979; Himmelfarb and Loar, 1979a; Lazerwitz, 1977b). The consistency of this finding makes denominational self-identification worthy of consideration as a good proxy for multiple measures of Jewish identification. It would be particularly efficient for use in surveys mostly devoted to other topics. We need to know in what way this measure is more representative of particular forms of Jewish identification than it is of others. It is probably more representative of a supernatural orientation to Jewish identification (ritual observance and doctrinal belief) than it is of other orientations (Himmelfarb, 1975). Lazerwitz's data indicate that a combination of denominational self-identification and membership would be an even more sensitive, yet still brief, indicator of current identification. Perhaps such a combination would be more balanced between communal and supernatural orientations.

One caveat should be inserted here. The efficacy of denominational self-identification as a measure of Jewish identification might dissipate over time. Recent analyses of the NJPS data (Himmelfarb and Loar, 1979a; Lazerwitz, 1979a) show that the proportion of Jews considering themselves nondenominational increases with each generation's distance from their foreign-born ancestors. Over a quarter of third-generation American Jews considered themselves nondenominational in 1970. If this proportion grows to as large as one-third of all American Jews, denominational self-identification will become a poor measure of Jewish identification since it will no longer differentiate between the various levels of identification held by many Jews. Perhaps social scientists can develop more discriminating labels for future use which could be popularized enough for most persons to be able to accurately label themselves.

Summary. Jewish identity and identification have been conceptualized and measured in numerous ways. There is a need for synthesis and consensus. Despite differences between studies there is also a considerable amount of agreement. A little time spent thrashing out remaining issues would probably yield some very usable measures which might even be verifiable with data already collected. When discussing issues of measurement it is important to keep in mind that identity and identification are distinct concepts and ought to be measured separately, and that there is a need for indices measuring multiple dimensions of identification as well as a short index of overall identification.

Findings

The most common approach to the study of Jewish identification in the last two decades has been to try to assess the relative influence of various institutions, experiences, and the general social milieu on an individual's Jewish identification. This was called "the socialization approach." In this section I want to review some substantive findings from these studies. In accord with the discussion on recent developments in survey design, I will concentrate on the findings of empirical studies using large representative samples and multivariate techniques of data analysis.

Social Context of Jewish Identification

Living in America presents numerous opportunities and challenges for Jews to be involved with Jewish life. These opportunities vary with the social milieu in which one lives. Studies of Jewish identification have researched the impact to some of these environmental factors.

Generation. It has been well documented for some time that almost all measures of Jewish identification decline with distance from the immigrant generation (Goldstein and Goldscheider, 1968; Axelrod, 1967; Sklare and Greenblum, 1967; Fowler, 1977; Himmelfarb, 1979). The only exceptions to this pattern seem to be with regard to certain rituals (attendance at a Passover Seder, lighting Chanukah candles) and Jewish school enrollment. Sklare and Greenblum (1967, p. 57) have explained the exceptions in the decline of ritual observances:

> Five criteria emerge as important in explaining retention of specific home rituals. Thus, the highest retention will occur when a ritual: (1) is capable of effective redefinition in modern terms,[14] (2) does not demand social isolation or the adoption of a unique life style, (3) accords with the religious culture of the larger community and provides a "Jewish" alternative when such is felt to be needed, (4) is centered on the child, and (5) is performed annually or infrequently.

This is a post hoc explanation of the retention of Chanukah and Passover observances in particular. The most important criterion is the third, and this can be readily seen if we take Purim as an example. Celebrated in March and not observed by a sizeable proportion of American Jews, Purim meets all of Sklare and Greenblum's criteria as well as Chanukah or Passover do, except that it does not provide a Jewish alternative to some Christian holiday as the latter do for Christmas and Easter. In Israel, where the "larger community" is Jewish, Purim receives more attention than Chanukah, although its observance often takes on more cultural than religious forms.

Regarding religious school enrollment, the implications for Jewish identification are ambiguous. Bock (1976) shows that while years of schooling increased with successive generations, the amount of time spent in the classroom decreased. Some suspect that since the early 1960s even the proportion of Jewish children receiving any Jewish schooling has decreased (Himmelfarb, 1976), although there is debate about that (Massarik, 1977). Analyses of the NJPS data (Bock, 1976; Himmelfarb and Loar, 1979a) show a tendency for decline in identification due to generational status to stabilize by the fourth generation at a low level.

Community. Goldstein and Goldscheider (1968) have shown substantial differences in Jewish identification between urban and suburban Jews. Suburban Jews are less identifying. Community size has a mixed effect. Studies of intermarriage (Rosenthal, 1963) have shown that it is substantially greater in communities where Jews are a smaller proportion of the total population than in larger Jewish communities. Intermarriage is also likely to be higher for Jews living in the Midwest and South (Lazerwitz, 1979b). Jews in smaller communities are much more likely to join and participate in synagogues and Jewish voluntary organizations. And Jews living in the Midwest are the most likely to attend synagogues and observe the Sabbath and holidays (Lazerwitz, 1977a).

Empirical data support the common-sense notion that the community in which one lives affects one's Jewish identification, but there is no simple relationship between Jewish concentration and identification. Apparently the relative presence or absence of Jewish neighbors and institutions affects one's opportunities and need to identify in different ways. To test the importance and substance of the community variable, we will need more studies with better controls.

Geographic Mobility. The relationship between geographic mobility and Jewish identification is not simple either. Early theories about geographic mobility followed the thinking of the "marginal man" idea arguing that mobility reduces ethnic group solidarity. However, empirical evidence has been lacking. Jaret's (1978) study of Chicago residents found that mobility and identification were only inversely related among Reform and nonaffiliated Jews. Among Orthodox and Conservative Jews more mobile individuals had higher levels of informal social relations with other Jews, were more activist in support of Israel and Soviet Jewry, and were more observant of religious traditions. Since most American Jews are likely to be Reform or nonaffiliated, increased geographic mobility is likely to reduce identification among the general population and create greater polarization in identification between more and less committed Jews.

Life Cycle. Marriage and children tend to make individuals more involved in Jewish life. Jewish identification among adults tends to reach a peak between the ages of forty and sixty. Sklare and Greenblum (1967) found the peak age to be around the time children are Bar and Bat Mitzvah. The life-cycle effect is more dramatic for those who are young, single, and childless. A combination of these characteristics produces very low levels of religious involvement. Individuals who are young and married but without children, and middle-aged singles without children, also have fairly low levels of Jewish identification. Life-cycle effects also tend to be most important for public types of identification such as participation in formal organizations and informal associations (Lazerwitz, 1977b). Whether these effects are a cause or a consequence of emphasis on family programming within Jewish organizations, or possibly an outgrowth of other forces affecting Jewish identification generally, remains to be determined. In any case, the life-cycle variable ought to assume greater importance as the trends for remaining single, postponing marriage, and having fewer or no children increase.

Socioeconomic Status. The relationship between socioeconomic status and Jewish identification is very slight. Lazerwitz (1977a), using the NJPS data, reports a negative relationship between years of education and overall Jewish identification (Beta = −.04) when other more important variables are held constant. He reports a slight positive relationship of equal magnitude to education between income and Jewish identification (Beta = .05). A study of Chicago Jews (Himmelfarb, 1974) also found a low negative relationship between education and "total religiosity," but a stronger positive relationship between income and "total religiosity." In a sample of New York City Jews, S. Cohen (1977) found a negative relationship between education and both Jewish endogamy and feelings of in-group solidarity, but no relationship between either education and intraethnic friendship or between income and endogamy, solidarity, or friendship. However, even the negative relationship between education and endogamy has not been a consistent finding (Goldstein and Goldscheider, 1968). The most consistent finding on socioeconomic variables is that income is positively related to philanthropic contributions and Jewish organizational participation (Axelrod, 1967; Fowler, 1977; Lazerwitz, 1973, 1977b; Himmelfarb, 1974), showing some degree of rationality behind these forms of identification. Cohen (1978b) found that occupation also has a small effect on the amount of Jewish philanthropic contributions. Self-employed individuals contribute more than salaried professionals and nonprofessionals, even when income is held constant. Attorneys are the most generous and physicians the least generous among self-employed professionals. Finally, there is some agreement among studies that education has its most negative effects on traditional beliefs (Lazerwitz, 1973, 1978; Himmelfarb, 1974). With these exceptions, we can conclude that socioeconomic factors do not have much impact on Jewish identification. This is also the general conclusion of the research on social class and Christian church participation (Mueller and Johnson, 1975).

Events of Jewish History (Anti-Semitism). Many observers have pointed out that Jewish identification increases particularly when Jews are attacked. The Holocaust, wars in Israel, the Munich massacre, the plight of Soviet Jews, the desire of neo-Nazis to march in Jewish neighborhoods, anti-Zionist sentiment and action in the United Nations and among civil rights groups, should all heighten awareness of Jewishness. In Lewin's terms, anti-Semitism should create a sense of group belongingness based on an "interdependence of fate."

Unfortunately, we do not have much data on this matter. Etzioni-Halevy and Shapira (1975) report that Jewish identification of Tel Aviv University students increased after the Six-Day War in Israel and two years later was higher than just a few months before the war. Records of the United Jewish Appeal in America show that both contributions and contributors increased after the 1967 and 1973 wars in Israel. We have no documentation that other forms of identification increased after these events and we do not know how long any impact lasted. We also do not know whether it is simply a threat to Jewish survival that heightens identification, or whether pride in success or widespread media coverage are what is important about these events. If it is the latter two, then we expect negative feelings of Jewish identity to heighten as political events and media coverage of Mideast politics become more critical of Israel.

Current Social Trends. At various times there are social movements, fads, or a societal atmosphere that can have an impact on Jewish identification. For example radicalism in the 1960s and feminism and fundamentalism in the 1970s have all had some impact on Jewish identification. What is interesting about these social trends, as with moderate anti-Semitism, is that most Jews are probably affected very little by them while for others they will have opposite effects. Organizations which arise as a response to these trends often bring some Jews to heightened Jewish identification and others to almost complete detachment from Jewish life. Both radicals and feminists saw the embodiment of the corruption they sought to change in Jewish institutions and many turned away from or against the Jewish establishment. Other Jewish radicals and feminists sought to activate their ideologies by changing Jewish institutions and became more involved in Jewish life. Similarly, the trend toward fundamentalism among large segments of American society caused many Jewish youth to turn to Christian or Eastern cults, while others sought their roots in Judaism and joined the growing ranks of *baalei teshuva*. Which individuals take these different routes is probably more determined by particular socialization experiences than by general societal trends.[15]

Socialization Experiences

Aside from the general social context which affects identification, there are particular socialization experiences that could reinforce or counter the other trends.

Family Influences. One of the most consistent findings in the Jewish identification literature is the positive relationship between an individual's Jewish identification and that of his parents (Rosen, 1976; Sklare and Greenblum, 1967; Lazerwitz, 1973; Dashefsky and Shapiro, 1974; Cohen, 1974; Bock, 1976; Himmelfarb, 1977b). The relationship extends from childhood to adulthood and is pervasive in the literature. Yet we know very little about parental socialization. For example, it has been argued (Himmelfarb, 1974) that parents affect adult identification indirectly by channeling children into other environments like schools, clubs, and marriage, which in turn have a more direct impact on identification in adulthood.

We also know very little about the qualities of family life that are important for identification, but the literature does suggest some areas for further research. Massarik and Chenkin (1973) found, somewhat surprisingly, that the highest percentage of intermarriage was not among those who described the Jewishness of their upbringing as "not at all Jewish," but among those who described their upbringing as doubtful or mixed. Parental ambiguity or conflict over religion has an even greater negative effect on Jewish identification than the absence of either positive or negative Jewish identification.

Caplovitz and Sherrow (1977) found that apostasy (not identifying oneself as belonging to any religious group) among college graduates was greater for those who had a poor relationship with their parents than for those who had a good one. For Jews, the correlation between relationship with parents and apostasy became very low when other variables were held constant. Weigert and Thomas (1972) found that perceived parental support and control is related to adolescent religiosity. However, one test of this relationship on Jewish adults found only low correlations (Himmelfarb, 1974).

In testing another family variable, Dashefsky and Shapiro (1974) found that in addition to parental religiosity, the presence of an older brother was an important influence on the adult identification of young Jewish men, but not on the identification of their fathers. All of this suggests that the relationship between the home environment and Jewish identification is complex and that many factors need to be further explored. Even the obvious trend of parental absence due to divorce and/or maternal employment has not been explored in regard to Jewish identification. We also know nothing about the effects of parental absence due to Jewish organizational activity, e.g. the "Nadav and Avihu syndrome."

Peer Influence. Rosen's study (1965) of Jewish adolescents found that peer influence had an important impact on Jewish identification. Where peer and parental influences on Jewish identification were contradictory, the peer group was often more influential, particularly if the adolescent chose his peers as a reference group over his parents. Dashefsky and Shapiro (1974) also report that adolescent peers were important influences of religious socialization on both the younger and older generations of adult Jewish men in their sample. Surprisingly, they were even more influential on the older generation than on the younger one, suggesting a long-term impact for that generation. In contrast to Rosen, they find parents more influential than peers.

Verbit's (1968) study of Jewish college students found that they perceived two opposing sets of referents for religion: "early socialization agents" (parents and rabbi) and "later socialization agents" (representatives of the larger culture — professors, intellectuals, fellow students, and future occupational colleagues). The students chose friends who supported them in their resolution of the conflict between the two referent sets. This suggests that the role of peers in the religious socialization process might be more as supporters of change (or status quo) rather than as initiators. This could help explain the findings of another study (Himmelfarb, 1974) that the influence of adolescent peers on adult identification becomes slight when other more direct influences are controlled. The impact of friends as supporters might also be important in studying religious converts, apostates, and *baalei teshuva*. Most research on individuals who change religions show that they are lonely, sometimes on drugs, or seeking self-definition in some way. If they find friends among religious groups, they are likely to adopt their norms.

Schools. Numerous studies have shown that there is a low to moderate correlation between amount of Jewish schooling and adult identification, even when controls for parental and other inputs are made. Some studies (Cohen, 1974; Himmelfarb, 1977b) find that schooling has an interaction effect, having greatest impact on those from highly religious homes. However, Bock (1976) studying the NJPS data does not find such an interaction. Two studies have found that hours of Jewish schooling, as a measure of quantity, does not impact adult identification in a linear manner. There is a minimum threshold below which Jewish schooling does not have any effect on adult Jewish identification and there are plateaus beyond which additional schooling has no impact (Bock, 1976; Himmelfarb, 1977a). One study (Bock) finds the threshold to be 1,000 hours in most cases. The other (Himmelfarb), finds it to be about 3,000 hours. There are numerous methodological reasons that can explain this discrepancy, for example, there were differences in the samples used and in the items constituting the Jewish identification scales and other variables in the two studies. In addition, Himmelfarb reduces much of the potential impact of Jewish schooling by controlling for spouse's religiosity before marriage. Bock did not have available a measure of spouse's religiosity in the NJPS data file. Despite these differences, the fact that both studies found a pattern of minimum threshold and plateau effects has important theoretical and policy implications and requires further exploration.

Both studies found that Jewish schooling has a different degree of impact on different measures of Jewish identification, and that different types of Jewish schools have differential impact on the various types of identification. One of them (Himmelfarb, 1977a) suggests that these various school differences might be related to different curricular emphases. We do not have one controlled study of a Jewish school innovation or curriculum design (other than the nonintensive versus intensive forms of schooling discussed above) which shows that one approach to Jewish instruction is more effective than another. The field is wide open for experimenting, testing, and evaluating.

Spouse. Several studies have looked at the impact of the spouse on adult Jewish identification (Pollack, 1961; Sklare and Greenblum, 1967; Mazur, 1971; Himmelfarb, 1974). Generally the studies show a substantial impact. One study found spouse's ritual observance before marriage to be the best single predictor of most types of adult Jewish identification. It also found that spouses could create substantial "conversion" effects, changing a person from the way he was raised and schooled (Himmelfarb, 1977b). Women are a little more likely to influence their husband's religiosity than vice versa.

The implications of spouse as a determinant of religious identification becomes striking when one considers the increasing rate of intermarriage.[16] Two-thirds of all Jewish intermarriages are Jewish men marrying non-Jewish women. If in fact, women are more likely to influence the religious identification of the home, the sex differences in propensity for intermarriage do not bode well for the identification level of most of those marriages. Actually though, almost half of the non-Jewish spouses of intermarriage consider themselves Jewish (although only one-third convert to Judaism), thus balancing the losses somewhat (Massarik and Chenkin, 1973; Lazerwitz, 1979b).

Intermarriage may heighten Jewish identification. Lazerwitz (1979b) found that where there is an intermarriage with a conversion, the family is likely to be more Jewishly identifying than intramarried Jewish couples. This happens only on religious, rather than ethnic, forms of Jewish identification (Lavender, 1976; Lazerwitz, 1979b). Once again, we find that the dynamics of family life as it impacts on identification is highly complex.

Other Settings for Religious Socialization. Numerous alternatives to formal Jewish education are sponsored in the Jewish community, the most prominent being youth groups, summer camps, trips to Israel, and more recently weekend retreats. No study has assessed the impact of any of these programs in a rigorous way. The most common flaw is lack of a proper control group. There are studies showing positive short-run effects of such programs (Farago, 1972; Wolfson, 1974; Lipnick, 1976) and there are numerous participant accounts of their efficacy. Little is known about their long-term effects, and without appropriate controls, even their short-run effects seem doubtful.

An exemplary study in this regard is Sheldon Dorph's (1976) assessment of the impact of Ramah Camps on teenage religious behavior (TRB) of Conservative Hebrew high school students (9th through 12th graders) in New York and Los Angeles. Dorph's design allowed him to compare the behavior of Jewish teenagers who had attended Ramah Camp for at least one month during the previous two summers to those who had attended some other Jewish camp during that time and to those who had not attended a Jewish camp for that length of time during those summers. He assessed the impact of family religious background, locality (New York or Los Angeles), and camping experience on teenage religious attitudes and behavior in the areas of prayer, ritual observance, Jewish study, Kashrut, Jewish and general charity, service to the Jewish community, service and volunteer work in the general community, and past and planned involvement with Israel. Dorph found that family religious background and location often have a greater impact than Jewish camp experience; and where Jewish camps seem to have an impact (whether Ramah or other Jewish camps), they seem to interact with family and location factors. Ramah camps showed a slightly greater impact than other Jewish camps, but on the whole Dorph (1976, p. 303) concludes that "Ramah has no consistent significant relationship to TRB." He argues that the behavior learned in camp is not carried over to the city unless the latter environment reinforces such behavior.

A study of Chicago Jews (Himmelfarb, 1974) tried to assess the relative impact of camps and youth groups on adult Jewish identification. It found that day camps have negligible effects and overnight camps have a low impact on adult identification. But when hours of Jewish schooling were held constant, even the impact of overnight camps became negligible. The study concluded that overnight camps can play a useful role in getting children to attend or continue attending a Jewish school. They can supplement, but not replace, an extensive formal Jewish education. Like Dorph, Himmelfarb sees the need to have the summer camp experience reinforced throughout the year.

Himmelfarb's study also examined youth group participation at four different ages: 9–11, 12–15, 16–18, and 19–22. It found that the strongest relationship between youth group participation and adult identification was participation during the college age years, 19–22. This relationship remained significant even when other variables were controlled. Participation in Jewish organizations during the college age years was the best single predictor of adult participation in Jewish organizations. These findings are exploratory. Much more work must be done in this area, particularly in trying to assess the impact of summer camps which seems to be very strong but has not proven to be so statistically.

Another exemplary study among recent attempts to evaluate alternative programs for heightening Jewish identification is Bernard Reisman's (1977) work on *havurot*. Reisman presents us with a good experimental model by comparing *havurot* members to other synagogue members and getting before and after measures on both groups. With this tighter experimental design than we usually get in such studies, claims for success are also much more modest than usual. Since *havurot* members and other synagogue members were not exactly comparable to begin with, it is not certain that even the modest gains reported by *havurot* members on some measures are actually due to the *havurah* experience. The evidence indicates that the *havurah* experiment is worthy of further exploration.

Summary. Studies of socialization point to the impact of family (of origin and of procreation), friends (including youth groups and possibly *havurot* and camps), and schools as the most important sources of Jewish socialization. But their interaction with each other and the previous variables discussed need more attention. The role of these various institutions as initiators or reinforcers of identity and identification needs to be clarified. Many of these matters will not be resolved until we begin doing longitudinal studies.

Prospects

This review of the literature shows that Jewish identity and identification have been studied by many researchers, using different conceptual perspectives and methodologies. There is no aspect of this topic that could not use more study. By way of illustration and summary, we shall briefly list the suggestions for further research which have been made throughout the previous discussion.

Areas for Further Research

1. There is need to clarify the relationship between identity and identification and the factors which affect each.
2. Psychological theories of social learning, child development, and attitude change need to be applied to the study of ethnic-religious socialization.
3. There is a need to view societal conditions affecting identity and identification from a comparative (cross-national) perspective. While historical evidence suggests what these factors might be, we do not have any quantitative historical studies or empirical contemporary studies to test the importance of the suggested factors.
4. Comparative studies of Jewish institutional arrangements would be useful. The comparisons can be across Jewish communities within the United States and between the United States and other countries. The latter can be combined with the comparative study of societal factors discussed above.
5. The study of Jewish organizations from the perspective of complex (formal) organizations is completely missing. This too can be studied comparatively, but at first we can use a few good case studies.
6. A review of studies of individual Jewish communities has shown a need for the study of larger, more "typical" Jewish communities and also follow-up studies of those communities previously researched.
7. More work needs to be done to develop low-cost sampling procedures for studies of American Jews. Perhaps the further development of "distinctive Jewish name" sampling or the use of the existent county level data of Halvorson and Newman would be useful.
8. There is a need for standardized measures of identity and identification to enable comparisons of findings in different studies. We need multiple scales for in-depth studies and short indices for other studies.
9. The effects of age, life cycle, and generation, which have been shown to have substantial effects upon identification, are often confounded with each other. Their relative importance is confounded by reliance on cross-sectional data. For example, we do not know whether the lower level of identification among younger Jews than among older Jews is predictive of future trends or whether the younger Jews will become more identifying as they grow older. To sort out these relationships, we need longitudinal data.
10. The study of socialization agents such as parents, peers, schools, and spouse and their effects on identity and identification has also suffered from a reliance on cross-sectional data. To measure the impact of some of these agents, we have often had to rely on retrospective information; and where we have contemporaneous information for compar-

ison with retrospective studies, it sometimes seems that agents having strong short-run influences may be different than those with strong long-run influences. Reliance on retrospective information has also handicapped our ability to gather information about socialization within settings such as families and schools. Longitudinal studies of individuals during childhood, adolescence, and adulthood, would help solve some of these problems.

11. To understand socialization it would be useful to study individuals who have made drastic changes in their lives — those who have opted for a much more intensive Jewish lifestyle than their upbringing would predict and those who have opted for another religion altogether. Intensive interviews with such persons would probably illuminate much about them and also about the socialization process that most other Jews experience.

12. There is a need to study the impact of "negative" forces such as anti-Semitism upon identity and identification. Such forces can be studied through laboratory experiments where the negative forces are introduced, and by collecting data on naturally induced negative forces from current and media events.[17]

13. We need studies of the long-term effects of summer camps, youth group participation, and trips to Israel. These studies should have adequate control groups to assess their impact.

14. All new experiments in enhancing Jewish identity and identification such as *havurot*, weekend retreats, parent education programs, or new school curricula, need to be rigorously evaluated. Every effort should be made to introduce an evaluative component into such programs before they begin and to control administration of the experiments so as to isolate variables and allow comparisons with a control group.

Some Priority Projects

The above list of areas for further research is long enough and broad enough to occupy researchers for some time. However, such a list raises the obvious issue of which items deserve priority. Whatever inherent merits a project might have, priorities will be largely dependent on the availability of funds and the interests and capabilities of the researchers. The following is a description of some suggested projects based on the perhaps naive assumption that funds would be available for any of them and colored by my own research interests.

Developing Standardized Measures. We are sufficiently advanced in the area of measurement to begin some closure. It is time to convene a group of scholars who have dealt with the questions of measuring identity and identification (who has not?) to consider the various conceptual approaches available in the literature and begin to achieve some consensus about what should be measured. Second, studies can be undertaken with existing data to develop scales of those dimensions for which appropriate measures are available. For others, appropriate measures would have to be devised and new data collected. What is needed are multiple scales for in-depth studies and two short scales of identity and identification which could be used in other studies of Jews or general polls with questions on religiosity and ethnicity. The scales need to be tested for validity and reliability and the short scales need to be compared to the multiple scales. Then, hopefully, the scales will be widely adopted by researchers and greater comparisons can be made between studies. It may also be possible to develop through this effort "quality of Jewish life indices" which could be used to assess identification levels of communities and countries over time.

A NJPS for the 1980s. The whole area of contemporary American Jewry will be severely lacking without updated national population information. The data from the first NJPS, which were never fully analyzed, are now old. Yet despite deficiencies in the first project, its value could be greatly enhanced if more recent data were available for comparison. It would be a good idea to begin a practice of decennial surveys of American Jewry. This might be done in conjunction with other religious groups to reduce costs. I raise this idea here, even though the NJPS was purportedly a demographic study, because it contains rich data about Jewish identification and its antecedents. To the extent that we find the Jewish identification measures on the first NJPS worthy of replication, we will be able to chart trends over time.

A Longitudinal Study of Religious Socialization. Studies have identified numerous factors which affect an individual's Jewish identification, but have been hindered in establishing a firm causal relationship between variables because of the use of cross-sectional data. It is time to study what happens to the same individuals over time. It might be possible to launch such a study from a subsample of the 1980s NJPS suggested above. Rather than randomly picking one adult member of each family to answer the detailed Jewish identification questionnaire (as was done in the previous NJPS survey), a predetermined member of the family based on age and sex would be selected as the respondent to the Jewish identification questionnaire. And those persons would be resurveyed at successive intervals, e.g., every five years.

Alternatively, several different subsamples could be chosen from the initial survey to study different perspectives of the socialization process. There could be a subsample of preteen children and another of college youths. There could be subsamples of adults of varying ages. We might want a subsample of entire families, or at least all siblings, to track how persons from the same families turn out differently. Such in-depth study of individuals over time would allow for more collection of information on personality characteristics and interpersonal relationships than has been possible with cross-sectional surveys.

A Comparative Study of Jewish Identity and Identification. A study of the factors which affect American Jewish identity and identification could be greatly enhanced if it were simultaneously conducted on Jews in another country. Israelis would be an interesting group for comparison because of the contrasts between minority and majority status and its effects on identity and identification.

Consequences of Identification. In recent years most researchers have assumed what earlier researchers strongly questioned. Today most researchers assume that greater identification has positive consequences for Jews collectively and individually. As we have seen, earlier researchers were very ambivalent about consequences for the individual, some assuming they were negative. Considering the low levels of behavioral identification among American Jews, one might conclude that they too assume some negative consequences from greater identification. Yet the testimony of "devotees" extols the virtues of such a lifestyle. Empirical research to support either position is lacking. Some consequences that might be studied are (1) the effect of Jewish identity upon the integration of other self-identities; (2) the impact of participation in Jewish life on participation in American society; (3) the impact of Jewish identification on occupational mobility and success; and (4) the impact of Jewish identification on family solidarity and individual happiness. To study these consequences questions could be incorporated into the longitudinal survey suggested above or some other survey of cross-sectional design. Psychological consequences could be studied by in-depth interviews or projective techniques. However, I would avoid trying to draw conclusions about the general Jewish population from case study notes of a clinical population, as those with a psychoanalytic perspective often attempt to do.

Conclusion

The vast literature on American Jews indicates that they have been a tremendously introspective people, even if not always perceptive. For many social scientists who have written about Jews, it has been mostly an avocation. Not until the last decade has a numerically significant cadre of scholars devoted most of their research time to the study of contemporary Jewish life. The possibilities for advancing our knowledge in this area is therefore greater than ever before. Throughout the accumulation of studies on American Jews, the topic of identity and identification has been of central concern. This review has attempted to show the broad range of issues that have been and need to be addressed, and the broad range of perspectives and methodologies which have been and still need to be employed. Hopefully, it will help future research in this field develop more systematically and rigorously.

Notes

1. Since Wirth (1928, p. 288–89) argues that the distinctiveness of Jews as an ethnic group would disappear over time as they were able to leave the ghetto and experience cosmopolitan life, the importance of studying Jews was diminished. Wirth (1943) only addressed Jewish issues one more time. Usually he concentrated on general urban problems.
2. For more comprehensive reviews of the literature and bibliographies, see Sanua (1962, 1963, 1964a, b, 1965), Fainstein and Feder (1966), National Jewish Welfare Board (1967?), Rosenfield (1970), Sklare (1974a, b), Brickman (1977).
3. For a review of studies that have looked at these types of reactions under varying rubrics, see Rothman (1965). Stonequist (1937), for example, calls these the nationalist role, the intermediary role, and assimilation and passing.
4. Implicit in many of these writings are assumptions similar to Heider's (1958) balance theory.
5. Perhaps many of us (including Glazer) do not think that the dividing line is quite as sharp today as it was then.
6. Studies of religious socialization are rare. See comments on this matter in the chapters by McCandless and by Campbell in the *Handbook of Socialization Theory and Research*, ed. David Goslin. The *Handbook* contains a chapter on minority group socialization but lacks one on religious socialization. In all of my literature review, I was able to find only one compendium of research studies on religious socialization (Strommen, 1971) and it is not available in many library collections.
7. To cite a personal example, when my daughter was three years old and mature enough to understand holiday stories, the events behind Chanukah, Purim, Pesach, and Yom Hashoa gave her a succession of tales of people who wanted to "hurt" Jews. Despite our emphasis on the happy ending to these stories, they gave her a frightening account of what being Jewish means. What do we know about child development that would help us relate the appropriate details of Jewish history and the appropriate experiences of Jewish living at an age that would maximize positive feelings about Jewish life?
8. See Sklare (1974) and Toll (1978) for useful bibliographies on historical studies of Jewish communities.
9. The Rothchild study is retrospective rather than a restudy and is more journalistic than scientific in the methods used.
10. See also Himmelfarb (1980) for a case study of a Jewish day school.
11. This subsection on measurement and the following section on findings borrow heavily from one of my other papers, "The Study of American Jewish Identification: How it is Defined, Measured, Obtained, Sustained, and Lost," *Journal for the Scientific Study of Religion* 19 (March 1980) p. 48–60.
12. Verbit and others have suggested that amount of knowledge is an indicator of religiosity. However, since knowledge is dependent on many things, including intelligence and prior education, it is not an unambiguous indicator of current involvement. Verbit also includes a more relevant aspect of an intellectual di-

mension — whether a person presently seeks knowledge such as by individual or group study, or in other ways (see the Growth and Striving scale of King and Hunt, 1972).

13. That is not to stay that verifying the internal consistency of scales is not a notable accomplishment. For example, work on the NJPS data has revealed that we can construct very reliable separate Guttman scales for ritual observance, synagogue attendance, and attitudes toward Israel from multiple-item indicators of those dimensions.

14. In terms of man's struggle for freedom, for example, rather than in terms of supernatural miracles.

15. The long-term societal trends of secularism, liberalism, and universalism have had more impact on Jewish life than any of the trends discussed above, except perhaps for anti-Semitism.

16. The rate of intermarriage may not be rising as fast as previously thought. Lazerwitz (1979b), using the NJPS data, estimates the intermarriage rate in 1971 to be closer to 14 percent rather than the 31.7 percent estimate of Massarik and Chenkin (1972) who use the same data. The disagreement is based on a technical point of whether the case base and weighting procedure of NJPS are sufficient to allow an accurate estimate of current intermarriage based on only a five-year interval or whether a ten-year interval is needed. Lazerwitz opts for the latter.

17. A "media event" is a news item exaggerated by the mass media out of all proportion to its actual occurrence. American Jews forcing the resignation of Andrew Young as U.S. ambassador to the United Nations is an example. Media events might be as real in their consequences as actual events.

References

Axelrod, Morris, Floyd J. Fowler, Jr., and Arnold Gurin, *A Community Survey for Long Range Planning: A Study of the Jewish Population of Greater Boston* (Boston: Combined Jewish Philanthropies, 1967).

Berkson, Isaac, *Theories of Americanization* (New York: Teachers College, Columbia University, 1920).

Bettelheim, Bruno, "How to Arm Our Children against Anti-Semitism? A Psychologist's Advice to Jewish Parents," *Commentary* 12 (September 1951): 209–18.

Bock, Geoffrey E., "The Jewish Schooling of American Jews: A Study of Non-Cognitive Educational Effects" (Ph.D. diss., Harvard University, 1976).

Brickman, William W., *The Jewish Community in America: An Annotated and Classified Bibliographical Guide* (New York: Burt Franklin Publishers / Lenox-Hill Publishing, distributors, 1977).

Campbell, Ernest Q., "Adolescent Socialization." In David A. Goslin (ed.), *Handbook of Socialization Theory and Research* (Chicago: Rand McNally, 1969).

Caplovitz, David, and Fred Sherrow, *The Religious Drop-outs: Apostasy among College Graduates* (Beverly Hills, Calif.: Sage, 1977).

Cohen, Arthur R., *Attitude Change and Social Influence* (New York: Basic Books, 1964).

Cohen, Eli, "On the Nature of Jewish Identity: A Methodological Approach" (Ph.D. diss., Indiana University, 1977).

Cohen, Steven M., "The Impact of Jewish Education on Religious Identification and Practice," *Jewish Social Studies* 36 (July-October 1974): 316–26.

Cohen, Steven M., "Socioeconomic Determinants of Intraethnic Marriage and Friendship," *Social Forces* 55 (June 1977): 997–1005.

Cohen, Steven M., "Will Jews Keep Giving? Prospects for the Jewish Charitable Community," *Journal of Jewish Communal Service* 55 (Autumn 1978a): 59–71.

Cohen, Steven M., "Assimilation and Coalescence: A Trend Analysis of Jewish Philanthropic Behavior in an American Metropolis, 1965–1975." Revised version of paper presented at the Tenth Annual Conference, Association for Jewish Studies, Boston (December 1978b).

Cohen, Steven M., "Trends in Jewish Philanthropy," *American Jewish Year Book* (1980): 29–51.

Cooley, Charles Horton, *Human Nature and the Social Order* (New York: Scribner, 1922).

Council for Jewish Federations and Welfare Funds, "Jewish Identity: Facts for Planning" (New York: CJFWF, 1974).

Dashefsky, Arnold, and Howard Shapiro, *Ethnic Identification among American Jews: Socialization and Social Structure* (Lexington, Mass.: Lexington, 1974).

Dodson, Dan W., "Human Relations and Post-War Metropolitan Growth," *Journal of Jewish Communal Service* 32 (Fall 1955): 61–70.

Dorph, Sheldon Arthur, "A Model for Jewish Education in America: Guidelines for the Restructuring of Conservative Congregational Education" (Ph.D. diss., Columbia University Teacher's College, 1976).

Durkheim, Emile, *The Elementary Forms of Religious Life* (New York: Free Press, 1965; orig. ed. 1915).

Eagly, Alice H., and Samuel Himmelfarb, "Attitudes and Opinions," *Annual Review of Psychology* (1978).

Elazar, Daniel J., *Community and Polity: The Organizational Dynamics of American Jewry* (Philadelphia: Jewish Publication Society, 1976).

Elkind, David, "The Child's Conception of His Religious Denomination: I. The Jewish Child," *Journal of Genetic Psychology* 99 (1961): 209–25. Also in Norman Kiell (ed.), *The Psychodynamics of American Jewish Life* (New York: Twayne, 1967).

Etzioni-Halevy, Eva, and Rina Shapira, "Jewish Identification of Israeli Students: What Lies Ahead," *Jewish Social Studies* 37 (Summer-Fall 1975): 251–66.

Fainstein, Norman, and Stanley Feder, "Bibliographies on Jewish Identity: Unannotated and Annotated." Prepared under the direction of Leonard J. Fein. (Cambridge: MIT, 1966, mimeo).

Farago, Uri, "The Influence of a Jewish Summer Camp's Social Climate on Camper's Jewish Identity" (Ph.D. diss., Brandeis University, 1972).

Festinger, Leon, *A Theory of Cognitive Dissonance* (Stanford: Stanford University Press, 1957).

Fishberg, Maurice, *The Jews: A Study of Race and Environment* (New York: Scribner, 1911).

Fishman, Joshua, "Negative Stereotypes Concerning Americans among Minority Children Receiving Various Types of Minority-Group Education," *Genetic Psychology Monographs* 51 (1955): 107–82.

Fowler, Floyd J., Jr., *1975 Community Survey: A Study of the Jewish Population of Greater Boston* (Boston: Combined Jewish Philanthropies of Greater Boston, 1977).

Gans, Herbert, "The Origin and Growth of a Jewish Community in the Suburbs: A Study of the Jews of Park Forest." In Sklare, Marshall (ed.), *The Jews: Social Patterns of an American Group* (New York: Free Press, 1958).

Ginsberg, Yona, *Jews in a Changing Neighborhood* (New York: Free Press, 1975).

Glazer, Nathan, "What Sociology Knows about American Jews," *Commentary* 9 (March 1950): 275–84.

Glazer, Nathan, and Daniel P. Moynihan, *Beyond the Melting Pot: The Negroes, Jews, Italians, and Irish of New York City* (Cambridge: MIT, 1963).

Goldstein, Sidney, and Calvin Goldscheider, *Jewish Americans: Three Generations in a Jewish Community* (Englewood Cliffs, N.J.: Prentice-Hall, 1968).

Gordon, Milton M., *Assimilation in American Life* (New York: Oxford University Press, 1964).

Gordon, Milton M., "Toward a General Theory of Racial and Ethnic Group Relations." In Nathan Glazer and Daniel P. Moynihan (eds.), *Ethnicity: Theory and Practice* (Cambridge: Harvard University Press, 1975).

Goslin, David A. (ed.), *Handbook of Socialization Theory and Research* (Chicago: Rand McNally, 1969).

Halvorson, Peter L., and William M. Newman, "A Data Archive of American Religious Denominations, 1952–1971," *Review of Religious Research* 20, no. 1 (1978): 86–91.

Halvorson, Peter L., and William M. Newman, "American Jews: Patterns of Geographic Distribution and Change, 1952–1971," *Journal for the Scientific Study of Religion* 18 (June 1979): 183–93.

Heider, Fritz, *The Psychology of Interpersonal Relations* (New York: Wiley, 1958).

Heilman, Samuel C., *Synagogue Life* (Chicago: University of Chicago Press, 1976).

Herman, Simon N., *American Students in Israel* (Ithaca, N.Y.: Cornell University Press, 1970a).

Herman, Simon N., *Israelis and Jews: The Continuity of an Identity* (New York: Random House, 1970b).

Herman, Simon N., *Jewish Identity: A Social Psychological Perspective* (Beverly Hills, Calif.: Sage, 1977).

Hill, Mozell C., "A Comparative Study of the Race Attitudes of the All-Negro Community in Oklahoma," *Phylon* 7 (1946): 260–68.

Himmelfarb, Harold S., "The Impact of Religious Schooling: The Effects of Jewish Education upon Adult Religious Involvement" (Ph.D. diss., University of Chicago, 1974).

Himmelfarb, Harold S., "Measuring Religious Involvement," *Social Forces* 53 (June 1975): 606–18.

Himmelfarb, Harold S., "Fertility Trends and Their Effects on Jewish Education." In "Zero Population Growth and the Jewish Community: A Symposium," *Analysis* no. 60 (November-December 1976 — Washington, D.C.: Institute for Jewish Policy Planning and Research of the Synagogue Council of America).

Himmelfarb, Harold S., "The Non-Linear Impact of Religious Schooling: Comparing Different Types and Amounts of Jewish Education," *Sociology of Education* 50 (April 1977a): 114–29.

Himmelfarb, Harold S., "The Interaction Effects of Parents, Spouse, and Schooling: Comparing the Impact of Jewish and Catholic Schools," *Sociological Quarterly* 18 (Autumn 1977b): 464–77.

Himmelfarb, Harold S., "Patterns of Assimilation-Identification among American Jews," *Ethnicity* 6 (September 1979): 249–67.

Himmelfarb, Harold S., "The Study of American Jewish Identification: How It is Defined, Measured, Obtained, Sustained, and Lost,"*Journal for the Scientific Study of Religion* 19 (March 1980): 18–60.

Himmelfarb, Harold S., "A Sociological Look at the Jewish Day School: A Case Study" (New York: American Jewish Committee, 1980a).

Himmelfarb, Harold S., and R. Michael Loar, "National Trends in Jewish Ethnicity: A Test of the Polarization Hypothesis." Paper presented at colloquium on Jewish Population Movements. (Ramat-Gan, Israel: Bar Ilan University, June 1979a).

Himmelfarb, Harold S., and R. Michael Loar, "How Distinctive Are Jews with Distinctive Jewish Names?" *Public Opinion Quarterly* (1982).

Hyman, Herbert, "The Psychology of Status," *Archives of Psychology*, no. 269 (1942).

Jaret, Charles, "The Impact of Geographic Mobility on Jewish Community Participation: Disruptive or Supportive?" *Contemporary Jewry* 4 (Spring-Summer 1978): 9–21.

Karpf, Maurice, *Jewish Community Organization in the United States: An Outline of Types of Organizations, Activities, and Problems* (New York: Bloch, 1938).

Kelley, Harold H., "Two Functions of Reference Groups." In G.E. Swanson, T.M., Newcomb, and E. L. Hartley (eds.), *Readings in Social Psychology* (New York: Holt, 1952).

Kelman, Herbert, "The Place of Jewish Identity in the Development of Personal Identity." In *Issues in Jewish Identity and Jewish Education*, Colloquium Papers (New York: American Jewish Committee, 1977).

King, Morton B., and Richard A. Hunt, "Measuring the Religious Variable: Amended Findings," *Journal for the Scientific Study of Religion* 11 (September 1972): 240–51.

Kohlberg, Lawrence, "Moral and Religious Education and the Public Schools: A Developmental View." In T. Sizer (ed.), *Religion and Public Education* (Boston: Houghton-Mifflin, 1967).

Kohlberg, Lawrence, *Stages in the Development of Moral Thought and Action* (New York: Holt, Rinehart, & Winston, 1969).

Kramer, Judith, and Seymour Leventman, *Children of the Gilded Ghetto: Conflict Resolutions of Three Generations of American Jews* (New Haven: Yale University Press, 1961).

Lavender, Abraham, "Jewish Intermarriage and Marriage to Converts: The Religious Factor and the Ethnic Factor," *Jewish Sociology and Social Research* 2 (Spring-Summer 1976): 17–22.

Lavender, Abraham (ed.), *A Coat of Many Colors* (Westport, Conn.: Greenwood, 1977).

Lazerwitz, Bernard, "Religious Identification and Its Ethnic Correlates," *Social Forces* 52 (December 1973): 204–20.

Lazerwitz, Bernard, "The Community Variable in Jewish Identification," *Journal for the Scientific Study of Religion* 16 (December 1977a): 361–69.

Lazerwitz, Bernard, "The Determinants of Religious Participation" (Ramat-Gan, Israel: Bar Ilan University, Department of Sociology, 1977b, mimeo).

Lazerwitz, Bernard, "An Approach to the Components and Consequences of Jewish Identification," *Contemporary Jewry* 4 (1978): 3–8.

Lazerwitz, Bernard, "Past and Future Trends in the Size of American Jewish Denominations," *Journal of Reform Judaism* 26 (Summer 1979a): 77–83.

Lazerwitz, Bernard, "Jewish-Christian Marriages and Conversions," *Jewish Social Studies* (1979b).

Lewin, Kurt, *Resolving Social Conflicts* (New York: Harper & Bro., 1948).

Liebman, Charles, *The Ambivalent American Jew: Politics, Religion, and Family in American Jewish Life* (Philadelphia: Jewish Publication Society of America, 1973).

Lipnick, Bernard, *An Experiment That Works in Religious Education* (New York: Bloch, 1976).

Lipset, Seymour M., "The Study of Jewish Communities in a Comparative Context," *Jewish Journal of Sociology* 5 (December 1963): 157–66.

Maslow, Will, *The Structure and Functioning of the American Jewish Community* (New York: American Jewish Congress, 1974).

Massarik, Fred, "New Approaches to the Study of the American Jew," *Jewish Journal of Sociology* 8 (December 1966): 175–91.

Massarik, Fred, "Trends on U.S. Jewish Education: National Jewish Population Study Findings," *American Jewish Year Book* 77 (1977): 240–50.

Massarik, Fred, and Alvin Chenkin, "Explorations in Intermarriage," *American Jewish Year Book* 74 (1973): 292–306.

Mayer, Egon, *Modern Jewish Orthodoxy in Post-Modern America: A Case Study of the Jewish Community of Boro Park* (Ph.D. diss., 1975, Rutgers University).

Mazur, Allan, "The Socialization of Jews into the Academic Subculture." In Charles Anderson and John Murray (eds.), *The Professors* (Cambridge: Schenkman, 1971).

Mead, George Herbert, *Mind, Self, and Society* (Chicago: University of Chicago Press, 1934).

Merton, Robert K., *Social Theory and Social Structure* (New York: Free Press, 1957).

McCandless, Boyd R., "Childhood Socializaton." In David A. Goslin (ed.), *Handbook of Socialization Theory and Research* (Chicago: Rand McNally, 1969).

Mueller, Charles, and Weldon Johnson, 'Socioeconomic Status and Religious Participation," *American Sociological Review* 40 (December 1975): 785–800.

National Jewish Welfare Board, "Religious Identification Bibliography" (Waltham, Mass.: National Jewish Welfare Board, Florence Heller Research Program at Brandeis University, 1967? mimeo).

Ostow, Mortimer, "The Determinants of Jewish Identity: A Maturational Approach." In *Issues in Jewish Identity and Jewish Education*, Colloquium Papers (New York: American Jewish Committee, 1977).

Park, Robert E., "Human Migration and the Marginal Man," *American Journal of Sociology* 33 (May 1928): 881–93.

Park, Robert E., "Introduction." In Everett V. Stonequist, *The Marginal Man* (New York: Scribner, 1937).

Park, Robert E., *Race and Culture* (New York: Free Press, 1950).

Park, Robert E., *Society* (New York: Free Press, 1955).

Poll, Solomon, *The Hasidic Community of Williamsburg* (New York: Free Press, 1962).

Pollack, George, *Graduates of Jewish Day Schools: A Follow-up Study* (Ph.D. diss., Western Reserve University, 1961).

Radke-Yarrow, Marian, "Personality Development and Minority Group Membership." In Sklare, Marshall (ed.), *The Jews: Social Patterns of an American Group* (New York: Free Press, 1958).

Reisman, Bernard, *The Havurah: A Contemporary Jewish Experience* (New York: Union of American Hebrew Congregations, 1977).

Ritterband, Paul, and Steven M. Cohen, "Study Design to Demographic Study of New York's Jews" (New York: City College and Queens College, Dept. of Sociology, 1978).

Rosen, Bernard C., *Adolescence and Religion* (Cambridge, Mass.: Schenkman, 1965).

Rosenfield, Geraldine, *What We Know about Young American Jews: An Annotated Bibliography* (New York: American Jewish Committee, 1970).

Rosenthal, Erich, "Studies of Jewish Intermarriage in the United States," *American Jewish Year Book* 64 (1963): 3–53.

Rothchild, Sylvia, "Return to 'Northrup,' Mass.," *Present Tense* 2 (Summer 1975): 36–41.

Rothman, Jack, *Minority Group Identification and Intergroup Relations: An Examination of Kurt Lewin's Theory of Jewish Group Identity* (New York: Research Institute for Group Work in Jewish Agencies in cooperation with The American Jewish Committee, 1965).

Rubin, Israel, *Satmar: An Island in the City* (Chicago: Quadrangle, 1972).

Sanua, Victor D., "Social Science Research Relevant to American Jewish Education: Fourth Bibliographic Review," *Jewish Education* 32 (1962): 99–114.

Sanua, Victor D., "Social Science Research Relevant to American Jewish Education: Fifth Bibliographic Review," *Jewish Education* 33 (Spring 1963): 162–75.

Sanua, Victor D., "Social Science Research Relevant to American Jewish Education: Sixth Bibliographic Review," *Jewish Education* 34 (Spring 1964a): 187–202.

Sanua, Victor D., "A Review of Social Science Studies of Jews and Jewish life in the United States," *Journal for the Scientific Study of Religion* 4 (Fall 1964b): 71–83.

Sanua, Victor D., "Social Science Research Relevant to American Jewish Education: Seventh Bibliographic Review," *Jewish Education* 35 (1965): 238–56.

Schoem, David, *Ethnic Survival in America: An Ethnography of the Jewish Afternoon School* (Ph.D. diss., University of California, Berkeley, 1979).

Sharot, Stephen, *Judaism: A Sociology* (New York: Holmes & Meier, 1976).

Sklare, Marshall, *The Jews: Social Patterns of an American Group* (New York: Free Press, 1958).

Sklare, Marshall, *America's Jews* (New York: Random House, 1971).

Sklare, Marshall, *The Jew in American Society* (New York: Behrman House, 1974a).

Sklare, Marshall, *The Jewish Community in America* (New York: Behrman House, 1974b).

Sklare, Marshall, "Change and Continuity in the Synagogues of Lakeville." Paper presented at the Tenth Annual Conference, Association for Jewish Studies, Boston (December 1978).

Sklare, Marshall, and Joseph Greenblum, *Jewish Identity on the Suburban Frontier* (New York: Basic Books, 1967).

Strommen, Merton P. (ed.), *Research on Religious Development: A Comprehensive Handbook* (New York: Hawthorn, 1971).

Toll, William, "Covenant and Mobility: Scholarship and Purpose in American Jewish Community History." Paper presented at the Tenth Annual Conference, Association for Jewish Studies, Boston (December 1978).

Verbit, Mervin, *Referents for Religion among Jewish College Students* (Ph.D. diss., Columbia University, 1968).

Verbit, Mervin, "The Components and Dimensions of Religious Behavior: Toward a Reconceptualization of Religiosity." In Phillip E. Hammond and Benton Johnson (eds.), *American Mosaic: Social Patterns of Religion in the U.S.* (New York: Random House, 1970).

Weigert, Andrew J., and Darwin L. Thomas, "Parental Support, Control, and Adolescent Religiosity: An Extension of Previous Research," *Journal for the Scientific Study of Religion* 11 (December 1972): 389–93.

Wirth, Louis, *The Ghetto* (Chicago: University of Chicago Press, 1928).

Wolfson, Ronald, *A Description and Analysis of an Innovative Living Experience in Israel: The Dream and the Reality* (Ph.D. diss., Washington University, 1974).

Zak, Itai, "Dimensions of Jewish-American Identity," *Psychological Reports* 33 (December 1973): 891–900.

3.

The Religious Life of American Jewry

Charles S. Liebman

In a forthcoming paper titled "The Sociology of Religion and the Study of American Jews" I note that whereas Jews in the United States often classify themselves as a religious group, they make use of concepts borrowed from a variety of social science disciplines to study themselves; but not concepts peculiar to the study of religious groups. They have relied on the fields of intergroup relations, minority group behavior, policy formation, and interest group behavior. The key concepts have been anti-Semitism, prejudice and discrimination, identity, acculturation and assimilation, and more recently pressure groups, lobbying, and public opinion. Few studies of Jews, even those which focus on internal aspects of Jewish life, make explicit or even implicit use of the sociology of religion.

One reason may be that there is no recognized field of study called American Jewish life. Students of contemporary American Judaism come from a variety of fields, bringing with them the tools and theories of their particular disciplines. If students of American Jewish life have not made use of the sociology of religion, perhaps the fault lies with that field. Why have not *its* practitioners studied American Judaism? The question is a fair one but does not entirely account for the absence of religious sociology from American Jewish studies. Disciplines are not so hermetically sealed in the social sciences that a person in one field cannot inform himself about another. Second, increasing numbers of young people are entering the social sciences with a primary interest in learning more about Judaism. Hence, if they or older scholars choose to study Judaism from the perspective of interest group behavior or minority group relations, it says something about the assumptions they make concerning what is or is not important in Jewish life. Sociology of religion plays a small role in studies of American Jews because students of American Jewish life do not consider the religious behavior of American Jews worthy of study. This bias may also have prevented their informing themselves about the concerns of the field.

This approach is unfortunate for a number of reasons. The one I wish to emphasize here is that understanding the religious behavior of American Jews is critical to understanding American Jews. The American Jewish community is a voluntaristic one. The basic fact of American Jewish life is that the survival of American Judaism depends on the commitment and will of American Jews to survive. Any understanding of American Jewish life must begin with questions of Jewish commitment, often mistakenly labeled as Jewish identity. Jewish commitment is a mental construct. It is a label we attach to certain attitudes and behavior patterns. There are many ways to measure Jewish commitment. One such measure is religious behavior; for example belief in God, or the performance of such rituals as candle lighting on Friday evening, celebration of a Seder, synagogue attendance, observance of kashrut. Other measures of Jewish commitment might include Jewish knowledge, Jewish education of one's children, the proportion of one's friends or neighbors who are Jewish, Jewish philanthropic contributions, attitudes toward Israel, concern for other Jews, attitudes toward intermarriage (Lazerwitz, 1973; Himmelfarb, 1978).

A striking finding of research on Jewish commitment is that the various measures are related and the most powerful one is religious behavior. This is found in studies of attachment to and identity with Israel (Sklare and Greenblum, 1967, pp. 231–34) — which is no less true for Jews outside the United States (Bensimon-Donat, 1970, pp. 124–26; Herman, 1977, pp. 187–91, 197–201), in studies of Jewish philanthropy (Cohen, 1978), of Jewish apostasy, i.e. accounting for those born Jewish who no longer identify themselves as Jews (Caplovitz and Sherrow, 1977), and for studies measuring Jewish commitment according to a variety of indices with a variety of consequences (Himmelfarb and Loar, forthcoming). There is a correlation between religious commitment and denominational identification. Orthodox Jews score higher on indices of religious behavior and belief than Conservative Jews, Conservative Jews higher than Reform Jews, and Reform Jews higher than Jews who do not identify themselves by denomination or who choose to call themselves "just a Jew" (Lazerwitz and Harrison, forthcoming). There are individual exceptions and sociodemographic factors such as age, income, education, generation in the United States, geographic location, which are related to the various measures of Jewish commitment. The best single measure of Jewish commitment, however one chooses to define it, is religious commitment. The synagogue is the Jewish institution to which the greatest number of American Jews are affiliated. The unaffiliated are unlikely to belong to other Jewish organizations, with the possible exception of Jewish community centers (Liebman, 1973b, pp. 142–44).

The religious behavior of American Jews is critical in understanding other aspects of their behavior. Even if one proceeds from the perspective of a complete secularist, even if one believes that religion is doomed, that Jews are really a nation or an ethnic group or a culture, that Judaism can survive without religion, that synagogue attendance or other ritual behavior is trivial because it engages so few Jews and is of little obvious consequence — the study of the religious behavior of American Jews remains central to a study of American Judaism. It does not really matter what the researcher thinks about religion or even what respondents report about the implications of religion in their lives. One cannot overlook the religious factor because, as the previous discussion suggests, it is critical in defining the essence of being Jewish. By overlooking the religious factor one does not know if one is studying Jewish behavior or behavior that happens to characterize American Jews and is accounted for by any number of other variables such as class or education.

It would be a mistake to confine our definition of religion to ritual observance or the affirmation of traditional Jewish beliefs. And therein lies a methodological problem which I do not pretend to have overcome. The task of isolating the religious aspect of American Jewish life is difficult — perhaps impossible, if not subjective and arbitrary. It is not entirely unreasonable to define the Jewish identity of American Jews as religious. In that case, perhaps every Jewish aspect of the life of American Jews is, by definition, of religious relevance. Organizational spokesmen for groups such as the American Jewish Committee have argued, at least until recently, that the Committee was a "religious organization," distinguishable from synagogue groups by its nondenominationalism but no less entitled to speak on behalf of the religious interests of American Jews. At the other extreme is the argument which most students of American Judaism have assumed — that most Jews express their Jewishness through modes and instrumentalities best accounted for by theories of ethnic behavior. American Jews, it might be argued, are predominantly an ethnic group. Some of their symbols bear the imprint of their religious tradition though their two most important symbols — Israel and the Holocaust — point to ethnic rather than religious orientations.

One can define religion in such a way that it encompasses activity and sentiment of a seemingly secular nature. If religion, for example, is defined as concern with questions of "ultimacy," that is questions of highest importance to the individual, then any intense commitment can be called religious. But in that case how are we to distinguish the morning prayers of the traditional Jew from the fears and hopes of the nontraditional Jew as he reads about Israel in his daily paper, or the activities of a B'nai B'rith lodge? The recital of morning prayers may have less to do with "ultimate concern" than the perusal of daily reports on Israel's predicament and threats to its survival. If ultimate concern or its symbols are the criteria of religiosity, Black ethnicity may be no less religious than Jewish concern for survival in the United States.

These and similar definitional problems are not unique to Judaism. They plague the study of religion in general and the sociology of religion in particular (Berger, 1974), though this does not mean that at a theoretical level sociologists of religion are confined to the extreme formulations suggested in the previous description of alternative definitions of American Jewish identity. (Susan Budd, 1973, provides a summary discussion of a number of different definitions articulated by the classical thinkers.) The Jewish problem is particularly troublesome because it cannot be an either/or proposition. Judaism, like other Eastern religions, recognizes no clear distinction between the realms of the religious and the nonreligious and, like Islam, sanctifies the "nation" of adherents. In addition, Jews remain vague about the religious and nonreligious aspects of their Judaism because it suits their own accommodation to American society and their own group interests to be able to press their claims in ethnic or religious terms as the occasion demands.

I have no adequate resolution to the problem. In the section below on the "State of the Field" I summarize a theoretical position with which I sympathize, but this does not resolve all the practical questions. One solution would be to define as *religious* those aspects of attitudinal, behavioral, and institutional life of American Jews always recognized as religious: attitudes and beliefs about God, Torah, prayer, ritual practice, the rabbi. From there one can proceed to the study of other phenomena which some may label quasi-religious or even secular but which seem appropriate subjects for the tools of religious analysis. In the course of such study one will undoubtedly confront the possibility of alternative approaches to the same phenomenon. This is to be expected. It is the reality of American Jewish life.

This study is not concerned with Judaism as a religion but with the religion of American Jews. Judaism, as a system of beliefs and practices defined by religious tradition, is an important component of the religion of American Jews but it is not an exclusive or independent focus of concern. It becomes relevant as it is filtered through the behavior and perceptions of American Jews. There is a distinction between the norms of tradition and those of American Jews. Their overlap, interrelationship, and conflict is of particular interest. Second, part of what constitutes the religion of American Jews may have nothing to do with Jewish tradition but nevertheless falls within our purview of concern.

Types of Information

There are almost no studies of Jewish religious life which approach the subject from the perspective of a study of religion asking the kinds of questions that a sociologist of religion might ask (Yinger, 1961, or on a broader and deeper level of concern, Berger, 1967). There are many studies of contemporary Jewry which include material relevant to a student of Jewish religious behavior. In the section that follows I have listed a variety of types of studies which might be helpful in understanding Jewish religious behavior. The typology is organized in terms of information available by method of collection (e.g. communal histories or opinion surveys) or subject matter (e.g. studies of synagogues), or potential source of information (e.g. newspapers). There is some overlap in the types of studies listed. Finally, the material described in this section has led me to include some areas of information (e.g. the religious life of *yordim* or *noshrim*) about which we know virtually nothing.

Communal Surveys

There are a number of surveys of Jewish communities generally undertaken by local federations which emphasize the demographic characteristics of the community. They often include responses to attitudinal and behavioral questions on denominational identification, synagogue membership and attendance, and observance of selected rituals. When correlated with demographic variables such as age, generational status, income, education, marital status, these surveys can yield interesting information. The most important data, however, is often left unpublished but is available on cards or tapes.

Communal surveys are of varying quality. The most useful is the Goldstein and Goldscheider study of Providence which formed the basis of their volume (1968) on generational changes among Providence Jews. The two surveys of Jews in metropolitan Boston assume special importance because they provide comparative data over a ten-year period (Axelrod et al., 1967; and Fowler, 1977). An appendix in Elazar (1976) provides a broad selected bibliography of Jewish community surveys as well as communal histories.

There are also studies of local communities or subcommunities undertaken by sociologists for the purpose of understanding aspects of American Jewish life. Some of these studies are very rewarding — for example Gans's (1958), and best known of all the study of Lakeville (Sklare and Greenblum, 1967), which includes an analysis of the religious attitudes and reported observance of individual Jews as well as the synagogue structure of Lakeville. A more recent study of a community which also comprises an important contribution to an understanding of contemporary Orthodoxy is Egon Mayer's study of Boro Park, New York (1975).

Communal Histories

Jewish communal histories are mostly undistinguished. Even the best of them, such as the history of Buffalo Jewry (Adler and Connolly, 1960), do not deal with the religious life of the local community in any depth. What emerges is a recounting of the development of local synagogues with some treatment of the internal tensions and external forces that led to the development of new synagogues. In reading some of these histories one is struck by the apparent absence of concern in the past with matters that would divide a traditional synagogue today (for example the introduction of an organ), and great concern with matters that would appear trivial today (for example the distribution of honors during services). The failure of most communal historians to evaluate the religious life of American Jewry stems in part from their lack of interest but also from the absence of an analytic framework to identify what was happening religiously. However, reading between the lines a portrait emerges, however fragmentary and sketchy, of the religious concerns of American Jews in historical perspective. This can provide an important benchmark in evaluating contemporary religious life.

Biography and Autobiography

The biographical literature sometimes tells us as much by its silence on religious matters as by its direct treatment of the subject. Most of the material is irrelevant for our purposes. There are exceptions including biographies of some rabbis (Noveck, 1978), cantors (Rosenblatt, 1954), or personalities prominent in Jewish life (Adler, 1941) which reveal something of the quality of Jewish religious life as well as some of its institutional dimensions. In many cases the reader will learn more by implication than by direct description or statement. Biographical studies, like communal histories, require a secondary analysis by students of Jewish religious life who can point out the implications of what is said and not said. A simple illustration of this point is Jan Peerce's biography (Levy, 1976). Peerce tells the story of his invitation to appear at a Rockefeller family reception in the 1930s, which included an invitation to dine. Peerce, who observed kashrut, could not accept the invitation. The anecdote revolves around the excuses he invented to avoid eating. He never raises the possibility of telling the Rockefellers that he observed kashrut. It is unreasonable to generalize from Peerce's anecdote. Perhaps it only reflects *his* problems of religious identity. But it also suggests an interesting hypothesis about the sensitivity of socially mobile Jews in the 1930s in admitting that they were ritually observant.

Newspapers

The most significant developments in Jewish religious life are not reported upon, much less analyzed in the general press or the Anglo-Jewish press since these developments tend to be incremental and require more sensitivity and sophistication in Jewish and religious matters than that which characterizes those reporting them. However, the general press provides all kinds of indirect measures of assimilation precisely because it does not focus on the Jewish behavior of Jews. Marriages, obituaries, society pages, theater columns, and sometimes even the activity of political personalities provide important data. The local Jewish press provides information on the formal activity of synagogues, how often and at what time services are held, sermon topics, guest speakers — all grist for the mill of the student of Jewish religious life. The Yiddish press is a more important source of information, particularly on institutional matters on the one hand and the religious underworld of Orthodox Judaism on the other.

Opinion Surveys

Systematic sampling of attitudes and opinions of the American population began almost fifty years ago. In the last three decades the number of surveys and polls has greatly increased and techniques have refined. There are too few Jews in national samples to permit correlation analysis of their religious attitudes or reported behavior with other variables. However, since the same questions often recur in different questionnaires, the size of the Jewish sample can be enlarged by combining Jewish respondents in a number of samples (Reed, 1979, combines data from 56 Gallup polls). Given the general dearth of information about Jews and the unreliability of many attitudinal surveys limited to Jews, it is important to make greater use of data from various surveys. Some research has been based on such sources (Caplovitz and Sherrow, 1977) with very useful results.

The National Jewish Population Study

The story of the trials and tribulations, the promise and disappointments of the National Jewish Population Study (NJPS) has yet to be written. Yet it does provide much useful information still untapped. NJPS data tapes are now available to researchers and can be utilized without the enormous technical difficulty associated with their use a few years ago. At least one doctoral dissertation has been written based on the NJPS data and a number of important studies and data reports relevant to Jewish religious life have been or will shortly be published (in addition to the NJPS *Reports* published by the Council of Jewish Federations and Welfare Funds see Lazerwitz, forthcoming; Lazerwitz and Harrison, forthcoming; Himmelfarb and Loar, forthcoming; Massarik, 1977). NJPS estimates of synagogue members probably overstate the total number of members by anywhere from half a million to a million. However, one can make certain assumptions about NJPS respondents, thereby salvaging information on respondents who report they are synagogue members and respondents who report they are not.

Other Jewish Surveys

Various other attitudinal and behavioral surveys have been conducted under a variety of Jewish auspices which vary in quality and scope. The American Jewish Committee conducted attitudinal surveys in four communities utilizing the scale developed for the Lakeville study on what it means to be a good Jew (Sklare and Greenblum, 1967). Surveys of the attitudes of rabbinical students, presidents of synagogues and B'nai B'rith lodges (Liebman, 1974), or of youth associated with Jewish community centers (Rosen, 1965) tell us something about what religion means to various segments of the population. Not all such studies have been published. A survey of religious opinions and behavior of delegates to a United Synagogue Youth convention in the late 1970s awaits analysis, as no doubt do other such studies.

Synagogue Studies

The first systematic effort to study the American synagogue is now being prepared for publication by Daniel Elazar. It is based on rabbis' responses to a mail questionnaire. The results will add to our knowledge but much basic research remains to be done. There are only a few synagogue histories, none of real merit. Even the best of them (Goldstein, 1930) are sociologically insensitive. The effort to utilize synagogue minute books of nineteenth-century Reform synagogues to write the early history of Reform Judaism in the United States (Jick, 1976) is not replicated for later periods or for other movements, although some communal histories carry information about local synagogue histories. Davis (1963) has something to say about some non-Reform synagogues of the nineteenth century.

The best study of a synagogue movement is Sklare's *Conservative Judaism* (augmented edition, 1972) — the richest source of insight on the religious life of American Jews. Sklare does draw upon individual synagogue histories but his formulations require testing through case studies of individual synagogues and groups of synagogues in a particular community. Heilman's keyhole peek at an Orthodox synagogue (1976) suggests how rich the raw material on synagogue life can be and how much remains to be explored. Reisman's study of synagogue as distinguished from independent *chavurot* (1977) is informative and reveals a level of sophistication beyond that which characterizes most contemporary Jewish research, but is limited by its reliance on survey data rather than participant observation.

Denominational Studies

There are a number of popular descriptions of the basic tenets of Orthodoxy, Conservatism, and Reform, but fewer studies that describe their organizational structure, the interrelationships of their various institutional components, or the impact of their organization on their ideology or vice versa. Sklare's study of Conservatism (1972) has no parallel among the other denominations though Liebman's studies of Orthodoxy and Reconstructionism (1974) are helpful. Liebman and Shapiro (1979) conducted a survey of opinions and behavior of an 8 percent random sample of Conservative synagogue members. Their report should be released shortly and their data made available to qualified students.

It is paradoxical that Reform Judaism, ostensibly the movement most sensitive to modernization and contemporary social currents and most accessible to social researchers, is the least known sociologically. Michael Meyer's study of Hebrew Union College (1976) is the best history of Reform Judaism in the United States, but his focus is too limited for the sociologist interested in contemporary Reform. The study of the Reform rabbinate (Lenn et al., 1972) and of members of selected Reform congregations (Fein, 1972) are important in their own right but do not significantly advance our understanding of the dynamics of Reform Judaism.

Among the Orthodox, the Lubavitcher movement has been the subject of a few studies (Shaffir, 1974), and other Hasidic groups have been the focus of a number of books and articles which are helpful in understanding their religious world (Kranzler, 1961; Poll, 1962; Gutwirth, 1978). A sociological study of the non-Hasidic Yeshiva world would be an important contribution (one such study is now in progress). Mayer (1975) is the best study of an Orthodox community. There are fewer studies of the religious outlook, behavior, and quests of modern Orthodoxy. Liebman has made two efforts in this direction (1974, 1979) and Heilman (1976) is of some help.

It is commonplace to bemoan the absence of theological concern among Jews. Yet there is a growing literature written by denominationally oriented theologians. Many of them tend to be sociologically self-conscious. Mordecai Kaplan, often treated as a theologian, maintained that he was a sociologist. Leading Reform thinkers such as Eugene Borowitz or Conservative thinkers such as Robert Gordis sometimes adopt a deliberate sociological stance and are sensitive to social conditions in their theological formulations. On the other hand, the sociological analysis of American Jewish theologians *is* fairly recent. The two works of this genre with which I am familiar are very illuminating (Eisen, 1978; Breslauer, 1978).

Special Groups

A variety of studies deal directly or peripherally with other aspects of the religious life of American Jews. None represent systematic sociological analysis of the subject. Some of the topics that have been touched upon include the following.

Rabbis. The training of rabbis was the topic of one study (Liebman, 1974) and the role of rabbis the topic of an older but still important study (Carlin and Mendlovitz, 1958). The psychological tensions built into the rabbinic role was the topic of a doctoral dissertation (Bloom, 1972). The paucity of scholarly information on rabbis compared to the relative wealth of information on ministers is striking.

The Nonsynagogue *Chavurah* **Movement.** This has elicited a great deal of attention in the popular media and a very fine article on its early development (Lerner, 1970) but no scholarly study.

Role of Women in Jewish Religious Life. This has attracted more attention than any of the other special topics listed here. Lerner (1976) surveys the women's movement in Jewish religious life and its achievements among the Orthodox, Conservative, and Reform movements. A comparison of the different roles open to women in different types of Conservative and Reform synagogues along with an effort to relate the changing role of women to other religious changes is documented in a recent monograph (Elazar and Monson, 1978). There is a recent effort at developing a theory of women's participation in different synagogue roles based on notions of the primal conception of the holy (Lazar, 1978).

Youth and College. We do not have a single good study of the religious behavior of Jewish teenagers, although there are a few suggestive studies (Rosen, 1965; Jewish Welfare Federation of New Orleans, 1966). A doctoral dissertation on one year's experience of Camp Ramah in New England is about the only careful study of the religious aspects of Jewish camping (Farago, 1972). There are a number of studies of Jewish college youth. Most are concerned with Jewish identity and provide measures of religious attitudes and observance (see Lavender, 1977, for a recent summary of the literature). Apostasy among Jewish college students and subsequent rates of return to Judaism is the subject of an important recent study (Caplovitz and Sherrow, 1977). Mervin Verbit's survey of Jewish college students has formed the basis of a number of conference papers but his written study has yet to appear.

Ba'ale T'shuvah. With the exception of a doctoral dissertation devoted to a study of the Lubavitcher Yeshiva in Morristown, New Jersey, an institution designed primarily for *ba'ale t'shuvah*, there are no studies of this phenomenon in the United States. The study of a Lubavitcher community in Canada (Shaffir, 1974) contains some material on their converts, and an interesting article (Shaffir, 1978) focuses on conversion techniques and the sociological significance of conversion from the point of view of the missionary organization. But the phenomenon of *ba'ale t'shuvah* is not confined to Lubavitch — it is not even confined to Orthodoxy. The American Jewish Committee is now undertaking a broader-based study of the phenomenon and two sociologists, Herbert Danziger and Janet O'Dea, are independently preparing manuscripts on *ba'ale t'shuvah* yeshivot in Israel. These institutions contain many Americans — some of them are composed almost entirely of Americans. A recent article (Glanz and Harrison, 1978) suggests a typology of *ba'ale t'shuvah*. The phenomenon will not be adequately understood unless it is compared and contrasted to the cult phenomenon and the attraction cults have for Jews. This is a subject eliciting enormous interest and talk in the Jewish community, yet no scholarly study has been forthcoming.

Intermarriage. There is a vast literature on intermarriage. Almost none of it is helpful in terms of understanding the religious life of American Jews. We know that the intensity of opposition to the intermarriage of one's children correlates with other measures of Jewish commitment, but we have little reliable data on the religious correlates of intermarriage — what are the religious characteristics of Jews who intermarry. We know even less about the religious behavior of intermarried couples. The most helpful study in this respect is that of Mayer and Sheingold (1979). However, given the somewhat haphazard method in which their sample was selected, the study is suggestive for further research rather than conclusive in its findings about the religious life of intermarried couples.

Yordim **and** *Noshrim.* The proportion of first-generation American Jews is growing as the declining Jewish birthrate is accompanied by growing numbers of immigrants from Israel and the Soviet Union. We know almost nothing about Jewish identity, much less the forms of religious expression of these new immigrants beyond the most impressionistic of materials. It is reasonable to assume that the vast majority of these immigrants do not participate in organized religious activity but that they do participate in some form of communal life of their own. This communal life, however informal its organization, probably bears the imprint of their Jewish origins. This was confirmed for me by student seminar papers, but we know almost nothing about this or about changes over time or among their children.

Civil Judaism. The penetration of religious symbols into secular Jewish life and the organization of nonreligious aspects of Jewish life in terms best comprehended by religious conceptions (ritual, myth) is suggested in the previous mention of *yordim* and *noshrim*. But this type of study can be expanded to include the entire gamut of Jewish communal life. Jonathan Woocher has undertaken a study of federations along these lines and his first results (1978) give promise of important conclusions.

State of the Field

Theoretical Observations

A few studies of the religion of American Jews are built on theoretical foundations, but there has been no systematic attention to the development of theory. Even the theoretical insights of sociologists of religion have been ignored by most of those who work in the field of Jewish sociology. Nevertheless, a start of some kind has been made.

Folk and Elite Religion. An earlier study (Liebman, 1973a) noted the importance of distinguishing folk from elite religion of American Jews. In this context religion refers to a formal organized institution with acknowledged leaders. Within the institution, certain rituals are acknowledged as legitimate modes for interacting with God, fulfilling His wishes, and reenacting historical religious experiences, and a set of beliefs is articulated as ultimate truths. Elite religion is composed of symbolic objects and expressions of rituals and beliefs which the leaders designate as legitimate. Elite religion is also the religious organization itself, its hierarchical arrangements, and the rights and obligations of the followers to the organization and its leaders.

Large numbers of people may affiliate with a particular religious institution, and even identify themselves as part of that religion, without accepting all aspects of its elitist formulation. A subculture may exist within a religion which the acknowledged leaders ignore or even condemn, but in which a majority of members participate. This is called "folk religion." It is not a separate religion, since its adherents share the same organization and recognize the authoritive nature of the objects, rituals, and beliefs articulated by the elite religion. Folk religion is not self-conscious; it does not articulate its own rituals and beliefs. As far as elite religion is concerned, folk religion is not a movement but an error shared by many people.

The rituals and objects of folk religion imply a belief system, but this tends to be mythic rather than rational and hence not in opposition to the more complex theological elaboration of the elite religion. Where the beliefs of the folk religion are self-conscious and articulated, they tend to be beliefs about which the elite religion is neutral. For example, a tenet of the folk religion of American Jews is the commitment to separation of church and state. This does not create a problem as long as elite religion does not claim the opposite.

The interrelationship between folk and elite religion is characterized by continual tension. The potential for folk religion to become institutionalized exists; if it happens it will become a separate religion, a denomination and/or an official heresy. Folk religion permits a more intimate religious expression and experience for many people, and may integrate them into organizational channels of elite religion. It is a mistake to think of folk religion as necessarily more primitive than elite religion. While its ceremonies and sanctums evoke emotions and inchoate ideas associated with basic instincts and primal needs, it is also more flexible than elite religion. Hence it is also capable of developing ceremonial responses to contemporary needs which may be incorporated into the elite religion; parts of the liturgy are an example.

The absence of an elaborate theology within folk religion and the appeal of folk religion to primal needs and emotions does not mean that folk religion is less attractive to intellectuals than elite religion. Quite the opposite may be true under certain circumstances. In contemporary Western society, elite religion has been forced to retreat before the challenge of science, biblical scholarship, notions of relativism implicit in contemporary social science, and the whole mood of current intellectual life. Most intellectuals cannot accept dogmatic formulations which purport to be true or to have arisen independently of time and place. The same intellectual currents which challenge religious doctrine can also serve to defend behavioral and even organizational forms against the onslaught of secular doctrines. Folk religion, with its stress on customary behavior and traditional practices, may be functionally legitimized without a rationalized prop. An intellectual may be attracted to folk religion because it provides comfort and solace, a sense of tradition, a feeling of rootedness, a source of family unity. His world view may remain secular, and from the point of view of elite religion, in error. But at least in the first instance, elite religion and not folk religion is challenged by a secular world view.

The folk and elite mixture and the interrelationships between the two vary in each Jewish denomination. Orthodoxy has lost its folk element and is increasingly confined to those with an elitist orientation. Reconstructionism was originally an elitist effort to express in ideological terms the folk religion of American Jews. This accounts for its failure to attract masses of Jews who are Reconstructionists in belief and behavior but embarrassed by a conscious articulation of what they consider their own private accommodation with Jewish tradition and the promise and demands modernity places upon them. In Conservatism and Reform the tension between folk and elite religion has declined in recent years. Within each denomination, folk and elite beliefs and practices have to some extent intermingled.

The notions of folk and elite lend themselves to theoretical elaboration and empirical testing. Despite the frequency with which the concept has been cited, no one has pushed it beyond its original formulation. Liebman described the rituals and beliefs of contemporary Jewish folk religion (1973a, b) based on a number of empirical studies already alluded to and some theoretical observations of Sklare. Sklare and Greenblum (1967, pp. 57–59) had already attempted to account for the pattern of ritual home observance among American Jews in terms of the kinds of needs ritual fulfilled for them.

The Problem of Meaning, Ritual, Belief, and Myth. A crucial concept in contemporary sociological studies of religion is meaning (Berger, 1967; Bellah, 1970; Geertz, 1973). Man seeks meaning — a sense of purpose, an understanding of who he is, of his role in life, of assurance that what he does and experiences transcends the immediate and sensory. Otherwise the suffering man undergoes or the knowledge of his own mortality would plunge him into despair. Human relationships would sour because they would be perceived as governed only by immediate needs. Neither friendship nor family have a place in a world where life, activity, or experience do not interrelate in any meaningful pattern; where the relationship itself is not grounded in some ultimate sense of rightness.

Family relations provide both example and paradigm for the foregoing. The traditional concept of family encompasses a variety of types of obligatory relationships based on the assurance that family is rooted in the very nature of life, complying in some way with the order of the universe. The family crisis which we are experiencing results in part from the breakdown of the meaning of family and its transformation into a set of contractual relationships. Commitments to family cease being obligatory once the balance of advantages and disadvantages shifts to one's disfavor.

Religion relates to family by legitimizing its ultimate meaning; by rooting it in ultimate reality. It does this by prescribing familistic behavior in law whose source is a transcendent authority, by binding family members together through ritual celebrated together, and by conveying the image of the family and its importance in myth.

Culture is the system of inherited conceptions of meaning expressed in symbols through which men communicate, perpetuate, and develop their knowledge about and attitudes toward life. Symbols are vehicles of cultural expression. They stand for patterns of meaning, but unlike signs they also shape these patterns because they are perceived as part of the reality they signify. In Geertz's (1973, pp. 93–94) terms, they are models *of* and *for*.

The concept of symbol can be illustrated with the example of New York's Lower East Side. (If American Jews have any sacred history it is surely the history of the Lower East Side and to a lesser extent its counterparts in other urban areas.) Like all symbols, the Lower East Side can mean different things to different people. It can even contain contradictory meanings and remains open to new meanings. Among its most important meanings are: hard work yields success; education is a basic Jewish value; Jews have suffered in the United States; Jews were once poor; Jews share a common history in the United States; the United States is the land of opportunity for those willing to work; Jews will succeed regardless of difficult conditions. But the Lower East Side is more than any one or all these meanings. It evokes a sense of awe and triggers a sense of Jewish belongingness and community as well as a sense of family because it points to genesis, to origins.

Religion is that set of symbols which root cultural conceptions into the general order of the universe. This is what makes symbols sacred. Because religion is expressed symbolically, it shapes our conceptions of meaning as it legitimizes them. To return to the example of family, religion legitimizes family relations by assuring us that family is part of the general order of the universe. The biblical story of Adam and Eve as a mythic symbol or the Seder as a ritual symbol serve these roles, among others. They not only legitimize the family but convey models for particular types of family relationships. A good example of a specifically religious Jewish symbol is kashrut. Among its other meanings, kashrut points to Jewish distinctiveness and separation. As Mary Douglas (1970) points out, our body and the ritualized uses we make of our body are symbols of our relationship to society. Emphasis on what we ingest symbolizes the emphasis on the distinction between ourselves and outer society. It suggests separation from others. Kashrut is a statement about relations between Jew and non-Jew and participation in this ritual enforces this separation socially and perceptually.

I am partial to the conception of religion as a system of meaning, although there is an anthropological and/or Protestant bias in a conception of religion which places so little emphasis on what any devout Jew, Muslim, and perhaps even Catholic experiences as central to religion: that it provides normative prescriptions of behavior. It is a system of law. This conception of religion can be incorporated into the formulation of religion as a meaning system, but if a Jew or Muslim were undertaking a definition of religion, the normative realm would receive more explicit formulation. Furthermore, if religion is a system of law, it is not mediated entirely through symbol.

Religion need not necessarily be institutionalized. We can conceive of religion as a set of symbols diffused within a culture which conveys meaning without a distinctive hierarchial organization, an elite, or an explicit structure. Religion was diffused rather than institutionalized in ancient Chinese culture. Those who talk of civil or political religion imply that a similar phenomenon may also be present in contemporary society. It can be argued that only diffuse religion is pure religion. Institutionalized religion means more and less than religion as a system of meaning. It means more because an institution generates its own needs, self-interests, an elaboration which may exist independently of its function. We cannot understand institutional religion without knowing a great deal about its recruitment procedures, personnel, finances, authority system, adherents, allies, relationships to other social institutions. All this will be related to its role in providing meaning, but is not the heart of the religious phenomenon.

Institutional religion may be something less than religion because other institutions may also provide and legitimize systems of meaning for an individual: professions, business corporations, some political groups, leisure time associations and (in less institutionized form) age groups — particularly the young and the elderly.

Religion viewed as a meaning system raises a number of questions about American Judaism. What is the Jewish meaning system as it is projected in ceremonial observances, American synagogues (which differ among themselves), Jewish schools, rabbinic sermons, prayerbooks, the Jewish press, statements by Jewish leaders, Jewish fiction? Is it only symbols themselves or what they refer to which distinguishes American Judaism from American Protestantism or Catholicism? There is no simple answer. And if we know little about the answer, it indicates we know very little about American Jews. Marshall Sklare has been among the few to have posed the question. But Sklare's achievement is flawed by the fact that he does not pose it explicitly or theoretically and therefore does not explore the problem in all its ramifications or specify those aspects which he does explore. For example, we want to know whether, where, and how American Judaism is speaking to the universal condition of a man who happens to be Jewish or to the specific condition of Jewishness. The two are not the same today though they may once have been. The sociology of religion alerts us to seek the answer initially in those Jewish symbols which evoke the greatest resonance. Israel and the Holocaust are the regnant Jewish symbols. This not only suggests that American Jewish meaning systems are rather particularistic, but how difficult it is to distinguish Jewish religion from Jewish ethnicity when one necessarily evokes the other in symbolic terms. The power of symbols is in their openness, their capacity to absorb new meaning and express various levels of meaning drawn from different domains of social experience and normative evaluations. Neither Israel nor the Holocaust need necessarily point to exclusively ethnic or parochial concerns, though they may for most Jews.

The major symbols through which religion is conveyed are rituals on the one hand and beliefs and myths on the other. Understanding of a meaning system means an understanding of the rituals, beliefs, and myths through which the religion is expressed. In this connection, the work of Mary Douglas (1970) is rich in theoretical insight. She addresses herself to the problem of accounting for why certain individuals, groups, and societies are more ritualistic than others. Given the correlation between ritual observance and other measures of Jewish commitment, it is surprising that only one study has utilized her observations in an effort to distinguish ritualistic from nonritualistic Jews (Liebman, 1979), and no one has sought to test her insights against the experiences of other groups of Jews. Whereas Woocher's (1978) study of civil Judaism is more concerned with belief than ritual, it is the only study of American Judaism to utilize Victor Turner's (1969) important contribution to our understanding of the role of ritual in creating the experience of community as distinct from structured differences.

The field of myth has been virtually ignored. Like ritual, it can be explored exegetically with emphasis on what the story relates and its different meanings, or it can be analyzed structurally. The latter type of analysis, which owes so much to the work of Lévi-Strauss, is most difficult to undertake in the case of contemporary myth. Nevertheless, one can study the types of protagonists, the level of relationships between them, the use of names. At the exegetical level the analysis is more obvious and likely to yield more demonstrable conclusions. For example, let us take the myth of New York's Lower East Side. What is it that Jews choose to tell one another and non-Jews about Jewish life there? American Jews are projecting images of themselves as they tell the story of their origins. What do they emphasize and what do they omit in their Hebrew school texts, organizational literature, fiction? How do American Jews recount the stories of Jewish holidays and in what ways, if any, does their recounting differ from other Jewish versions? Unfortunately, we have no such studies.

Americanization of Judaism. Sklare's *Conservative Judaism* (1972) is the most important theoretical statement on the Americanization of Jewish religion. Sklare showed how upwardly mobile, second-generation American Jews transformed the synagogue and its meaning in accordance with dominant values of middle-class American culture to further their own integration into American society while they simultaneously sought to retain their group identity and further Jewish survival. Unfortunately, some have made Americanization into an organizing concept for every phenomenon in Jewish life (Blau, 1976), without distinguishing whether in responding to their environment Jews are simply assimilating aspects of the environment, transforming it, or creating structures to resist it. The term *environment* requires definition. Every living organism responds to its environment. If *environment* simply stands for the equivalent of American culture it is inadequate, because there are aspects of the culture to which Jews have been indifferent (Liebman, 1977).

The Americanization of Jewish religion must be placed in two comparative contexts before it can be adequately understood; it must be compared with the responses of other religious groups to the American environment — a subject upon which there is a flourishing literature, particularly in the last decade — and the responses of other Jewish communities to their respective environments, a subject on which there is a paucity of material (for one attempt see Sharot, 1976).

American Religion and Jews. Herberg's model of American religion (1960, 1962) has become widely accepted in its general outline without our always being aware of our debt to its creator. In accordance with this model, Americans participate in a private and a public religion. The private religion, whether Protestant, Catholic, or Jewish, is oriented to problems of individual meaning and/or maintenance of group ties, but also relates the individual to the larger social order and socializes the religious adherent into the values of society. A classic illustration of the interrelationship between private religion and public order was the large number of Americans who attended church and synagogue services immediately following President Kennedy's assassination. The president's funeral was another illustration.

In addition to the private religion there is a public religion referred to with increasing frequency in the literature as the civil or civic religion of America (Bellah, 1970, pp. 168–89). Whatever reservations one may have about the definition and nature of American civil religion it is indisputable that there are rituals, celebrations, myths, and objects which point to the American national experience and to the American people in transcendent terms and which involve large numbers of Americans in their celebration without the mediation of church or synagogue.

This model deserves systematic examination rather than casual acceptance. If it is an accurate portrayal of reality, it has enormous implication for the study of the religion of American Jews. The intersection between private and public religion needs to be explored and we want to know whether Jews celebrate the public religion in a particular way. Are the rituals, beliefs, myths, and other significant symbols which bear no ostensible relationship to Judaism, but to which American Jews relate, unique to them in some way? Do Jews interpret these symbols and enact their non-Jewish religion in ways peculiar to them? Or is their public religion indistinguishable from the public religion of non-Jews of comparable social and demographic characteristics?

Empirical Observations

We know a great deal about the ritual observance of American Jews — how much is observed by how many. We also know a great deal about the demographic correlates of observance. We know relatively little about the specifics of observance and their demographic correlates and even less about the dynamics of abandoning or undertaking ritual observance. Sklare's empirical and theoretical contributions in this regard are only a first step.

There is very useful empirical data on synagogue membership and comparisons of members and nonmembers. We are still left with many unanswered questions about the nature and meaning of synagogue membership, particularly to those whose social characteristics and pattern of observance is no different from that of nonmembers.

We know a little but not much about the dynamics of synagogue life, roles and changing roles of rabbi and layman, the correlates of increased professionalization among laity, the changing role of women and its implications for male participation, ritual aspects of the synagogue that do or do not engage the laity, what can and cannot be changed, and the dynamics of change.

A growing body of data supports the notion that religious observance is the most powerful measure of Jewish commitment. We know much less about the correlation of religious belief and observance with political, economic, and educational variables. The few studies we have suggest that Jews of high socioeconomic status and liberal or leftist political propensities are the least committed and observant. Groups whose socioeconomic status is low are least likely to be affiliated with synagogues. But synagogue affiliation is another excellent measure of Jewish commitment exceeding in some cases religious observance. There is need for more information in this regard.

We have some notion about the distribution of synagogue members among the different denominations, the socioeconomic correlates of the different denominational members, and about differences among denominations in terms of synagogue size and training of rabbis. When Elazar's study is published we should know more about differences in rabbi-congregant relationships by denomination. We know much less about the politics of denominational relationships, and about relations between and within denominations.

Data Collection, Archival Projects, and Research Projects

Some archival and data collection projects are of a higher-order priority. First in importance is the establishment of a unit to systematically and periodically survey the attitudes, opinions, and reported behavior of Jews on a variety of topics — religious as well as nonreligious. My model is the Detroit Area Study conducted by the Survey Research Center of the University of Michigan, where each year a sample of Detroit area residents were surveyed with respect to a different topic of concern to social scientists. The Boston area is an ideal location from which a periodic Jewish sample could be drawn. Specifying the kind of staff and facilities necessary for the maintenance of such a unit falls beyond the scope of my knowledge, but it is fairly easy to identify crucial topics upon which periodic surveys could focus. Some questions would be replicated each year, while others would center on the special topic(s) chosen for that particular survey.

A second major project is the gathering, editing, and reproducing on tape of information obtained from past Jewish and non-Jewish, local and national surveys and polls. The information would be packaged and made available to accredited scholars. Some of it might even be reproduced in printout form to facilitate its use.

A third project involves gathering all items of relevance to Jewish religious behavior in the general and Jewish press. Serious attention must be given to an appropriate classification system. It would be foolish to confine this project to exclusively religious matters. The categories I am suggesting are very tentative. They would have to mesh with categories from other areas of Jewish concern. I am only suggesting broad categories. One might want to consider a variety of subcategories within each of the following: (1) Jewish/non-Jewish relations; (2) Jewish civil religion (religious or quasi-religious manifestations in Jewish public life); (3) religious behavior of Jews in non-Jewish contexts (information about Jewish celebrations of Thanksgiving, Christmas, etc.); (4) intra- and inter-Jewish denominational relations; (5) religious institutional items (synagogues, *chavurot*, groups of synagogues, rabbinical groups, seminaries); (6) *yordim* and *noshrim*; (7) *ba'ale t'shuvah*; (8) belief; (9) ritual and its observance; (10) conversion and apostasy; and (11) rabbis, cantors, and Jewish educators.

A fourth key project which will form the foundation of many subsequent research proposals is a synagogue data collection project. Its purpose would be to ascertain the number of synagogues in the United States and Canada, their location, their denominational affiliation and/or orientation, the presence or absence of a rabbi, their size, cost of their physical plant, budget, activity, membership, attendance at services, and recent changes in these characteristics. Even if the data on change is unreliable, the data on the present condition of synagogues will provide a benchmark for future studies.

This is an extensive undertaking. It should begin with the data collected by Elazar in his synagogue study. This can be supplemented with letters, phone calls, and visits to known synagogues which did not respond to his questionnaire. A greater problem will be the identification of smaller synagogues, *shteiblach*, and informal *minyanim*. One method is to utilize the municipal rolls of tax exempt properties which specify which properties are used for religious purposes. One will probably have to rely upon at least one correspondent in most major Jewish communities. In New York City where the number of small synagogues is greatest and the problems of identification most acute, one will have to rely on the assistance of knowledgeable people in a number of different neighborhoods.

Research Proposals

The proposals that follow all relate to the theoretical and empirical observations outlined in the previous section on the "State of the Field." They seek to either expand the empirical knowledge we have or fill a vacuum while they rely upon and contribute toward construction of theory. A number of proposals relate to more than one theoretical observation. I have not elaborated upon the theoretical bases for each proposal because they are obvious; I wanted to avoid redundancy, but I also believe the individual researcher ought to develop the proposal along the theoretical lines with which he is most comfortable.

The Dynamics of Ritual Observance and Change in the Synagogue, *Chavurah,* and Home. This proposal should include both the home and the synagogue or *chavurah* in order to explore the interrelationships between home and institutional observance. The sample would include a small group of individuals, *chavurot,* and synagogues to be studied very intensively for a year or longer. The purpose would be to collect detailed information on what rituals are observed, how they are observed, why the celebrants report they observe them, and changes that have taken place in the pattern of observance. We want to know what is and is not important to the celebrant and what is being celebrated. Does the observance or celebration encourage the individual's sense of self, ethnic ties, or a universal human bond? Is the ritual observance formal and mechanical and/or very personal? The *chavurot* are of special interest because of their greater self-consciousness with respect to ritual. Subjects, whether individuals or institutions, ought to be selected in terms of a distribution by denomination, age, region, family status, and socioeconomic status.

Religion and Change. A separate proposal related to the former is a study of religious responses to change. In this case, the independent variable is "change" and the question raised is its impact, if any, on the religious adherent and the religious institution. Changes can be personal (in occupation, status, age, residence) or communal (composition of the neighborhood, politics, status and acceptance of Jews, the condition of Israel). The dependent variables are changes in belief, private ritual, synagogue affiliation, participation, or ritual, synagogue activity, and expectations of the rabbi.

Research methods are the same as in the previous proposal, except that cases for study ought to be chosen on the basis of types of changes. The individuals, *chavurot,* and synagogues studied in the previous proposal might serve as control groups for the present study.

In a study of this nature one must guard against looking for dramatic religious responses, overlooking more subtle incremental changes that only become obvious over an extended period. Responses may be expressed in the activity surrounding the ritual rather than the ritual itself. For example, Friday night candles may be lit as they always were but changes will be reflected in the clothing worn by the person lighting the candles, the amount of time taken in reciting the blessing, the presence of other people during the ceremony, placement of the candles, care exercised in their preparation, etc. Ducey (1977) is a model for a study of religious response to change in an institutional setting.

An alternative or supplementary method of study for a project of this nature is the examination of children's books and school texts. For example, one can take a home ceremony such as candle lighting and note how it is portrayed (in pictures as well as texts) over the last forty or fifty years holding denominational sponsorship constant. A student seminar paper on this topic indicated that such sources provide high yields.

Ba'ale T'shuvah. For operational purposes I would define a *ba'ale t'-shuvah* (BT) as an individual of Jewish birth of college age or above, who observes traditional Jewish practices far more intensively than would have been anticipated by his parents and high school peers. There are BTs among all denominations. The study of BTs falls into two related though somewhat independent categories. First, an estimate of the number of BTs in the United States, their social characteristics, the period in their lives in which they become BTs, and their relative distribution among Jewish denominations. Such a project can be undertaken through systematic sampling of rabbis, most of whom are aware of the identity of BTs in their congregations and familiar with their life histories. If necessary, individual synagogues can be sampled to arrive at estimates. Rabbis ought also to be queried about recidivistic behavior among BTs.

A sample of BTs themselves ought to be selected and interviewed in extended sessions. We want to know their life histories, what first led them to religious affirmation, what attracts them now to Judaism, how they feel about other types of Jews, what if anything they cannot accept in Judaism. Various conversion theories lend themselves to testing as well as a variety of theories about Jewish identity. For example, are BTs more religiously rather than ethnically orientated when compared to their peers? Are they less sympathetic to Israel? Finally, the interaction between the BT and his immediate Jewish community ought to be studied; particularly in the case of the Orthodox where the presence of BTs — however welcome in theory — raises considerable problems of absorption and has led, in some cases, to the establishment of the functional equivalent of halfway houses.

Religion and Jewish Public Life. Woocher is undertaking an important study of the symbols and symbolic referents of public Judaism. Without duplicating this study one can expand its thrust and build on its formulations and findings. Two important areas of extension seem appropriate. First, Woocher's focus on federations means we only have a partial portrait of civil Judaism for two reasons. Federations are built on the basis of communal consensus and are careful not to offend any segment of the community. Second, while their celebration of civil Judaism engages the elite of the Jewish community, it involves fewer Jews than do other organizations. It should prove extremely useful to look at the public expression of civil Judaism among more specialized groups — the American Jewish Committee, B'nai B'rith, Hadassah, the National Council of Jewish Women, and Women's ORT are obvious choices. We want to know how they conceive of Judaism and Jewish purpose, what major Jewish symbols they invoke, what these symbols mean to them, and how they integrate their Jewish and American orientations.

The second direction in which Woocher's study needs expansion is in a study of the private religious orientations of Jewish organizational leaders and professionals; changes that may have taken place among them in the last few decades and the manner in which their private and public orientations interrelate. These interrelationships operate in two directions. Jewish professionals — younger people in particular — come increasingly from the ranks of traditional Jews. The question is whether this affects their performance and whether their public role affects their private observance and belief patterns. My impression is that the interrelationship is considerable. I am less confident about what effect Jewish public activity has on the lives of organizational lay leaders. A recent study of the New York Federation of Jewish Philanthropies (Liebman, 1978) suggests there has been an effect but it is difficult to document. Nevertheless, the contrast in attitudes toward religious observance by past and present leaders is striking.

Correlates of Religious Traditionalism. What are the consequences of Jewish commitment in the lives of individual Jews? A number of sample surveys point to the correlation of observance and other measures of commitment. We know less about the correlates of religious belief and other measures of Jewish commitment. There is also a very important contribution by Goldstein and Goldscheider (1968), but we need to know more about the association between religious traditionalism and variables such as family size, child rearing practices, political attitudes and behavior, occupation, education, and so forth. This is the kind of research undertaken by Gerhard Lenski (1961) which proved so useful despite its controversiality. Such a study should begin with a secondary analysis of data obtained by Goldstein and Goldscheider (1968), Himmelfarb and Loar (forthcoming), and the NJPS data which is already somewhat dated. But independent field study, particularly in the area of political activity and family life, is necessary. Boston provides an ideal locale for the sample survey given the heterogeneity of its Jewish population and the availability of recent demographic information.

Jewish Religious Leadership and Role Models. Spiritual leaders, for our purposes, are defined as people to whose formulations other Jews are receptive or from whom they expect to hear about what is or is not moral, right, just, or Jewishly appropriate. Role models are people after whom Jews feel they ought to pattern their lives. A Jewish religious role model, by definition, is a spiritual leader for Jews, but not every spiritual leader is a religious role model. The following research questions are suggested by this definition of terms:

1. Are the spiritual leaders of American Jews all Jews, or do Jews distinguish between particularist and universalist levels of morality, ethics, and religion and respond to two different sets of spiritual leaders?

2. What is the scope of particularist leaders' authority, assuming Jews do distinguish a particularist from a universalist level?
3. Do universalist spiritual leaders tend to be Jewish? If not, might they also be Christian personalities or are they more likely to be religiously unidentified?
4. How prominently do rabbis, professors of Jewish studies, Jewish organizational leaders, and other types of Jewish leaders loom as spiritual personalities? From what other groups do Jewish spiritual leaders come?
5. What role, if any, do psychological therapists play as spiritual leaders and/or in determining attitudes toward spiritual leaders?
6. How common is it for Jews to have religious role models?
7. How significant are rabbis as religious role models? Others (professors of Jewish studies, Orthodox Jews, etc.)? Are rabbis being replaced as religious role models?
8. Do those who serve as religious role models resist or welcome their role and what impact, if any, does their attitude have on their role?
9. Does overtly religious behavior carry status among American Jews without regard to whether the religious actor is viewed as a spiritual leader or role model?
10. What are the differences with respect to all these questions among different groups of American Jews as distinguished by their socioeconomic, biosocial, and religious characteristics?

This is an area study based on a carefully designed questionnaire to be administered to a random sample of Jews in a metropolitan area and supplemented by interviews with rabbis, professors of Jewish studies, therapists, and others.

Yordim and/or *Noshrim.* The proposal is to identify three or four groups of *yordim* and/or *noshrim* in different settings and to study them individually and as a group. The proposal does not pretend to report on a random sample of *yordim* and/or *noshrim.* Its purpose is to explore group ceremonials (broadly understood) and note the usage and meaning given to symbols derived from the Jewish, Israeli (or Russian), and American experience of group members. The extent to which those ceremonials involve spouse and children and whether they serve as alternatives, obstacles, or catalysts to involvement in American Jewish religious life should be specified. It is important to relate these ceremonials to the explicit ideologies of participants and their cognitive expressions of religious identity in general and Jewish identity in particular.

The groups ought to be studied in a variety of settings. For example, groups meeting under the aegis of a Jewish community center and/or organized by the center, those meeting in private homes having assumed the initiative for their own organization, and those meeting under religiously neutral sponsorship. The proposal involves intensive case study, ideally by participant observers who are *yordim* or *noshrim* and who can learn a great deal about the subjects and their families before the stage of formal interviews.

Judaism as a Diffused or Institutionalized Entity. One of the marked differences among the world's religions is the nature of their relationship to society. Diffuse religions (ancient China, Hinduism, Islam) lack an elaborate independent religious hierarchy and are organically related to the culture and key social and political institutions of the society in which they are the majority religion. Institutionalized religions (Buddhism, Catholicism) are more independently structured and generate agreements or understandings rather than being interrelated in their essence with key institutions of their society, even when they constitute the religious majority (Smith, 1970 uses the terms "organic" and "church religio-political systems").

Judaism, in relation to Jewish society and culture, is closer to the model of diffused rather than institutionalized religion. Since Jews internalize their religion rather than objectifying it in some representative institution, they are often convinced they know what Judaism means or says despite the fact that they are ignorant of the traditional literature. This diffuse nature of Judaism helps account for the relative absence of sentiment in favor of religion/state separation in Israel or the sense of any group that the institution of a chief rabbinate is really a requirement.

Let us put the matter in a comparative context. The Catholic conceives of his church as something apart from himself. Catholic history is the history of the Church. But if we were to write a religious history of Judaism, it would be a history of Jews. This is not the same as saying that Judaism is an "ethnic church," though the concepts are interrelated. There are powerful ethnic groups among Catholics for whom the church nevertheless exists as an objectified entity in a way that Judaism is not objectified.

There are groups and individuals who conceive of Judaism in a more institutionalized-objectified manner and less so. My hypothesis is that those most committed to and alienated from Judaism are those who view it in objectified terms — as an independent system of symbols apart from themselves, which imposes obligations the individual either affirms or rejects. This and corollary hypotheses stemming from such a conception of Judaism can be tested through survey methods. It should be interesting and helpful to use American Catholics and Protestants as controls.

References

Adler, Cyrus, *I Have Considered These Days* (Philadelphia: Jewish Publication Society, 1941).

Adler, Selig, and Thomas E. Connolly, *From Ararat to Suburbia* (Philadelphia: Jewish Publication Society, 1960).

Axelrod, Morris, Floyd T. Fowler, Jr., and Arnold Gurin, *A Community Survey for Long Range Planning: A Study of the Jewish Population of Greater Boston* (Boston: Combined Jewish Philanthropies, 1967).

Bellah, Robert, *Beyond Belief* (New York: Harper and Row, 1970).

Bensimon-Donat, Doris, "North African Jews in France," *Dispersion and Unity* 10 (Winter 1970): 119–35.

Berger, Peter, *The Sacred Canopy* (New York: Doubleday, 1967).

Berger, Peter, "Some Second Thoughts on Substantive versus Functional Definitions of Religion," *Journal for the Scientific Study of Religion* 13 (June 1974): 125–34.

Blau, Joseph, *Judaism in America* (Chicago: University of Chicago Press, 1976).

Bloom, Jacob, *The Rabbi as Symbolic Exemplar* (New York: Columbia University Teacher's College, 1972).

Breslauer, S. Daniel, *The Ecumenical Perspective and the Modernization of Jewish Religion* (Missoula, Mont.: Scholars Press, Brown University Judaic Studies, 1978).

Budd, Susan, *Sociologists and Religion* (London: Collier-Macmillan, 1973).

Caplovitz, David, and Fred Sherrow, *The Religious Drop-outs* (Beverly Hills, Calif.: Sage, 1977).

Carlin, Jerome E., and Saul H. Mendlovitz, "The American Rabbi: A Religious Specialist Responds to Loss of Authority." In Marshall Sklare (ed.), *The Jews* (New York: Free Press, 1958).

Cohen, Steven M., "Will Jews Keep Giving? Prospects for the Jewish Charitable Community," *Journal of Jewish Communal Service* 55 (Autumn 1978): 59–71.

Davis, Moshe, *The Emergence of Conservative Judaism* (Philadelphia: Jewish Publication Society, 1963).

Douglas, Mary, *Natural Symbols* (New York: Random House, 1970).

Ducey, Michael, *Sunday Morning* (New York: Free Press, 1977).

Eisen, Arnold, "Choosing Election: Mission, Exclusivity, and Covenant in American Judaism, 1930–1960" (Jerusalem: Hebrew University, doctoral diss., 1978).

Elazar, Daniel J., *Community and Polity* (Philadelphia: Jewish Publication Society, 1976).

Elazar, Daniel J., and Rela Geffen Monson, "The Evolving Role of Women in the Ritual of the American Synagogue" (Philadelphia: Center for Jewish Community Studies, 1978).

Farago, Uri, "The Influence of a Jewish Summer Camp's Social Climate on Campers' Jewish Identity" (Waltham, Mass.: Brandeis University, doctoral diss., 1972).

Fein, Leonard, et al., *Reform Is a Verb* (New York: Union of American Hebrew Congregations, 1972).

Fowler, Floyd J., Jr., *1975 Community Survey: A Study of the Jewish Population of Greater Boston* (Boston: Combined Jewish Philanthropies, 1977).

Gans, Herbert, "The Origins and Growth of a Jewish Community in the Suburbs: A Study of the Jews of Park Forest." In Marshall Sklare (ed.), *The Jews* (New York: Free Press, 1958).

Geertz, Clifford, "Religion as a Cultural System." In Clifford Geertz, *The Interpretation of Cultures* (New York: Harper & Row, 1973).

Glanz, David, and Michael Harrison, "Varieties of Identity Transformation: The Case of Newly Orthodox Jews," *Jewish Journal of Sociology* 20 (December 1978): 129–42.

Goldstein, Israel, *A Century of Judaism in New York* (New York: Bnai Jeshurun, 1930).

Goldstein, Sidney, and Calvin Goldscheider, *Jewish Americans: Three Generations in a Jewish Community* (Englewood Cliffs, N.J.: Prentice-Hall, 1968).

Gutwirth, Jacques, "Fieldwork Method and the Sociology of Jews: Case Studies of Hassidic Communities," *Jewish Journal of Sociology* 20 (June 1978): 49–58.

Heilman, Samuel, *Synagogue Life* (Chicago: University of Chicago Press, 1976).

Herberg, Will, *Protestant, Catholic, Jew* (New York: Anchor Books, rev. ed., 1960).

Herberg, Will, "Religion in a Secularized Society: The New Shape of Religion in America," *Review of Religious Research* 3 (Spring 1962): 145–58.

Herman, Simon, *Jewish Identity* (Beverly Hills, Calif.: Sage, 1977).

Himmelfarb, Harold, "The Study of American Jewish Identification." Paper presented to the Tenth Annual Meeting of the Association for Jewish Studies, Boston, 1978.

Himmelfarb, Harold, and R. Michael Loar, "National Trends in Jewish Ethnicity: A Test of the Polarization Hypothesis." Forthcoming.

Jewish Welfare Federation of New Orleans, *A Study of Jewish Adolescents of New Orleans* (New Orleans: Jewish Welfare Federation, 1966).

Jick, Leon A., *The Americanization of the Synagogue, 1810–1870* (Hanover, N.H.: University Press of New England, 1976).

Kranzler, Gershon, *Williamsburg: A Jewish Community in Transition* (New York: Philipp Feldheim, 1961).

Lavender, Abraham, "Studies of Jewish College Students: A Review and a Replication," *Jewish Social Studies* 39 (Winter-Spring 1977): 37–52.

Lazar, Morty M., "The Role of Women in Synagogue Ritual in Canadian Conservative Congregations," *Jewish Journal of Sociology* 20 (December 1978): 165–72.

Lazerwitz, Bernard, "Religious Identification and Its Ethnic Correlates," *Social Forces* 52 (December 1973): 204–22.

Lazerwitz, Bernard, "Past and Future Trends in the Size of American Jewish Denominations," *Journal of Reform Judaism* (forthcoming).

Lazerwitz, Bernard, and Michael Harrison, "American Jewish Denominations: A Social and Religious Profile," *American Sociological Review* (forthcoming).

Lenn, Theodore, et al., *Rabbi and Synagogue in Reform Judaism* (New York: Central Conference of American Rabbis, 1972).

Lenski, Gerhard, *The Religious Factor* (New York: Doubleday, 1961).

Lerner, Ann Lapidus, " 'Who Hast Not Made Me a Man': The Movement for Equal Rights for Women in American Jewry," *The American Jewish Year Book* 77 (Philadelphia: Jewish Publication Society, 1976).

Lerner, Stephen, "The Havurot," *Conservative Judaism* 24 (Spring 1970): 2–15.

Levy, Alan, *Bluebird of Happiness* (New York: Harper & Row, 1976).

Liebman, Charles, *The Ambivalent American Jew* (Philadelphia: Jewish Publication Society, 1973a).

Liebman, Charles, "American Jewry: Identity and Affiliation." In David Sidorsky (ed.), *The Future of the Jewish Community in America* (New York: Basic Books, 1973b).

Liebman, Charles, *The Religious Behavior of American Jews* (New York: Ktav, 1974).

Liebman, Charles, "American Jews: Still a Distinctive Group," *Commentary* 64 (August 1977): 57–60.

Liebman, Charles, "Leadership and Decision-making in a Jewish Federation: The New York Federation of Jewish Philanthropies," *American Jewish Year Book* 79 (Philadelphia: Jewish Publication Society, 1978).

Liebman, Charles, "Orthodox Judaism Today," *Midstream* 20 (August 1979).

Liebman, Charles, and Saul Shapiro, "The Conservative Movement Today." Unpublished report submitted to the chancellor of the Jewish Theological Seminary, 1979.

Massarik, Fred, "Affiliation and Nonaffiliation in the United States Jewish Community: A Reconceptualization," *American Jewish Year Book 78* (Philadelphia: Jewish Publication Society, 1977).

Mayer, Egon, *Modern Jewish Orthodoxy in Post-Modern America* (New Brunswick: Rutgers University, doctoral diss., 1975). Forthcoming under the title *From Suburbia to Shtetl* (Philadelphia: Temple University Press).

Mayer, Egon, and Carl Sheingold, *Intermarriage and the Jewish Future* (New York: American Jewish Committee, 1979).

Meyer, Michael A., "A Centennial History." In Samuel E. Karff (ed.), *Hebrew Union College–Jewish Institute of Religion at One Hundred Years* (Cincinnati: Hebrew Union College Press, 1976).

Noveck, Simon, *Milton Steinberg: Portrait of a Rabbi* (New York: Ktav, 1978).

Poll, Solomon, *The Hasidic Community of Williamsburg* (New York: Free Press, 1962).

Reed, John Shelton, "Ethnicity in the South: Some Observations on the Acculturation of Southern Jews," *Ethnicity* 6 (March 1979): 97–106.

Reisman, Bernard, *The Chavurah* (New York: Union of American Hebrew Congregations, 1977).

Rosen, Bernard, *Adolescence and Religion* (Cambridge, Mass.: Schenkman, 1965).

Rosenblatt, Samuel, *Yossele Rosenblatt: The Story of His Life as Told by His Son* (New York: Farrar, Straus, & Young, 1954).

Shaffir, William, *Life in a Religious Community* (Toronto: Holt, Rinehart, & Winston, 1974).

Shaffir, William, "Witnessing as Identity Consolidation: The Case of the Lubavitcher Chassidim." In Hans Mol (ed.), *Identity and Religion* (Beverly Hills, Calif.: Sage, 1978): 39–57.

Sharot, Stephen, *Judaism: A Sociology* (Devon: David & Charles, 1976).

Sklare, Marshall, *Conservative Judaism,* new aug. ed. (New York: Schocken, 1972).

Sklare, Marshall, and Joseph Greenblum, *Jewish Identity on the Suburban Frontier* (New York: Basic Books, 1967).

Smith, Donald E., *Religion and Political Development* (Boston: Little, Brown, 1970).

Turner, Victor, *The Ritual Process* (Chicago: Aldine, 1969).

Woocher, Jonathan, " 'Civil Judaism' in the United States" (Philadelphia: Center for Jewish Community Studies, 1978).

Yinger, J. Milton, *Sociology Looks at Religion* (London: Macmillan, 1961).

4.

Toward an Agenda for Research in Jewish Education*

David A. Resnick

Setting research agendas in Jewish education has enough of a history that one need not feel the trepidation that would accompany an entirely new venture. Golub (1940, p. 88) begins an article with the statement that "eleven years ago Dr. Maller read a paper before this conference analyzing the research that was needed in 1929. Eleven years have passed, but notwithstanding the fact that some researches have been made in the field, substantially the list can still stand; and I might have satisfied the requirements of my paper by rereading it." Thirty-nine years have passed and there is some temptation to reproduce the rest of Golub's paper as meeting *my* requirements. There have been some changes, more in the way research needs are conceived than in the particular projects deemed vital. To avoid the activity that Ecclesiastes might have characterized as "the making of many agendas is without limit," a more thoroughgoing analysis of Jewish educational research is required. The beginnings of that analysis followed by guidelines and suggestions for research constitute the substance of this chapter.

Impediments to Setting a Research Agenda

As urgent as the desire to improve Jewish education may be, it would be unwise to propose a research agenda aimed at ameliorating the current situation without first examining the foundations on which such a research venture must rest. The areas in which the foundations are weak must necessarily affect the setting of any agenda. Five problematic areas will be outlined in this section with some additions and elaborations in subsequent sections.

First, the absence of a clearly articulated philosophy of Jewish education makes it impossible for educators to chart a course toward specific goals (Fox, 1973; Chazan, 1972). An adequate philosophy of education is not limited to a discussion of goals, but also includes methods to achieve its

125

goals (Fox, 1968). The educational program is not formulated by philosophers or administrators in isolation from the community which must ultimately endorse and support it (Fishman, 1958–59). Yet even the most recent curricular efforts are notable for the unclarity of their goals and means. Take the following example:

> Develop at least two approaches on how one relates to supernaturalism and the miracles in the Bible, particularly in the book of Shemot [reference here is to the Burning Bush, Moses' Rod, and the parting of the Red Sea]. Depending upon the school and teacher, the approaches may be fundamentalist, folkloristic, may rely upon the explanation of literary license, may be midrashic, may rely upon comparative literature (e.g. Melton Research Center methodology), may be historical-archaeological (e.g. Ben-Gurion's reconsideration of the numbers who participated in the Exodus), or may be didactic (ignoring the apparent problem while using the story for its lesson value) (Stern, 1978, p. 230).

While a curriculum must have a clearer philosophic stance than the one just quoted, it should be obvious that there is not one monolithic philosophy of American Jewish education. Each ideological group must develop a philosophy appropriate to its own educational system.

The absence of a discussion either of goals or means makes it impossible for researchers to assess how well the process of education meets its goals or what methods might better meet those goals than methods currently in use. Consequently, researchers generate their own goals for education ("Jewish identity" is a favorite) and assess how well various educational institutions and programs further their goals. Educational programs might further a goal for which they were not explicitly designed, but any such progress is likely to be fortuitous. Researchers should neither have to nor be allowed to set educational goals.

The second impediment to setting a research agenda is less direct than the first. There does not now exist an ongoing research enterprise in Jewish education. There is a certain amount of census gathering by a few national organizations, but even these have been beset by anomie (Bennett et al., 1979). There is neither a nucleus of researchers nor a lore unique to Jewish educational research about which topics are worthy of study or which methods of research are most useful. Should an agenda be generated even without either of these, there is no reason to expect that any group of researchers exists to pursue it. "There are practically no scholars or researchers in the field of Jewish education . . . How can we hope to train proper personnel or look at Jewish education reflexively if there are no experts to undertake these tasks?" (Fox, 1973, pp. 267–68).

Third, the research that does exist is reported in journals published under Jewish auspices. More than twenty years ago Fishman enumerated the undesirable consequences of this practice. (The three largest sources of published research at that time appear to be the same today: *Jewish Education, Jewish Social Studies,* and the *Journal of Jewish Communal Service.*) Since so little has changed it is worth quoting Fishman (1957–58) directly:

> Social research on American Jewry is, by and large, outside of the mainstream of American social research. It is published in journals not commonly accessible to (or scanned by) the majority of American social scientists. It is not subjected to the critical reading, to the methodological standards, or to the theoretical insemination that more frequently marks social research under general auspices.

While there may have been some improvement on this score in general Jewish social research (Heilman's [1976] *Synagogue Life* is one example), the situation in Jewish educational research has not improved.

The major exception to the questionable quality of Jewish educational research is contained in doctoral dissertations. The volume of this type of research has always been substantial and shows no signs of abating. The number of dissertations germane to Jewish education (as contained, for instance, in the periodic "Reviews of Doctoral Dissertations Relevant to Jewish Education" in *Jewish Education*) is generally underestimated in reviews since they usually depend on the key word *Jewish* appearing in the title. Dissertations have the advantage of having to hew to the canons of research and making contact with relevant literature beyond the Jewish field. They have the disadvantage of remaining inaccessible. The perplexing question which dissertation research raises is what happens to the authors of this research in Jewish education. The number of dissertations might suggest that there is a sophisticated audience for Jewish research, contrary to Fishman's analysis. Yet no journal for such research exists. It might not be a wasted research effort to study the career development of these tyro researchers in Jewish life to determine what use has been made of their skills.

The fourth impediment touches on a complex issue which can be mentioned here only briefly: the politics of research in education. As in general education (Orfield, 1979), the initiation and funding of educational research are not neutral acts. Many people are affected by research findings (principals, teachers, students, and parents, to mention the largest constituencies), yet few ever have a role in shaping research topics. Ironically, those with the most direct power over education — local school boards — rarely commission research. Research is generally initiated by outside funding agencies or by those with a stake in education but no direct power. The largest funder of educational research in the United States is the U.S. government, which has no direct control over state and local school boards. It can influence local practice only by presenting research evidence which it hopes will sway local school officials directly or cause pressure to be exerted on them. There are parallels here for Jewish education, but it is difficult to spell them out since a good study of the politics of American Jewish education has yet to be done. One further caveat in this area is in order. The field of Jewish education (as education generally) is not serene, it is beset by a large number of warring factions — parents, students, teachers, administrators, and clergy, to name a few. Conflicting research needs and the utilization or subversion of research findings by the various groups is a reality which cannot be ignored even if it is not likely to be changed (Fishman, 1957-58).

The fifth area is more problematic than outright obstructive. I mention it here only briefly since it will be dealt with more fully below. The issue is the nature of the relationship of research in the fields of secular and religious education to that in Jewish education. I will argue against the conventional wisdom that chastens Jewish educators for looking too readily to the general educational field. The only justified grounds for chastisement in the past were that reference to general educational research was neither critical (in the sense of exercising careful judgement and evaluation) nor thorough. Given the superiority of personnel, expertise, and funding in the field of general educational research, it would be negligent to overlook its methods and findings. Nonetheless, one must exercise caution in two areas before indiscriminately adopting existing research conclusions. First, one must be slightly skeptical of the level of sophistication presumed to prevail in the general field:

> There are Jewish educators who think that if there were minimal conflict among them concerning the philosophic underpinnings of their profession, and if the current desperate conditions under which they must function were alleviated, there would be a great deal to learn from scientific advances in general education. But unfortunately, that assumption borders on naiveté. General education's "state of the art" is nowhere near maturity, much as we'd like to think so (Tannenbaum, 1968, p. 3).

Second, Jewish educators must determine whether there are aspects of Jewish education to which importations from non-Jewish education might be irrelevant or even destructive. Current preoccupation with the individual and his needs as opposed to strengthening social and community bonds might be one example. For instance, note the emphasis on the personal in this opening paragraph of a "Statement of Religious Principles and Policy" (1979) for a Solomon Schechter Day School (though the attempt to articulate such a statement is in itself a rare and praiseworthy venture):

> The SSDS-BC is a Conservative Jewish Day School committed to presenting Jewish experience to our children as a positive, substantial, varied, and accessible source of personal values and strength. Our primary commitment is

to the study of Jewish experience, past and present. We are searching for elements of our past which have personal meaning and value for us today. We affirm our identification with the Jewish people at the same time that we recognize and acknowledge our involvement in contemporary American society.

What We Know about Jewish Education

Having set forth the problematic preconditions for research in Jewish education, there is one step remaining before setting a new agenda. It is worth trying to summarize the fruits of previous research both to avoid duplication and to guide future research efforts along promising paths.

The most striking fact when reviewing research in Jewish education is the lack of studies of short-term effects and the excess of studies of presumed long-term outcomes. Most researchers seem untroubled by the vapid, nonoperational definitions they offer of the purpose of Jewish education, e.g., "the broad purpose of Jewish education is to contribute to the continued existence of Jews as an identifiable group" (Weinberger, 1971). In educational terms, formulations of this type do not "avoid the common error of failing to identify a small number of important objectives that will be meaningful to children, that will arouse their interest and effort, and that can be learned under the existing conditions" (Tyler, 1972). The work of Jacoby (1970) on characteristics of students who drop out of or continue in Jewish education following graduation from elementary school is exceptional in its focus on short-term effects. He found that the students' sense of accomplishment at the end of the elementary years was a prime factor in whether they continued into some program of high school education. He found that 50 percent of those continuing in a rigorous postelementary program indicated that they had learned "a great deal" during the elementary years, a sentiment with which only 27.8 percent of the dropouts concurred. The reasons for achievement and continuation may be beyond the control of the school. Thus, when ranking eight objectives of the Hebrew school, dropouts rank "to prepare for the bar/bat mitzvah" in second place while continuers rank it seventh. In the sample of Hebrew school students studied, there seemed to be a degree of self-fulfilling prophecy. Students who acquired a view of elementary education as a terminus, terminated; those who did not often continued, especially when they found the experience worthwhile.

Even Jacoby's study was limited to graduates' perceptions of and attitudes toward their education. Studies of more objective short-term effects — e.g. achievement — were abandoned long ago, which was inevitable given the prevailing definition of Jewish education unconcerned with short-term effects. Since the stated goal of education is adult identity, it does not seem to matter to researchers what in particular transpires in the schools so long as some kind of identity emerges fifteen to twenty years later. Consequently we do not know what happens in Jewish schools regarding curriculum construction, implementation, achievement, teaching methods, and so on. Weinberger (1971, p. 237) is correct when he states that "there is a dearth of well-designed empirical studies comparing the results of different educational efforts." Similarly, there is little research linking particular short-term effects (aside from attending a certain type of school for a specified number of years) to long-term effects.

The preoccupation with Jewish identity as the outcome of Jewish education is particularly perplexing since most investigators have found that personal Jewishness is more influenced by the home than by the school (Bock, 1972). On important public issues, Jews seem to be educated more effectively by the media and Jewish social norms than by the schools. Geller (cited in Weinberger, 1971) found only slight differences regarding positive attitudes toward Israel among adolescents from very different school settings.

Before turning to long-term studies, it must be noted that there does exist a sizable amount of demographic information about Jewish schools. Local bureaus of education and some national Jewish educational organizations publish data on school enrollment, per capita student expenditures, average class size, etc. All these factors are, however, related to school achievement only at the grossest extremes.

Long-term studies are mostly correlational. All investigators have found that participation in more intense forms of Jewish education correlates with more intense adult Jewish identity. Such studies often fall prey to the correlational fallacy and confuse correlation with causation. Bock (1972, p. 4) states that "by simply having been inside the Jewish schoolhouse door, individuals are 'more Jewish' in their outlook about these issues (Jewish self-esteem, etc.)." They also overlook the fact that commitment to increasingly intense educational experiences is almost certainly caused by increasingly committed Jewish home life, the factor Bock found a more potent predictor of identity than education.

We have almost no systematic knowledge about Jewish education in terms of its current operation and short-term effects. There is considerably more research on long-term outcomes, but not of the kind that can have an appreciable impact on what goes on inside schools, other than recommendations to increase the number of hours students are exposed to school settings (Bock, 1972; Himmelfarb, 1975).

Enduring Dilemmas of Research in Jewish Education: Items on an Agenda

In the first section I outlined impediments to the research venture, questions of policy, philosophy, and poverty of the field. In this section I will proceed as if those problems did not exist (though it will become clear that one cannot completely ignore them), and pose the most serious issues that face a researcher who turns his attention to Jewish education. In some cases, the dilemmas call for a tactical decision. Other resolutions may arise from the researcher's personal preferences. In any case, an enumeration of these issues will itself generate a healthy list of questions to be researched or otherwise resolved.

Without shrinking from the task at hand, one must still guard against the expectation that completing some discrete number of investigations would somehow untie the Gordian knot of Jewish education or, indeed, of education generally. Like teacher education, we are only now beginning to isolate the variables which are the prelude to fruitful research:

> The main research effort of the past eighty years has been built on the assumption that one can skip over all the little intermediate questions that may lie in the path of any given line of inquiry and answer the ultimate question at once. It is as if biologists set as their single-minded purpose the discovery of the secret of life. We might as well admit that the secrets of success in teaching, if they are knowable at all, are a long way from being revealed and are particularly impregnable to a direct assault. The big question is too formidable, too imposing, too cosmic to ask directly. We have to sneak up on it (Kleibard, 1973, p. 21).

Educational researchers must proceed with a large measure of humility and be careful not to raise unfulfillable expectations, as if comprehensive insights were about to be discovered.

Current State of Jewish Education in Terms of Educational Outcomes

There is an urgent need to establish a valid baseline against which future changes in Jewish education can be measured. The task here is not the usual census-taking (though that may be needed as well) nor the manufacture of a single set of achievement tests to be administered on a national scale. On the contrary, criterion- rather than norm-referenced tests would be more appropriate since they "tend to be more useful for evaluating instructional programs" (Lindeman and Merenda, 1979, p. 125). But let me backtrack for a moment.

We need a small but representative sample of the best of each configuration of schools (e.g. Reform Sunday schools, Conservative afternoon schools, Orthodox day schools) to outline in some detail and in behavioral terms the goals for their students upon graduation and the few years immediately thereafter. ("Behavior" and "behavioral terms" are to be construed meaningfully — cf. Chein, 1972.) These goals could be knowledge, skill, observance and attitudinal goals — e.g. know the names of the months of the Jewish year, be able to recite *havdala*, study a daily *mishna* on one's own or with a friend, support Israel. In addition to statements of goals, each group of schools would identify the aspects of their curriculum (broadly defined to include all educational activities sponsored by the school) meant to achieve the goals. Finally, the graduates (and a graduating class a few years removed) would then be assessed vis-à-vis the school's stated goals as well as on other relevant demographic variables.

Such a study would be the basis for a number of fruitful hypotheses and interventions. It might even be the first step toward a definition of "Jewish identity" in terms of necessary and sufficient conditions. I assume that schools may be able to supply some of the conditions necessary for an adult Jewish identity (e.g. ability to read Hebrew), though schooling on its own could hardly ever constitute the sufficient condition, except perhaps in a totalitarian society (Bronfenbrenner, 1970). How many graduates can read Hebrew at a stated level of comprehension and do so outside the school context? What variables account for skill attainment (IQ, family reinforcement, etc.) and which for subsequent exercise of the skill (membership in junior congregation, reinforcement from the rabbi, etc.)? What percentage of graduates maintain and exercise these skills three (or X) years after graduation? What accounts for the sustained behavior — membership in a youth group, Jewish summer camping, or what? Only questions of this order of specificity can shed light on the current state of affairs and generate hypotheses for changes in curriculum, informal education, social support groups, and so on. Short of a longitudinal study of educational effects, this is the best way to begin to link the behavior (including attitudes) a school can hope to inculcate with the behavior a mature, independent adult will exhibit. The further removed the arena of adult life is from the conditions of schooling, the greater must be general societal support of desired behavior.

Though the previous suggestion has some similarities to the National Assessment of Educational Progress currently underway in general education, there are important differences. For example, the NAEP is assessing all public schools in the United States on a single set of items in ten subject areas (citizenship, science, music, mathematics, etc.). For Jewish education, I have suggested different subject areas for different types of schools. That is because less of a consensus exists in Jewish education as to what are desired educational attainments. The sole exceptions may be the teaching of Israel (Chazan, 1979) and the Holocaust, and a single set of items might be prepared in those areas. In this case, as in the NAEP, the goal should be to document educational attainment by broad geographic area or type of school (e.g. day school vs. Sunday school) rather than by individual cities or ideologies (e.g. Conservative vs. Orthodox).

There is much to be emulated in the NAEP, and not in methodological design alone. The healthy debate NAEP generated among school and lay people on the meaning, uses, and limits of education, accountability, and evaluation could be an invigorating boost to the Jewish educational enterprise. Inclusion in NAEP of such areas as music, citizenship, art, literature, and career development as well as the more traditional academic subjects speaks well for its designers' concern for a broad, meaningful conception of education. Some recent (undeserved) criticism of the NAEP notwithstanding (Ebel, 1977), an appropriate adaption of the NAEP to Jewish education is a worthy long-term goal.

Should Research in Jewish Education Focus on Uniqueness or on Common Features with General Education or Non-Jewish Religious Education?

The question of the uniqueness of religious phenomena has been raised by many psychological investigators (Dittes, 1969) though never resolved. In the field of research in teaching, the parallel question is whether teaching should be studied in general (across ages and subject areas) or in specific domains limited by pupil characteristics (age, motivation, etc.) and subject matter. There the response has also been that it is too early to reach a definitive answer, but that there are likely to be some aspects of teaching which are highly specific (Gage, 1979). In the present context the question is valuable because it forces Jewish educators to articulate a conception of Jewish education as it differs from or overlaps with general education.

At first glance and on pragmatic grounds one rushes to endorse the uniqueness position (cf. Slesinger, 1963). Given limited time and research resources, the emphasis should be on questions to which investigators in the general field will never address themselves. For instance, to the extent there is subject matter specificity, research on methods of teaching the hermeneutics of Jewish law have few parallels elsewhere. On the other hand, it is an open empirical question to what extent research in non-Jewish education would be germane to areas of Jewish education. For example, at what age can students understand the symbolism of the Midrash (for a Christian perspective compare Berryman, 1979)? What are the prospects for supplementary Hebrew-language instruction (for an international bilingual perspective compare Fishman, 1976)? What are strategies for getting students to read the Bible closely yet creatively (for a general approach to teaching literature and literary classics compare Moffett, 1968)?

It might be argued that it is not any particular subject matter which makes Jewish education unique but rather the entire milieu in which it takes place. The voluntary and supplementary nature of Jewish education (Ackerman, 1969) is the source of its uniqueness. There are other educational ventures which are both voluntary and supplementary, but research in those areas has yet to be examined for implications for Jewish education.

Music educators, for example, struggle with most of the same problems that plague Jewish education: a demoralized teaching corps concerned more with subject matter than pedogagy; the challenge of making a classical curriculum relevant to a pop culture; students forced to attend class against their will. How woefully similar is the music teacher's lament about practice to the Hebrew teacher's lament about homework:

> Perhaps you have heard a child say, "I just don't like music." Does this young person really dislike music, or is it that the frustration of practice is too much to bear? Teachers have all heard, at some point, some of the following remarks from students: "I couldn't practice this week because I had too much homework." "I couldn't find time to practice because we had basketball . . . play rehearsal . . . school paper" (you name it!). "I couldn't practice because I was ill for two days and had extra homework to make up." "I just didn't like that piece so I didn't practice it" (Pace, 1977, p. 11).

There are conflicting trends in music education research, but our ignorance of their endeavors and insights is inexcusable.

There are other models which might shed light on Jewish education in addition to the music model just mentioned. Himmelfarb (1975) has shown how a cultural deprivation model of Jewish education can generate educational policy (though the parallel was first suggested by Schanin, 1963). In sum, I am urging that research in Jewish education can best formulate its unique challenges by assuming a comparative educational stance.

Formulating Goals for Jewish Education

This challenge is closely linked to the existence of a clearly articulated philosophy of Jewish education. But there are research possibilities even prior to the outcome of the philosophical quest. For instance, it should be possible to characterize the nature of Jewish life in a community where any given level of success has been achieved. Such characterizations would be creative extensions of the lives of actual communities. The goal is to show what difference it makes in the lives of individuals and their community when students can understand Hebrew at a given level, can blow the shofar, know how and want to recite the kiddush, etc. Such projections would be similar to those which determine a desired level of health care by projecting the number of health care practitioners per thousand people in a population. The problem is that the level of health care is determined not only by the training and availability of a corps of professionals but also on the level of health care sophistication and attitude toward treatment among nonprofessionals. This quantitative outlook is also implicit in the midrashic statement (*Vayikra Raba* Parsha Bet) that of every 1,000 students that began the study of Torah, only one advanced to the mastery of

Talmud. Similarly, the quality of religious life depends on how the relatively untutored 999 are educated to relate to the Talmudic master. There is room here for research in the history of Jewish education. Some myths of widespread high levels of literacy in former times might well fall to careful historical investigation. (Such a work on literacy in biblical times has already been completed by Demsky, 1976). The midrashic ratio of 1/1000 cited earlier may be no better than our current rate.

The issue of levels of Jewish literacy has an ironic side. Definitions of literacy vary widely, and no thoughtful definition for the modern American Jewish scene has been articulated. Nonetheless, the implicitly accepted definition of Jewish literacy seems to be declining (Borowitz, 1961). The opposite is true in American education. Only in this century have high standards of literacy been projected as the goals for mass and elite education. Maybe these higher standards contribute to the feeling that education is failing to meet its objectives (Resnick and Resnick, 1977). The irony is that the same feeling of failure arises in Jewish education despite *lowered* objectives.

Pending some analytic definition of success, it would be worthwhile to have in-depth descriptions of schools, youth programs, teachers, principals, widely regarded as successful. Such descriptions would serve two functions. First, they shift the focus away from preoccupation with the failures of Jewish education. Second, careful analyses of success may yield specific variables to be refined and introduced experimentally in new settings. The pitfall here is to be able to identify genuine instances of success rather than mere legends or impressions of success. There are schools popularly regarded as successful which may not either succeed in fact or claim credit for a large share of their success. Illustrative of the first point (from a very different domain) is the Hemphill and Sechrest (1952) study of the effectiveness of Korean War bomber crews. They used effectiveness ratings to identify successful crews and found high reliability from officers and men as to which crews were most effective. Direct observation of bombing performance showed that bomber crew accuracy was inconsistent from day to day and unpredictable. Nonetheless, reliable *legends* about crew accuracy grew up around random incidents and persisted. Unfortunately, the legends did not even have the power to generate self-fulfilling prophecies.

Another reason clear definitions of success are needed is that they are the logical prerequisite for evaluations of effectiveness of educational programs. "The process of evaluation begins with the objectives of the educational program" (Tyler, 1949, p. 110). Most studies of the effects of Jewish education correlate years of schooling with some set of adult Jewish attitudes without regard to the objectives of the educational program. There are three fallacies at work. First, even if the desired adult attitude (e.g.

"belief in and experience of God" as in Himmelfarb, 1975) was included in the list of school goals, chances are that such a goal was never translated into curriculum and from there into classroom activity and practice. The more likely case is that the desired adult behavior (organizational participation, child-rearing practices, etc.) are far removed from any possible connection to the school curriculum. Schools ought to be judged on the degree to which they accomplish the task at hand, not some task remote in time and relation.

The second fallacy — and the reason for my advocating anecdotal reports of educational success — is that correlational studies lump together all kinds of schools, thereby obscuring the very relationships they seek to reveal. The positive impact of successful schools is neutralized by the negative effect of unsuccessful schools. This yields a net educational effect of zero. Of real interest is whether schools organized in certain ways, staffed by teachers of particular training and talent, using specific curricular materials have an effect different from schools, teachers, and materials of another type. This leads to the third fallacy, which elevates sheer quantity of an (unspecified) educational experience to the level of a major independent variable. Time by itself is no explanation of change.

One might be interested in the overall impact of large-scale educational enterprise, but then the relevant comparison (as Gage [1978] has pointed out regarding the overall effectiveness of teaching) would be to those outside the enterprise. In our case, that means contrasting adults who received no formal Jewish education with those who did. In such a comparison the effect of Jewish education will be far more successful than heretofore demonstrated, although comparisons of this sort may highlight the powerful impact of education which takes place outside the scope of formal schooling by the home, neighborhood, peer group, etc.

There is a highly speculative research topic which links the previous school/no-school effect to the first topic in this section on characterizing communities of various preset achievement levels. A pessimistic view of Jewish education is that educational institutions provide the setting for only some low level of random success, on the order of 10–15 percent (following Himmelfarb's 12 percent "conversion" effect for students from families of low religiosity who nonetheless become highly religiously involved adults). Were there no settings at all, even these successes could not occur. Can there be positive long-range consequences of this low random success rate, perhaps by molding the random success group into an elite? The difficulty with elites in our egalitarian society is more with educating the masses to accept the leadership of the elite than in the education of an elite per se.

Which Research Methodology Is Most Productive in Jewish Education?

There are two main dichotomies regarding research methodology, but they have aspects in common. The first dichotomy is whether research should be basic or applied; the second is whether it should be quantitative or qualitative. When portrayed as dichotomies a tone of irresolvability is introduced which needs to be overcome. Fortunately, there is deep sympathy in Jewish culture for the notion that "both are correct."

Presently it is the "basic" half of the first dichotomy which needs defense. In times of crisis — and everyone assumes that Jewish education is one long, agonizing crisis — basic research is regarded as an indulgence. Yet human history is replete with seemingly dramatic breakthroughs that were the result of long-term basic research enterprises. Penicillin is one such example:

> Penicillin did not simply drop into our laps in the mid 1930s nor did sulfanilamide. These agents, and their successors, could not have been dreamed of in the 1930s or now had it not been for the preceding sixty years of steady, intense, and often brilliant basic research which established first off that there were such things as microbes and microbial diseases and then succeeded in sorting out the various infectious diseases by name so that we knew with certainty which ones were caused by which bacteria or virus. This astonishing body of work . . . represents a landmark advance in human affairs (cited in Gage, 1978, p. 92).

Gage (1978) concludes that "research on teaching may well be in a stage similar to the sixty-year prepenicillin stage of medicine — one in which the necessary knowledge and understanding must accumulate so that breakthroughs can be exploited" (p. 92).

Religious development is a prime area of basic research fundamental to Jewish education in need of support at the present time. We do not know what it means to speak of religious development in general, let alone Jewish religious development. There are tentative attempts in the non-Jewish sphere (Fowler and Keen, 1978; Gleason, 1975) but none in Jewish religion (aside from Elkind's 1961 study which deals with the development of the use of the label "Jewish"). Such research is unlikely to yield early answers to questions of classroom management, staff development, or language instruction. Yet it is difficult to envision a sound lifelong theory of Jewish education without a commensurate research-based theory of religious development. Educators with a more cultural-ethnic bent would want similar research on the development of ethnic identity. Both ventures will have to be as much sociological as psychological — religion and ethnicity have different expressions in Boston, New York, and Los Angeles. If Kerlinger (1977) is correct, in the long run basic research more than applied research is likely to make important contributions to educational practice.

As for the second of the two dichotomies — qualitative vs. quantitative — research in Jewish education has generally not risen to a level of sophistication requisite to entering the fray. Spotts (1965) observed the low level of Jewish educational research. It is usually limited to questionnaires, casual interviews, or analyses of published descriptive materials as if they were a true reflection of actual processes and outcomes (Dushkin, 1970). Perhaps research in Jewish education is still in the natural history, descriptive stage. A more accurate assessment might be that it has yet to enter even that stage. There is now finally one rigorous, ethnographic description of an afternoon Hebrew school (Schoem, 1979). Studies of similar rigor are now needed of day schools, Jewish teacher training, suburban Jewish home life, youth groups, and so on. While descriptive studies do not verify relationships, they are the seedbed of ideas for "quantitative" researchers to pursue. Action research — attempts to involve local personnel in the solution of a particular problem — can be viewed in the same light. While providing an important local service, its value lies in generating hypotheses whose generalizability needs to be investigated with subsequent, better-controlled procedures.

Turning to quantitative research, the guiding paradigm should probably be the "descriptive-correlational-experimental loop" of Rosenshine and Furst (1973). A body of descriptive work in Jewish education already exists, usually attitude surveys, e.g. Kelman (1979). Few of the descriptive studies progress to the correlational stage, that is linking different descriptive measures in a correlational matrix. The correlational studies which do exist tend to utilize such global variables (e.g. years of schooling) that they do not yield fruitful relationships worth translating into experimental interventions. I know of no research in Jewish education that has traversed this entire route. Certainly none of the doctoral dissertations surveyed by Pollack (1979) and covering 1964–78 do so.

Jewish education is wallowing in attitude surveys while there is a dearth of studies on behavioral (including attitude) *change*, whether on the part of students, teachers, or parents. If the essence of education is change, that emphasis should be prominent in research projects, which it is not. Quantitative research must assume a more interventionist stance, though not in its most manipulative, authoritarian forms. We do not need to know so much about what the educational marketplace can bear in its current configuration, but rather more about how to alter that configuration.

It may be instructive to illustrate how current research could profitably be redirected into the descriptive-correlational-experimental loop. Frazin (cited in Pollack, 1979)

> investigated the relationship between Jewish religious values and self-esteem among Reform Jewish adolescents attending religious schools as related to

sex, grade levels, and degrees of isolation from areas of Jewish concentration. He found that factors of sex, grade levels, and residential locations are significant variables in relation to religious values and self-esteem of Reform adolescents. The author urges further investigation of the factors mentioned.

This research began at the descriptive level with measures of demographic and psychological variables. Then progress was made to the correlational level by computing correlations and positing relationships between the variables. Thus we assume that the further one lives from areas of Jewish concentration, the weaker are his Jewish religious values and self-esteem. Of course we shrink from positing a causal link between area of residence and psychological variables. That link must be established at the experimental level, the step Jewish educational research never takes. It would have been interesting to try to increase religious values and self-esteem experimentally with a number of different interventions. For instance, which of the following hypothetical interventions intended to overcome isolation might actually affect values and self-esteem, in which direction, and to what degree: (1) a mail campaign (weekly, biweekly, or monthly?) of education materials sent to the adolescents' homes; (2) a telephone campaign (weekly, biweekly, or monthly?) from the local rabbi, youth leader, or peer inviting participation in local events or "just to rap"; (3) an advertising campaign in local media to raise Jewish consciousness; and (4) a home visitation campaign by rabbi, youth leader, or peer.

While this specific suggestion may be pedestrian, it illustrates the general direction research ought to take. It would be best if interventions had some theoretical rationale, since "research not guided by general theoretical formulations and arguments is likely to be inconsequential" (Hawkins, 1972, p. 287). Thus, is there isolation from sources of information, from institutional identification, or from peer support? What theories lead us to believe each of these might be important?

Jewish educators who implement interventions rarely research results in any systematic way. A recent mail-order library outreach program to youngsters in isolated communities (Winter, 1979) seems to be the action response to the Frazin challenge, yet the chances are nil that the effectiveness of Winter's program will be researched. If there is a general research recommendation lurking here, it might be the assignment of research personnel (on a permanent or rotation basis) to local educational institutions to help in formulating and redesigning existing programs in a way that makes them of greater theoretical interest and more amenable to follow-up evaluation.

Contexts of Jewish Education and Corresponding Goals

A taxonomy of Jewish educational settings exhibits healthy variety. Lacking is some coherent sense of the dominant role of each setting in furthering particular educational goals. One expects formal school settings to be primarily involved in teaching academic skills and concepts, while informal settings may stress group cohesion and social attitudes. There has been an unwillingness to assert which settings shall be recommended or restricted to which student populations. In general comparative education (Kerr, 1979), theorists have not shrunk from analyzing configurations of education as being of elite vs. universal access or as individualized vs. monolithic. The universal form of Jewish education has been centered in the school with informal programs given less attention. What would happen if priorities were reversed and membership in an educational youth movement was required (i.e. prerequisite for bar/bat mitzvah) with formal schooling reserved for the leadership elite of that movement?

The term *education* turns out to be too global. When researching the effectiveness of education one would have to specify which goals were sought and in which contexts. If Jewish identity is the goal, it might be better achieved through informal rather than formal programs. A broader perspective on contexts and settings of education investigates how they relate to one another (see Cremin's [1976] "ecology of education"). Such studies in the past have tended to focus on formal schooling and home support as the only two important determinants of educational outcome. There are clearly many more possibilities. As Cremin points out, much has been made of the incidental or deutero-learning produced by organizational patterns of educational settings (Grannis, 1967). No education can afford to be unaware of such learning, especially where they may run counter to the intended educational lesson. Undue focus on unintended outcomes betrays the notion of education as a deliberate process. Greater expertise in intended outcomes would generate more favorable unintended outcomes as well.

Conclusion

There is a temptation to continue generating a shopping list of research topics. But serious attention needs to be given to research in Jewish education as an enterprise per se as well as to specific research topics within that enterprise. The five research areas sketched above are worthwhile both on theoretical and practical grounds. Still, it would be difficult to defend them a priori as vastly superior to other possible areas of study. Their worth must be judged by the insights and results they produce.

Table 4.1

Taxonomy of Jewish Educational Settings

| | Religious | | | | Cultural | | | |
| | Formal | | Informal | | Formal | | Informal | |
	Supplementary	Full-time	Supplementary	Full-time	Supplementary	Full-time	Supplementary	Full-time
Preschool	schools	—	—	—	schools	—	—	—
Elementary	Sunday/afternoon schools	day schools	Junior congregation; youth groups	camps	schools	—	youth groups; museums; centers	camps
Secondary	Sunday/afternoon schools	day schools	youth groups; tours	camps tours	schools	—	centers; youth groups; museums	tours; camps

Some educators have altogether despaired of educational research in general as well as research in Jewish education. On their behalf I have not plastered over the various weaknesses and shortcomings of educational research. Nonetheless, countless educational decisions and innovations are made daily. There must be some reflective stock-taking of these decisions and their effects else education proceeds willy-nilly and loses one of its defining characteristics: purposiveness. Empirical research need not be the sum total of required evaluation and analysis, but neither can such an analysis endure without an underpinning of empirical research. It is certainly time to begin.

Note

* The author acknowledges the helpful suggestions and criticism of Professors Miriam Goldberg and Joseph Lukinsky as well as the cooperation of the Education Department of the Jewish Theological Seminary of America.

References

Ackerman, W., "Jewish Education: For What?" In M. Fine and M. Himmelfarb (eds.), *American Jewish Year Book* 70 (New York: American Jewish Committee, 1969).

Bennett, A., et al., "Perceptions of Bureau Executives Concerning the Future Role of the American Association for Jewish Education," *Jewish Education* 47, no. 2 (1979): 22–25.

Berryman, J., "Being in Parables with Children," *Religious Education* 74, no. 3 (1979): 271–85.

Bock, G., *Does Jewish Schooling Matter?* (New York: American Jewish Committee, 1972).

Borowitz, E., "Problems Facing Jewish Educational Philosophy in the Sixties." In M. Fine and M. Himmelfarb (eds.), *American Jewish Year Book* 62 (New York: American Jewish Committee, 1961).

Bronfenbrenner, U., *Two Worlds of Childhood: U.S. and U.S.S.R.* (New York: Basic Books, 1970).

Chazan, B., "The Nature of Contemporary Philosophy of Jewish Education." In M. Raywid (ed.), *Philosophy of Education, 1972.* Proceedings of the 28th Annual Meeting of the Philosophy of Education Society (Southern Illinois University, 1972).

Chazan, B., "Israel in American Jewish Schools Revisited, *Jewish Education* 47, no. 2 (1979): 7–17.

Chein, I., *The Science of Behavior and the Image of Man* (New York: Basic Books, 1972).

Cremin, L., *Public Education* (New York: Basic Books, 1976).

Demsky, A., "Literacy in Israel and among Neighboring Peoples in the Biblical Period" (Doctoral diss., Hebrew University, Jerusalem, 1976).

Dittes, J., "Psychology of Religion." In G. Lindzey and E. Aronson (eds.), *The Handbook of Social Psychology,* vol. 5, 2nd ed. (Reading, Mass.: Addison-Wesley, 1969).

Dushkin, A., *Comparative Study of the Jewish Teacher Training Schools in the Diaspora* (Jerusalem: Institute of Contemporary Jewry, Hebrew University, 1970).

Ebel, R., Review of "Measuring Educational Progress: A Study of the National Assessment" by W. Greenbaum et al., *Teachers College Record* 79, no. 1 (1977): 147–49.

Elkind, D., "The Child's Conception of His Religious Denomination: I. The Jewish child," *Journal of Genetic Psychology* 99 (1961): 209–25.

Fishman, J., "Social Science Research Relevant to American Jewish Education," *Jewish Education* 28, no. 2 (1957–58): 49–60.

Fishman, J., "Educational Evaluation in the Context of Minority Group Dynamics," *Jewish Education* 29, no. 1 (1958–59): 17–24.

Fishman, J., *Bilingual Education: An International Sociological Perspective* (Rowley, Mass.: Newbury House, 1976).

Fowler, J., and Keen, S., *Life Maps: Conversations on the Journey of Faith* (Waco, Tex.: World Books, 1978).

Fox, S., "Prolegomenon to a Philosophy of Jewish Education." In *Essays in Education Presented to Akiva Ernst Simon* (Jerusalem, 1968), Hebrew.

Fox, S., "Toward a General Theory of Jewish Education." In D. Sidorsky (ed.), *The Future of the Jewish Community in America* (New York: Basic Books, 1973).

Gage, N., *The Scientific Basis of the Art of Teaching* (New York: Teachers College Press, 1978).

Gage, N., "The Generality of Dimensions of Teaching." In P. Peterson and H. Walberg (eds.), *Research on Teaching* (Berkeley, Calif.: McCutchan, 1979).

Gleason, J., *Growing Up to God: Eight Steps in Religious Development* (New York: Abingdon, 1975).

Golub, J., "Some Needed Research in Jewish Education," *Jewish Education* 12, no. 2 (1940): 88–96.

Grannis, J., "The School as a Model of Society," *Harvard Graduate School of Education Alumni Bulletin* 12 (Fall 1967): 15–27.

Hawkins, D., "Human Nature and the Scope of Education." In L. Thomas (ed.), *NSSE Yearbook* 71, pt. 1 (Chicago: University of Chicago Press, 1972).

Heilman, S., *Synagogue Life: A Study in Symbolic Interaction* (Chicago: University of Chicago Press, 1976).

Hemphill, J., and Sechrest, L., "A Comparison of Three Criteria of Aircrew Effectiveness in Combat over Korea," *Journal of Applied Psychology* 36 (1952): 323–27.

Himmelfarb, H., *Jewish Education for Naught: Educating the Culturally Deprived Jewish Child (Analysis* 51) (Washington, D.C.: Institute for Jewish Policy Planning and Research, 1975).

Jacoby, E., *Continuation and Dropout in Conservative Congregational Schools* (Los Angeles: University of Judaism, 1970).

Kelman, S., "Parent Motivations for Enrolling a Child in a Non-Orthodox Jewish Day School," *Jewish Education* 47, no. 1 (1979): 44–48.

Kerlinger, F., "The Influence of Research on Education Practice," *Educational Researcher* 6, no. 8 (1977): 5–12.

Kerr, C., "Five Strategies for Education and Their Major Variants," *Comparative Education Review* 23, no. 2 (1979): 171–82.

Kleibard, H., "The Question in Teacher Education." In D. McCarty (ed.), *New Perspectives on Teacher Education* (San Francisco: Jossey Bass, 1973).

Lindeman, R., and Merenda, P., *Educational Measurement*, 2nd ed. (Glenview, Ill.: Scott Foresman, 1979).

Moffett, J., *A Student-Centered Language Arts Curriculum, Grades K-13: A Handbook for Teachers* (New York: Houghton Mifflin, 1968).

Orfield, G., "The Politics of Research Design: A Reply to Mornell," *School Review* 87, no. 3 (1979): 314–23.

Pace, R., "Practice! Practice! Practice!" *Piano Quarterly* (Summer 1977): 11–13.

Pollack, G., "A Review of Doctoral Dissertations in Jewish Education," *Jewish Education* 47, no. 1 (1979): 35–43.

Resnick, D., and Resnick, L., "The Nature of Literacy: An Historical Explanation," *Harvard Educational Review* 47, no. 3 (1977): 370–85.

Rosenshine, B., and Furst, N., "The Use of Direct Observation to Study Teaching." In R.M.W. Travers (ed.), *Second Handbook of Research on Teaching* (Chicago: Rand McNally, 1973).

Schanin, N., "A Review of American Pedagogic Literature Relevant to Jewish Education," *Jewish Education* 33, no. 2 (1963): 97–113.

Schoem, D., "Ethnic Survival in America: An Ethnography of a Jewish Afternoon School" (Doctoral diss., University of California, Berkeley, 1979).

Slesinger, Z., "Research: The Missing Ingredient in Jewish Education," *Pedagogic Reporter* (May 1963): 6–9.

Spotts, L., "Current Research in Jewish Education: Description and Evaluation," *Jewish Education* 36, no. 1 (1965): 30–37.

Statement of Religious Principles and Policy (draft) (Teaneck, N.J.: Solomon Schechter Day School of Bergen County, 1979).

Stern, J. (ed.), *A Curriculum for the Afternoon Hebrew School* (New York: United Synagogue Commission on Jewish Education, 1978).

Tannenbaum, A., *What General Education Might Contribute to Jewish Education* (Cleveland: Cleveland College of Jewish Studies, 1968).

Tyler, R., *Basic Principles of Curriculum and Instruction* (Chicago: University of Chicago Press, 1949).

Tyler, R., "Conditions for Learning Religion," *Religious Education* (July-August 1972), 2: 31–34.

Weinberger, P., "The Effects of Jewish Education." In M. Fine and M. Himmelfarb (eds.), *American Jewish Year Book* 72 (New York: American Jewish Committee, 1971).

Winter, N., "Regional Judaica 'Library' Reaches Out," *United Synagogue Review* (Summer 1979): 14.

5.

Jews and Other People:
An Agenda for Research on Families and Family Policies

Sheila B. Kamerman

The family is still the only institution we have that is capable of producing future generations; and it is the primary institution any society has for socializing each new generation into its values and desired behavior patterns. Where the Jewish family is concerned, the functions are the same. There is nothing uniquely Jewish about this view of the family. Other religions stress the sanctity of the family and its role as the transmitter of values. The literature of several countries identifies the family as the carrier of history, tradition, and cultural identity across generations. The role and value of the family are certainly not at issue here.

There are several countries which place the family in a far more central role than we do in the United States. In some countries, public policies are explicitly designed to support family life and well-being, albeit from very different perspectives. And there are innumerable political ideologies which espouse the family and its significance in elaborate rhetoric.

There can be no single, monolithic policy perspective on families which would be acceptable in a pluralistic society. American society, with its disparate belief systems, epitomizes a pluralistic society. Even the American Jewish community encompasses diverse values and is unlikely to support a uniform policy perspective. I have no intention of proposing such a policy here.

The family — Jewish and non-Jewish — does not function in a vacuum. It acts and is acted upon. It is an agent of change, a responder to change, and a keeper of tradition and the status quo. The Jewish family in the United States today is urban, largely middle class, living in a highly industrialized society, in a particular political, economic, and sociocultural environment — the United States — with a particular historical-cultural-religious identity — Jewish. American Jewish families range on a continuum from those which define themselves as American and only peripherally

Jewish to those which are Jewish at the core, with barely any national identification. Most are somewhere in the middle, which is why our concern should be with the quality and quantity of that middle. In other words — How will families which identify themselves as Jewish (regardless of why) continue to exist in the United States? What will be the nature of their Jewish identification and how can it be strengthened?

We cannot identify a totally separate and distinct Jewish family in America any more than we can distinguish a "Jewish family" in the world as a whole. Any brief visit to Israel today — with Sephardic Jewish families resembling Moslem families far more than they do their Western European Jewish brethren in regard to many social patterns and practices — would disabuse us of the notion of a single, distinct "Jewish family" type. Just as we may talk of "the American family" and discover that the statistical reality is very unlike the conventional myth — and even that reality varies enormously when statistical norms are disaggregated — the same is probably true for the Jews. I say "probably" because we do not have statistical data on the Jewish family to confront the myths. Even without that data, I think we would all agree that there is no one "American Jewish family."

To understand what is happening to American Jewish families, we must know something of what is happening to American families generally, in particular families with similar socioeconomic characteristics — and then attempt to analyze trends, comparing similarities and differences. Unfortunately, the paucity of reliable data — indeed almost any data — on Jewish families, makes any rigorous comparative analysis impossible. It underscores the recommendation made by Waxman (with which I strongly concur) that the first priority in the proposed center would be the design and implementation of a regularly scheduled and systematic survey of Jews and Jewish families in the United States. Without such data in hand, any analysis is limited.[1]

The remainder of this chapter will be devoted to the following:

1. Highlight selected trends for American families which seem to have special relevance for Jewish families (and for which it would be important to have firm comparable data) and trends specific to Jewish families from available data.
2. Discuss the implications of these developments for families generally and for Jewish families in particular.
3. Distinguish between developments and/or problems which are universal and warrant a governmental policy response for the society at large, and those which are specific to Jewish families and suggest the need for response by the Jewish community.

4. Discuss the types of responses that could be developed in each category and the nature of relevant research and existing experience.
5. Suggest a possible research agenda that would include both types of research.

American Families in the 1980s[2]

My premise here is that the American Jewish family is becoming increasingly similar to its counterpart among American families: White, urban, middle class, educated. Thus demographic trends for these families have growing significance for American Jewish families generally. Some of these trends have already been noted elsewhere; others have not, or at least have not received the attention they warrant. Some of the most significant changes have occured over the last decade, a period for which data on American Jewish families are most inadequate.

Despite the increase in the number of families over the last decade, the percentage of families in the United States having at least one child under 18 has declined steadily. The average number of children per family with children has decreased from 2.4 in 1968 to 1.96 in 1978. Since 1972, levels of fertility in the United States have been below those required for long-run replacement of the population. The annual total fertility rate has decreased each year, with very few exceptions, since the peak of the baby boom in 1957. The average number of children implied by the 1978 rate is about 1.8 per woman, well below the rate of 2.1 required for natural replacement.

Although overall the median age at first marriage and at birth of first child reflect a small but significant increase, there has been a very sharp increase in the percentage of women remaining unmarried in their early twenties. Almost half of those 20–24 were single in 1978, an increase of two-thirds since 1960, and one-third since 1970. The proportion of those aged 25–29 who were single increased by two-thirds since 1970 (from 10.5 to 18 percent). These trends are even more significant for the more highly educated. The divorce rate has continued to move upward, almost doubling since 1970, and the rate has risen most dramatically for young adults, especially those under 30. Despite these developments, about 95 percent of all adults in the United States have been married at some time — the highest proportion married in any Western country — and close to 90 percent of those married have been married only once.

There has been a significant increase in the numbers of adults living alone (now 20 percent of all households are one-person households). Although the largest group of these, over 40 percent, are elderly, the most substantial rate of increase was among White youths aged 14–24. Since

1970, the number of young unmarried adults living together has more than doubled, to over 1.1 million households in 1978, primarily unmarried couples under age 35, with no children.

The number of families maintained by women increased extraordinarily since 1960, from 4.5 million to 8.2 million. The major increase occurred in the 1970s with the number almost doubling from 5.6 million in 1970, a 44 percent increase. Fourteen percent of all families, but 18 percent of those with children under age 18, were female-headed in 1978. The women maintaining these families were more likely to be younger, have children, be divorced, and Black than their earlier counterparts. Although the proportion of female-headed families is disturbingly high for Black families (almost half), it still represents a very high and growing proportion of White families with children. Fourteen percent of these are female-headed; most of these women are divorced.

Although there has been a significant decline in the percentage of the population living in poverty over the last two decades — and the percentage of White families living in poverty is considerably lower than for Blacks — the change in composition of the poverty population is particularly important. Half the poor families are female-headed and more than half of those families maintained by women are poor; another significant proportion are near-poor. The percentage of poor families headed by an adult in the labor force has declined significantly, as has the percentage of aged who are poor.

The growth in female labor force participation has been described by several commentators as the most significant development in the twentieth century for the Western world. Women accounted for 60 percent of labor force growth in the United States since 1960. Most dramatic is the increase in the labor force participation rate of married women with children, especially young children. Their rate has more than doubled during these years, and the rate for those with preschool children has tripled. The most rapid growth in labor force participation rates since 1970 has been among married women under age 35, with children under age 3. Mothers have higher labor force participation rates than women without children, and married women with children are as likely to work as those with none. Half of all adult women work today (60 percent of those who are nonaged) — about two-thirds full-time. Close to 60 percent of those with school-age children, 50 percent of those with children aged 3–6, and 40 percent of those with children under age 3 are in the labor force today. In contrast, labor force participation rates for married men, historically the status with the highest rates, has been declining steadily, although those with children continue to have rates over 90 percent, the highest for any group.

Regardless of whether a wife has children, the more highly educated she is the more likely she is to be in the labor force. Over two-thirds of the wives who are college graduates were in the labor force in 1978. The largest single family type today in the United States is the two-earner, husband-wife family. In about half of husband-wife families, both spouses worked in 1978. If we add to this group single-parent families, families with working women are clearly the dominant type. In addition to these major trends described above, I would note:

1. More children (almost all) live with at least one parent than ever before in American history, although almost half of all children born in the mid-1970s are likely to experience living with only one parent at some time in their lives.
2. Median family income in two-parent families is far higher than it has ever been, especially in those families in which husbands and wives both work.
3. The 1980s will be a decade in which for the first time in over ten years there will be a larger potentially marriageable group of young adult males for young women; and delay in the age of first marriage may be reflected in a decrease (or at least a leveling) of the divorce rate.
4. The population group which will peak in the 1980s is that aged 25–44.

The baby boom population is now reaching the age where adults are most likely to be married, to have young children, and to be in the labor force. Every previous decade since the baby boom began has reflected the dominant presence of this group. The 1950s saw a surge in baby food and other baby-related industries; schools and universities expanded during the 1960s, a decade which also experienced a variety of other, less socially approved youth-related developments and trends; and the 1970s saw a disturbing increase in youth unemployment (at the same time as it experienced a dramatic increase in youth employment!), young couples living together, and so forth. Recent expansion in the housing industry is already reflecting the growing numbers of young families.

Regardless of where else and how their presence will be reflected, there will be a rapid growth in the numbers of young families with children in the 1980s in the United States. This group should be of major interest to those concerned with American Jewish families as well as American families generally. Their lifestyle has particular significance for us, yet has not received sufficient attention thus far. Although these trends may vary in extensiveness in other countries, the same pattern characterizes all Western industrialized countries today. In particular, there has been a steady decline in birth rates and family size (although more pronounced in several countries than in the United States), an increase in the number and percentage of female-headed families (although far less in most countries than in the United States), and an increase in female labor force participation, especially for married women with children.

Existing data for Jewish families in America suggest that these trends are the same, with some variations: fertility rates may be slightly lower but are probably comparable to those for the more highly educated; the percentage of single-parent families is slightly lower; median age at first marriage and birth of first child are probably about the same as for American women generally, and certainly for educated women. There are no data for Jewish female labor force participation. Using education as an indicator, I would estimate significantly higher rates for Jewish women than current national rates. All these data, as well as trends over time, would be extremely important to have. In addition, there is the rapid growth of intermarriage over the last decade, a trend sufficiently documented in the Jewish community not to require further comment here.

What are the implications of these developments? What is the state of knowledge and the nature of existing responses? What is known about effectiveness or ineffectiveness of interventions?

Implications for American Jewish Families

Our concern is with factors affecting the quantity or quality of subsequent generations of Jews. My focus is on families with minor children, not on the aged. This is not to minimize the significance of the elderly in the Jewish community, but rather to suggest that if our concern is with the family as a transmitter of Jewish values and identity, it is families with children, especially those with young children, which must be the target of attention. Public response to the needs of the elderly has been much more extensive over the past two decades than to the needs of families with children. It may be time to redress some of this imbalance.

Only those developments which affect very large numbers in the general population can (and should) generate a national policy response. If there is to be any successful federal public policy intervention, it can only be in relation to developments of concern to groups other than Jews. It is especially important to distinguish universal developments which are also significant for Jews, from concerns germane only or primarily to Jews.

To summarize our picture of American Jewish families: There are fewer families with children and those families with children have fewer of them; there has been a rapid growth in the number and percentage of two-earner families and of single-parent, working-mother families (usually a consequence of divorce); Jewish children born in the last quarter of the twentieth century are more likely to experience living in a one-parent family, in a reconstituted family, in a family with working parents, in a family with one parent who was not born Jewish. Despite all this, individuals are likely to get married, have children, and continue to assert that a happy family life is the single most important factor in contributing to their own sense of well-being.[3] The question is: "Will they be Jewish?"

The quantity of children produced is a direct result of fertility rates (number of children produced by each woman) and probably of the inter-marriage rate (whether those children are considered Jews). The quality of children is affected by many factors, including the quantity and quality of the time parents invest in their children, family income, mother's education, the quality of family life and of the environment in which children are reared.

Increasing the Quantity of Jewish Children

Our goal is the survival of the Jewish community in America. Some may argue that this is an inappropriate goal. Yet without some quantity of children, any discussion of the quality of Jewish survival is irrelevant. Thus we begin with the problem of childbearing, and explore what existing experience there is regarding efforts to influence fertility decisions and behavior. Subsequently, I will address the question of intermarriage.

There is a very extensive literature dealing with efforts at influencing fertility, both to increase and decrease birth rates. There is no evidence that any public policies are effective in influencing individual fertility decisions in either direction for a sustained period of time. Several European countries have attempted to increase birth rates — an implicit goal of much of the discussion regarding American Jewish families — without any sustained success. The most extensive research and most sophisticated analysis of existing experience has been made by demographers at the Institut National d'Etudes Démographiques (INED) in France, a country which has tried unsuccessfully for almost forty years to increase its birth rate. The leading expert in this field is the director of this institute, Gérard Calot. The general consensus is that even with deliberate, multiple, and extensive pronatalist policy incentives, there is as much evidence to indicate no effect on fertility as to indicate success.

Three European countries have made extraordinary efforts to increase birth rates: Czechoslovakia, the German Democratic Republic, and Hungary. Policies have included up to nineteen separate but cumulative incentives in one country (Czechoslovakia) to have children, including a variety of cash bonuses, increased child allowances, housing priorities, and so forth. Those countries with the most extensive efforts are also countries with highly centralized and authoritarian governments as well as long histories of very low birth rates. Even under these circumstances the fertility effects thus far have been only calendar effects.[4] Even where there has been an impact, the accomplishment has been that women have had two children. Very few women have shown any indication to have a third child, regardless of what incentive is offered. We might hypothesize, since in many Western countries the two-child family continues to be the preferred size, whether the development of these policies may not have acted to attenuate the impact of previous, implicitly antinatalist policies which made child rearing a particularly heavy burden. The group for which these policies have had the least impact is that of highly educated women. Educated parents continue to have one child, and only sometimes a second, despite all efforts in these countries thus far.

Over the next decade or so the United States may become more concerned about declining birth rates, but that time has not yet arrived. There is no evidence to suggest that even if concern increased, there would be any general consensus around pronatalist policies, much less that these policies would be effective. Research on fertility decisions suggests a complicated amalgam of factors influencing individuals to have children, including the state of the economy, attitudes toward the future, and the comfort and ease of daily living.

Any efforts at direct and massive intervention to influence fertility decisions are (1) unlikely to be implemented in the United States at any time; (2) unlikely to be effective regardless; and (3) likely to be most ineffective with families such as American Jewish families. Nor is there any evidence that efforts at providing harsh disincentives regarding contraception and abortion are any more effective.[5] For a U.S. example of what might be described elsewhere as the ineffectiveness of a policy combining a pronatalist incentive and an abortion disincentive, we have only to note the decrease in the size of the typical AFDC family despite higher benefit levels and restricted public funding of abortion.

Analysis of fertility trends and what is known about fertility decisions and behavior suggests that one large constraint on having children — especially more than one — is the problem of coping with work demands while managing family responsibilities. Numbers of children as well as their age are a constraint on labor force participation of women. Once mothers, especially of young children, are in the labor force, some attention to how these women manage suggests that some relief for those carrying the double burden of family and work is essential, if adults are to be expected to bear and rear children. The tension between work and family life, though longstanding, has become visible only as it has been universalized — as more and more women enter the labor force.[6] When one parent was prepared to remain at home full time, the tension between work and family could be managed, if often only just barely. Now the situation is very different.

Women are in the labor force to stay and for the same reasons men are — for pecuniary and nonpecuniary reasons. The numbers are increasing and projections are for the increase to continue.[7] If we are concerned about adults continuing to be productive in the family, at home, and in the community — even as they are productive in the labor force — some attention must be paid to attenuating the tension between work and family life; and this attention must go beyond an assumption that it is only a woman's problem. Unless it is defined as a problem for the whole society, policy interventions are bound to be skewed, with less than satisfactory results. Restructuring the relationship between work and family life is an appropriate target for national public policy as well as for attention by private industry and organized labor. Successful intervention here could make a major contribution to improving the quality of family and community life for all families.

The growing rate of intermarriage is a problem for the Jewish community since intermarriage affects whether children are reared as Jews as well as the kind of Jews they may become. In a very basic way, it has consequences for both the quantity and quality of children produced. Given certain trends among young Americans generally in the 1970s, it is likely that this trend is greater today than a decade ago. As several others have pointed out, no strategy for dealing with the problem has emerged on the Jewish communal agenda. There is an attitude that intermarriage is inevitable and the community will have to learn to live with it.

Intermarriage is a significant problem, but it is one which can only be addressed by the Jewish community itself. Although no strategy for reducing the trend has been developed, I am not prepared to say none can or will be. It is pointless for the community to continue its exclusionary stance toward the non-Jewish spouse, especially one who has converted or expressed interest in conversion. For many non-Jewish young adults, it may be precisely the idea of community — and/or family — which represents part of the attraction in marrying a Jew. If we are concerned about losing Jews, why exclude any who might identify as Jews and raise their children as Jews? Acceptance of reality is not necessarily whole-hearted approval, but just as we are noticing a variety of changes in families and in society, intermarriage may have meanings other than those previously assumed. Our goal should be to encourage into the community those who want to have some identification with it.

Quality of Children

The quality of children is influenced most by the family in which they are born and then by the society in which they live out their own life experience. There is extensive research to indicate that the cognitive capacities of children in school are highly correlated with the education of their mothers — a reassuring piece of data given the high education levels of many Jewish women.[8] Some brief comments follow, with regard to the most frequently posed questions:[9]

1. There are no known negative consequences for children resulting from their mothers' working.

2. There is substantial evidence that adolescents with working mothers function better in school, are better adjusted, have higher self-esteem.
3. There is some evidence that some younger children whose mothers work develop better than children whose mothers do not work.
4. There is significant evidence that women who work (in industrialized countries such as the United States) are happier; and some evidence to suggest that women at home full time have a higher incidence of depression.
5. There are no known negative consequences of group care for infants and toddlers.
6. There is some evidence and extensive consensus that chldren aged 3–6 develop better when participating in group experiences with peers.
7. There is a growing body of research devoted to the use and allocation of time, especially in two-earner families, suggesting that internal roles in such families are different from those in traditional, one-earner families.
8. There is no research on the effects on children of fathers working.
9. There is no research on the effects on children of nonparticipation in group activities when most peers are participating (or having a full-time mother at home when most peers do not like having an unemployed father at home all the time).
10. There is no adequate research on the amount of time full-time, at-home mothers spend with their children, or the nature of that experience for most children.
11. There is no research on the effects on families of current lifestyle for most families with preschool children — complex amalgams of multiple child-care arrangements organized and managed by mothers.
12. There has been little research in the United States on the cost of rearing a child and who carries what proportion of the cost (individual families, local communities, the federal government?)[10]

The "Jewishness" of children is probably a function first of the values of their parents and/or caregivers, and second of their immediate social environment. Neither of these — nor even both combined — is a guarantee of children choosing to be identified and affiliated Jews, but they seem to increase the likelihood of this occurring. It would seem especially important to develop, encourage, and/or maintain an attachment to the Jewish community regardless of the form of the attachment. The most critical times for forming such an attachment are when young people are approaching the stage of family formation and when young families (young parents, young children) experience a time and money crunch as they first attempt to cope with intensive work and family pressures.

Thus far, I have described major demographic trends for U.S. families generally which have special significance for American Jewish families, and supplemented these by discussion of trends specific to the American Jewish community. I have analyzed these in the context of distinguishing those which might respond to support by broad-based public policies — or a broad-based research program — from those which are of concern only to the Jewish community. I have tried, albeit briefly, to summarize the state of knowledge today regarding some possible responses or solutions. I turn now to some suggestions of where limited resources might have the greatest research payoff and/or where a policy focus might have the most leverage.

Toward a Research Agenda

Resources (money, expertise, time) are limited. Therefore items should not be included on a research agenda unless they satisfy one or more of the following criteria.

1. Salience for the Jewish community as well as for the American community at large, and an issue not now receiving adequate attention.
2. Potentially greater significance for the American Jewish community than for the larger community (here the proposed center could build on work being done elsewhere to the benefit of the Jewish community).
3. Potential for developing applied programmatic strategies to meet immediate needs within the Jewish community.

Without baseline data any such center would be severely constrained in its development. The prime requisite for a center — recognizing all the caveats — would be implementation of a national survey of Jews, instituted regularly. Despite the inadequacy of available data, I would support proceeding with certain studies regardless, given the probability of significant trends.

A final premise with regard to the research agenda is that the program should be multidisciplinary. Depending on the kinds of expertise available, certain of the proposed items would be more or less feasible. The proposed "Research Program on American Jewish Families Today" would include three parts: (1) a family policy research program; (2) a family research program; (3) a Jewish community research and demonstration program.

A Family Policy Research Program

The proposed center could take a leadership role and make a significant contribution in the area of work and family life. This is a subject now emerging as a central family policy concern. It is an important issue for

American families generally because the two-earner family is now the dominant family type in the United States and it is a family lifestyle with major implications for childbearing and child rearing. It is of particular significance for American Jewish families because they are especially likely to follow this lifestyle. One strategy for achieving a higher birthrate is to attenuate the strain of managing work and family life (or reduce the conflict between domains) for all adults. An additional consequence might be higher "quality" children, as parents have more time and energy, without suffering economic penalty.[11]

The knowledge base is limited at present and there are only a small number of researchers working in the field.[12] The United States has not developed any statutory policies in this area, unlike most of Europe. Thus the potential impact of any positive development could be substantial.

A Family Research Program

There are five areas which offer significant potential for the proposed center: (1) intrafamily gender roles and division of labor in the family; (2) application of a historical life course perspective to modern American Jewish families; (3) the role of the family as educator; (4) cults, particularly youth cults; (5) more specifically, the study of intrafamily gender roles including time allocation and use, as well as the division of roles within the family are an increasingly important subject for research as family lifestyles change and as two-parent, two-earner (and single-parent/earner) families predominate in society. If restructuring of work-family life implies the need for a new perspective in the public policy and industrial policy arena, it also implies continued attention to what is occurring within the family. How family and home roles (tasks, decision making) and the family economy adapt to these changes and on occasion stimulate change, have major consequences for marital and parent-child relationships.[13]

There is some evidence that changes are occurring in families with two working spouses.[14] It would be important to know whether there is anything uniquely Jewish about this experience. For example — Are there special factors which facilitate or impede intrafamily changes for Jewish families, and what are the consequences for marital relationships and their stability? It would also be important to know whether there are differences between the ways in which dual-career couples and dual-worker families adapt, since we might hypothesize that Jewish families are more likely to be dual career. Working parents suffer from a time shortage. How do Jewish working parents spend this scarce resource and where are they likely to be "pinched"? Ultimately, we would want to learn more about the phenomenon generally and what is unique for Jewish families, in order to identify the strengths of this family type and the needs for particular support services not now available.

Application of a historical life course perspective to family and social history offers an exciting approach to integrating macro–social history and change with a lifecycle perspective, by means of historical and sociological analysis. Given our particular concern with young American Jewish families today and over the next decade, it would be important to understand how the life experience of a cohort shapes its views and behavior as adults. For example, most of these young adults will have been born in the 1950s (of parents who lived during World War II) and experienced adolescence in the 1960s. What impact did growing up in the 1960s have on them? A greater understanding of the relationship between social change and individual and family change (and vice versa) would be of special importance to the Jewish community in the United States as well as in Israel and elsewhere.[15]

The role of the family as educator[16] would be an obvious research focus given the assumption about how children are socialized into Jewish values. A related counterpart effort might be a longitudinal study comparing the Jewish identification patterns of children who attend Jewish day schools with those who do not. What is it that makes a difference in identification patterns?

From a very different perspective, cults — what they represent, who joins them, with what consequences, and especially why they are so attractive to middle-class Jewish youth — could be another item, given our concern about youth.[17] All organized religions are losing young people when it comes to any formal affiliation. Although it is clear that those who are attracted by cults have already lost their Jewish identification, there is no reason to assume that alternative structures must by definition be non-Jewish. Existing research on some of these cults suggests that some youths who join are severely disturbed before joining (and may even be sustained outside of institutions by their identification with these groups), but a large proportion of entrants might have chosen any one of several alternatives. The search for a surrogate family to replace one viewed as unsatisfactory, the desire to belong to a group or community, the fascination with the mystical or spiritual — are all part of what attracts these young people and, if understood better with regard to Jewish youth, could be incorporated into alternative Jewish communities.

Some Jewish youth are lost through intermarriage, while others find their way to non-Jewish cults or other groups. It would be important to know what these young people are looking for and why the Jewish community cannot provide satisfactory answers for them through other than conventional institutions.

A Jewish Community Research and Demonstration Program

Some attention to the problem of intermarriage would be central here. I would urge a multifaceted approach to include:

1. Increasing understanding of the phenomenon (who intermarries and why; whom do they marry and what happens) and the process of Jewish identification and affiliation more broadly defined.
2. Developing alternative experiences for youth who are "searching" for something different.
3. Expanding opportunities and programs for conversion and development of support services (self-help groups?) for those who have converted in order to strengthen their Jewish identification.

Of equal significance would be the careful and thoughtful development of a program for community-based Jewish family support services. The focus would be on developing innovative programs to respond to changes in Jewish family lifestyles, particularly working and single-parent families, reconstituted families, and families with a converting or converted spouse. Existing Jewish family services are not yet responding to the new realities of family life (nor are non-Jewish family service agencies), certainly not in any uniquely Jewish way. One aspect to study might be the uniquely Jewish component of such services and what role they could play in increasing Jewish identification and supporting family life. What kinds of services would be most helpful to these families, with what kinds of consequences? Here the focus would be on developing the specific kinds of support services needed and making them attractive, accessible, and reasonably priced. The goal would be to encourage identification and affiliation with the Jewish community by providing what young families need and want. We would want to explore how Jewish values and culture could be integrated into such services — and what approaches are most effective — as well as what the relative payoff is for Jewish philanthropy invested in such programs rather than some of the other more prestigious but seemingly less centrally "Jewish" philanthropic targets.

Among the types of support services I would stress are child care programs for infants and toddlers as well as preschool programs; practical helping services for single-parent or working families (a reliable baby sitter and information and referral service, a family day care registry); self-help groups; family life and parent education programs. A much larger list could be made, nor do I mean to exclude all traditional counseling services. The Jewish community has not begun to serve the needs of the large "middle" group of Jewish families central to any continuity of the Jewish community. In contrast, it continues to heavily invest in supporting institutions and services which may have high visibility and prestige but much less significance for the concerns expressed here or for the Jewish community.

In conclusion, I would like to underscore the central thesis in this chapter. Families are changing, as is society around us. Change may be and usually is painful; but neither death nor disaster is inevitable for the Jewish community. New family lifestyles offer a significant potential for improving the quality of life for all members, as men and women become more equal and as both share more in the larger society and in their roles as parents. Children have much to gain as societies recognize their value more explicitly, parents become more involved with child rearing, and children participate more in the world around them.

For the Jewish family to survive in America, society at large must first be supportive to all family life. In that context, the Jewish community must direct its attention to learning more about what Jewish families are experiencing and need, and then responding to these needs. Family and community are what people identify as most important in their lives. The Jewish community cannot survive without Jewish families and vice versa; and neither can survive without some support from the larger society. This mutual interdependence needs some creative attention at this time.

Notes

1. I acknowledge my debt to the review of data on the American Jewish family in Chaim I. Waxman, "The Threadbare Canopy: The Vicissitudes of the Jewish Family in Modern American Society," and to a variety of material provided by the American Jewish Committee. Apart from several standard sources (e.g. *American Jewish Year Book*; Sidney Goldstein, "A Demographic View of the Jewish Community in the 1980s," paper presented at the YIVO Conference, May 1978, and in another form at the J.W.B. Greater Northeast Convention, April 1979). I have made no effort to explore any primary source material.
2. Unless otherwise indicated, the primary sources for the following overview are: Paul L. Glick and Arthur J. Norton, "Marrying, Divorcing, and Living Together in the U.S. Today," *Population Bulletin* 32 (October 1977); U.S. Bureau of the Census, *Current Population Reports*, series P-20, no. 336, "Population Profile of the United States, 1978" (Washington, D.C.: U.S.G.P.O., 1979); U.S. Bureau of the Census, *Current Population Reports*, Special Studies, series P-23, no. 77, "Perspectives on American Husbands and Wives" (1978); Arthur J. Norton, "One-Parent Families in the United States," paper presented at the Ditchley Conference on One-Parent Families, Ditchley, England, 1979 (to be published); U.S. Senate, Hearings before the Committee on Labor and Human Resources, pt. 1, January 31 and February 1, 1979, *The Coming Decade: American Women and Human Resources Policies and Programs* (Washington, D.C.: U.S.G.P.O., 1979). See esp. appendix C, Alexis Herman, Women's Bureau, D.O.L., pp. 319–62, and Congressional Research Service, "Women in America: A Source Book," pp. 1343–58.
3. A recurrent theme in "quality of life" surveys. See for example Angus Campbell, Phillip E. Converse, and Willard Rogers, *The Quality of American Life* (New York: Russell Sage, 1976).

4. By this I mean that women may have first children earlier and a second child close to the first, but they do not have *more* children than they would have had, regardless.
5. The antiabortion stance of some Orthodox Jewish groups represents an invasion of personal privacy and choice. It is also a denial of the prevalence of illegal abortion both in Israel and in the United States until abortion was legalized. Moreover, as should be obvious, the quality of children reflects whether they are born wanted or not.
6. For a discussion of this point see Sheila B. Kamerman and Alfred J. Kahn, *Child Care, Family Benefits, and Working Parents* (forthcoming); Sheila B. Kamerman and Alfred J. Kahn, "A Comparative Analysis in Family Policy," *Social Work* (November 1979); Sheila B. Kamerman, "Work and Family in Industrialized Societies," *SIGNS: The Journal of Women and Culture in Society* (Summer 1979); Sheila B. Kamerman, "Managing Work and Family Life." In P. Moss and N. Fonda (eds.), *Work and Family* (London: Maurice Temple Smith, 1980).
7. For U.S. female labor force projections see Ralph Smith, *Women in the Labor Force in the 1990's* (Washington, D.C.: Urban Institute, 1978). For some discussion of these trends in Western mixed economies see *Equal Opportunities for Women* (Paris: OECD, 1979).
8. See Robert LeVine, "Women's Education and Maternal Behavior in the Third World: A Report to the Ford Foundation" (Cambridge, Mass.: Harvard Graduate School of Education, 1978). See also comments on the German Democratic Republic as quoted in Kamerman and Kahn, *Child Care, Family Benefits, and Working Parents.*
9. Much of this research is reviewed and/or discussed in Kamerman and Kahn, ibid. The most definitive and updated review of research on children of working mothers is Lois W. Hoffman, "Maternal Employment, 1979," *The American Psychologist* (forthcoming).
10. The most extensive research on the cost of a child has been done in Europe in relation to setting the level of family allowances. See for example Bureau d'Informations et de Prévisions Economiques, *Cout de l'enfant et consommation familiale* (Paris: CNAF, 1977).
11. This whole issue is discussed extensively in Kamerman and Kahn, *Child Care, Family Benefits, and Working Parents.*
12. Among the leaders are: James Morgan and Greg Duncan, University of Michigan; Rosabeth Moss Kanter, Yale University; Jerome Rostow, Work in America Inst., White Plains, N.Y.; The Urban Institute Program on Women and Family, Washington, D.C.; and our Cross-National Family Policy Research Program at Columbia University.
13. Among those working in this field are: Frank Stafford, University of Michigan; John Robinson, Indiana University; Katherine Walker, Cornell University; Joseph Pleck and James Levine of Wellesley College on changing male roles; and a number of women scholars on changing women's roles.
14. For example, my own study of working families in one suburban New York county suggests that working parents may spend more time with their families (children, parents, other relatives) and less in community, recreational, and social activities. See Sheila B. Kamerman, *Parenting in an Unresponsive Society: Managing Work and Family Life* (New York: Free Press, 1980).
15. Among leaders in this field are: Glen Elder, Cornell University; Tamara Hareven, Clark and Harvard Universities; John Demos, Brandeis University.

16. Hope Leichter at Columbia University directs such a research program. The U.S. Department of Health, Education, and Welfare, National Institute of Education held a conference on this subject in 1978.
17. Harold Visotsky, Medical School, Northwestern University, is among those who have studied youth cults.

6.

The Family and the American Jewish Community on the Threshold of the 1980s: An Inventory for Research and Planning*

Chaim I. Waxman

One basic problem in attempting to determine any demographic features of America's Jews is the difficulty of obtaining reliable data. The doctrine of separation of church and state has been interpreted to preclude questions on religious affiliation in surveys conducted by the Bureau of the Census. In the mid-1950s, the Bureau of the Census did conduct a special survey of about 35,000 households, in which respondents were able to voluntarily answer a question on religion, and a brief report of that survey was published (U.S. Bureau of the Census, 1958). This report and two later studies derived from data in the report were for many years the only sources of national information on the religious characteristics of the American population. Given the many shifts and changes in American society and culture during the past twenty years, it is doubtful that these data can be used to indicate anything more than speculation about the characteristics by religion of the American population in general and American Jews in particular, at the dawn of the 1980s.

For more or less current information on the Jewish population in the United States, there are two main sources. The most widely used and quoted, and probably most reliable for the decade of the 1970s, is the National Jewish Population Study, sponsored by the Council of Jewish Federations and Welfare Funds. This study, the nearest to a national census of American Jewry ever conducted in the United States, provided a wealth of information previously unavailable. However, a complete report of the findings was never published. For a variety of reasons, only a series of brief reports which summarized data relating to issues of concern to those involved in community planning within local Jewish federations, were issued. Since the data were collected during the late 1960s and early 1970s, there is some question as to validity. It seems reasonable to assume that significant changes have taken place in the characteristics of American Jewry during the 1970s.

Another source of information on the American Jewish population is in the series of community surveys periodically conducted by local Jewish federations. The quality of these surveys, in terms of social research techniques, varies widely, and the degree of representativeness, even for the local community, has been questioned in many cases, since they frequently survey only those Jews affiliated with local Jewish institutions. Questions have also been raised as to the degree to which a particular community is representative of American Jewry as a whole. In this respect, Goldstein (1971) reports that his review of the community surveys revealed surprisingly uniform patterns.

One final source of information is in the limited number of specialized studies conducted by social scientists and reported in academic journals. Many criticisms raised with respect to the community surveys are applicable here as well. Given the limitations of reliable data, the following discussion of family patterns of America's Jews should be taken as tentative. The current situation is not much better than it was almost a decade ago when Marshall Sklare (1971, p. 73) bemoaned "the paucity of substantial research studies on the American-Jewish family." Yet since the data come from a variety of sources and findings are more or less similar, there is reason to assume that the picture which emerges approximates reality.

Marriage

Jews and Judaism have traditionally placed a high priority on marriage as an intrinsic value, and data indicate that a high proportion of America's Jews are married, and that the vast majority marry at least once. In their study of Providence, Rhode Island, Goldstein and Goldscheider found that Jews had a higher rate of marriage than non-Jews (1968, pp. 102–3). In a more recent study of Rhode Island, Kobrin and Goldscheider found marriage to be virtually universal among Jews, with the proportion of ever married increasing over the years (1978, p. 38). That those findings are fairly representative is evident when compared with figures reported from the National Jewish Population Study (NJPS). In the table showing "Percent Distribution of Households' Age of Head, by Marital Status, U.S. Jewish Population — 1971," less than 5 percent of respondents aged 30 and over are single. More than 95 percent are listed as married, separated or divorced, or widowed (Chenkin, 1972, p. 16). This high rate of ever-married would seem to indicate that American Jews continue to abide by the biblical dictum that "it is not good for man to be alone" (Genesis 2:18).

Andrew Greeley (1974, p. 45) reports different findings in data derived from seven NORC surveys. He found that "among the three major religious bodies, the Jews (at least if they are Eastern European and "Other") are rather surprisingly less likely to be married than the Catholics, and the Catholics are less likely to be married than the Protestants." His figures show a somewhat higher rate of never married than reported by Chenkin. Without specifying age cohort, Greeley found that for American Jews of German background 3.2 percent were never married, for those of East European background the percentage rose to 11.3, and for "Other" American Jews 15.7 percent were never married (p. 46, Table 6). The discrepancy between the NORC and NJPS data cannot be explained at this point. Nevertheless, it should be noted that Greeley's data are more commensurate with the preceptions of many observers of American Jewry that the rate of marriage is now considerably lower than reported in pre-1970s studies (cf. Goldscheider, 1978).

One source of relatively recent data, which also provides for comparison with data collected a decade earlier, is the study of the Boston Jewish population sponsored by the Combined Jewish Philanthropies of Greater Boston (Fowler, 1977). Recognizing that the Jewish population of Boston is atypical of American Jewry as a whole in that the Boston population has a disporportionately high number of Jews involved in academia, its trends may nevertheless be indicative of patterns which will spread to other American Jewish communities in time. A number of changes in family patterns from the mid-1960s to the mid-1970s are significant. Whereas in 1965, 73 percent of the adult Jewish population of Greater Boston was married, by 1975 this figure had declined to 56 percent (p. 13). More specifically, in the 21-29 age cohort the percentage of those married dropped from 58 percent in 1965 to 42 percent in 1975 (p. 14). Overall, Jewish population remaining single rose from 14 percent in 1965 to 32 percent in 1975, and those currently divorced or separated rose from 1 percent in 1965 to 4 percent in 1975 (p. 13).

Preliminary data from a more recent study of the Jewish community in Greater Los Angeles suggest different patterns. While 35.8 of respondents aged 18-39 remained single, less than 4 percent of those aged 40-59 and 3 percent of those 60 and older remained single (Phillips, 1980). While there are no data from the previous decade with which these figures can be compared, they may suggest a tendency toward later marriage, rather than nonmarriage. If this were the case, it would simply be a continuation and extension of a pattern which, as discussed below, has been evident since the early 1960s — that American Jews marry later than others.

Insofar as age at first marriage is concerned, most of the evidence suggests that Jews marry later than their non-Jewish neighbors. Kobrin and Goldscheider found "that only a very small proportion of Jewish males marry at ages 20 or younger compared to Protestants and Catholics" (1978, p. 78), and that "Jewish women marry at older ages on average than Protestants and Catholics in both age cohorts" (1978, p. 83). Sklare cites a study conducted in New York City during 1963-64 from which he concludes that "native-born Jews marry later than their peers but when they reach what they consider an appropriate age they out-distance all others" (1971, p. 75). While this finding is borne out by every study of American Jews, Greeley's studies of American Catholics produced somewhat different findings. He reports data which show that "Catholics are much less likely than either Protestants or Jews to be married before their twenty-first birthday" (1977, p. 187). Since he does not provide precise information on the source of his data and the number of Jews in his sample, it is difficult to even attempt to reconcile Greeley's findings with the majority of studies which uniformly report later marriages for Jews than for non-Jews.

Divorce

Despite the high priority on marriage in the Jewish tradition, Judaism has never viewed marriage as an absolutely permanent and indissoluble bond during the lifetime of both spouses. Though betrothal is defined as a sacred bond — the Hebrew term for which is *kidushin,* from the term *kodesh* which translates as "sacred" — Judaism provides for an institutionalized ceremony through which people can dissolve that bond, should remaining together become intolerable. In considering divorce rates, therefore, and especially when analyzing the comparative rates of different groups, it must be emphasized that the absence or infrequency of divorce is not necessarily an indication of strong and positive relationships between spouses. As Goldberg (1968) points out in his survey of Jewish and non-Jewish divorce rates in Europe since the nineteenth century, of parts of Africa and Asia including Israel, and of the United States and Canada, attitudes toward divorce vary from society to society and group to group. In societies where Jews had a larger percentage of divorce than non-Jews, the reason was frequently the product of Jewish emphasis on human dignity, rather than the marital bliss of the non-Jewish population. In examining data from various communities in the United States, Goldberg found that "separation and divorce are less prevalent among Jews than among the general white population" (p. 8) In his Detroit sample, Lenski (1961, p. 198) found a lower divorce rate for Jews than for Protestants and Catholics, as did Goldstein and Goldscheider (1968) and Kobrin and Goldscheider (1978) in their studies of Providence, Rhode Island. Among Jews themselves, Goldstein and Goldscheider found the divorce rate to be higher among those born in the United States than among those born elsewhere, and higher among Reform than among Conservative and Orthodox Jews

(p. 113). In contrast to a number of studies indicating that among the general American population the more educated have lower divorce rates, Goldstein and Goldscheider found divorce and separation to be higher among those more highly educated. They suggest that this may be attributed to the fact that more highly educated Jews are more secularized and acculturated, and that their rates would therefore be more similar to those of non-Jews (p. 112). If their data were representative of national Jewish patterns, one could have predicted a growing divorce rate among Jews.

While there are no reliable data on current divorce rates among American Jews, there is consensus among rabbis and other Jewish communal workers that the American Jewish divorce rate has risen dramatically in recent years. Some have gone so far as to claim that the American Jewish divorce rate is identical with the general divorce rate (Smolar, 1979; Postal, 1979). When pressed for reliable evidence, most will admit that their conclusion is based on intuition and personal observation rather than data. Preliminary data from Greater Los Angeles do not support their claim. The data indicate a doubling of the divorce rate between 1968 and 1979, but in 1979 the Jewish divorce rate was still significantly lower than the general divorce rate (Phillips, 1980).

While it has been an article of faith until recently that the Orthodox Jewish divorce rate is very low (both relatively and absolutely), some claim that it too is rapidly changing. For example, for three consecutive years, 1977–79, the leaders of the largest Orthodox rabbinic organization, the Rabbinical Council of America, highlighted the issue of the rapidly increasing Orthodox Jewish divorce rate at the organization's annual convention (*The Jewish Week*, January 30, 1977, p. 4; February 5, 1978, p. 17; June 24, 1979, p. 22). These reports are based on intuition and personal observation, with no reliable supporting data (see the exchange of letters on this subject between Mayer and Waxman, *The Jewish Week*, July 1, 1979, p. 38; July 15, 1979, p. 22). The sole item approximating empirical data is the report by Kranzler (1978) of a girls' day high school in Boro Park, Brooklyn, the largest Orthodox Jewish neighborhood in the United States. The guidance counselor at the school estimated that about 8 percent of the approximately one thousand students came from homes in which the parents were divorced. Given that this is a highly traditional Orthodox school in an intensely Orthodox neighborhood, the 8 percent figure comes as a surprise. Since these data relate to cases of divorce in which there are high school-age children, it seems reasonable to assume that if younger and/or childless divorced Orthodox Jews were included the percentage would be even higher.

Single-Parent Family

A related aspect of American Jewish life, which has recently become an issue of concern to survivalists within the community, is that of single-parent families (Waxman, 1980).

There are no solid data on the number of such families nor on rates of increase. Nevertheless, there are indices within the community of significant increases and reliable data showing sharp increases within the American middle class. Such information strongly suggests that there has been a significant increase in the number of American Jewish single-parent families in the 1970s.

From the standpoint of the group, the causes for concern lie in the central role the family, in its two-parent form, has played in Jewish socialization, and in evidence of disaffiliation and alienation from community among American Jewish single parents. Concerned as they are about the rate of increase, leaders of institutionally affiliated American Jewry have not yet resolved the dilemma of successfully integrating single-parent families into a two-parent, family-centered communal life. There are structural and cultural elements to this dilemma. The main structural component of Jewish communal life is the two-parent family, and there is a dialectical relationship between the structure and the religious-cultural value of the centrality of that family form. The perception of alienation on the part of many single parents derives from the structure which implicitly excludes single parents, the religious-cultural value which does likewise, and from the rejection of the demand by some single parents that the Jewish community not only accept and integrate them as individuals, but that the community legitimize single parenthood as an equal and viable alternative to the two-parent form. With increasing numbers of Jewish single-parent families, it may be anticipated that there will be increasing pressure on the organized Jewish community to take cognizance of and accommodate the needs of such families.

Fertility

Presumably, all self-conscious minority groups are concerned about group size, since it is anticipated that the larger the size of the group, the greater its chances for survival in the majority/minority situation. The areas where this is most clearly articulated, if not acted upon, among America's Jews are fertility and intermarriage. That both of these facets of Jewish family life are perceived by some as determining the very survival of the Jewish community in the United States is evident from even the titles of many of the most quoted writings on the subject, such as "The Vanishing American Jew" (Morgan, 1964) and "Intermarriage and the Jewish

Future" (Sklare, 1964). A former president of the New York Board of Rabbis is quoted as having urged the American Jewish community to exempt itself from the nationwide trend toward zero population growth and increase its numbers. Otherwise, "it will grow weaker and will face a threat to its existence." "Three children should be the minimum number for Jewish families," he asserted, "but the larger the better" (Spiegel, 1974).

Most demographers would probably view this perception as alarmist, if not downright paranoid (cf. Jaffe, 1978; Berelson, 1978). There is another approach within which fears about American Jewish population decline are well founded. Goldscheider (1978) has perceptively summarized two contrasting perspectives on the issue:

> To an outsider, the concern about the disappearance of American Jewry or the vanishing American Jew appears exaggerated or alarmist, if not ludicrous. At best the issue appears rhetorical or artificially created, to be rejected with the obvious retorts about the strength of American Jewish life. One does not have to go beyond a regular reading of the press to know that Jews are conspicuously present in a wide range of political and social activities (p. 121). An insider who knows the strength and weaknesses of the Jewish community goes beyond the superficial indicators and below the surface, however. Other signs appear, more powerful and challenging, subtle and destructive, which provide an alternative perspective (p. 123).

A look at a number of demographic variables of American Jewry provides substance to the "insider" perspective.

According to the *American Jewish Year Book* (Chenkin and Miran, 1979, p. 177), the size of the American Jewish population numbers 5,781,000, or about 2.67 percent of the total population of the United States. When these figures are compared with those of the past, the 1930s for example, when Jews were 3.7 percent of the total population, it can be readily seen that American Jewry is becoming an increasingly smaller part of the overall American population. This does not necessarily mean that American Jewry is shrinking. These figures may reflect the traditional pattern of Jews maintaining a lower birth rate than their non-Jewish counterparts. As Goldscheider (1967) has demonstrated, the lower birth rate of Jews is not only characteristic of contemporary American Jewry but has been the pattern in the United States since the nineteenth century. This pattern is found in Europe as well. Goldstein (1981) puts it succinctly: "Already in the late nineteenth century, the Jewish birthrate was lower than that of the non-Jewish population. This differential has persisted to the present. Jews marry later than the average, desire and expect to have the smallest families, have had the most favorable attitudes toward the use of contraceptives, have used birth control to a greater extent than other groups, and have been among its most efficient users."

Closer inspection reveals that American Jewry is not only becoming an increasingly smaller proportion of the total population, but that the American Jewish birth rate is at and possibly below the replacement level, which is generally accepted to be an average of 2.1 children per family. For American Jewry the issue is not that of zero population growth, but of negative population growth. Studies of the fertility expectations of women of childbearing age, which suggest a narrowing of the gap between the birth rates of Jewish and non-Jewish women, leave no room for optimism with respect to the Jewish birth rate, because the projected decline in the differential is not due to a rise in the Jewish birth rate but to an anticipated decline in the non-Jewish birth rate (Goldstein, 1981; Cohen and Ritterband, 1981). If current trends of religious intermarriage continue, as will be discussed below, the rate of Jewish fertility seems likely to decline even more significantly, since, as Goldstein indicates, couples in which one of the spouses is Jewish have significantly fewer children than couples in which both spouses are Jewish. For Jewish women married to Jewish husbands, the average is 2.1 children, whereas for Jewish women married to non-Jewish husbands the average is 1.6. Similar patterns prevail when the focus is on Jewish husbands married to Jewish and non-Jewish wives. The reasons for this differential are beyond the scope of this chapter. Within this context, the significant issue is that the differential exists and intermarriage is rising.

There are a number of qualifications to these projections and predictions. First, there are the limitations inherent to demography. Second, as most demographers of American Jewry caution, the limitations of those studies whose samples are significantly Jewish and the small number of Jews represented in national surveys, make for an even greater risk in predicting Jewish demographic patterns. A third limitation is the serious bias in samples in all the surveys and studies upon which the predictions are based. There are groups of American Jews, such as Hasidim and other Orthodox Jews, who live not only in Brooklyn but in sections of practically every large city in the United States who are not represented in the samples. Because they are not likely to talk about private family matters, because they live in highly insular communities and are even less likely to discuss such matters with outsiders, because they have a greater tendency to remain within their own primary groups — their chances of being queried as respondents and interviewees in demographic studies are remote, if not nil. But these groups' demographic patterns may be radically different from the mainstream, sufficiently so as to offset the trends of the majority. For example, it has been suggested that families with more than a half-dozen children are common among these groups. If that continues to be the case, their high birth rate could compensate for the low birth rate of the majority and thus curtail the American Jewish population decline. This is merely a highly speculative point within a discussion of the limitations of demographic prediction.

There have arisen a number of ideological movements in American society that have had a direct impact on the family and fertility and in which there appear to be an at least proportional number of Jews affiliated, but about which there are little reliable data. Included among these are the "gay" movement, the radical feminists, and those who favor marriage without children. The organized Jewish community is not quite certain as to how to deal with these movements, although the Union of American Hebrew Congregations, the national agency of the Reform synagogues, has accepted gay congregations into its ranks. Whether and how these movements will affect mainstream American Jewry and its pattern of family life remains to be seen. This area begs empirical analysis.

Intermarriage

As is the case for all social groups, Jews reserve one of the most severe sanctions — intense ostracism — for those members who reject and deny the group. Historically apostasy has been deemed an even more serious affront than the violation of religious codes. The former is perceived as a rejection of both the religion and the group, whereas the latter is limited to the Jewish religion.

Until recently intermarriage was considered such an act of rejection. Among traditionalists not only was intermarriage not condoned, but the Jewish spouse was considered "dead" and his or her family observed many of the traditional rites of mourning. Even in the minority of cases where the non-Jewish spouse converted to Judaism, in which situation the evidence of rejection, if any, was not clearly present, there was strong disapproval from the Jewish community. The community feared that the conversion was religiously insincere, and that while the couple may not have explicitly rejected the Jewish community, their children would surely be lost to it. It was inconceivable that the offspring of such parents would be socialized as Jews. Intermarriage, even when involving conversion, was perceived as harmful to the Jewish people, which has a strong sense of corporate identity.

With the advent of the modern era the socioeconomic position of Jews in the United States and in the urban centers of Europe improved. Along with rising political and social equality there were increased informal social contacts and interpersonal relationships between Jews and non-Jews. Predictably, the intermarriage rate of Jews increased somewhat (Barron, 1946, pp. 177–89), but the group as a whole remained highly endogamous. In his review of studies of Jewish intermarriage Rosenthal (1963) reported that data from a study of Washington, D.C. by Stanley Bigman indicated an overall Jewish intermarriage rate of 13.1 percent, with that rate rising to about 18 percent for third-generation American Jews. "The Washington data revealed that children in at least 70 percent of mixed families are lost to the Jewish group" (p. 32). By 1965, the National Jewish Population Study estimated the intermarriage rate to be 29.1 percent and rising. As of 1972, it estimated that the rate of intermarriage had risen to 48.1 percent (Massarik 1973, p. 11).

As evidence of rising intermarriage rates mounted during the 1960s, public expressions of concern for the Jewish future of intermarried couples and their children grew louder. In 1964, Marshall Sklare (1964, p. 48), widely regarded as the foremost authority on the sociology of American Jewry and whose analyses emanate from a survivalist perspective (Waxman, 1977-78), decried "Jewish complacency about the rate of intermarriage." Contrary to prevalent arguments used by those attempting to dissuade couples from intermarrying by suggesting that intermarriage is symptomatic of individuals with psychological maladies and that it invariably leads to marital instability, Sklare asserted that "it is precisely the 'healthy' modern intermarriage which raises the most troubling questions of all to the Jewish community." He warned that the rising intermarriage rate posed a formidable threat to "the Jewish future." In 1970 he reiterated his warning, asserting that this threat overshadowed recent positive developments in the American Jewish community. "It strikes," he argued, "at the very core of Jewish group existence" (Sklare, 1970, p. 51).

Despite the stern warnings and dire predictions of Sklare and many others, no strategy for dealing with the issue has emerged on the Jewish communal agenda. There appears to have developed an attitude of inevitability — that the community will have to reconcile itself to "living with intermarriage" (Singer, 1979) and making the best of it. In an attempt to resolve the tensions of the resulting "cognitive dissonance" (Festinger, 1957), a number of students of Jewish intermarriage now argue that what appeared as a threat may actually be a blessing in disguise. Fred Massarik (1978, p. 33), who was scientific director of the National Jewish Population Study, has reconsidered the data and suggests that the issue for Jewish survival is not intermarriage but fertility, and that "the net effect of intermarriage may be an increase in Jewish population rather than a decrease." While not arriving at an unequivocal conclusion, Massarik argues that the issue of intermarriage as it affects the Jewish future is more complex than was previously evident. It is only one variable which itself has many complex features, such as whether the non-Jewish spouse undertakes conversion, or whether the Jewish spouse is male or female. Each of these variants has a differential impact on the future identification and plans for involvement of the intermarried couple and their children with the Jewish community and Jewish religious-cultural life.

In their summary report of a national study (Mayer, 1978) sponsored by the American Jewish Committee on "Intermarriage and the Jewish Future," Mayer and Sheingold (1979) argue that the rate of Jewish intermarriage will continue to increase in the foreseeable future. Their study confirmed earlier findings by Lazerwitz (1971) that what they term "conversionary marriages," in which the previously non-Jewish spouse converts to Judaism, compare favorably, in terms of religious affiliation and observance, not only with "mixed marriages," in which the non-Jewish spouse does not convert, but also with endogamous Jewish marriages. "The Jewish community would do well to examine what steps it can take to encourage" conversion (Mayer and Sheingold, 1979, p. 32). While they accept the inevitability of an increasing rate of intermarriage and call for steps to encourage conversion, they do not go so far as to say that intermarriage is not a threat. On the contrary, they conclude that the data "tend to reinforce the fear that intermarriage represents a threat to Jewish continuity," primarily because "most non-Jewish spouses do not convert to Judaism; the level of Jewish content and practice in mixed marriages is low; only about one-third of the Jewish partners in such marriages view their children as Jewish; and most such children are exposed to little by way of Jewish culture or religion" (p. 30).

In two subsequent publications, Egon Mayer, director of the AJC study, focuses and elaborates on his outreach proposal. In the lengthier of the two written for the National Jewish Conference Center (1979a), he urges that the Jewish community change its traditional stance of discouraging prospective converts and establish "conversion outreach centers" which "should bridge the gap between the religious Jewish community and the potential convert" (p. 7). However, he maintains that the majority of mixed-marriage spouses are probably not receptive to conversion in any case, and therefore there is virtually no chance that they will ever become wholly integrated into the Jewish community. Moreover, their Jewish spouses, who may serve as their Jewish role models, rarely, if ever, manifest any religious behavior. To the extent that they are active Jews they are so within secular rather than religious frameworks. Mayer maintains that there are many non-Jewish spouses in mixed marriages who identify as Jews in that they have positive feelings toward Jewry and participate in secular Jewish activities, such as serving on committees of Jewish community centers, on the boards of local Hadassah chapters, and in federation fund-raising activities. Given this growing group of mixed-marriage spouses who, according to Jewish religious law, *halachah*, are not Jewish but feel themselves to be somewhat Jewish in a secular and perhaps even ethnic sense, Mayer recommends that a new category of Jew be created — those who are members of the "people" but not of the "faith" (p. 7). In a second article on this subject, Mayer (1979b) is even more explicit in calling for a kind of "ethnic conversion," which will respond to the desire of many of the intermarried to see themselves and be seen as Jews, but without religious conviction. Motivated by a desire to improve the demographic outlook, Mayer sees hope in the minority of spouses in mixed marriages who, he claims, "are Jews through the alchemy of sociology, not of *halachah*" (p. 64).

Whether he is correct in his estimate of the number of potential "cultural" Jews who would respond to outreach efforts aimed at "ethnic conversion" is a moot point. For better or worse the organized Jewish community is not quite harking to Mayer's urgings. It is not embarking on an organized outreach campaign. Neither has it developed any strategy for stemming the rising intermarriage rate.[1] While the community no longer perceives intermarriage as a curse, neither does it perceive it as a blessing. The community has come to begrudgingly accept intermarriage with the implicit faith that it can be successfully endured. Empirical research on the next generation may reveal the degree to which that faith is warranted. If the five "half-Jews" interviewed by Span (1979) are in any way representative of this group, there are grounds for skepticism about the extent to which the children of mixed marriages serve as a potential source of strength for the American Jewish community.

Extended Familism

With respect to patterns of kinship relationships, the ideal household of the American Jew, like that of the middle class generally, consists of parents and their minor children (Sklare, 1971, p. 94), in contrast to the three-generation household typical among Jews in Eastern Europe. The American Jewish family appears to be relatively unique with respect to maintenance of strong kinship ties. This characteristic is so out of line with what one would have predicted on the basis of the group's socioeconomic status, that Berman (1976) has pointed to it as "an inconsistency in theory" (see also Balswick, 1966; Westerman, 1967; Winch, Greer, and Blumberg, 1967; Sklare, 1971, p. 95; for a study of the interesting development of family clubs and cousins' clubs among Jews in New York City, see Mitchell, 1978). With the increasing rate of intermarriage, it remains to be seen to what degree the extended familism of American Jews will prevail and to what extent this kind of extended family will serve to reinforce and transmit Jewish identity and identification.

Centrality of the Family

It was argued at the beginning of this chapter that an examination of the contemporary American Jewish family is warranted, particularly because of the central role it plays in defining and transmitting Jewish identity and identification. The foregoing examination indicates that though certain unique family patterns persist, the American Jewish family has changed significantly from the traditional Jewish patterns, and that it is increasingly manifesting the same patterns as the general American middle-class family. If that is the case, it would be appropriate to raise the question of the probability of Jewish group survival in American society. Developments within the American Jewish community during the last decade appear to suggest that the prognosis for the survival of American Jewry is more positive than it appeared in the early 1960s. For example, in his assessment of recent changes in the suburban Jewish community of Lakeville, Sklare (1979, pp. 333–405) points to "many positive signs of Jewish survivalism," which, he implies, might mitigate the "negative signs, most obviously the rise in intermarriage" (p. 404). Do such findings support the argument of those, such as Kutzik (1977), that the family plays a subsidiary role in Jewish identification, and that communal institutions, such as the synagogue and social welfare institutions, play the more basic role? And if so, is the scarcity of data on the contemporary American Jewish family justified by its secondary nature? Our response to both these questions is negative. To begin with, we have argued that although the family plays a central role in Jewish identity formation and transmission, it cannot be viewed in a vacuum, without the support of the more formal institutions of the Jewish community (Waxman, 1977, pp. 5, 7). On this matter Kutzik agrees (1977, p. 35). His position on the primacy of communal institutions and secondary nature of the family is based on his view of "the limited . . . role of the contemporary American family in . . . enculturation or sociocultural identification." The contemporary family, "whether Jewish or not," he asserts, "is structurally incapable of carrying out enculturation on its own" (p. 11). Here Kutzik is echoing Rosenberg and Humphrey (1955, p. 27), who assert "the secondary nature of primary groups." They argue:

> Agencies of socialization transmit culture; they do not necessarily create it. Primary groups may be the nursery of a human nature whose shapes and contours they do not determine. A sacred society will use its neighborhoods in one way, a secular society in another. The child must always be socialized within a small group, but the norms it is obliged to "interiorize" have another and a larger locus. The child is plastic, and he is molded to a large extent by his family, his play group, and his neighbors, but all these take their essential character from courses external to them.

While there is no disagreement as to the family's inability to function in this manner "on its own," Kutzik underestimates the significant degree to which the family of the past and present, Jewish or not, is involved in identity formation. The family is not only a "haven in a heartless world" (Lasch, 1977); it is a "small world" (Luckmann, 1970) in which the self emerges and in which the individual acquires a stable sense of identity and reality.

In terms of Jewish identity and identification, likewise, the family plays the central role in primary socialization and provides the foundation for the complementary roles of formal communal institutions. This does not mean that strong traditional family ties will necessarily provide that foundation — those with no Jewish self-consciousness will not. As Rosenberg and Humphrey point out in their analogy of the primary group and the conveyor belt, "the belt is *eo ipso* a neutral object, which must be adjusted to work norms and end products impersonally thrust upon it" (1955, p. 27). We are dealing with families which have a Jewish consciousness and the central role the family plays in defining and transmitting that consciousness to the next generation. Communal institutions are important in providing the structural context for realizing and living out that identity and for reinforcing it, but they are still secondary to the primary role of the family. Recent studies by Cohen (1978) indicate that those living in "alternate families" are considerably less Jewishly active than those living in traditional normative families. Apparently, nontraditional forms of family are unable to provide the framework within which the individual would acquire a stable sense of Jewish identity and Jewish reality, and therefore does not seek out those structural contexts within which Jewish identity is operationalized.

If, as the evidence suggests, changes in the American Jewish family have been most dramatic within the past two decades, it may be premature to take solace from recent positive signs of Jewish survivalism which Sklare and others have found. They may be but short-term patterns resulting from a number of events which took place both within the Jewish and general American communities during the late 1960s and early 1970s (cf. Glazer, 1972, pp. 151–86). But their staying power may be limited, especially as both the American cultural milieu and the American Jewish family have changed.

Those positive signs are found among American Jewry. This is not the contradiction it appears to be. There is a basic difference between being an American Jew and being a member of the American Jewish community — between those who are nominally Jewish and those affiliated with the organized community. While it is difficult to get precise figures, indications are that the unaffiliated comprise a large portion of the American Jewish population. For example Elazar (1976, pp. 70–74) has divided the American Jewish population into seven groups, represented as a series of seven uneven concentric circles, ranging from the hard-core "integral Jews" to those whose Jewish status is least clear, "quasi Jews." If we add up his estimates of those who are "peripherals" and beyond, we find that 25-30 percent of the American Jewish population is completely uninvolved in Jewish life. Another group, "contributors and consumers," who "clearly identify as Jews but are minimally associated with the Jewish community as such, comprise about 25 to 30 percent of all American Jews" (p. 73). The condition of contemporary American Jewry is one in which there is a "shrinking middle" (Goldscheider, 1978, p. 125). There is a polarization with respect to Jewish commitment. The positive signs discussed by Sklare are manifested only within that approximately 50 percent of the American Jewish population affiliated with the American Jewish community. The weakening commitment of the other half, the unaffiliated, has distinct implications for the qualitative survival and well-being of the whole.

Implications: Research and Policy

American Jewish organizations have long been opposed to the inclusion of questions relating to religion on the national census, and it is assumed that no change in that position will occur in the foreseeable future. As a result, one of the most fruitful resources for obtaining basic demographic information on American Jewry is foreclosed. In lieu of the publicly supported census, the Council of Jewish Federations and Welfare Funds had funded the National Jewish Population Study during the late 1960s and early 1970s. A full report of the findings was never published, and in any case, those data are now ten years old.

As a first step, there is the need for a commitment to provide resources for a census of the American Jewish population on a regular basis, and that the information derived from the census be made available to both social scientists and American Jewish organizations for purposes of analysis and planning. It may be that there is an historical aversion to a census on the part of Jews, in addition to pragmatic resistance to undertaking a census. Unless these resistances are overcome, American Jewry will continue to remain in the dark as to current trends among its population and will not be able to engage in meaningful planning. Basic demographic data is a prerequisite for communal planning and policy.

Second, the recommendation has been made for the establishment of a national Jewish family center which would have ties with universities and other research institutions and which would conduct, sponsor, and disseminate information to guide the formulation of communal policy, program proposals, and the training of professional and lay leadership on matters relating to Jewish family life (Waxman, 1979). Some efforts in this direction are being undertaken by the Jewish Communal Affairs Department of the American Jewish Committee, but it is too early to determine the extent to which the proposal will be realized. It is significant that one of the largest and most prestigious American Jewish organizations is making an effort to place the issue of Jewish family life on its list of priorities. If other American Jewish organizations should make similar commitments, this might have an impact on both American Jewish values and general American cultural values.

If American Jewish norms and values are similar to those of White middle-class America, it is likely that the changing status of women has had significant impact on American Jewish family life. At the very least, employment by both spouses in a marriage poses numerous problems for the institution of marriage, the birth rate, the socialization of children, the roles of both parents, and the quality of Jewish family life. We need data on the extent of careerism among American Jewish women, to what degree it influences prospects of marriage and children, and the ways in which American Jewish women have been able to successfully integrate professional and family roles.

While most American Jews do not work within Jewish communal institutions, those institutions might nevertheless serve as forerunners in undertaking careful self-analyses by conducting family impact studies such as the one recently prepared by the American Jewish Committee's National Jewish Family Center to determine to what extent their policies and procedures are supportive or disruptive of family life and, where disruptive, how they might be changed to be supportive of wholesome family life in general and Jewish family life in particular. Grandiose as this recommendation may appear, it should be recalled that American Jewish organizations have a history of being in the vanguard of social change and have frequently been supportive of innovations which initially appeared as utopian.

Although there is a minority of opinion which argues, with respect to the fertility issue, that the significant element is quality rather than quantity and that therefore the low birth rate need not be a matter of concern, most survivalists agree that quantity is a prerequisite to quality because communal institutions are composed of people and the fertility outlook casts serious doubts on the ability of many American Jewish institutions to withstand impending depletion. Admonitions to increase the birth rate are met with resistance and opposition from many circles on both ideological and pragmatic grounds. Ecologists argue that having more than two children per couple is detrimental to the natural environment. Feminists argue that children are more of a burden to mothers than to fathers and that therefore profertility exhortations are inherently sexist. Beyond ideological sources of opposition, there is no escaping the reality of institutional arrangements in both American society as a whole and in the American Jewish community in particular, which render children a financial burden. A source of the low fertility of America's Jews may lie in the fact that to be part of the American Jewish community is a very expensive proposition. While synagogue membership is family membership and would cost no more for those with larger families, almost all the incidentals which go along with that membership involves greater expenditures for those with larger families. If we add only the increased cost for Jewish education, the expense becomes unbearable. A colleague in the Orthodox community remarked several years ago that day school tuitions have accomplished what zero-population-growth ideologists never would have — the decline of the modern Orthodox birth rate. This decline, apparent in Leff's (1974) survey of members of Young Israel synagogues (see also Mayer and Waxman, 1977), is more likely due to prohibitively heavy financial burdens than to an ideology of low fertility.

The problem is exacerbated by our ignorance of how to deal with the fertility issue even if the community had the resolve to take a profertility stance. While it is easy to point to any number of ways in which our communal organization inhibits an increase in the fertility rate, there is no evidence that changes in those arrangements would result in a higher birth rate. For example, while it seems reasonable to suggest that the absence of quality Jewish day-care facilities has a negative impact on the fertility rate, the experience in countries which do provide quality day care indicates that the birth rate has not increased accordingly, even in those countries which take an official profertility stance. The same is true for other social services in countries seeking to increase the birth rate. The birth rate continues to decline in the face of the expansion of social services. There is a universal inverse relationship between social class and fertility, with those who ostensibly have the greatest need for family policies having the largest families. Increasing the birth rate appears to involve much more than changing institutional arrangements to reduce economic burdens.

Goldscheider (1967, p. 207) has argued that minority status has been the source of the low birth rate among Jews: "The aspirations of Jews for social mobility, their desire for acceptance in American society, and the insecurity of their minority status tended to encourage small families." This suggests that if the American Jewish community wishes to increase its fertility rate, it must exert much stronger efforts at reducing the minority status and economic insecurity of American Jewry. Only when Jews have become more acculturated, integrated, and economically secure in American society will the birth rate increase. Yet the reality of the American Jewish experience indicates the reverse. American Jewry has been disproportionately successful economically, has become increasingly acculturated and integrated into American society, and the birth rate has continued to decline. The fertility rate is higher among the more highly Orthodox Jews, presumably less acculturated and less affluent than their less Orthodox and non-Orthodox coreligionists. In addition to urging adoption of a profertility stance by agencies, organizations, and institutions of the

American Jewish community, in coalition with other groups with similar interests, and instituting operating procedures reflecting that stance, research is needed on the sources of the low fertility rate and what can be done to reverse that trend.

As to the divorce rate, data is needed with respect to the actual rate. We should research such questions as discernible patterns of divorce, the nature of the relationship prior to divorce, the impact of involvement with the organized community on the divorce rate, and vice versa. This kind of information is required before there can be any realistic research on new approaches and the impact of communal preventive measures.

Some of these data are not too difficult to obtain, but an organized communal effort is a prerequisite. While we do not know what percent of those getting divorced avail themselves of the services of a rabbi, either for receiving a Jewish divorce, a *get*, or even for counseling, this population may be a good place to begin research on divorce. The major American Jewish religious groups have central rabbinic organizations, and several even have special departments dealing with divorce. Each might be approached by a sociologist to encourage them to maintain uniform records, so that they would be subsequently available for analysis. While those records would not reveal all that we seek to know about American Jewish divorce patterns, they would be a valuable beginning for a data bank. No great expenditures would be required to set up this initial data bank. The major requirement would be a record-keeping system and the training of those involved in gathering information.

Such records would also provide information on single-parent families. We might then be in a better position to study the important questions of the impact of being reared in a single-parent family upon the general and Jewish identity of children. For this we also need to explore ways of reducing the perceived alienation of single parents from the Jewish community. We would have to investigate the extent of that perception, whether the impact of prior involvement in the community is a significant variable, and whether that feeling of alienation is short or long range. I have made some preliminary suggestions for integrating single parents and their families within the Jewish community (Waxman, 1980), but much more attention, in terms of both research and policy, is called for.

The issue of intermarriage is the most difficult and complex of all those discussed in this chapter. Jewish identity involves more than self and more than group identity and identification — it involves very deep and personal religious issues (cf. Lichtenstein, 1977, 1978). I prefer to abstain from making policy recommendations on intermarriage. Much more extensive research is required, regardless of ideological proclivities, on the long-range impact of both conversional and mixed marriages on both spouses and children. The couple involved should be made fully aware of the potential religious and communal complications which may result from their marriage.

Returning to the basic issue of the lack of social-scientific data on the American Jewish family, it is recommended that proposals be made for systematizing the study of Jewish communities in the United States. Since many communities carry out periodic studies of their Jewish populations, careful planning is needed to coordinate and improve the level of this research. The time is ripe to begin discussion and work which would expand our knowledge of the American Jewish community and put all those concerned in a much better position to plan for the future of American Jewry. If a Jewish social research center at Brandeis can further this effort it will make an important contribution to knowledge and ultimately to Jewish communal policy.

Notes

* A section of this chapter appeared in somewhat different form as "The Threadbare Canopy: The Vicissitudes of the Jewish Family in Modern American Society," *American Behavioral Scientist* 23, no. 4 (March-April 1980), pp. 467–86. The gracious assistance of Cyma Horowitz, director of the Blaustein Library of the American Jewish Committee, is deeply appreciated.

1. A proposal for outreach similar to Mayer's was offered at the quarterly meeting of the board of the Union of American Hebrew Congregations on December 2, 1978, and made the front page of the *New York Times* the following day. (The proposal, together with reactions of four Jewish leaders and a discussion with a number of converts, appears in *Moment* (March 1979). Theodore Friedman (1979) has also published a number of articles recently in which he advocates a change in the Jewish stance toward conversion. There are quite a few Reform rabbis and a number of Conservative rabbis who do engage in conversionary outreach. But none of these represents an organized communal response.

References

Balswick, Jack. 1966. "Are American Jewish Families Close Knit? A Review of the Literature." *Jewish Social Studies* 27 (July): 159–69.

Barron, Milton C. 1946. *People Who Intermarry* (Syracuse: Syracuse University Press).

Berelson, Bernard. 1978. "Ethnicity and Fertility: What and So What." In Milton Himmelfarb and Victor Baras (eds.), *Zero Population Growth — For Whom? Differential Fertility and Minority Group Survival:* 74–118 (Westport: Greenwood Press).

Bergman, Elihu. 1977. "The American Jewish Population Erosion," *Midstream* 23 (October): 9–19.

Berman, Gerald S. 1976. "The Adaptable American Jewish Family: An Inconsistency in Theory," *Jewish Journal of Sociology* 18 (June): 5–16.

Chenkin, Alvin. 1972. "Demographic Highlights: Facts for Planning," *National Jewish Population Study* (New York: Council of Jewish Federations and Welfare Funds).

Chenkin, Alvin, and Maynard Miran. 1979. "Jewish Population in the United States, 1978." In Morris Fine and Milton Himmelfarb (eds.), *American Jewish Year Book* 79: 177–89 (New York and Philadelphia: American Jewish Committee and Jewish Publication Society of America).

Cohen, Steven M. 1978. "Will Jews Keep Giving: Prospects for the Jewish Charitable Community." Paper delivered at the Tenth Annual Conference of the Association for Jewish Studies (Boston, December 18).

Cohen, Steven M., and Paul Ritterband. 1981. "Why Contemporary American Jews Want Small Families: An Interreligious Comparison of College Graduates." In Paul Ritterband (ed.), *Modern Jewish Fertility* (Leiden: Brill).

Elazar, Daniel. 1976. *Community and Polity: The Organizational Dynamics of American Jewry* (Philadelphia: Jewish Publication Society of America).

Festinger, Leon. 1957. *Theory of Cognitive Dissonance* (New York: Harper & Row).

Fowler, Floyd J. 1977. *1975 Community Survey: A Study of the Jewish Population of Greater Boston* (Boston: Combined Jewish Philanthropies of Greater Boston).

Friedman, Theodore. 1979. "Jewish Proselytism: A New Look," *Forum* 34 (Winter): 31–38. A shorter version appeared, under the same title, in *Congress Monthly* 46 (June): 8–11.

Glazer, Nathan. 1972. *American Judaism,* 2nd ed. (Chicago: University of Chicago Press).

Goldberg, Nathan. 1968. "The Jewish Attitude toward Divorce." In Jacob Freid (ed.), *Jews and Divorce* (New York: Ktav).

Goldschieder, Calvin. 1967. "Fertility of the Jews," *Demography* 4 (no. 1): 196–209.

Goldscheider, Calvin. 1978. "Demography and American Jewish Survival." In Milton Himmelfarb and Victor Baras (eds.), *Zero Population Growth — For Whom?* (Westport: Greenwood Press).

Goldstein, Sidney. 1971. "American Jewry, 1970." In Morris Fine and Milton Himmelfarb (eds.), *American Jewish Year Book* 72: 3–88 (New York and Philadelphia: American Jewish Committee and Jewish Publication Society of America).

Goldstein, Sidney. 1981. "Jewish Fertility in Contemporary America." In Paul Ritterband (ed.), *Modern Jewish Fertility* (Leiden: Brill).

Goldstein, Sidney, and Calvin Goldscheider. 1968. *Jewish Americans* (Englewood Cliffs: Prentice-Hall).

Greeley, Andrew M. 1974. *Ethnicity in the United States* (New York: Wiley).

Greeley, Andrew M. 1977. *The American Catholic* (New York: Basic Books).

Jaffe, Frederick S. 1978. "Alarms, Excursions, and Delusions of Grandeur: Implicit Assumptions of Group Efforts to Alter Differential Fertility Trends." In Milton Himmelfarb and Victor Baras (eds.), *Zero Population Growth — For Whom?* (Westport: Greenwood Press).

Kobrin, Frances E., and Calvin Goldscheider. 1978. *The Ethnic Factor in Family Structure and Mobility* (Cambridge: Ballinger).

Kranzler, Gershon. 1978. "The Changing Orthodox Jewish Family," *Jewish Life* 3 (Summer-Fall): 23–36.

Kutzik, Alfred J. 1977. "The Roles of the Jewish Community and Family in Jewish Identification." Paper prepared for the American Jewish Committee, Jewish Communal Affairs Department (mimeographed).

Lasch, Christopher. 1977. *Haven in a Heartless World* (New York: Basic Books).

Lazerwitz, Bernard, 1971. "Intermarriage and Conversion: A Guide for Future Research," *Jewish Journal of Sociology* 13 (June): 41–63.

Leff, Bertram A. 1974. "The Modern Orthodox Jew: Acculturation and Religious Identification" (M.A. thesis, Adelphi University).

Lenski, Gerhard. 1961. *The Religious Factor* (Garden City: Doubleday).

Lichtenstein, Aharon. 1977. "Patterns of Contemporary Jewish *Hizdahut* (Self-Identification)." In Moshe Davis (ed.), *World Jewry and the Jewish State* (New York: Arno).

Lichtenstein, Aharon. 1978. "Of Jewish Identity and Unity: The Halakhic Perspective," *Congress Monthly* 45 (March-April): 4–8.

Liebman, Charles S. 1979. "Leadership and Decision-Making in a Jewish Federation: The New York Federation of Jewish Philanthropies." In Morris Fine and Milton Himmelfarb (eds.), *American Jewish Year Book* 79: 3–76 (New York and Philadelphia: American Jewish Committee and Jewish Publication Society of America).

Luckmann, Benita. 1970. "The Small Worlds of Modern Man," *Social Research* 37 (Winter): 580–96.

Massarik, Fred. 1973. "Intermarriage: Facts for Planning," *National Jewish Population Study* (New York: Council of Jewish Federations and Welfare Funds).

Massarik, Fred. 1978. "Rethinking the Intermarriage Crisis," *Moment* 3 (June): 29–33.

Mayer, Egon. 1978. *Patterns of Intermarriage among American Jews* (New York: American Jewish Committee, Jewish Communal Affairs Department).

Mayer, Egon. 1979a. "Intermarriage among American Jews: Consequences, Prospects, and Policies," *Policy Studies* 79 (New York: National Jewish Conference Center, February 15).

Mayer, Egon. 1979b. "A Cure for Intermarriage?" *Moment* 4 (June): 62–64.

Mayer, Egon, and Carl Sheingold. 1979. *Intermarriage and the Jewish Future: A National Study in Summary* (New York: American Jewish Committee, Institute of Human Relations).

Mayer, Egon, and Chaim I. Waxman. 1977. "Modern Jewish Orthodoxy in America: Toward the Year 2000," *Tradition* 16 (Spring): 98–111.

Mitchell, William E. 1978. *Mishpokhe: A Study of New York City Jewish Family Clubs* (The Hague: Mouton).

Moment Magazine. 1979. "The Issue Is Conversion," *Moment* 4 (March): 17–35.

Morgan, T.B. 1964. "The Vanishing American Jew," *Look* (May 5): 42 ff.

Phillips, Bruce. 1980. *Los Angeles Jewish Community Survey: Overview for Regional Planning* (Los Angeles: Jewish Federation — Council of Greater Los Angeles).

Postal, Bernard. 1979. "Postal Card," *The Jewish Week* (March 11).

Rosenberg, Bernard, and Norman D. Humphrey. 1955. "The Secondary Nature of Primary Groups," *Social Research* 22 (Spring): 25–38.

Rosenthal, Erich. 1963. "Studies of Jewish Intermarriage in the United States." In Morris Fine and Milton Himmelfarb (eds.), *American Jewish Year Book* 64: 3–53 (New York and Philadelphia: American Jewish Committee and Jewish Publication Society of America).

Singer, David. 1979. "Living with Intermarriage," *Commentary* 68 (July): 48–53.

Sklare, Marshall. 1964. "Intermarriage and the Jewish Future," *Commentary* 37 (April): 46–52.

Sklare, Marshall. 1970. "Intermarriage and Jewish Survival," *Commentary* 49 (March): 51–58.

Sklare, Marshall. 1971. *America's Jews* (New York: Random House).

Sklare, Marshall, and Joseph Greenblum. 1979. *Jewish Identity on the Suburban Frontier,* 2nd ed. (Chicago: University of Chicago Press).

Smolar, Boris. 1979. "Easy Marriages Bring Easy Splits: Jews in the 1 in 3 Divorce Scene," *New Brunswick Jewish Journal* (March 8).

Span, Paula. 1979. "Half-Jews: Sooner or Later the Children Grow Up," *Present Tense* 6 (Summer): 49–52.

Spiegel, Irving. 1974. "Rabbi Deplores Small Families," *New York Times* (January 24): 40.

Sussman, Marvin B. 1978. "The Family Today: Is It an Endangered Species?" *Children Today* 7 (March-April): 32–37, 45.

United States Bureau of the Census. 1958. "Religion by Civilian Population of the United States." *Current Population Reports,* series P-20, no. 79 (February).

Vitz, Paul C. 1977. *Psychology as Religion: The Cult of Self-Worship* (Grand Rapids: Eerdmans).

Waxman, Chaim I. 1977. "Perspectives on the Family and Jewish Identity in America" (New York: American Jewish Committee, Jewish Communal Affairs Department).

Waxman, Chaim I., 1977–78. "Psalms of a Sober Man: The Sociology of Marshall Sklare," *Contemporary Jewry* 4 (Fall-Winter): 3–11.

Waxman, Chaim I. 1979. *Task Force Report on Jewish Family Policy* (New York: American Jewish Committee, Jewish Communal Affairs Department).

Waxman, Chaim I. 1980. *Single-Parent Families: Challenge to the Jewish Community* (New York: American Jewish Committee, National Jewish Family Center).

Westerman, Jacqueline. 1967. "Note on Balswick's Article: A Response," *Jewish Social Studies* 29 (October): 241–44.

Winch, Robert F., Scott Greer, and Rae Lesser Blumberg. 1967. "Ethnicity and Familism in an Upper Middle-Class Suburb," *American Sociological Review* 32 (April): 265–62.

7.

The Jewish Community as a Polity

Daniel J. Elazar

There is every prospect that the 1980s will prove to be the decade in which systematic Jewish political research comes into its own, just as the 1970s brought the burgeoning of systematic Jewish sociological research. This is not the place to discuss the reasons why this is likely. Let us consider what should be done systematically in the realm of American Jewish political research — the structure and organization of the Jewish community, its functions and political dynamics, and its public affairs.

Elsewhere I have discussed Jewish political studies as a field of inquiry in some detail (Elazar 1974b). What do we mean when we define "Jewish political studies" as a field, and what are its concerns? Politics is concerned with both power and justice — who gets what, when, and how (in the words of Harold Lasswell), and the search for the good political order. Jews share these concerns when they function as a corporate body as well as in their individual capacities. Political or public concerns are those involving the community as a whole, the collective interests of people living in the community, activities in society that have a communal bent or character, and the concerns of individuals insofar as they relate to community life and interests. While acknowledgement of some distinction between public and private concerns is crucial, no sharp division between the two spheres can ever be drawn, even for reasons of convention. Jewish life can be conceived as revolving around a core of political concerns, e.g., the life of the community or the provision of certain public services, surrounded by concentric circles of concern that move out toward the private realm and into a gray area of matters than can be considered "public" for some purposes, and "private" for others.

The delineation of Jewish political studies raises certain additional problems by virtue of its Jewish aspect. In the Western world, where the separation between public and private starts from firmly established premises and the political and religious aspects of life are separated with equal clarity, public affairs are resolved into questions of the immediately or essentially political. Within the framework of Jewish civilization, distinctions

186

between public and private, political and religious, are blurred. The lack of clearly political institutions to help set the formal boundaries of public affairs (at least in the diaspora) requires examination of Jewish social and communal life with a more careful and penetrating eye. Our knowledge of things political gives us an advantage over preceding generations. Social scientists have discovered in Afro-Asian cultures blurrings of public and private, political and religious matters similar to those found in Jewish life, that give us some new points of comparison (Easton, 1953; Almond and Coleman, 1960; Dahl, 1963; Macridis and Brown, 1968).

While Jewish political studies have only recently begun to develop a literature of their own, many of the questions dealing with their purview of concern have been discussed, directly or obliquely, by social scientists, historians, and theologians. Critical examinations of relevant works in these categories published since the mid-1960s have been published in the *American Jewish Year Book* on a regular basis (Elazar, 1967, 1969a, 1972b; Waller, 1975, 1977). An overview of the literature of Jewish public affairs (Burke, 1970) and an initial bibliography of relevant titles (Siegal, 1970) have been made available through the Center for Jewish Community Studies.

A series of studies of aspects of the Jewish political tradition has appeared recently under the auspices of Workshop on Covenant and the Jewish Political Tradition jointly sponsored by Bar Ilan University and the Center for Jewish Community Studies. Topics dealt with include preliminary observations on the Jewish political tradition (Elazar, 1979), the theocracy question (Belfer, 1978), Jewish political theory (Susser and Don Yihye, 1978), covenant as the basis of the Jewish political tradition (Elazar, 1978c), and rabbinic conceptions of covenant (Freeman, 1981). A multiauthored volume presenting an overview of the subject is presently in press (Elazar, 1981).

The subject matter of Jewish political studies falls into three major divisions: Jewish political institutions and behavior, Jewish political thought, and Jewish public affairs. A variety of areas of concern can be identified on the basis of those divisions as reflected in current literature: Jewish political thought; religious movements, ideologies, and public persuasions; defining the boundaries of Jewish society; Jewish political culture; Jewish political behavior; Jewish political organization; Jewish public law; Jewish political and communal institutions; Jewish organizations and interest groups; civic education; public personalities; Israel; subdivisions of the Jewish people; country, community, and area studies; intercommunity relations; external relations; the course of Jewish public affairs; contemporary issues; and research approaches and methods. This division into subfields offers a way to frame the questions of Jewish political research under contemporary conditions of Jewish political life. Not all of these are of concern to us here; we shall focus on a few of them.

Religious movements, ideologies, and public persuasions reflect that point of contact between abstract political ideas and realities of the Jewish community. Historically, divisions in the Jewish community that have maintained the diffusion of power among many centers have been derived from movements that emerged to embody the different understandings of common theopolitical ideas in the real world. In the United States, regardless of the significance of Jewish thought in the larger framework of Jewish public affairs, the public life of the American Jewish community has been oriented toward its religious movements as the institutional embodiments of the public persuasions of American Jews.

The term *public persuasions* is used advisedly. While religion in America is commonly conceived to be primarily concerned with the private sphere, institutionalized Jewish religion is a reflection of public persuasions rather than personal behavior or belief. Only a small percentage of Jews formally affiliated with Jewish religious movements conduct their private lives according to the patterns prescribed by their movement. Institutional affiliation reflects public commitments Jews wish to make, more than the state of their personal lives as Jews. This subfield concerns itself empirically with communal manifestations of ideologies and persuasions as well as their intellectual abstract religious meaning.

The problem of *defining the boundaries of Jewish society* is a particularly modern one in Jewish history. The question of who is a Jew is raised in every corner of the Jewish world today, where freedom of choice is not only a theoretical phenomenon but an immediately practical reality faced almost daily by millions of Jews. The Jewish community of today consists of many ill-defined concentric circles shading out from a central core of fully committed Jews through the progressively less committed and into a gray area where people's very Jewishness is no longer clear (Elazar, 1976a). From the perspective of Jewish political studies, this is a problem insofar as it concerns the corporate behavior of the Jewish community, whether in determining participation, tasks, or official attitudes.

The problem of defining the boundaries of the Jewish people has been complicated by the addition of a new phenomenon in the post–World War II era — conversion to Judaism, raising the question of communal "citizenship" in new ways. These factors, coupled with the reestablishment of the Jewish state, have transformed the problem into a political as well as a legal or "religious" one, with considerations of the status of religious movements involved and the political arena within which crucial decisions are made (Liebman, 1978b).

Political culture — the underlying pattern of orientations toward politics, the community, and public issues — is one of the most significant factors shaping the responses of Jews to the needs, demands, and problems of Jewish public life. The study of Jewish political culture has barely begun.

The classic Zionist view, presented with great force in the last two generations, is that Jews existed for seventeen centuries as political objects because they were stateless — political slaves of majorities in the various
countries in the diaspora. More recent studies, including our own, strongly
take issue with this view and document the ways in which the Jewish people remained politically alive in the diaspora (Schorsch, 1976). In the process, a Jewish political culture was kept alive. Among the elements of the
dominant political culture among Jews, are, in Milton Himmelfarb's
words, "an actively positive attitude toward society and community, growing out of their life in their own society and community; and potentially
positive attitude toward government, growing out of a Jewish tradition that
affirms the worth of government and out of their strong feelings for the social and communal." Himmelfarb (1965) concludes that even during their
exclusion from the political life of their host countries, the Jews were "already civic," and simply "wanted to be citizens." Pursuing the idea of political culture in a different direction, Herman Israel (1966) has argued
that Jewish tradition, by its very nature, promotes the limitation and diffusion of authority, and that the social organization of modern Western society is a direct result of the influence of biblical concepts on the Puritans,
first in England and then in the United States and elsewhere. These points
suggest the lines of inquiry in this subfield.

Jewish political culture leads directly to certain kinds of political behavior, both within the Jewish community and in relationship to the larger society. The way Jews conduct the business of their own communities is one
aspect of the study of Jewish political behavior. Quite different but equally
a part of this subfield is the way in which Jews as a group relate to the
larger political scene in the societies of their residence. Voting studies,
community power studies, and group interaction studies dominate this subfield.

In recent years there has been an increase in scholarly efforts to understand the nature of *Jewish political organization*, both past and contemporary. This concern, much of which emanates from Israel, reflects a
transcending of the Zionist view that Jews had no political life except in an
independent state of their own. Contemporary studies explore the varieties
of Jewish political organization during periods of independence, autonomy,
and even nominal nonexistence.

Writings on the political organization of the American Jewish community pose difficulties unprecedented in the literature of earlier Jewish communal experience. There is an absence of significant research into the
operation of the organized Jewish community in the United States. Most
published materials are collections of simple demographic data, catalogues
of the numerous organizations and their interconnections, or polemical
works discussing immediate problems of organized Jewish life. The occa-

sional pieces going beyond these categories are almost invariably historical accounts (e.g. Gartner, 1975).

A major share of the attention given to Jewish public affairs throughout Jewish history has focused on institutions serving the public welfare in various assistance, relief, and rehabilitation capacities. In our own time, the work of these institutions has often constituted the major share of Jewish public affairs in the diaspora, and their problems are therefore of special import in the study of Jewish public affairs.

Jewish public law, once a major consideration of Talmudists in another context, fell into a state of disrepair with Jewish emancipation and the destruction of the last remaining corporate Jewish communities in the diaspora. Today, outside of Israel, students and scholars at best devote themselves to laws regarding the status of Jews within the general community (Elazar and Goldstein, 1972), but even this is confined to a relatively small group. In Israel there is a revival of concern with Jewish public law as many Israelis, both in the religious camp and outside, seek to find ways to build the law of the new state upon Jewish jurisprudential precedents (Blidstein, 1981; Elon, 1981; Gartner, 1968). Current work in this subfield reflects the search for ways and means to adapt Talmudic precedents to contemporary situations.

One of the major functions of Jewish educational institutions is to foster *civic education*. In the United States, the increased interest of Jewish welfare federations in Jewish education is in direct proportion to federation leaders' concern with the problems of civic education of a new generation of Jews. A particular problem is lack of commitment by the younger generation of Jews, a commitment necessary for the continuation of the federations' operations and of their related agencies and programs. Civic education, whether defined as the kind of "Torah education" designed to produce an Orthodox "citizen," or the kind of peoplehood-oriented education of other groups, ranks very high on the agenda of Jewish public affairs today.

Concern for civic education extends deeply into matters of curriculum. Zalman Slesinger (1965) has suggested eight major fields of social studies concern in the American Jewish community: structure and dynamics of the American Jewish community, unity in diversity (intracommunal pluralism), preserving tradition, relations with Israel, maintaining Jewish society in the United States, community leadership, community finance, and the Jews' role in general public affairs.

The study of Jewish public affairs would be incomplete without reference to the powerful and not-so-powerful *public personalities* who are the leaders of the Jewish community. Biographies of such leaders that look toward an understanding of the sources and uses of their power must necessarily occupy a significant place in the field. Such works are rare enough.

While all topics of concern in the field of Jewish political studies also include the Israeli dimension, the special place occupied by Israel in the structure of Jewish civilization puts the State of Israel in a special category. Analysis of Israel's political institutions and processes in light of the voluntaristic origin of the country's settlement leads to the conclusion that the state's political background is not merely a product of Eastern European culture, but also a direct outgrowth of the autonomous Jewish *kehillah* with its congregational, republican, and federal principles which for many generations provided the training ground for Jewish political leaders and ultimately influenced those who became Israel's leaders (Baeck, 1965; Elazar, 1980). The dilemmas of contemporary Israeli politics are at least partly rooted in the contradictions between the foreign ideological institutions brought from Eastern Europe and the political culture of the Jewish people.

Subdivisions of the Jewish people: The Jewish people are divided organizationally and sociologically along several lines. Under the system of political organization developed early in Jewish history, the local community or congregation became, and has remained, the foundation of Jewish communal life. Local communities have grouped together in different ways at different times, depending on external circumstances. From these groupings emerged the major worldwide religious-cultural bifurcation into Sephardim and Ashkenazim, and regional cultural divisions such as "German" and "Polish" Jews, "Litvaks" and "Galitzianer," Yemenites and Moroccans. With the rise of the modern nation-state, countrywide groupings of local communities have taken on historical permanence and legal status that mark one from the other within the overall "confederation" of Jewries. Each of these Jewries requires study from the political perspective. Such studies usually fall within the category of specific Jewish communities on the countrywide, local, and regional levels. The character of the material available is varied, ranging from casual travelers' reports to serious social science studies of the organized Jewish communities in most parts of the world. Data on the United States is best, while material on the smaller countries of Asia, Africa, and Latin America is sparse indeed. To date, there is not even a proper bibliography of what exists.

Intercommunity relations: An aspect of Jewish public affairs commanding growing attention is the relationship between the various Jewish communities in the world (Stock, 1975b), particularly between Israel and the diaspora (Liebman, 1975, 1977; Stock, 1972), between the United States and smaller diaspora communities (Elazar, 1977a), and the problem of the relationship between Soviet and world Jewry. To date, most attention has been paid to the first and last of these.

External relations: Traditionally, one of the most important concerns in Jewish public affairs has been relations between the Jewish people and the rest of the world. This has been so significant that it has become common-place to think that all political concerns of Jews are wrapped up in the problems inherent in these external relations. This is emphatically not the case. Nevertheless, the importance attached to this problem is reflected in the sheer volume of written and published material about it. Discussion of the place of the Jewish people in the modern world has been recurring for two centuries or more. Mala Tabory and Charles Liebman have prepared a book-length annotated bibliography on Jewish corporate involvement in the international arena since the Congress of Vienna in 1815. This should serve as a major introduction to this aspect of Jewish political research and as a model for such works.

Concern with *contemporary public issues* is part and parcel of the field. Jewish public policy is a matter of interest as the point at which the theoretical and the practical meet. This may range from problems of Jewish unity to poverty in the Jewish community.

Delayed Emergence of the Field

The emergence of Jewish political studies as a systematic field of inquiry has been a relatively late development in modern Jewish scholarship for both historical and ideological reasons. The founders of the scientific study of Judaism in the nineteenth century thought they were giving the Jewish "corpse" an honorable burial by studying its past achievements and glories to leave a record of Jewish civilization for future generations. As such, they were eager to put forward Judaism's "best face" as they understood it, which meant ignoring aspects of Jewish civilization which ran contrary to the spirit of their age. For them, the science of Judaism was a tool for the advancement of Jewish emancipation; they used the past as a basis for justifying their own right of entry into the host societies in which they resided. Any "unpleasant" elements in Jewish history and tradition were to be ignored or downplayed, whether kabbalah or, more important for our purposes, the autonomous existence of Jewish communities in the diaspora.

The presentation of the Jewish people as a state within a state, maintaining its own law, organization, institutions, and politics did not serve the image which emancipationist Jews wished to project. Hence that dimension of Jewish life was downplayed considerably. The view of Jews as impotent in the years in which they did not possess citizenship in their countries of residence, was a desideratum and was emphasized and reemphasized. Thus the foundations for modern Jewish studies were laid in such a way as to reflect the ideological biases of the emancipationists and create a historical base which denied the reality of Jewish polity. This had to be overcome to recover the sense of the Jewish people as an *edah* — in its original meaning of a constitutionally assembled community rather than in its later sense of a religious congregation.[1]

While American Jewry was not directly affected by the scholarly currents of the *judische Wissenschaft*, American Jews shared its emancipationist biases and, because of the possibilities inherent in the American experience, were even more prone to simply forget about the autonomous political basis of Jewish communal life. Yet because integration into the United States was relatively easy, American Jewry emerged without any built-in resistance to viewing the Jewish people as a polity and, as time and tides shifted, have proven capable of dealing with both the real history of the Jewish experience in that respect and with the character of contemporary Jewry as a political phenomenon.

One of the results of the earlier American Jewish experience was a neglect of the study of organized Jewish life. American Jewish scholarship begins with filiopietistic history, an attempt to discover the involvement of American Jews in the American experience of nation building at the critical junctures of American history. By its very nature, that history looked to the role of individual Jews, particularly in the Colonial period or in connection with participation in America's wars. Organizational matters were treated only to the extent of examining the founding of congregations, so as to demonstrate that Jews did have an organized presence in the American colonies and states beginning in the colonial period. But this was a secondary matter and focused on the introduction of Jewish cemeteries and congregational worship, not on the organization of congregational institutions. For example, none of the standard histories are particularly interested in when the Jews of New York City ceased to be simply a *minyan* and began to function as a *kahal kadosh*. At best there is some interest in when the first building of Shearith Israel was built. Only when it comes to nineteenth-century foundings, where matters are clear in and of themselves, do we get the records that combine both.

Filiopietistic history subsequently developed into more serious historical studies, although only in the past decade have there been studies even by noted historians which have begun to emancipate themselves from a strong antiquarian dimension.[2] Few of them have focused on questions of organization. Rather, they have sought to link with another trend that had emerged in the interim — the sociological study of Jews (as distinct from Jewry or the Jewish community).

Beginning in the 1940s, the contemporary condition of Jews in America became the object of research interest. Marshall Sklare (1958) was not only the pioneer in developing this interest, but was the only one to look at Jews in a systematic, comprehensive way. For most other researchers, more specific subjects became the focus of their interest, whether Jewish demography, religious practices or beliefs, or Jewish affiliation. The starting point was the individual Jew; the attempt was made to see how the individual Jew related to Judaism or Jewishness and only marginally to the

Jewish community. Even community studies focused on the aggregate of individual Jews and paid almost no attention to Jewish community organization. As a new generation of historians began to look beyond antiquarian concerns, they too adopted this approach.

The only work done within American Jewry that contributed to the understanding of the organized Jewish community (beyond the minimum of background provided by sociological and historical studies) was a few insiders' books produced by Jewish organizational professionals to describe the object of their life's work. The *Journal of Jewish Communal Service* was a major outlet for this kind of consideration of Jewish organizational matters, particularly in social service fields and, to some extent, in Jewish education and fund-raising. Beginning in the 1920s, surveys of specific Jewish communal services were undertaken by the staffs of countrywide Jewish social service and educational agencies at the behest of local community agencies.[3] The latter's aim was analyzing particular services in an effort to improve them, not undertaking organizational studies in an academic sense. Nevertheless, they were the first systematic efforts in the field and remain important sources for the contemporary researcher.

In the meantime, beginnings were being made in the Jewish world as a whole toward examining the larger question of the Jewish people as a polity. These beginnings were inevitably related to the development of Zionism. Zionist polemic viewed Jewish history through emancipationist eyes, as the story of Jewish abandonment of the political arena for "two thousand years," adding further justification for the Zionist effort to return Jews to that arena.

The Zionist idea produced a generation of scholars, principally historians, imbued with a sense of the Zionist mission but who went far beyond the polemics of Zionist politics. These historians, led by Yitzhak (Fritz) Baer and Ben Zion Dinur, founded a new "school" of Jewish history at the Hebrew University, beginning in the late 1920s.[4] Contrary to the Zionist polemic, their work focused on the way in which Jews had organized themselves into autonomous communities in the years of exile and preserved a corporate Jewish life throughout that period. Through painstaking but clearly directed research, these Zionist historians restored a picture of autonomous Jewish communal life in the years between the destruction of the second temple and emancipation. After the establishment of the State of Israel, they were joined by students of Jewish jurisprudence, principally under the leadership of Menachem Elon, who extended the investigation to Jewish public law and the legal basis for communal governance, principally through an exploration of the *responsa* literature.[5]

In the United States, a more modest but parallel manifestation of the same phenomenon is represented by scattered articles, many of which originated as term papers by former yeshivah students who sought to synthesize their academic and traditional studies (Golding, 1966; Israel, 1966). Ben Halpern applied Zionist criteria and the Zionist sense of Jewish peoplehood to the study of contemporary Jewish history and the American Jewish community (Halpern, 1956). By 1960, the stage was set for a more focused effort.

First Steps

The first sociologists of American Jewry have already been mentioned. To the extent that they attempted to provide a larger view of individual Jewish communities or movements, thereby reintroducing their audiences to the idea that the Jews functioned in some respects in organized ways, their work was a precursor of the restoration of concern with Jewish organizational life. However, because it was not their purpose to focus on the organizational dimension, their role in this regard was limited and their heirs did not pick up on the comprehensive or systemic view, but turned to further exploration of individual dimensions of Jewish behavior.

Beginning in the 1960s, a number of younger political scientists began to concern themselves with questions and politics of Jewish organizations and life (Elazar, 1961). Younger classical Jewish scholars became interested in the political dimensions of Jewish history and classic Jewish texts (Blidstein, 1973a, b).

During the 1968–69 academic year, several of those who had been moving in this direction came together to undertake what may have been the first systematic worldwide study of organized Jewish community life in the contemporary world. This study was initially commissioned by the Institute of Jewish Affairs of the World Jewish Congress and cosponsored by the Center for the Study of Federalism of Temple University. After 1970, it became the first project of the then newly organized Jewish Community Studies Group, precursor of the Center for Jewish Community Studies. It was designed to map the structures, functions, and institutional dynamics of all the organized Jewish communities in the world, or at least as many as possible given limited funds. In the course of a decade, all of the larger countrywide Jewish communities in the world have been mapped (see Appendix A for list of studies completed and published). Most of the largest, such as the United States (Elazar, 1976a), Canada (Waller and Elazar, 1981), and France (Greilsamer and Salzberg, 1978), have been studied in depth. Many smaller communities have been mapped as well. This study has not only produced a number of individual products, but has served to expand the network of researchers working in the field, developing some basic research methodologies and strategies.

With the emergence of the Jewish state, the study of its political system generated interest among political scientists and others (Bernstein, 1957;

Eisenstadt, 1968; Fein, 1967; Horowitz and Lissak, 1978). To the extent that the State of Israel can be considered an organized Jewish community, there is a linkage between those studies and the topic at hand (Avineri, 1972; Elazar, 1978). Political scientists studying Israel's political system viewed it from a strictly political science perspective, as they would any other nation-state, applying the same methodologies and models and ignoring any consideration of Israel's possible relationship to a Jewish political tradition. The first works on the subject in English tended to be quite formalistic, following a style of political science rapidly going out of fashion in the profession.

In academic journals and in a few selected volumes (Avineri, 1972) there was an effort to apply more current political science methodologies and techniques to the study of the Israeli polity; there, too, almost exclusively without reference to any specifically Jewish dimension other than the fact that Israel had been established as a homeland for Jews. Only in the 1970s was some effort made to bridge this gap, mostly by the same people who had been involved in the development of Jewish political studies generally (Penniman, 1979).

In the 1970s, these efforts to study the Jews as a community began to find an audience. The restoration of Jewish political life as a result of the Zionist revolution and creation of the State of Israel led to a revival of Jewish concern with matters political in the diaspora as well. This revival was resisted as long as emancipationist ideologies remained strong and the task of integrating into host societies remained preeminent. Nevertheless it began to grow as a result of certain realities, the principal being the State of Israel and demands made upon Jews everywhere to mobilize politically in its support.

The development of organized Jewish communal life in the United States is intimately wrapped up with the emergence of Israel as the main item on the American Jewish agenda. The emergence of local Jewish federations, the Council of Jewish Federations, and the UJA as preeminent instruments of American Jewry in its corporate capacity, and the growth of the role of local Jewish community relations councils relative to that of the old-line community relations agencies are both intimately connected with their roles vis-à-vis Israel (Elazar, 1976a). The events of 1967 and 1973 did their share (Davis, 1974; Stock, 1975a).

The first half of the post–World War II generation was devoted to completion of Jewish entry into American society, making any considerations of Jewish separateness outside of the religious sphere subordinate. (This was the heyday of the period denying that there was such a thing as a Jewish vote, despite such phenomena as 90 percent plus for FDR in Jewish neighborhoods.) By the 1960s, American Jews were sufficiently integrated to begin to respond to new ethnic stirrings, stimulated in part by the Black civil rights movement. These phenomena, coming together with the Six-Day war and its aftermath as well as a certain disillusionment with the American dream, especially among youth, due to the all-embracing source of moral values which resulted from the Vietnam war, opened the door to more active political expression on the part of Jews as Jews. As is usually the case, scholarship began to follow the headlines.

The phenomenon as a whole represented an almost total reversal of emancipationist dicta. The statement of Haskala poet J.L. Gordon that a Jew should be a Jew in his home and a man in the street gave way to just the reverse. Jews who no longer knew how to be Jews in their homes were willing to go out and demonstrate politically in the streets on behalf of Jewish causes: Israel, Soviet Jewry, and the like — causes that were unequivocally political in nature. The leadership of Jewish organizations, particularly federations in the United States and their networks, including the UJA, became increasingly aware of the political character of what they were doing, although there is still a certain ambivalence about recognizing that fact. The reconstitution of the Jewish Agency at the end of the 1960s added to this politicized climate, as key American Jewish leaders for the first time were thrown into a clearly Jewish political situation (Liebman, 1975; Stock, 1972). The groundwork was laid for developing scholarly concern with organizational and political matters.

Systematic Efforts

Three strands can be identified as having developed into systematic efforts. While most sociologists remained concerned with the Jews as individuals or as aggregates but not collectivities, a few began to move over into the field of Jewish organizational research. This is perhaps the least well developed strand of the three.

Early in the 1970s, a small group of scholars trained in policy research developed an interest in the Jewish field. An outstanding example of systematic effort of this kind was that undertaken by the Institute for Jewish Policy Planning and Research under the direction of Ira Silverman. In the few years of its existence as an independent body, the Institute began to develop serious policy research which examined organizational matters and policy issues within the Jewish community. Its publication *Analysis* was widely hailed as an important contribution to understanding contemporary Jewish life.

The initial success of the Institute for Jewish Policy Planning and Research in attracting the sponsorship of the Synagogue Council of America and its role in bringing the latter at least partially into the limelight of American life, is testimony to what a policy research program can do even in a community that is not geared to such matters. Personnel changes in the Institute and the Synagogue Council contributed to its demise, particularly in the latter case where new leadership was unable to recognize the value of such research and was fearful of its costs and controversial character. The major drawback to research on contemporary Jewish policy problems is that in a community dedicated to submerging controversy wherever possible, policy research by its very nature is likely to get involved in controversial matters. So, too, with regard to organizational research. It is much easier to study questions of Jewish demography or identity, behind which there is general agreement in Jewish ranks regarding what is desirable and undesirable, than to get involved in policy matters such as synagogue-federation relations, the federation allocation process, or the role of the rabbi.

Within the Jewish world most policy research has revolved around Israeli issues. Perhaps the most extensive effort of this kind has been that launched by a group of laymen and directed by Steven Spiegel of UCLA and a Fellow of the Center for Jewish Community Studies to prepare policy papers dealing with matters affecting Israel. It has produced a large number of such papers, many of which have been circulated to policymakers in various arenas and some of which have been published in major journals of opinion such as *Commentary*. This effort has not supported original research, but has provided modest honoraria to induce scholars to prepare papers for a specialized audience based upon knowledge already gained. Even these papers have dealt principally with external factors affecting Israel rather than with Israel itself.

The third strand emphasizes the study of the contemporary Jewish community as part of the continuing political history and tradition of the Jewish people. It grows out of the discipline of political science and views Jewish political studies as a legitimate area of study within that discipline as well as an aspect of Jewish studies. The Center for Jewish Community Studies has provided the major focal point for that effort, and its Fellows represent the major portion of those engaged in it. The Center evolved from the group which came together in connection with the worldwide study of Jewish community organization. Recognizing their common interest in the study of the organized Jewish community, present and past, and in Jewish public affairs, in 1970 they and other like-minded scholars formed the Jewish Community Studies Group as an academic consortium. As the work of the consortium expanded, its Fellows concluded that further institutionalization was necessary and reorganized as the Center for Jewish Community Studies in 1972. The Center has its headquarters in Jerusalem, maintains a major office in Philadelphia at Temple University, and other offices in Montreal and Paris.

The Center and its Fellows have launched research projects in a wide variety of fields. In addition to the initial mapping project, they include a study of the American synagogue as a major element in the organized Jewish community and as an organization itself; studies of Israeli-diaspora relations, policy studies dealing with various current issues on the American, Israeli, and world Jewish agendas, and an exploration of Jewish political tradition (see Appendix A). Today, the CJCS is the only academic institute with a central commitment to the study of Jewish public policy. The Center is also involved in preparing materials for Jewish civic education in the United States, Israel, and Latin America.

Of related interest is research being done under the auspices of the School of Jewish Communal Service of the Hebrew Union College-Jewish Institute of Religion in Los Angeles. Candidates for masters' degrees must prepare theses on topics which often fall within the purview of Jewish political studies. The body of work produced over the past decade, while of mixed quality (some theses are first-rate), represents the largest single resource of studies of local community institutions, functions, and policies available. The emphasis of the School of Jewish Communal Service reflects the emergence of a Jewish communal organization profession parallel to Jewish political studies as a discipline and the relationship between the two. Characteristic of this third approach is its academic commitment to the study of the Jewish people as a corporate entity in every age, not simply as part of contemporary Jewish studies. It speaks for a discipline, not simply an area or policy interest.

What Has Been Done and What Needs to Be Done

Studies of Individual Organizations

With the exception of a few historical studies which, because they were sponsored by the organizations involved, did not probe beneath the surface (Agar, 1970; Cohen, 1972), there have been no systematic studies of individual Jewish organizations in the United States. The two organizations best served have been the American Jewish Committee and the American Jewish Joint Distribution Committee, with the former being somewhat more open to scholarly critique but, even so, limited in what it will support in that regard. B'nai B'rith and the Council of Jewish Federations have had books written about them, but none are more than highly selective insiders' views of organizational activities for a particular period. A number of local institutions have been the subject of memoirs or reminiscences, in some cases composite in character, which offer raw material for an organizational study in the same way that the studies of countrywide organizations do. But that is not the same as a systematic study. There are also a few doctoral dissertations which are organizational studies of specific organizations or institutions. The greatest single source of research is the library of masters' theses developed at the HUC-JIR School of Jewish Communal Service.

This is as close to a virgin field as there exists in the world of social research. There is hardly a Jewish organization in the United States that could not be considered a target for study. What is needed, first of all, is a proper sense of what is to be studied, going beyond historical treatments to look at these organizations as social and even political entities. The field is so vast that it is necessary to establish a set of priorities.

The task is made additionally complex by the fact that many of the most interesting organizations are also the most difficult to study. For example, the American Israel Public Affairs Committee (AIPAC) would offer the opportunity for a fascinating study of the organizational mechanics of the "Jewish lobby." The work of AIPAC has been studied along with other elements of the Jewish lobby by political scientists looking at the interplay of interests in Washington, but it has never been studied as a component of the organized Jewish community or as an organization structured around a loose network of community leaders. In all likelihood, those who have access to the information would not be willing to expose the full story to the public, even the scholarly public, for good and sufficient reasons. Much the same would be true in the case of the Conference of Presidents of Major Jewish Organizations. But there is no reason why the national community relations organizations cannot be studied thoroughly with profit.

The various countrywide coordinating bodies, such as the National Jewish Welfare Board and the American Association for Jewish Education, could also be studied and each would provide its own kind of payoff in understanding the American Jewish community. The Council of Jewish Federations (CJF) has benefited from Harry Lurie's insider's study, *A Heritage Affirmed*, but as an organization it remains to be systematically examined. This is an appropriate time to do so, given that the CJF has recently completed a major review of its purposes, structure, and functions whose recommendations are now being implemented. The review committee interviewed some 1,200 people around the country, including all major Jewish leaders, regarding the CJF, its operations, and role in the American Jewish community. While use of this data is likely to be restricted, the very fact of the study can be a starting point for a more scholarly effort.

Similar studies are needed of individual federations, community relations councils, bureaus of Jewish education, and Jewish community centers, particularly in the key cities in which the bulk of American Jewry is located. Without such studies, no proper examination of organized Jewish life in the United States is possible. At present we have Charles Liebman's (1978a) study of the New York Jewish Federation and Ernest Stock's (1970) study of how the Combined Jewish Philanthropies of Boston functioned during the Six-Day war emergency, plus some doctoral dissertations and masters' theses.

Synagogues also need to be studied as organizations. There have been some important sociological studies of synagogues as institutions, principally those of Marshall Sklare (1972), and others of synagogues as mobilizers of Jewish commitment, but very little about synagogues as organizations.

Leadership Studies

There is a similar paucity of studies of Jewish leadership. In some respects, the American Jewish community represents a continuation of traditional forms of Jewish leadership, and in other respects, it represents a substantial adaptation and transformation of those forms (Elazar, 1976a). Little of this has been studied. Marshall Sklare's (1972) pioneering work on the rabbinate remains basic, supplemented by Charles Liebman's (1968) study of the training of American rabbis. The transformation of the role of the American rabbi deserves further study.

Studies of voluntary leadership are few and far between. The roles of voluntary leaders, the way they are recruited and mobilized, the differences in character and style of voluntary leadership in different organizations, all deserve serious attention. For example, work done suggests substantial differences between the kind of people attracted to synagogue leadership and those attracted to federation leadership. Jewish folk wisdom supports this view in many ways. To take another topic, the question remains as to what extent there is continuity in forms and patterns of Jewish leadership between the old world and the new. It is a generally accepted piece of conventional wisdom that American Jewish leaders are drawn from among the wealthy. Like most conventional wisdom it is to some extent true, but not as fully as it would seem. Studies of leadership recruitment might be revealing as to sources of leadership, their backgrounds, and their resource material.

Among the questions presently on the Jewish agenda in this connection is what happens to the sons and daughters of contemporary Jewish leaders. Do they follow in their parents' footsteps or do they drift away? With regard to rabbis, impressionistic evidence suggests that there is a tendency for children of rabbis to continue in the Jewish field creating, if not dynasties, at least an intergenerational network of people deeply involved in Jewish life often on a professional basis, who intermarry and form a special subset within the overall American Jewish community. This question is equally important with regard to voluntary leadership whose positions reflect their ability to make major contributions in support of Jewish activities, that is to say, wealthy Jews. Do their children assume equivalent positions when they come of age, or do they turn elsewhere, thereby depriving the Jewish community of the same measure of access to family resources (Cohen, 1980)? This issue has been repeatedly raised in discussions among Jewish leaders, who have indicated a concern with the trend on the part of children of successful businessmen to go into salaried occupations, and who are therefore less likely to contribute on the same scale even if they retain an interest in participating in Jewish community life. There is also some evidence that, as new generations of Jewish entrepreneurs develop, a proportion of them will seek civic expression through the Jewish community and make their newly-earned resources available just as their predecessors have.

Studies of the Jewish Civil Service

Another dimension of the leadership issue, which also relates to the overall structure of contemporary Jewish life, is the emergence of a Jewish civil service. A substantial number of people now earn their livelihoods by serving the Jewish community in administrative and professional capacities on a career basis. The Jewish civil service is a particularly American phenomenon which is only now beginning to find its way into other parts of the Jewish world. It follows the general American commitment to professionalization and specialization.

The first outlines of a Jewish civil service extending beyond the traditional Jewish occupations came with the emergence of community-sponsored Jewish and educational institutions around World War I. In the interwar period, the development of such professional cadres remained modest, albeit increasing, held back principally by the Depression. The flowering of the Jewish civil service came after World War II, as Jewish communities acquired resources to employ more people and interest in expanding the services provided under their auspices.

Despite its importance, there is no study of the Jewish civil service, no count of how many Jews are employed by Jewish institutions on either a full- or part-time basis, no examination of the range of positions supported by the Jewish community, no study of the ways and means of recruitment, and only one recent effort to assess present and future demand and the kind of training provided Jewish civil servants (Gurin, 1979). None of these, or any of the questions which represent standard subjects of inquiry in the field of public administration, have been studied. At best, there have been a few staffing surveys conducted in local communities either locally or by national agencies to deal with immediate practical problems of recruitment and replacement of personnel.

Studies of Interorganizational Relationships

The network of organizations and institutions which together comprise the American Jewish community (Table 7.1) also requires more study. This writer has laid out the basis for such a study and models helpful in approaching the question of interorganizational relationships (Elazar,

1976a). Here too, little else has been done. For example, over the years since the MacIver Report, Jewish community relations organizations have changed their internal organization to develop local branches or chapters, have realigned their mutual relationships to better divide the tasks before them and eliminate the most unproductive duplication the report cited, and have moved from heavy emphasis on the fight against anti-Semitism to deep involvement with non-Jewish human rights groups in a common front against all forms of discrimination, back to a more defensive posture on behalf of the Jewish community. None of this has been studied. The entire sphere of community relations needs mapping and in-depth study.

The same can be said of other spheres. While there have been studies of synagogues and their movements from a sociological point of view, almost nothing has been done to study those movements as organizations or networks of interorganizational relationships. What shapes relationship between individual seminaries and their respective movements? How does the rabbinical placement system relate to those relationships? Who governs the countrywide networks of each synagogue movement?

Similar kinds of studies can be undertaken in the educational-cultural sphere; for example, the creation of the Joint Cultural Appeal and its consequences. The communal-welfare sphere has undergone significant changes within the Council of Jewish Federations, in relations between the CJF and its related agencies, and especially in the local parallels of the latter. In the Israel-overseas sphere, studies of the UJA are clearly in order. What lies before us is a virgin field for which we now have some theory and a basic outline but very little in the way of empirical research to fill in the details of the theory, test, and modify it where necessary.

Both countrywide and local interorganizational networks need to be studied — as complete networks and in terms of partial linkages. It is now well accepted that the federations have moved to center stage as the framing institutions of the American Jewish community. How do they relate to other institutions in the "community" — those formally linked to them and those not formally linked but affected by their presence and activities? What kinds of relationships prevail among the various groupings of countrywide institutions and why are they where they are? What is happening with the emergence of regional networks that go beyond the traditional boundaries of local communities?

Policy Studies

While the above have immediately recognizable policy implications, there is room for more overtly policy-oriented research in the American Jewish community. Elsewhere I have suggested that such policy research has not developed because of the way in which "mavenology" is so widespread in Jewish life (Elazar, 1978f). Every leader believes he is a *maven*

TABLE 7.1
Spheres, Institutions, and Organizations

		Institutions and Organizations	
Sphere	Local	Countrywide	Worldwide
Religious-Congregational	Synagogues Orthodox Outposts Rabbinical Courts Kashruth Councils	Synagogue Council of America Synagogue Confederations Seminaries and Yeshivot Rabbinical Associations	Israeli Rabbinate Knesset International Synagogue Federations
Educational-Cultural	Synagogues Communal, Secularist and Day Schools Colleges of Jewish Studies Central Agencies of Jewish Education Jewish Studies Programs in Universities Local Cultural Institutions and Groups Jewish Community Centers	American Association for Jewish Education Torah Umesorah National Jewish Welfare Board B.B. Hillel Foundations Jewish Colleges and Universities Scholarly Associations Jewish Foundations (i.e., National Foundation for Jewish Culture) CJFWF Educators' Associations Jewish Cultural Institutions and Organizations	Jewish Agency and Subsidiaries Memorial Foundation for Jewish Culture

Community Relations	Jewish Community Relations Councils Local Chapters or Offices of AJ Committee, ADL, AJ Congress, JWV, Jewish Labor Committee	Presidents' Conference CJWF NJCRAC American Jewish Committee Anti-Defamation League American Jewish Congress Jewish Labor Committee Jewish War Veterans Professional Associations Special Purpose Groups (e.g., Soviet Jewry)	Consultative Council of Jewish Agencies Coordinating Board of Jewish Organizations World Jewish Congress Israeli Government
Communal-Welfare	Jewish Federation Social Service Agencies Jewish Community Centers Local Jewish Press Hospital/Health Care	CJFWF Jewish Welfare Board B'nai Brith American Jewish Committee American Jewish Congress United HIAS Service	Israeli Government Jewish Agency International Professional/ Functional Associations
Israeli-Overseas	Jewish Federations Local Zionist Chapters Local Zionist Offices Local Israeli Bond Office Local "Friends" of Israel or Overseas Institutions	CJFWF UJA-IEF Zionist Organizations Israel Bonds United HIAS Service "Friends" of Israel or Overseas Institutions JNF	Israeli Government Jewish Agency Jewish National Fund Joint Distribution Committee ORT Claims Conference Keren Hayesod

For the most complete available listing of countrywide institutions and organizations, local Jewish federations, and the Jewish press, see the annual directories in the *American Jewish Year Book*.

and therefore does not need studies. There is some truth in the fact that in a circumscribed sphere, intelligent leaders do develop a good understanding of their situation. Many of those who have presented themselves to do policy research often know less about the Jewish community than the leaders whom they hope will commission them to undertake such studies.

The growing complexity of Jewish life, which only matches that of life in general, requires systematic study of policy issues, that can go beyond what all but the wisest and most far-sighted leaders can possibly learn simply by observing what goes on around them. The whole question of projecting Jewish fund-raising capabilities has come to the fore recently (Cohen, 1980). There has been a decline in Jewish giving, partly as a result of inflation and recession in the United States and the world, partly because the situation in Israel does not seem to be in crisis, partly because the children of wealthy Jews are moving into fields where they are no longer generating the kind of entrepreneurial income that affords substantial contributions. Simple observation can provide a list of reasons, but only systematic study can sort them out and help us with their consequences. There are a number of questions about the future of Jewish political influence in the United States — what it is likely to be, what can be done to enhance it, what kinds of proposed reforms in the American political system are likely to weaken it. All these are questions which can be studied. On another dimension, there are organizational studies which can be undertaken to develop a better set of priorities for organized American Jewry or for any particular Jewish community. The whole question of federation-synagogue relations which on one level belongs in the category of interorganizational relationships but on another involves pressing policy studies, needs to be considered.

Community Finance

The fiscal issues of contemporary Jewry go hand in hand with organizational issues. They are only separable to a degree. It is not surprising that we have already mentioned a number of such issues under earlier categories. A thorough study of Jewish public finance is well in order, looking at income and expenditures in detail on all planes and in all facets. Included in this would be a study of the growing phenomenon of governmental support of Jewish-sponsored institutions, not simply hospitals which are nonsectarian and provide a neutral service, but day-care centers sponsored by various Hasidic groups and Jewish community center programs established to impart Jewish content to participants. The implications of this funding of institutional programs and policies needs to be examined.

Conclusion

The research agenda in this field is wide open with only the most preliminary tools available to do the job. We have the outlines of a theory, a number of probing studies, and a nucleus of people who have developed the interest and capability for working in the field. Beyond that, we have very little. For example, there is no program in the United States for training people to do research in this field, other than on-the-job training after going through some other program of studies, Jewish, general, or combined.[6] We even lack a basic bibliography for prospective researchers to enable them to know what materials do exist.

Finally, the institutional framework for doing such work is spotty. There are the research capabilities of the American Jewish Committee and, to a lesser extent, the Anti-Defamation League. There are survey departments (usually consisting of one person) in the major service agencies for their respective functional groups. (For example, the American Association for Jewish Education can send someone to do a study of a local bureau of Jewish education, and the National Jewish Welfare Board can study the program needs or the necessity to reorganize a Jewish community center.) And we have the Center for Jewish Community Studies. That exhausts the list. Funds for research are very limited. Commissions are made on the basis of minimal budgets, so that only the most superficial kind of work can be done except insofar as a scholar does more, utilizing his own or university resources. All this adds up to considerable opportunity to do serious work at minimum cost in a frontier area but in a still problematic research environment.

Notes

1. The term *congregation* evolved from a polity constituted on the basis of a theological commitment (an *edah*) as it was used during the frontier and Puritan era in the sixteenth and seventeenth centuries, to a definition of a strictly religious organization. See *Oxford English Dictionary*.
2. The publications of the American Jewish Historical Society, founded in 1892, are a case in point. The AJHS has yet to fully free itself from this tendency. Even well-known historians of Jewish background who have been brought onto the AJHS board and whose own work is far from antiquarian seem willing to accept that approach to the study of American Jewish history.
3. The best single "archive" of these studies is in the offices of the Council of Jewish Federations whose files, while not organized for research purposes, are an unexplored treasure trove of reports, field notes, minutes, and the like covering the organizational life of the communal-welfare and related spheres of North American Jewry, locally and countrywide since the 1920s.
4. *Tzion*, the journal of the Israel Historical Society, is their principal outlet.

5. See the publications of the Hebrew University's Institute of Hebrew Law (founded by Elon), particularly their annual reviews.
6. The Department of Political Studies at Bar Ilan University offers a program in Jewish political studies leading to the B.A., M.A., and Ph.D, with research training an integral element of the advanced degree programs. It is the only such program available anywhere.

APPENDIX A
Community Studies Produced by the Study of Jewish Community Organization

Aschheim, Steven, *The Communal Organization of South African Jewry.**

Bowerman, Jennifer K., *The Governance of the Jewish Community of Edmonton.*

Chazzan, Baruch, *The Jewish Community of Bulgaria.*

Cohen, Alan M., *The Governance of the Jewish Community of London (Ontario).*

Cohen, Stuart A., *The Conquest of a Community? The Zionists and the Board of Deputies in 1917* (Jerusalem: Turtledove Publishing, forthcoming).

Elazar, Daniel J., *Community and Polity: The Organizational Dynamics of American Jewry* (Philadelphia: Jewish Publication Society, 1976).

Elazar, Daniel J., *The Jewish Community of Iran.*

Elazar, Daniel J., *The Jewries of Scandinavia.*

Elazar, Daniel J., *The Sunset of Balkan Jewry.*

Elazar, Daniel J., with Peter Medding, *Three Jewries at the Great Frontier: Argentina, South Africa, and Australia* (New York: Holmes & Meier, forthcoming).

Friedenreich, Harriet, *The Jewish Community of Yugoslavia.*

Geller, Henryk Zvi, *The Jewish Community of Italy.***

Glickman, Yaakov, *The Governance of the Jewish Community of Toronto.*

Gordon, Anna, *The Governance of the Jewish Community of Winnipeg.*

Greenspan, Louis, *The Governance of the Jewish Community of Hamilton.*

Greilsamer, Ilan, *The Democratization of French Jewry.*

Greilsamer, Ilan, *The Jews of France: From Neutrality to Involvement.*

Greilsamer, Ilan, and Marc Salzberg, *The Jewish Community of France.*

Kay, Zachariah, *The Governance of the Jewish Community of Ottawa.*

Liberles, Adina Weiss, *The Jewish Community of Denmark.*

Liberles, Adina Weiss, *The Jewish Community of Finland.*

Liberles, Adina Weiss, *The Jewish Community of Sweden.*

Liberles, Adina Weiss, and Simcha Werner, *The Jewish Community of Norway.*

Liebman, Seymour B., *The Jewish Community of Mexico.*

Mandel, Stephen, and R.H. Wagenberg, *The Governance of the Jewish Community of Windsor.*

Oberman, Edna, *The Governance of the Jewish Community of Vancouver.*

Oren, Esther, *The Jewish Community of Rumania.***

Rich, Harvey, *The Governance of the Jewish Community of Calgary.*

Salzberg, Marc, *French Jewry and American Jewry.*

Waller, Harold, *The Governance of the Jewish Community of Canada.*

Waller, Harold, and Sheldon Schreter, *The Governance of the Jewish Community of Montreal.*

Weiss, Adina, *The Jewish Community of Belgium.*

Weiss, Adina, *The Jewish Community of Greece.*

Weiss, Adina, *The Jewish Community of the Soviet Union.***

Weiss, Adina, *The Jewish Community of Turkey.*

Weiss Adina, and Joseph Aron, *The Jewish Community of Camden, New Jersey.***

Weiss, Adina, and Joseph Aron, *The Jewish Community of Delaware.*

Weiss, Adina, and Joseph Aron, *The Jewish Community of Norristown, Pennsylvania.*

Notes

* Unless otherwise indicated, the studies were published by the Center for Jewish Community Studies.
** Unpublished study available in the files of the Center for Jewish Community Studies.

References

Adler, Cyrus, *I Have Considered These Days* (Philadelphia: Jewish Publication Society, 1941).

Adler, Selig, and Thomas E. Connolly, *From Ararat to Suburbia* (Philadelphia: Jewish Publication Society, 1960).

Agar, Herbert, *The Saving Remnant* (New York: Viking, 1970).

Almond, G., and J.S. Coleman (eds.), *The Politics of Developing Areas* (Princeton: Princeton University Press, 1960).

Avineri, Shlomo, "Israel: Two Nations?" *Midstream* 18 (May 1972): 3–20.

Baeck, Leo, *This People Israel* (Philadelphia: Jewish Publication Society, 1965).

Baron, Salo, *The Jewish Community* (Philadelphia: Jewish Publication Society, 1938–42, 3 vols.).

Belfer, Ella, *Al HaShniut Bekayon HaBrit vHakshara el Reayon Ha-Mashiah* (Philadelphia: Center for Jewish Community Studies, 1978).

Berger, G., "American Jewish Communal Service, 1776–1976: From Traditional Self-Help to Government Support," *Jewish Social Studies* 38 (July 1976): 225–46.

Bernstein, Marver, *Politics of Israel: First Decade of Statehood* (Princeton: Princeton University Press, 1957).

Blidstein, Gerald J., "Notes on Hefker Bet-Din in Talmudic and Medieval Law," *Dine Israel* 4 (1973a): 35–49.

Blidstein, Gerald J., "A Note on the Function of 'The Law of the Kingdom is Law' in the Medieval Jewish Community," *Jewish Journal of Sociology* 15 (December 1973b): 213–19.

Blidstein, Gerald J., "Individual and Community in the Middle Ages: Halachic Theory." In Daniel J. Elazar (ed.), *Kinship and Consent* (Jerusalem: Turtledove, 1981).

Brickman, William W., *The Jewish Community in America: An Annotated and Classified Bibliographical Guide* (New York: Burt Franklin, 1977).

Burke, Estelle, *The Literature of Jewish Public Affairs: Organizing the Published Materials* (Philadelphia: Center for Jewish Community Studies, 1970).

Carlin, Jerome E., and Saul H. Mendlovitz, "The American Rabbi: A Religious Specialist Responds to Loss of Authority." In Marshall Sklare (ed.), *The Jews* (New York: Free Press, 1958).

Cohen, Naomi W., *Not Free to Desist: The American Jewish Committee, 1906–1966* (Philadelphia: Jewish Publication Society, 1972).

Cohen, Steven M., "Will Jews Keep Giving? Prospects for the Jewish Charitable Community," *Journal of Jewish Communal Service* 55 (Autumn 1978): 59–71.

Cohen, Steven M., "Trends in Jewish Philanthropy," *American Jewish Year Book* (1980): 29–51 (Philadelphia: Jewish Publication Society, 1980).

Dahl, R.A., *Modern Political Analysis* (Englewood Cliffs, N.J.: Prentice-Hall, 1963).

Davis, Moshe (ed.), *The Yom Kippur War, Israel, and the Jewish People* (New York: Arno, 1974).

Dresner, Samuel, "Federation or Synagogue: Alternatives in the American Jewish Community," *Forum* 27 (1977): 73–95.

Easton, D., *The Political System* (New York: Knopf, 1953).

Eisenstadt, Shmuel, *Israeli Society* (New York: Basic Books, 1968).

Elazar, Daniel J., "A Constitutional View of Jewish History," *Judaism* (Summer 1961): 256-64.

Elazar, Daniel J., "The Pursuit of Community: Selections from the Literature of Jewish Public Affairs, 1965–66," *American Jewish Year Book* (1967): 178–229 (Philadelphia: Jewish Publication Society, 1967).

Elazar, Daniel J., "The Rediscovered Polity: Selections from the Literature of Jewish Public Affairs, 1967-68," *American Jewish Year Book* (1969): 172–237 (Philadelphia: Jewish Publication Society, 1969a).

Elazar, Daniel J., "The Reconstitution of Jewish Communities in the Postwar Period," *Jewish Journal of Sociology* 11 (December 1969b): 187– 226.

Elazar, Daniel J., *Israel: From Ideological to Territorial Democracy* (New York: General Learning Press, 1971a).

Elazar, Daniel J., "The Institutional Life of American Jewry," *Midstream* (June-July 1971b): 31–50.

Elazar, Daniel J., "The Activity Spheres of the American Jewish Community," *Gratz College Annual of Jewish Studies* (1972a): 120–33.

Elazar, Daniel J., "Confrontation and Reconstitution: Selections from the Literature of Jewish Public Affairs, 1969-1971," *American Jewish Year Book* (1972): 301-83 (Philadelphia: Jewish Publication Society, 1972b).

Elazar, Daniel J., *Studying Jewish Communities: A Research Guide* (Philadelphia: Center for Jewish Community Studies, 1972c).

Elazar, Daniel J., "Decision Makers in Communal Agencies: A Profile," *Journal of Jewish Communal Service* 49 (Summer 1973a): 281-85.

Elazar, Daniel J., "The Decision Makers: Key Divisions in Jewish Communal Life," *Dispersion and Unity* 19–20 (1973b): 20–30.

Elazar, Daniel J., "United States of America: Overview." In Moshe Davis (ed.), *The Yom Kippur War, Israel, and the Jewish People* (New York: Arno, 1974a).

Elazar, Daniel J., "Jewish Political Studies as a Field of Inquiry," *Jewish Social Studies* 36 (July-October 1974b): 220–33.

Elazar, Daniel J., "Kinship and Consent in the Jewish Community: Patterns of Continuity in Jewish Communal Life," *Tradition* 14 (Fall 1974c): 63–79.

Elazar, Daniel J., "Perspectives on Jewish Political Studies on the American Campus," *American Jewish Historical Quarterly* (June 1974d).

Elazar, Daniel J., *Community and Polity: The Organizational Dynamics of American Jewry* (Philadelphia: Jewish Publication Society, 1976a).

Elazar, Daniel J., "Training Executives for the Jewish Community," *Journal of Jewish Communal Service* (1976b).

Elazar, Daniel J., *Israel-American Jewish Relations in the Context of the World Jewish Polity* (Philadelphia: Center for Jewish Community Studies, 1977a).

Elazar, Daniel J., "The Compound Structure of Public Service Delivery in Israel." In Vincent Ostrom and Francis Pennell Bish (eds.), *Comparing Urban Service Delivery Systems* (Beverly Hills: Sage, 1977b).

Elazar, Daniel J., "The Political Tradition of the American Jew." In Stanley M. Wagner (ed.), *Traditions of the American Jew* (New York: Ktav, 1978a).

Elazar, Daniel J., "Synagogue/Federation Relations: Overlapping Spheres." In Alvin Kass (ed.), *Proceedings: The United Synagogue of America 1977 Biennial Convention,* 1978b.

Elazar, Daniel J., "Covenant as the Basis of the Jewish Political Tradition," *Jewish Journal of Sociology* 20 (June 1978c): 5–37.

Elazar, Daniel J., "Toward a Jewish Vision of Statehood for Israel," *Judaism* 27 (Spring) 1978d: 233–44.

Elazar, Daniel J., "What Indeed Is American Jewry?" *Forum* (Winter 1978e).

Elazar, Daniel J., "What We Know and What We Need to Know about the Status of Jewish Social Research," *Journal of Jewish Communal Service* 54 (Spring 1978f).

Elazar, Daniel J., "The Constitutional Periodization of Jewish History: A Second Look" (Philadelphia: Center for Jewish Community Studies, 1979).

Elazar, Daniel J., *The Kehillah* (Bar Ilan University and Center for Jewish Community Studies, 1980).

Elazar, Daniel J., *Kinship and Consent: The Jewish Political Tradition and Its Contemporary Uses* (Jerusalem: Turtledove, 1981).

Elazar, Daniel J., and Stephen Goldstein, "The Legal Status of American Jewry," *American Jewish Year Book* (1972): 3–94 (Philadelphia: Jewish Publication Society, 1972).

Elbogen, Ismar, *A Century of Jewish Life* (Philadelphia: Jewish Publication Society, 1944).

Elon, Menachem, "Power and Authority: Halachic Stance of the Traditional Community and Its Contemporary Implications." In Daniel J. Elazar (ed.), *Kinship and Consent* (Jerusalem: Turtledove, 1981).

Fein, Leonard, *Politics in Israel* (Boston: Little, Brown, 1967).

Freeman, Gordon, "The Rabbinic Understanding of Covenant as a Political Idea." In Daniel J. Elazar (ed.), *Kinship and Consent* (Jerusalem: Turtledove, 1981).

Friedenreich, Harriet Pass, *Yugoslav Jewry between the Wars* (Philadelphia: Jewish Publication Society, 1979).

Gartner, Lloyd, "Roumania, America and World Jewry: Consul Peixotto in Bucharest, 1870–1876," *American Jewish Historical Quarterly* 58 (September 1968).

Gartner, Lloyd, *Bibliography of Jewish Law: Modern Books, Monographs, and Articles in Hebrew* (Harry Fischel Institute, 1975).

Goitein, S.D., "Congregation vs. Community," *Jewish Quarterly Review* 44 (April 1954): 291–304.

Goldberg, S.P., "Jewish Communal Services: Programs and Finances," *American Jewish Year Book* (1978): 172–221 (Philadelphia: Jewish Publication Society, 1978).

Golding, Martin P., "The Juridical Basis of Communal Associations in Medieval Rabbinic Legal Thought," *Jewish Social Studies* 28, no. 2 (April 1966): 25–33.

Goren, Arthur, *New York Jews and the Quest for Community: The Kehillah Experiment, 1908–1922* (New York: Columbia University Press, 1970).

Graetz, Heinreich, *History of the Jews* (Philadelphia: Jewish Publication Society, 1891).

Greilsamer, Ilan, and Marc Salzberg, "The Organized Jewish Community in France" (Hebrew), *Tefutzot Israel* 16, no. 4 (1978).

Gurin, Arnold, *Final Report of the Personnel Committee* (Council of Jewish Federations, 1979).

Halpern, Ben, *The American Jew: A Zionist Analysis* (New York: Herzl Press, 1956).

Himmelfarb, Milton, "The Jew: Subject or Object," *Commentary* 40 (July 1965): 54–57.

Horowitz, Dan, and Moshe Lissak, *Origins of the Israeli Polity: Palestine under the Mandate* (Chicago: University of Chicago Press, 1978).

Israel, Herman, "Some Influences of Hebraic Culture on Modern Social Organization," *American Journal of Sociology* 71 (January 1966): 384–94.

Kanner, Ted, "Federation and Synagogue: A New Partnership for a New Time," *Journal of Jewish Communal Service* 53 (September 1976): 21–28.

Karpf, Maurice, *Jewish Community Organization in the United States: An Outline of Types of Organizations, Activities, and Problems* (New York: Bloch, 1938).

Kessler, A.A., *On the Study of Financing of Jewish Community Activities* (Philadelphia: Center for Jewish Community Studies, 1970).

Levin, Morris, "Establishing Priorities for Jewish Communal Service," *Journal of Jewish Communal Service* 47 (Fall 1970): 43–54.

Liebman, Charles S., "The Training of American Rabbis," *American Jewish Year Book* (1968): 3–112 (Philadelphia: Jewish Publication Society, 1968).

Liebman, Charles S., *Dimensions of Authority in the Contemporary Jewish Community* (Philadelphia: Center for Jewish Community Studies, 1970).

Liebman, Charles S., "Diaspora Influence on Israel: The Ben-Gurion 'Exchange' and Its Aftermath." *Jewish Social Studies* 36 (July–October 1974).

Liebman, Charles S., "Does the Diaspora Influence Israel? The Case of the Reconstituted Jewish Agency," *Forum* 23 (Spring 1975): 18–30.

Liebman, Charles S., *Pressure without Sanctions: The Influence of World Jewry in Shaping Israel's Public Policy* (Cranbury, N.J.: Associated University Presses, 1977).

Liebman, Charles S., "Leadership and Decision-making in a Jewish Federation: The New York Federation of Jewish Philanthropies," *American Jewish Year Book* (1979): 3–76 (Philadelphia: Jewish Publication Society, 1978a).

Liebman, Charles S., *On the Study of International Jewish Political Organization* (Philadelphia: Center for Jewish Community Studies, 1978b).

Lurie, Harry, *A Heritage Affirmed* (Philadelphia: Jewish Publication Society, 1960).

Macridis, R.C., and B.E. Brown (eds.), *Comparative Politics, Notes, and Readings* (Homewood, Ill.: Dorsey, 3rd ed., 1968).

Medding, Peter Y., "Towards a General Theory of Jewish Political Interests and Behavior," *Jewish Journal of Sociology* 19 (December 1977): 115–44.

Meyer, Michael A., "A Centennial History." In Samuel E. Karff (ed.), *Hebrew Union College-Jewish Institute of Religion at One Hundred Years* (Cincinnati: Hebrew Union College Press, 1976).

Noveck, Simon, *Milton Steinberg: Portrait of a Rabbi* (New York: Ktav, 1978).

Penniman, Howard (ed.), *Israel at the Polls: The Knesset Elections of 1977* (Washington, D.C.: American Enterprise Institute for Public Policy Research, 1979).

Poll, Solomon, *The Hassidic Community of Williamsburg* (New York: Free Press, 1962).

Raab, Earl, "The End of Jewish Community Relations," *Journal of Jewish Community Relations* 54 (December 1977): 107–15.

Roseman, Kenneth, "American Communal Institutions in Their Historical Context," *Jewish Journal of Sociology* 16 (June 1974): 25–37.

Rosenstock, Morton, *Louis Marshall: Defender of Jewish Rights* (Detroit: Wayne State University Press, 1965).

Schorsch, Ismar, *On the Political Judgement of the Jew* (New York: Leo Baeck Institute, 1976).

Siegal, Daniel, *Jewish Political Theories and Institutions: A Bibliography* (Philadelphia: Study of Jewish Community Organization, 1970).

Sklare, Marshall, *The Jews: Social Patterns of an American Group* (New York: Free Press, 1958).

Sklare, Marshall, *America's Jews* (New York: Random House, 1971).

Sklare, Marshall, *Conservative Judaism,* new aug. ed. (New York: Schocken, 1972).

Sklare, Marshall, *The Jew in American Society* (New York: Behrman House, 1974a).

Sklare, Marshall, *The Jewish Community in America* (New York: Behrman House, 1974b).

Sklare, Marshall, "Change and Continuity in the Synagogues of Lakeville." Paper presented at the Tenth Annual Conference, Association for Jewish Studies (Boston, December 1978).

Sklare, Marshall, and Joseph Greenblum, *Jewish Identity on the Suburban Frontier* (Chicago: University of Chicago Press, 1979).

Slesinger, Z., "The Need for Jewish Social Studies Programs," *Pedagogic Reporter* 17 (December 1965): 9–10, 29–30.

Stock, Ernest, "In the Absence of Hierarchy: Notes on the Organization of the American Jewish Community," *Jewish Journal of Sociology* 12 (September 1970): 195–200.

Stock, Ernest, "The Reconstitution of the Jewish Agency: A Political Analysis," *American Jewish Year Book* (1972): 178–193 (Philadelphia: Jewish Publication Society, 1972).

Stock, Ernest, "How 'Durban' Reacted to Israel's Crises," *Forum* (Spring 1975a): 38–60.

Stock, Ernest, *Jewish Multi-Country Associations* (Philadelphia: Center for Jewish Community Studies, 1975b).

Susser, Bernard, and Don-Yihye, Eliezer, *A Prolegomena to the Study of Jewish Political Theory* (Bar Ilan University and Center for Jewish Community Studies, 1978).

Swichkow, Louis J., and Lloyd P. Gartner, *The History of the Jews of Milwaukee* (Philadelphia: Jewish Publication Society, 1963).

Tabory, Mala, and Charles S. Liebman, *Jewish International Relations: An Annotated Bibliography* (Ramat-Gan, Israel: Turtledove, 1980).

Tarshish, Alan, "The Board of Delegates of American Israelites," *Publications of the American Jewish Historical Society* 49 (September 1959): 16–32.

Toll, William, "Covenant and Mobility: Scholarship and Purpose in American Jewish Community History." Paper presented at the Tenth Annual Conference, Association for Jewish Studies (Boston, December 1978).

Vorspan, Max, and Lloyd P. Gartner, *History of the Jews of Los Angeles* (Philadelphia: Jewish Publication Society, 1970).

Waller, Harold, "Reassessment and Retrenchment: Selections from the Literature of Jewish Public Affairs, 1972–1974," *American Jewish Year Book* (1976): 199–222 (Philadelphia: Jewish Publication Society, 1975).

Waller, Harold, "Selections from the Literature of Jewish Public Affairs, 1975–76," *American Jewish Year Book* (1978): 222–49 (Philadelphia: Jewish Publication Society, 1977).

Waller, Harold, and Daniel Elazar, *The Governance of Canadian Jewry* (New Brunswick, N.J.: Transaction, 1981).

Weinberger, Paul, "Conflict and Consensus in Jewish Welfare Fund Allocations," *Jewish Social Studies* 34 (October 1972): 354–64.

Woocher, Jonathan, *"Civil Judaism" in the United States* (Philadelphia: Center for Jewish Community Studies, 1978).

8

Jews Among Others

Earl Raab

Former States of the Art

For more years and in more societies than any other historical group, Jews have been at the "wrong" end of some design of "majority/minority relations." Jews were always aware of the difficulties attendant upon these varying relationships; and usually did about as well as they could. When the world became much more organized and self-conscious about its social behavior and the hopeful management thereof, the Jews developed concerns and agencies entitled "external relations," "defense," "intergroup relations," and "community relations." All the titles have to do with the ability of Jews and their communal institutions to flourish as a minority in a host society without disadvantage. "Without disadvantage" is subject to different measures and expectations. In certain times and places, it has meant little more than sheer survival. In America today, it means everything: survival, equal opportunity, and access to all the world has to offer; and even, to some, the absence of hostility.

There have been two kinds of broad perceptions: external relations governed by power and those governed by good (or ill) will. In earlier days, power relationships were clearly determinant. The object was to get the king or prince to protect the Jews; and to use whatever power the Jews could muster to serve the needs of that king or prince. In many cases it was a commercial service of one kind of another. When modern "liberal" societies emerged, many Jews added to their philosophy of defense a belief in the power of good will. They were now supposed to have equal status, and it would be denied only if people held ill will toward them. That would happen only if their fellow citizens clung to the hostile and mistaken anti-Jewish stereotypes developed in the Dark Ages.

The Zentralverein Deutscher Staatsbürger Jüdischen Glaubens — the German Jewish defense agency founded just before the turn of the century — stated its purpose this way: "We intend to express openly before the whole world how we feel and what we think. The systematic slanders will not cease therewith to cover us with their poison. But the neutral will not deny their sympathy to a serious and respectably conducted defense, and those who today do not know us, who are unable to get to know us because our entire life is strange to them, will testify for us: 'These Jews of Germany are not less loyal citizens than we, just as self-sacrificing patriots, just as noble human beings.'" The Anti-Defamation League launched its major campaign against anti-Semitism in America in 1930 with this statement of purpose: "To educate the great mass in the truth concerning the Jew and to demolish the foibles and fictions that are now part of the mental picture of the Jew in the public mind."[1]

Yet the weight of evidence was that direct cognitive assault against anti-Semitic stereotypes was not successful. Practical results seemed incommensurate with the money and energy spent on that assault. In addition, a new and more sophisticated application of the "good will" construct was becoming dominant by way of dynamic psychology: an approach to the emotional rather than cognitive elements of prejudice. Theories of frustration-aggression, anxiety-aggression, projection and scapegoating, and psychogenic character structure, such as the authoritarian personality, were developed and applied, and by and large seemed illuminating. This approach prospered in the years immediately following World War II, and particularly fit the wartime image of Hitlerism as consummate personal diabolism and pathology.

However valid this causative perspective may have been, it provided no strong remedial seat. Neither individual nor group therapy, nor family life retraining, produced or promised that much. Besides, a new social science approach began to dominate the field. Social structure rather than psychopathology became the analytic fulcrum. Values and conflicts were perceived to be created by the social systems in which people were trapped. This approach was also in tune with the political temper developing in America, although it came into conflict with cruder forms of economic determinism. The latter had been around for some time and had always been found seriously wanting as a total explanation of intergroup hostility.

The field of external relations moved in another direction. The objective was not individual or intercultural therapy, but societal therapy. The metaphor of the civil rights movement was to bypass individual attitudes and reform the social structure out of which such attitudes grew. The focus on power, rather than good will, again took center stage in the discussion about majority/minority relations. None of these trends entered or exited neatly, but, in roughly the sequence described, layered on the information and influences which brought us to present circumstances.

Current State of the Art: Theoretical Framework

We know a great deal about the apparent extent of the good will which the American public holds toward Jews. Measured in terms of negative stereotypes by a continuing series of surveys, the American public has not changed much. A little more than a third of Americans held some systematic pattern of anti-Semitic attitudes in the 1930s, and a little less than a third do so now. There is a formidable reservoir of anti-Semitism out there, the heritage of a couple of millenia. Information suggests that this is not the most direct threat to Jewish security; nor indeed does the most direct threat reside in those who hold these images.

There is another mass out there which is more critical. These are the people who are not actively anti-Semitic; but neither are they actively committed in any way *against* anti-Semitism. They are the low-resisters. When the American public was asked whether a congressional candidate's anti-Semitic platform would cause them to be for him, against him, or whether it would make no difference, a third of the respondents said the latter (only about 5 percent said they would support him on that account).[2] Apparently there was no significantly higher proportion of explicit anti-Semites among Father Coughlin's followers than among the rest of the American public, but they were all nevertheless supporting a dangerous anti-Semitic movement.

The work of Philip Converse and others suggests that among the mass of people, no comprehensive ideology, good or bad (including anti-Semitic ideology) is operative. The nature of political thinking is geared to the concrete rather than the abstract. In light of his findings, and discussing the Nazis, Converse concluded: "Under comparable stresses, it is likely that large numbers of citizens in any society would gladly support *ad hoc* promises of change without any great concern about ideological implications." One is inevitably reminded of that marvelous subtitle of Hannah Arendt's book on Eichmann: *The Banality of Evil.*

While stresses trigger anti-Semitic believers, they create active anti-Semites out of low-resisters. They draw on the cultural reservoir of anti-Semitic conventions, but at the same time they replenish that reservoir. The working premise is that there is nothing remarkably pathological about low-resisters. It is rather the high-resisters who are "remarkable" and deserve special attention. According to this approach, social circumstances rather than psychopathology distinguish the low-resisters from the high-resisters. This approach can also take into account the fact that Jews are often subject to conditions of disadvantage which are not best described as "anti-Semitism," such as mandatory Christian observances in public schools.

There are three levels to be considered in the etiology of Jewish disadvantage. There are the precipitating stresses: economic depressions, plagues, and other social cataclysms. There are the individuals, the ultimate actors. And in between the two are the systems — the institutions and institutional behaviors of society — which presumably differentiate the ways in which a society reacts to stresses (as well as contributing to the nature of the stresses). This intervening structure primarily stamps the attitudes and behavior of individual citizens.

On the direct relationship between institutionalized behavior and individual attitudes, there is a mass of evidence. When people are required to work together on an equal basis, prejudiced attitudes toward working together diminish. When people are forced by residential design to live in proximity on an equal basis, prejudiced attitudes toward living together diminish. When people live in proximity on a less equal and less integrated basis, prejudiced attitudes toward living together tend to increase.

When there is an attempt to predict behavior toward housing integration by pretesting attitudes, the prediction fails because of intervening institutional factors, e.g., lending practices of banking institutions. Attempts to predict behavior toward school integration by pretesting prejudicial attitudes would also fail. In one Southern city, college graduates were as prejudiced against having Blacks in their schools as were grade-school graduates. But the college graduates were much less resistant to the idea of desegregation, because they had other institutional (systems) investments.

As to the relationships between cataclysmic stresses and the intervening systems, one can only draw inferences from available information. Surveys conducted during the 1930s indicate that the level of popular or folk anti-Semitism in the United States was not significantly less than that of Germany. And while objective stresses were much greater in Germany than in the United States, no one doubted that the stress on America was well within the range of the dangerous. Yet although the attempt was made, organized anti-Semitism never became a viable political instrument in the United States as it did in Germany. The intervening institutions and structure of the United States presumably made a difference. This intervening structure is not only determinative, but more directly subject to remedial action than either individual attitudes or cataclysmic stresses.

What elements of this intervening structure seem particularly pertinent to the enterprise of Jewish external relations? A comprehensive political construct has developed in which the axis of democratic pluralism/extremism has replaced the axis of prejudice/nonprejudice. *Democratic pluralism* falls easily into cliché unless it is elaborated as connoting the "double freedom" so critical for Jewish security: equal opportunity for the individual and working legitimacy for the group and its institutions. In Jewish history, host societies have often offered one or the other but not both, and the results have been disastrous for both. *Democratic pluralism* also connotes an orderly and peaceable arrangement for the exercise of this double freedom. And extremism in this framework means a political attack on those orderly and peaceful arrangements.

At this point, much may seem to be in the eye of the beholder. A very militant Black group was picketing Goldwater outside the hotel in which he made his remark about the virtue of extremism in the pursuit of freedom. When this remark was relayed outside, the head of the picket line said "Right on!" The fighters of the Warsaw ghetto were disrupting an "orderly arrangement" with as much violence as possible. In this framework *extremism* is a judgement call, depending on one's assessment of the state of democratic pluralism, one of whose correlates is the possibility of peaceful change. The prevalent perception among American Jewry is that American democracy and democratic pluralism *have* worked to a degree never reached by any other host society.

Within this framework of democratic pluralism/extremism — What are the relevant components of the intervening structure in America? First there are the laws of society: there are laws which protect equal opportunity for the individual; laws to protect the individual's due process; freedom of association; there are laws which protect a religious group against official second-class citizenship; laws which favor peaceful change by protecting free speech and assembly. It is important to understand the social process underlying commitment to the law in general, and commitment to the laws of democratic pluralism in particular. The descriptive construct of "social disorganization" applies. Commitment to the official rules of society depends on the state of allegiance to that society and to its traditional groups, which are involved in the primary transmission of values. Such allegiances are strained by a number of circumstances in which the interdependent systems come unglued: loss of function by the society and its traditional groups; value conflict, when influences pressing on individuals are not mutually reinforcing; conflict between means and ends; conflict between rules and aspirations; conflict between aspirations and achievement.

This approach illuminates the earlier prescription that it is more important for the populace to be committed *against* the violation of Jewish rights than it is for them to like Jews. Thus it was more important for the law to prevail in the desegregation of certain Southern institutions, than it was for the Southern populace to be unprejudiced against Blacks. Such a sociological model fits the political framework (democratic pluralism/extremism). The dysfunction of groups, value conflicts, the disruption of expectations, tend to identify two forces in society. There are the have-nots who feel strongly about their disprivilege; and there are those relatively privileged who feel that their status and well-being are threatened. In both cases, when these forces are politicized, the equilibrium of the system is threatened. These are the circumstances in which extremist movements, of the Left or Right, arise. With the rise of extremist movements and the dilution of resistance to them, the phenomenon of organized political anti-Semitism emerges. The model of extremism typically carries the luggage of racial or ethnic scapegoats, some featured in a comprehensive conspiracy theory which legitimizes abandonment of the democratic process.

One practical aspect of the American political process notably relates to this framework: coalition politics. There has always been a direct relationship between factional and extremist politics. The heterogeneous nature of American society and its multiplicity of interest associations have required, for political stability, that the major political entities themselves be interest-bargaining mechanisms. The major political parties have invariably swallowed up strong factional extremist movements in American history by becoming responsive to some of the goals they have digested, while suppressing the more extremist procedural goals. The institutions of coalition politics, of compromise politics, are the first line of practical defense against the rise of extremist movements.

The genesis of extremist movements is related to objective situations in society and concomitant social conditions: unmet aspirations, often associated with raised expectations; and status anxiety, usually associated with threatened displacement. Extremist movements often come in such a matched pair, Left and Right, at any given time; and one's interest in political stability, as one's concern about extremism, depends on one's personal evaluation of the state of democratic pluralism and the possibilities of orderly change. Whatever one's personal evaluation on that score, the above framework partly integrates the conflict theory approach, which emphasizes the exploitive nature of group relations amid scarcity situations, with the functional-systems approach which emphasizes the effect of the intervening social structure.

The implications in this framework for socialization shape the approach to formal education. The emphasis is not on education "about Jews." It is not even on intergroup relations education in general, although the beneficial effects of integration are still a conventional article of belief. The emphasis is on the kind of education which will help socialize the young with respect to the broader values of society and of democratic pluralism. As Selznick and Steinberg put it: "The uneducated are cognitively and morally unenlightened because they have never been indoctrinated into the enlightened values of the larger society and in this sense are alienated from it."[3]

Level of education was repeatedly found to be the prime independent variable related to intensity of anti-Semitism, as measured by the acceptance of negative stereotypes. Quality and quantity of education were found to have a consistent effect. However, with the minimization of the negative stereotype as an index of potential political anti-Semitism, the chief focus becomes the relationship of education to high resistance, to strong democratic restraint, to commitment to societal values and democratic pluralism. Again, level and quality of education were consistently found directly related to attitudes on these matters. Education is often a function of one's general status in society, of one's vested interest in its systems and values. But holding socioeconomic status constant, education and knowledge about the institutions of democratic pluralism make a significant difference, for at least a significant leadership segment of our society.

American democratic institutions have flourished because some people understood them and the rest were loyal to them. In recapitulation, that loyalty relates to the dynamics of stress and of the intervening social structure described above, in a political framework of democratic pluralism/ extremism. But there is at least one other kind of meshing framework which can be used: integration-assimilation-subordination.

This would suggest a more narrow preoccupation with such traditional matters as ethnic stratification and mobility; or intermarriage and other forms of intercultural accommodation. From the point of view of Jewish external relations, as currently perceived, this is a vintage framework as compared to a more political cast. Subsumed under the larger political construct, this framework can provide useful vantage points relating more directly to other subjects of internal Jewish concern.

Another large dimension that must be added to any discussion of Jewish external relations is the security of Jews outside the United States and *their* problems of minority/majority relations. The security problems of Israeli Jews have dominated the agendas of American Jewish community relations agencies at least since 1967. The problems of Soviet Jewry have received much attention. So have the problems of Syrian Jews, Iranian Jews, Argentinian Jews, Ethiopian Jews. The framework in which the security of American Jews is perceived does not apply to these Jewries elsewhere. At its most abstract, such a framework might apply to postindustrial countries such as Nazi Germany or the Soviet Union; but it is of little use at its most abstract — and besides, the American Jewish community would have no direct remedial leverage. In other countries or regions in which Jews are in trouble, the framework does not apply at all. The art of external relations with respect to other Jewries has to do with trying to bring to bear the leverage of the United States.

This objective brings the current external relations theory full circle, on two counts. First, the kind of American society in which American Jews will be able to most effectively influence American foreign policy on behalf of foreign Jewries, is exactly the kind of American society in which American Jews will themselves have the most security. Therefore the theme of democratic pluralism is replicated. Beyond that, the "theory" of external relations on behalf of foreign Jewries is based on a simple power approach: the power of the United States to affect other nations, and the power of American Jews to affect the United States. This is congruent with the current perception of how American Jews must attempt to affect their fate *within* the United States. The political structure and the intervening social structure to which modern community relations theory is addressed are seen as determined by power relations, rather than by the promulgation of "good will." In that sense, in a much more sophisticated way and in a much more complicated world, the Jews have returned to their instincts of the twelfth century.

What We Do Not Know

What is it that we do not know in these matters? What important gaps still exist? The trouble with such questions is that they are necessarily asked from a blind alley. The current state of information and of theory about Jewish external relations have been pieced together from Jewish history and social science study, for the most part derivatively applied to problems at hand; and shaped by academic fashions as well as by the predilections of its reporters. As A.N. Whitehead once said: "There is only one difficulty with clear and distinct ideas. When we finally achieve them, we can be sure that something is left out."[4] In short, much of what we do not know, and of what we know mistakenly, will be revealed in the course of future study which we cannot anticipate. However, it is likely that such future study would be facilitated by some systematic attention to the subject, which has not been the case to date.

The study of external relations — and application of general knowledge to the field — has been in the hands of relatively isolated students or national agencies set up by the American Jewish community to handle this problem. These agencies, to varying degrees, have amassed helpful bodies of information, have maintained a certain level of continuing analytic discussion, and at times have stimulated and funded some landmark studies. But they suffer from certain disabilities with respect to the systematic study of external relations. Their primary mandate is action, not study; they are competitive; they have constant need to deal with the expressive needs of their constituencies, which are not always in full consonance with the instrumental needs of external relations; they are institutionally self-conscious.

At a time when American society may be in a state of transition, there is a need for more systematic attention to the field of Jewish external relations. Since the state of American society and that of Jewish external relations strongly intersect, such systematic attention would be of benefit to both. It is impossible to anticipate all the avenues such systematic attention might travel, but certain paths of exploration and systematization can be suggested. If there is any order in their presentation, it is from the more obvious to the less so.

Analysis of Public Opinion

While the state of public opinion toward Jews, in America or elsewhere, is not central to the current theoretical framework drawn, its constant measurement remains useful for diagnostic purposes. It is also the field most often plowed, with the support of national agencies. Every decade or so there is an effort to pull together available data for more serious analysis. These efforts have typically been by way of "afterthought," rather than with a core of planned long-term studies. These *ad hoc* efforts are marred by such flaws as the need to interpret inconsistent wording, and most of all by the failure to systematically sample opinions in immediate conjunction with certain relevant world events. The surveys would be more useful if they concentrated more often and more systematically on the opinions of lawmakers, public officials, intellectuals, and generally those closest to affecting the "intervening structures" which still more often shape than follow general public opinion.

Intergroup Relations

The study of interaction among the various ethnic and racial groups in America has increasingly been left to journalistic accounts, often at times of crisis, self-serving, impressionistic, and polemic. The Hispanic population of America, for example, is destined to be a paramount force in shaping some of those future institutions which are also of prime interest to Jews. But there is no studied analysis of Hispanic aspirations as they are emerging, and as they may affect both relationships with the Jews and public affairs objectives of the Jews. The same lacuna exists with respect to the enlarged Black middle class. When the "Andrew Young affair" struck, the Jewish community seemed stunned by the nature of Black reaction; it should not have been.

The Nature of Democratic Pluralism

Most of the work on those aspects of American society and its intervening structure which are of central interest to Jewish external relations will properly be accomplished in general studies. However, there has been little systematic application of these general studies to the theoretical framework developed in the field of Jewish external relations. From that vantage point, for example, what is the stake of the Jewish community in the populist, "participatory democracy" impulses which have affected a number of American political institutions? Many Jewish public affairs agencies have supported such impulses without an informed sense of what their import might be for coalition politics in general. Jews had a strong instinct for the dangers of factionalized major-party conventions, but were more vague about the effects of the direct primary movement. Some Jewish agencies took a position against radical changes in the electoral college; but that position was based on a concern about immediate loss of voting power. The more far-reaching implications for factionalism and an extremist temper were not explicated.

To examine such phenomena from a specialized vantage point does not mean to examine them from a biased and fixed position. But to do the first without the second is more likely to be within the capability of an institution with an academic cast than one with an organizational cast. Such examinations by a cross-cut of historians, political scientists, sociologists, and other scholarly observers, will not be contained by the bias of any given theoretical framework, but will inevitably test and alter that framework. Systematic attention to such matters means not just the ongoing application of general knowledge to external relations, but also the stimulation of special studies which would illuminate aspects of the larger field — not just for Jews, but for the other actors in the political and intellectual world.

American Foreign Policy

American foreign policy has never been an area of expertise for Jewish external relations. There has been concern for the status of oppressed Jewry abroad and for the security of Israel. But there has been no systematic examination of how American foreign policy in general affects either of those concerns or the security of the American Jew. There is reason to believe that there are such interrelationships. The state of democratic pluralism in America depends on the position of America in the world; as well as on America sustaining a free-world sector. The image of *1984* is compelling with respect to the kind of totalitarian extremism that concerns informed Jews.

The Jewish community has a special stake in the way America deals with political developments in countries which are "turning over," such as Nicaragua, Rhodesia, Iran; or the security and stability of Western Europe and South Korea; or the defense posture of the United States. But the framework within which the field of external relations operates, does not seriously include any working consideration of such general foreign affairs. This could be a serious flaw if the state of democratic pluralism is increasingly affected by the conduct of foreign affairs. There are also practical questions: How can the field of external relations relate to such special expertise, which it does not now have? How can the various agencies in the field of external relations find a consensus, which they do not now have? Those questions require a new examination of relevant Jewish institutions.

Even within the limited area of American foreign policy vis-à-vis Israel, external affairs agencies have proceeded on conventional wisdom, without a systematic body of knowledge or theoretical framework. In the past several years, Stephen Speigel, a professor of political science at UCLA, has managed a kind of "committee of correspondence," commissioning, collecting, and circulating papers by experts on specific aspects of American foreign policy and Israel. This highly useful project is a minimodel of what may be needed on a broader and more systematic basis. It also suggests that a "think tank" for this kind of "basket subject" does not require that its product issue exclusively or even primarily from a body of residents.

Social Action and Relevant Jewish Institutions

If the political process and its effect on the social structure is central to the course of external affairs, so is the role of the American Jew as an actor in that process. That Jewish role is perhaps the most ignored aspect of the external relations field. Democratic pluralism, as distinct from extremism, is the most hospitable mode for a small Jewish minority. In such a system, ideally, power is not exercised directly but strained through neutral laws and institutions. Much is made of the fact that laws cannot be drawn for particular individuals or groups, but must apply generally. Behind and beyond the laws and in their administration, there is the constant exercise of differential power. But this system allows more room than otherwise for indirect and partial power, variously applied. What is the nature of American Jewish power in such a system?

One classification of power bases distinguishes among "expert power," "reward power," and "coercive power."[5] As applied to the American situation, most attention has been paid to the supposed "reward power" of American Jews in the political process. Jews are presumably able to reward legislators and public officials by dint of their voting power and political activism, thus gaining some leverage in the shaping of public policy and institutions. There is much literature on this subject, but most of it is journalistic and indecisive. From the perspective of external relations, that may be just as well. If it were definitively established that Jews exercise a great deal of such power, it would fit a standard item in the catalogue of anti-Semitic beliefs: "Jews have too much power." If, more likely, it were definitively established that Jewish political power is quite marginal, limited, and situational, a useful fiction would be destroyed.

Our information and reflection on this subject is quite primitive. We are guessing most of the time. At the least, we should be more aware of what our demographic shifts might mean politically (if we only knew what our demographic shifts were). For that matter — What is the effect of a mass writing campaign? Of a demonstration, of a highly placed delegation, of editorial comment in a local newspaper? The dynamics that apply in the case of the National Rifle Association may not apply for the Jewish community. Light could be thrown on such matters by research designed and ready to be triggered by specific events and policy issues. It may turn out that the Jewish community has overestimated its "reward power" and underestimated its "expert power" and even its "coercive power," in the modern sense of affecting the climate of ideas. What is the role of the Jewish influential: the Jewish individual who is a public official or aide, writer, professor, or just a public activist? How connected are such influentials with the Jewish community, how informed are they on the urgencies of Jewish external relations, and what are the trends with respect to their connection?

There are signals that in recent years a trend of double dissociation has been taking place. On the one hand, the guess is, there has been a fall-off of young Jews involving themselves in public life. This trend would be a result of post-1967 preoccupation with Israel, combined with turmoil on the American scene dating from about that time. This is the phenomenon of the "turning in" of the Jewish community which has been often and loosely commented upon. On the other hand, the guess is, there have been a number of Jewish individuals out there in public life who have been less connected with the Jewish community agenda, with the Jewish external relations "framework," than their counterparts would have been a generation ago.

This is directly related to Jewish community relations effectiveness and to the broader question of "what is happening to the American Jew." It is probably true that Jews in active public life were once more "naturally" informed in these matters by values and knowledgeable instincts of "mother's milk" origin. Such Jews were not produced by Jewish agencies; they produced and comprised the Jewish agencies. In the past thirty years we have seen the rapid growth and dominance of Jewish external relations agencies — for mixed reasons and with mixed results.

These agencies — both the older national agencies and the newer local agencies in over one hundred communities — flourished in the aftermath of the Holocaust, out of the civil rights successes of the 1950s and early 1960s, and then because of special concerns with the security of Israel, which depends so greatly on U.S. governmental support.

Sometime during that period, the burden of Jewish external relations seemed to have "tipped," from a body of naturally informed individuals to a structure of agencies established by the communities. This "tipping" occurred for a number of reasons. There was the diminution of "naturally informed" Jewry. There were the extended boundaries of external relations. And there was just the bureaucratic momentum of the agencies themselves. There was another related development: organizational centralization. One of the failures of the American Jewish community in the 1930s was its fragmentation. The Jewish community set about to repair that failure, and managed to set up coalition and consensus mechanisms, nationally and locally, in the area of public affairs. But the older agencies themselves, flushed by success and Parkinsonian impulse, became more consensual in their search for broader membership. Once these organizations had represented different caucuses in Jewish life. Now they began to resemble each other more and more, and became less inclined toward factionalism.

In its drive for centralization and consensus the organized Jewish community became narrower in boundary and less capable as a community to deal with the broadening exigencies of modern external relations. The agencies, as a body, have taken on a certain horse-and-buggy character. These narrowing boundaries in a broadening public affairs world have exacerbated the double dissociation referred to earlier. Some Jews, caught in the organizational boundaries, have remained inordinately "turned in." Others, out there in public life, have become inordinately "turned off" with respect to Jewish organizational connection. These developments cry out for a new examination of these Jewish institutions. It may be that some decentralization is called for, and some reformation of the function of these institutions. Perhaps they must deemphasize their function as position takers and spokesmen, and function more as training grounds and wellsprings for informed Jewish individuals acting more autonomously in the public arena while remaining connected to the community.

There is another dimension. The above proposal has a certain artificial sound about it: the "creation" by public affairs agencies of active individuals informed by Jewish values and knowledge. The ability to replicate "naturally informed" Jews is at least questionable. It would seem that the complex of Jewish institutions — educational, religious, public affairs — would need to be more integrated toward this task. Here is another place where the external relations needs of the Jewish community intersect with its total needs.

There should be little expectation that Jewish institutions would be able to conduct a self-examination, or do so in isolation. Some detached, systematic, and disciplined study of Jewish institutions related at least to external relations is called for. In sum, much is known — although not enough — about the conditions of Jewish security. But the Jewish community is flying by the seat of its pants with respect to implementing that knowledge.

Interfacing

A number of issues have been raised which are simultaneously "external relations" issues and "internal Jewish life" issues. Many of these fall within the integration-assimilation-subordination framework cited earlier.

For example, we are in a period presumably emphasizing ethnocentrism, including our own, which is often called "Jewish identity." How do we best mesh ethnocentrism and pluralist equilibrium? Such questions should occasionally be addressed from a cosmic point of view, because they have implications for a number of different fields in Jewish life. Examination of certain questions in external relations should often relate to other examinations of Jewish life and vice versa. There is currently no institutional way to facilitate such cross-seeding.

Such systematic examination of external relations vis-à-vis total Jewish life might result in more informed and serious thought about the nature of *American* Jewish identity. External relations are now being defined as vitally intersecting with the very nature of democratic pluralism. Democratic pluralism is perceived by some as the "calling" — even the spiritual calling of the formal American society. The role of Jews is perceived as important, or potentially important, in supporting this aspect of American life. If these perceptions are valid and can be further developed, they may help to further not only a sense of authenticity as Jews, but a sense of authenticity as Jews in America.

Notes

1. Proceedings of the Thirteenth General Convention of B'nai B'rith (Cincinnati, Ohio, April 27, 1930), pp. 507–58.
2. NORC survey reported in S.M. Lipset and Earl Raab, *The Politics of Unreason* (Chicago: University of Chicago Press, 2nd ed., 1978).
3. Gertrude J. Selznick and Stephen Steinberg, *The Tenacity of Prejudice* (New York: Harper & Row, 1969), p. 157.
4. Quoted in R.A. Schermerhorn, *Comparative Ethnic Relations* (New York: Random House, 1970), p. 22.
5. J.R. French and B. Raven, "The Bases of Social Power." In D. Cartwright (ed.), *Studies in Social Power* (Ann Arbor: University of Michigan Press, 1959).

9.

Research Needs of National Jewish Organizations

Ira Silverman

National Jewish organizations in the United States perceive little need for social research of the sort (sociological, psychological, demographic, political) under discussion in this volume.[1] They occasionally commission or engage in such research, but it is often for reasons other than to fill gaps in the knowledge they need to achieve their organizational mandates. Social research pertinent to the work of these organizations could significantly enlighten and guide their work. Their current operational styles make it difficult or unlikely for them to promote such research in the absence of clearly perceived needs.

Use of Social Research

Before looking at current and potential research needs of Jewish organizations, it may be helpful to consider the utilization of social research by policymaking and action agencies generally. According to a recent essay by Carol H. Weiss on the subject,[2] people say that social science research should be used, but many of those doing the saying are social scientists who, like Tugwell on his way to Roosevelt's Washington, expect to "speak truth to power." Such a posture, in Weiss's words, "presupposes that a) there is a clear and single truth, b) they have it by the tail . . . , c) powerful decision makers will heed this truth, and d) decisions embodying such 'truth' will be better and wiser than decisions reached on other grounds."

I hold no such assumptions across the board, but I believe that in many instances of complex problems, social science can provide both theoretical direction and empirical guideposts to help the policymaker reach sound decisions. This holds true even if one discounts the social scientist's natural interest in achieving personal status or in influencing policy decisions. No social science research is value-free. By the concepts it uses, its theoretical premises, its focus on certain issues, by the normative bases of its recommendations, research takes a stand.[3] Research is nevertheless useful as long as the decision maker accepts or at least recognizes and accounts for a given set of values.

How can social research be useful? Decision theory puts forth at least two elementary models describing the use of social research for policy-making. The first and most commonly conceived pattern is the problem-solving or "decision-driven" model. The policymaker faces a problem on which he must make a decision — issue a statement, support or oppose legislation, join a coalition. Information is lacking to generate a solution or to choose among alternatives. Research then provides the missing knowledge, leading to a solution. Instrumental social research can provide evidence of several types. It can be qualitative and descriptive (such as an observational account of relations between Jews and members of another ethnic group). It can be quantitative data on "soft" indicators (such as public attitudes about Israel) or "hard" matters (such as the dollar distribution of Jewish philanthropic funds). Or it can be a mix of these, including generalized conclusions about the associations between factors or even theories in terms of cause and effect.[4] If the needed research does not antedate the policy problem, in which case it could be drawn on in need, it can be commissioned to fill the knowledge gap. This "decision-driven" model assumes that policymakers have a clear idea of their goals and alternatives, but lack some item of understanding which can be supplied by the social researcher. The expectation is that research generated in this sequence will have direct applicability in the decision-making process — it will be "used."

An alternative pattern is described by the "knowledge-driven" model. Research can be used for policymaking not only in the case of a problem that requires elucidation but also when the research itself engenders new ideas which suggest applications for policy. Although examples of this model generally come from the physical sciences (e.g. basic biochemical research produces contraceptive pills), this model can also apply in the social policy realm.[5] (A basic Jewish demographic survey, for example, could reveal high incidences of divorce, poverty, or other "pathologies" which could then be treated; or more positively, general research into ethnotherapy could yield several strategies for Jewish identity transmission from generation to generation.) In these cases, either the problem itself or a suggested solution to a recognized problem is brought to light by social research not specifically intended for that purpose.

There are several other ways in which social research may be used. It can be employed to back up a predetermined position on an issue — as political ammunition for the side that finds the research supportive of its stand. Or it can be used to delay action ("let's have a study"); to avoid taking responsibility for a decision ("the experts say . . . "); to gain prestige for the agency that hires a renowned scholar to do the research; to help publicize or gain recognition for a decision or planned program. These are not illegitimate uses, but they are less fundamental and germane to our purposes of assessing the research needs of national Jewish organizations — despite the fact that Jewish agencies, like most others, often commission or engage in research for these reasons.

These models of research utilization fit into the four points presented at the outset. First, organizations only rarely perceive the need to use social research directly for problem solving, as in the decision-driven model. Second, they do commission or engage in research, but most often for the (legitimate but less policy-useful) purposes mentioned above. Third, there is significant potential guidance to be gained by the Jewish community from greater general support of policy-oriented social research, as in the knowledge-driven model. Fourth, as currently structured, Jewish organizations are not likely to pursue that route.

Postwar Social Research for National Jewish Organizations

A brief historical review of American Jewry's postwar affair with social research is in order. As early as 1948 H.L. Lurie, writing for YIVO, expressed concern about the lack of systematic use of social research by American Jewish organizations. He wrote:

> It will be noted that for the greater part of this [last] period of fifty years, Jewish researches were fragmentary or sporadic or consisted of occasional or continuing gathering of welfare agency statistics. Special surveys or studies were made in response to a specific need for help in the administration of welfare programs. Such projects involved for the most part statisticians and practical social welfare administrators rather than specialized social research personnel. Not until American Jews were becoming acutely aware of the growth of anti-Semitism in the 1930s and uncertain about the efficacy of their "practical" programs of protesting prejudices and combating discrimination do we find any serious attempt to utilize the methods and skills of sociologists, economists, psychologists, and historians. For most of this time there has been relatively little community interest in the Jewish experience of the past and its meaning for contemporary Jewish life, considered to be merely the curiosity of specialists and scholars. Except for some of the research scholars associated with some of the Jewish agencies there is little interest expressed in American Jewish experience as a subject for historical and sociological research. Hundreds of thousands of dollars are raised annually to study the proper methods for combating anti-Semitism, or to assemble information on the war efforts of Jewry, lesser but substantial sums to record philanthropic activities or to study current social welfare services. The amounts available for basic population and demographic data, economic and social analysis, cultural and personality development are exceedingly meagre.[6]

Lurie's prognosis was less gloomy, although along the same lines of thought. It was prescient in its emphasis on health and welfare services, Israel, and anti-Semitism, but probably overly pessimistic regarding American Jewish sociology:

> We may expect that there will be continuing interest and financial support of organized research which is considered to be immediately useful to programs for health and welfare services in the United States, for the expenditure of funds for overseas and Palestine programs and for all those activities which are related to the campaigns against anti-Semitism. We may also anticipate that these studies will improve progressively both in content and in the calibre of the professional workers engaged in this research. On the other hand, the lag may continue in those phases of research which are primarily concerned with knowledge about American Jewry, the processes of social and economic adjustment, and the changes in culture that the various immigrant stocks which comprise American Jewry have undergone. We may hope, however, that a recognition of the importance of such studies may gradually be achieved by those research workers and by the agencies that employ them in studying contemporary agencies and programs and that through such recognition they will influence the development of basic research. Perhaps out of our preoccupations with anti-Semitism and how to resolve it, we may be led into the productive task of thinking more deeply about ourselves, and go on from introspection toward study and analysis.[7]

Fifteen years later, in a survey of the needs of Jewish social science research, Victor Sanua echoed these concerns and called for Jewish organizations to address several key issues:

> There is definite need for a more systematic study of Jewish personality and Jewish life in America, particularly because Jewish life is undergoing many changes. What do these changes mean to the self-concept of the Jews? What are some of the values we need to maintain in order to perpetuate and strengthen Jewish identification? What are the aspirations and views of Jewish adolescents concerning the present and the future? These are some of the areas which could and should be investigated. With the founding of the state of Israel, the position of the Jews in the United States has become more complex. What is the degree of allegiance which American Jews, young and old, feel toward Israel? The recent controversies over the meaning of Zionism make this type of research even more pertinent. A thorough analysis of the reactions of various segments of American Jewry towards Israel would provide illuminating data.[8]

Sanua also made the point that while there had been a lack of research on the "Jewish personality," many studies had been published on the "anti-Semitic personality," culminating in the monumental work of Adorno et al., *The Authoritarian Personality* (sponsored by the American Jewish Committee and published in 1952). Although Sanua commended these efforts, he expressed serious concern that the study of the biased individual had been overemphasized to the neglect of studying the object of this bias, members of minority groups themselves.[9]

By 1963, the year of Sanua's survey, Marshall Sklare was well on his way to the fatherhood of American Jewish sociology. Not only had he begun addressing many of the questions put by Lurie and Sanua, among others, but he also analyzed the state of the art at that time. In his essay "The Development and Utilization of Sociological Research: The Case of the American Jewish Community,"[10] Sklare suggested that American Jewry might wish to enhance the study of itself: "Jewish agencies may sponsor research as an aid to solving specific problems of programmatic concern or because of a desire to attain a better understanding of the general position of the group on whose behalf they labor."[11] Sklare asserted that despite this attractive possibility, such research was exceedingly modest both in quantity and quality. In trying to ascertain why this was the case, he analyzed four fields of inquiry which in his view should have been ripe for study by organized American Jewry: demography, philanthropy, religion, and intergroup relations. It is worth reviewing his assessments of sixteen years ago.

On demography and social characteristics, Sklare noted that protest by Jewish agencies against data collection by governmental bodies had not given rise to the establishment of any demographic research agency conducted under Jewish auspices. The field was thus left mostly to local Jewish population surveys, with the result that knowledge of Jewish demographic and social characteristics was spotty and incomplete; even the data collected were not generally subjected to anything approaching exhaustive analysis.

On philanthropic behavior, research was also left largely to local communities, mostly to local federations — with similarly incomplete and underutilized results. Regarding religious behavior, some national groups — most notably the Union of American Hebrew Congregations and to a lesser extent the United Synagogue of America — had begun to conduct research, but results were not satisfactory. The regular UAHC surveys of its (Reform) congregations (covering membership statistics, sources of income, nature of expenditures, types of congregational activity, religious school organizations, personnel practices) were comprehensive, but of limited utility since they were more descriptive than analytical. Sklare suggested several questions that should be asked about American Jewish religious life, which, as we shall see, were subsequently addressed by agency-sponsored research.

It was in the field of intergroup relations, particularly anti-Semitism, that agency-sponsored efforts were most extensive by the time of Sklare's 1963 survey. Research on anti-Semitism, according to Sklare, differed from the study of Jewish demography, philanthropy, and religious behavior both quantitatively and qualitatively. Unlike those other fields, the study of anti-Semitism was characterized by a sharing of interest and responsibility between Jewish agencies and private scholars. Sklare cited comments about the excellent working relations between the scholarly researchers who prepared *The Authoritarian Personality* and its sponsor, the American Jewish Committee.

What use was made by the agencies of this relatively extensive and good research they promoted? Sklare wrote that an adequate answer must await the definitive histories of the agencies as well as analyses of their techniques to combat anti-Semitism, but that the general result of the research was clear:

> It has been in the direction of increasing agency sophistication. The ideas once shared by some laymen and professionals which research has modified include the following: anti-Semitism is a phenomenon which can be combated by the distribution of materials containing accurate information about the in-group; prejudice is a reaction to particular qualities or actions of the in-group; the predisposition toward anti-Jewish sentiment grows as rapidly at one stage in the life-cycle as another.[12]

A dozen years after Sklare's analysis of Jewish social research, Daniel Elazar addressed the 1975 General Assembly of the Council of Jewish Federations on the same subject, and brought the picture up to date.[13] Studies of Jewish demography, Jewish identity, and intermarriage had advanced the knowledge of those fields, but Elazar's evaluation differs little from Sklare's. He added one major item to the menu of Jewish social research. Not surprisingly, it emerges from his own field, political science. He stated:

> We are now seeing the emergence of yet another element in the Jewish social research package, to be added to the others, and that is the emergence of Jewish political research. Studies in this discipline have taken two forms. One is policy research, the study of how Jews as a community should cope with the political problems that face them externally and internally. . . . The second form involves research into the structure and dynamics, the organization and functions, of Jewish communities, their processes of decision-making, budgeting, and the like.

Although Elazar was little more sanguine than Sklare about the extent and quality of agency-sponsored Jewish social research, the fact is that each of the fields analyzed by Sklare has had significant development in the last fifteen or so years since Sklare's essay. Several key items of such agency-sponsored research deserve mention here.[14]

Recent Agency-Sponsored Research

It is in the demographic field that the single most monumental agency-sponsored research has been undertaken. The National Jewish Population Study (NJPS)[15] was launched in 1970 by the Council of Jewish Federations and Welfare Funds, and ultimately resulted in a survey of some 10,000 Jewish households distributed across the country. Despite participation in the project of some of the best demographers and sociologists available to the Jewish community, NJPS has since been criticized for having serious sampling and technical problems, and for having inadequately analyzed the data collected. These criticisms have put in doubt whether NJPS was worth its $600,000 cost. An answer to that question awaits a determination of how, if at all, the NJPS findings are used in the planning of national and local agencies to which the results are made available. Accurate data on demographic issues — family size, birth rates, marriage and divorce, residential mobility, income and education — could be very valuable for the policy planning of national groups and for the financial considerations of local federations which, through CJF, paid for the project.

Sklare's "Lakeville" studies — published as *Jewish Identity on the Suburban Frontier*[16] in 1967 — were undertaken directly by the American Jewish Committee, and remain the model for Jewish identity research. Since that study, national agencies have supported several inquiries into Jewish identity and religious behavior, but all on a smaller scale. Such works include the UAHC's *Reform Is a Verb* by Leonard Fein,[17] the CCAR's *Rabbi and Synagogue in Reform Judaism* by Theodore Lenn,[18] several analyses based on NJPS data by Bernard Lazerwitz sponsored by the Institute for Jewish Policy Planning and Research of the Synagogue Council of America,[19] and Egon Mayer's study of intermarriage for the American Jewish Committee.[20]

Since the authoritarian personality studies there have been several further agency-sponsored inquiries into anti-Semitism, attitudes toward Jews, and so forth, but none on that scale. Among the notable products were the Anti-Defamation League's University of California Study[21] and its book *The New Anti-Semitism*.[22] The American Jewish Committee has most recently helped support the work of William Schneider, analyzing public opinion data regarding Jews and Israel, to be published in the near future.[23]

Daniel Elazar contributed significantly to fulfilling the need he saw for research into Jewish community structure, through the publication of his *Community and Polity*.[24] Research funds to assist that project were made available from, among others, the Synagogue Council's Institute for Jewish Policy Planning and Research, which also sponsored some related work in progress by Samuel Klausner on the dynamics of a synagogue in a changing community.

Current and Future Research Needs

It is beyond the scope of this chapter to project which issues will dominate the national Jewish communal agenda in the years ahead,[25] and hence to suggest just which problems could use some social research input — but some current and expected trends can be discerned. In the absence of any unanticipated crises, national Jewish agencies will continue to focus on problems of Jewish life in America, engendering public and governmental support for Israel, combating anti-Semitism and other discrimination, and on alleviating the plight of imperiled Jews in other parts of the world. These agencies will also seek to ensure their own institutional well-being and survival. Given these anticipated general goals, what kinds of additional Jewish social research are likely to be useful to these agencies? The following five categories are the most important.

Demography

In order to address many central problems of Jewish life in America — assimilation, intermarriage, declining population, and even the economic status and political influence of Jews — Jewish organizations will need more and better demographic research about Jews in the United States. It would be wise to reconsider and reverse official Jewish opposition to inclusion of a religious identification question in the U.S. Decennial Census. Regardless of whether that option is taken, the agencies will need — and the community should supply — a regular flow of data on family size, birth rates, marriage and divorce, residential mobility, income, education, etc. of American Jewry.

Jewish Attitudes and Political Behavior

Although there is no pressing need for more studies of Jewish identity formation, indices, etc., the agencies could benefit from regular gauging of Jewish attitudes and political behavior: what Jews think about Jewish issues (marriage patterns, resettlement of Soviet Jews, Israeli government policies) as well as general social issues (unemployment, inflation, affirmative action, public education) and how they act in political terms (voting patterns, partisan affiliation, organization memberships). Our organizations gain some indication of these matters from their own members, but even that is not done on a systematic basis. While Jewish organizations need not necessarily base policy decisions on a tabulation of community sentiment, they should take better and more systematic cognizance of what Jews think and how they act on the issues.[26]

U.S. Public Opinion and Behavioral Trends

Inasmuch as national Jewish organizations will continue to concentrate on engendering official and public support for Israel and pressing for other public stands on issues of concern, as well as combating anti-Semitism and other attitudes hostile to Jewish interests, they will need the best information about public opinion on these matters. While much information on public attitudes regarding Israel is readily available from routine polls of such commercial operations as Gallup and Harris, we could benefit from much more regular and intensive examination of public opinion trends — investigating the views of the general public as well as those of selected key subgroups such as opinion leaders, Blacks, university students, various church memberships, regional groups. This information would be supplemented by another type of needed research, namely trend analysis — what these public opinion data, along with reports of incidence of violence, organizational growth, propaganda activities, etc., tell us about social trends to which we should be alerted, such as the strengthening of extremist groups on the Right or Left, or the growth of Arab economic and political influence in America.

Condition of Jewish Communities Abroad

Although there may be less technical or theoretical appeal in the study of the situation of Jews in other parts of the world (than there is, say, in Jewish identity research or in public opinion analysis), this kind of research is imperative if Jewish organizations are to fulfill their mandate of relieving the plight of imperiled Jewish communities. We must have more detailed and current information on the political and economic condition of Jews in all countries, but particularly those outside of North America and Western Europe (the Soviet Union, Rumania, Hungary, Argentina, South Africa, Iran). Such research is being commissioned by the *American Jewish Year Book* and the World Jewish Congress's Institute of Jewish Affairs in London, among others, but more will be needed.

Institutional Survival

National Jewish organizations like community federations will have to address questions pertaining to their own survival: where will money and membership come from; how to relate, externally, to federations and umbrella groups, and internally to local chapters; how to manage their bureaucratic organizations more efficiently; and how to develop institutional leadership for the future. Such recent studies as Steven M. Cohen's analysis of Jewish philanthropic patterns[27] and Charles Liebman's work on the New York Federation[28] and the American Jewish Congress are illustrative of the kind of research which may be needed in this category.

Such research will be useful to national Jewish organizations in the years ahead. One problem is that organizations do not always recognize the need for such research in advance of their having to take steps toward the solution of problems which the research could elucidate (as in the "decision-driven" model). The customer does not always know what he wants. Another function of social research for the Jewish organization would be to help in agenda setting: analyzing issues likely to confront Jews and determining a pertinent research agenda well in advance of crises. In each of these categories social researchers could assist agencies in connecting research findings to current policy problems — setting forth the problem, marshalling pertinent data, and outlining options. Agencies should consider increased sponsorship of basic research in the categories described above, in order to elicit data and analysis which would be on hand for dealing with unanticipated crises and which could suggest new problems or new directions for solving old ones (as in the "knowledge-driven" model).

Organizations do not usually operate in a style conducive to such policy analysis or broad research sponsorship. Their program departments address current, immediate problems. If they have specialized research departments, for budgeting and public relations reasons they are often not in a position or inclined to engage in basic research projects. Few agencies have the luxury of adequate budget and insulation from immediate pressures to pursue long-term research and systematic policy analysis (which was the aim of such single-purpose research operations as the Synagogue Council's Institute for Jewish Policy Planning and Research, now closed, and the World Jewish Congress's Institute of Jewish Affairs).

Research Sponsorship

How is the research to be generated and conducted? One option would be for the organizations, either singly or in some cooperative fashion, to develop their own research arms and endow them with the funds and insulation (from other pressures) necessary to fulfill their aims. Such departments could both engage in "in-house" research and commission studies by outside scholars, when appropriate. In view of my own former association with the Synagogue Council's institute, it should be clear that I have supported such efforts, although I recognize numerous difficulties (of funding and organizational relationships) which may hinder their achievement.

Another option entails the establishment of one or more centers, under university auspices, devoted to the study of contemporary Jewry and available to service some research needs of national Jewish organizations. Such a center could prove extremely valuable. The idea of a university-based center to conduct research for American Jewry is not new. In his 1948 paper cited above, Max Weinreich broached the idea:

From whatever angle we approach it, a well equipped central planning, research, and training institution in the domain of Jewish social science is essential. For the time being, while the universities cannot yet be counted upon, this institution is indispensable. Once it is firmly entrenched, the efforts of individual scholars outside of it will obviously become infinitely more meaningful. But even with a score of Jewish chairs all over the country, the usefulness of a central clearing house for documentation and planning is self-evident and the call for coordination will be even more urgent than at present.[29]

Sanua, too, advocated such a center, advancing the idea to locate it in a Jewish institution:

It is our feeling that if a secure place is to be developed for Jewish social science, a well-financed organization should be established with responsibilities to encourage and initiate support of research, and to disseminate its findings. To enhance the prospect of community support, such an organization should be established within the framework of a general institution of Jewish learning. Many of the major universities have established research divisions which have been given various names such as Human Relations, Social Relations, etc. A Jewish university, by the same token, could establish a similar organization primarily focusing its interests on Jewish social studies.[30]

And Sklare, sixteen years ago, foreshadowed this development stating that "Jewish-sponsored institutions of higher learning, having fully established their academic respectability as general institutions of higher learning, may move in the direction of seeking to emphasize the distinctive character of the institution and thus may encourage scholarship on the contemporary Jewish community and its problems."[31]

If and when such a center develops the respect and trust of national organizations, its scholars could assist the agencies in the research and agenda-setting function described above. They could then be available, according to field of competence, to accept commissions to engage in basic or policy research the organizations determine they need or wish to sponsor. Not all the categories described above are likely to be in the field of specialization of scholars of contemporary American Jewry, but certainly some of the demographic, attitudinal, and instructional questions would be.

The agencies have developed some expertise in trend analysis, and have developed contacts to assist with public opinion research and overseas research, but these areas, too, could benefit from the academic expertise of scholars who might be associated with such a center. Presumably the scholars to be at such a center already stand available, on an individual basis, to perform research services for the organizations. The advantages of a center which would assemble such people are numerous. Not only would they benefit from the interchange which characterizes a university department, but they would be at a single address easily reached by client agencies, and would have as one of their fundamental aims the conduct of research needed by those agencies.

Sklare wrote in 1963 that should scholars be ready to work in contemporary Jewish studies, and should appropriate institutional frameworks be established, "the burden of proof will be shifted. Social science will be confronted with the question of whether it is equal to the tasks being thrust upon the discipline."[32] We now may be near that task; but so also will the national Jewish agencies have to prove wise enough to identify their research needs, raise and allocate the funds required to obtain the studies, conduct or buy the best research available, and then *use* it to inform its policy decisions. Several agencies are ready for that challenge.

Notes

1. By national Jewish organizations I refer primarily to the major community relations agencies (the American Jewish Committee, the American Jewish Congress, the Anti-Defamation League of B'nai B'rith), the Zionist agencies (Hadassah, the Zionist Organization of America), the synagogal agencies (the Synagogue Council of America and its six constituents, most notably in this context, the Union of American Hebrew Congregations and the United Synagogue of America), and some key special constituency or special purpose groups (the National Council of Jewish Women, the Jewish War Veterans, the Jewish Labor Committee). Additionally, the major national coordinating agencies (The Council of Jewish Federations for the federations, the National Jewish Welfare Board for the community centers, the NJCRAC for the community relations councils, etc.) have been instrumental in promoting research, and so the needs of these groups and their constituents are also taken into consideration. Although I have conferred with leaders of most of these agencies on their research needs, in general and for the purpose of this chapter, the views presented here are attributable only to myself.
2. Carol H. Weiss (ed.), "Introduction." In *Using Social Research in Public Policy Making* (New York, Lexington Books, 1977).
3. Ibid., p. 10.
4. Ibid., p. 12.
5. For the opposing view — that this model is less applicable in the social sciences — see Weiss, p. 13.
6. H.L. Lurie, "The Status of Basic Jewish Social Research in the United States" (New York: YIVO, mimeo, 1948), p. 6.
7. Ibid., p. 8. For an interesting rejoinder to Lurie, see "Jewish Social Research: Status and Prospects" by Max Weinreich, also in a 1948 YIVO paper. For example (p. 3):

> The necessity of gathering facts about Jewish community life, as Mr. Lurie shows, has been gradually recognized. But isn't it a truism that the very definition of a pertinent fact depends upon the particular frame of reference? Probably, nobody will doubt the desirability of a study concerning the adjustment of a group of DPs in some Mid-Western city and it would be most

reassuring to any of us to learn that within a year all of them have found jobs and study English in night school. So far, so good. But haven't also the "indigenous" Jews been affected by the recent arrivals, intellectually or emotionally? And what about the impact of the increase in the Jewish community upon the non-Jewish population? Such a question immediately makes us think of adverse effects, but it need not do so. Couldn't it be that the effect was different upon different strata of the population? Because of the lack of research, we hardly know how to put the questions intelligently. But one thing we know for certain: the fate of the Jews the world over, in our times as before, affects the fate of the Jews in this country, too. To what degree? In what respects particularly? How has the Jew's concept of himself, and other people's concept of him, been changing? It is not sufficient to indulge in generalities; and there is no specific knowledge without meticulous research. By the way, this knowledge, indispensable to the Jews, is also highly valuable to the general social scientist because of the wealth of relevant new material that would be placed at his disposal.

8. Victor D. Sanua, "A Survey of the Needs of Jewish Social Science Research," *Journal of Jewish Communal Service* (Fall 1963), p. 48.
9. Ibid., p. 50.
10. Marshall Sklare, "The Development and Utilization of Sociological Research: The Case of the American Jewish Community," *Jewish Journal of Sociology* 5 (December 1963).
11. Ibid., p. 168.
12. Ibid., p. 182.
13. Daniel J. Elazar, "What We Know and What We Need to Know about the Status of Jewish Social Research." Presented at the General Assembly of the Council of Jewish Federations and Welfare Funds (Miami Beach, November 22, 1975). Reprinted in the *Journal of Jewish Communal Service* (Spring 1978).
14. Those mentioned are only some of the many examples of agency-sponsored research; they were selected either because of their signal importance or their representative nature.
15. Council of Jewish Federations and Welfare Funds, *National Jewish Population Study*. Mimeo reports published 1973–75; summary article by Fred Massarik in *American Jewish Year Book* 75 (1974–75): 296–304.
16. Marshall Sklare and Joseph Greenblum, *Jewish Identity on the Suburban Frontier: A Study of Group Survival in the Open Society* (New York: Basic Books, 1967). 2nd ed. (Chicago: University of Chicago Press, 1979). Companion volume by Benjamin B. Ringer, *The Edge of Friendliness: A Study of Jewish-Gentile Relations* (New York: Basic Books, 1967).
17. Leonard J. Fein, *Reform Is a Verb* (New York: Union of American Hebrew Congregations, 1972).
18. Theodore I. Lenn, *Rabbi and Synagogue in Reform Judaism* (New York: Central Conference of American Rabbis, 1972).
19. Among others, see Bernard Lazerwitz, "Past and Future Trends in the Size of American Jewish Denominations," *Journal of Reform Judaism* (Summer 1979).
20. Egon Mayer and Carl Sheingold, *Intermarriage and the Jewish Future* (New York: American Jewish Committee, 1979).

21. Charles Y. Glock and Ellen Siegelman (eds.), *Prejudice U.S.A.* (New York: Praeger, 1969).
22. Arnold Forster and Benjamin R. Epstein, *The New Anti-Semitism* (New York: McGraw Hill, 1974).
23. William Schneider, "Anti-Semitism and Israel: A Report on American Public Opinion" (New York: American Jewish Committee, December 1978, mimeo).
24. Daniel J. Elazar, *Community and Polity: The Organizational Dynamics of American Jewry* (Philadelphia: Jewish Publication Society of America, 1976).
25. The American Jewish Committee is aiming to determine such an agenda for the 1980s, through a series of task forces which will address the issues likely to dominate national Jewish agency attention in the decade ahead. Such an effort was undertaken for the 1970s, resulting in the publication of task force reports and collections of essays on *The Future of the Jewish Community in America, World Politics and the Jewish Condition,* and *Group Life in America.*
26. Eight years ago Erich Rosenthal suggested that social research ought to focus similarly on Jewish attitudes and behavior: "The next step in Jewish social research ought to be a thorough analysis of the third and fourth generation (grandchildren and great-grandchildren of the immigrants) with regard to Zionism, to assimilation (intermarriage), internal migration (the move from the large Jewish population centers), social mobility (what comes after the rapid rise in socioeconomic status?), and social disorganization (especially drug addiction)." Erich Rosenthal, "The Current Status of Jewish Social Research," *Midstream* (April 1971).
27. Steven M. Cohen, "Will Jews Keep Giving?" *Journal of Jewish Communal Service* (Fall 1978).
28. Charles S. Liebman, "Decision Making in the Jewish Community: The New York Federation of Jewish Philanthropies," *American Jewish Year Book* 79 (1979).
29. Weinreich, p. 5.
30. Sanua, p. 57.
31. Sklare, p. 184.
32. Ibid.

10.

Research Needs of Local Jewish Communities: Current Trends and New Directions

Bruce A. Phillips

Much Jewish social research has been conducted by or about local communities, a tradition which goes back to the early twenties.[1] While many of these studies exhibit a timid intellectual scope and questionable intellectual rigor, many classic works in Jewish sociology have been community studies. At the turn of the century Charles Bernheimer produced the first volume of research on the social conditions of American Jews.[2] Bernheimer's volume was a collection of community studies conducted in New York, Philadelphia, and Chicago. Louis Wirth's *The Ghetto* is a study of the areas of first and second settlement in Chicago.[3] More recently Sklare and Greenblum's study of "Lakeville" is a community study in the grand tradition of "Yankee City" and "Middletown."[4] Even our knowledge of intermarriage has been largely based on findings from local Jewish community studies.[5]

The ambitious scope of the National Jewish Population Study conducted in 1970 has not altered the trend of local Jewish research. Since the NJPS over twenty local communities have conducted local surveys on their own: Akron (1974), Allentown (1976), Boston (1975), Dallas (1974), Erie (1977), Hamilton, Ontario (1978), Houston (1978), Jersey City (1978), Kansas City (1976), Minneapolis (1972), New Orleans (1973), Norfolk (1974), Oakland (1979), Omaha (1976), Pittsburgh (1976), Portland, Oregon (1977), St. Petersburg (1972), Salt Lake City (1976), San Diego (1975, 1979), Seattle (1978), Vineland (1977), and Los Angeles (1980). Local Jewish federations probably represent a larger group of social research consumers than does the community of scholars. In the West an interest in social research has even taken root in the synagogue community. In Los Angeles, for example, one of the larger Conservative synagogues in the city recently commissioned a major survey of its membership. The Pacific-Southwest Council of the Union of American Hebrew Congregations is currently working with individual Reform synagogues to include research as part of a larger effort to encourage long-range planning at the local level.[6] On the national scene the Conservative movement has launched an ambitious research effort for long-range planning on a wider scale.[7]

Through the proposed Center for Modern Jewish Studies the academic community could make a significant contribution toward enhancing both the scope and quality of local Jewish communal research. Despite the importance of nationally conducted research, the local Jewish community itself should be considered a priority on the center's scholarly agenda. In the first part of this chapter I shall discuss the current state of local Jewish research along with new directions and standards which the center could be instrumental in developing. In the second part I shall argue for the importance of the local Jewish community as a research setting and object of research. I shall conclude with some recommendations for the agenda of the center itself with regard to the local Jewish community.

Local Jewish Research at the Dawn of the Eighties

Local Jewish communal research is conducted by and for the local federation, and it is this body that will be the focus of attention here. As Daniel Elazar has pointed out, federation-sponsored research is applied research —in the sense that it is designed to be used in decision making rather than as the exploration of causes or trends.[8] The current state of applied research in the federations is both promising and disturbing. It is promising in that new directions are developing; disturbing in that many conceptual and methodological problems have remained unresolved over the years. I have divided my remarks into two categories here: the more traditional area of Jewish communal research, and the new areas being explored in agency-related research.

The Community Population Estimates and Demographic Surveys

Estimates of the local Jewish population are the most prevalent type of local social research. The *American Jewish Year Book* published estimates for communities as small as one hundred persons. Sampling techniques used in community surveys use the same basic techniques as population estimates and are thus weakened by similar methodological shortcomings. Both survey sampling and population estimates must identify Jewish households within the general population. Over the years a number of techniques have been used for population estimates including Yom Kippur school absences, extrapolating from U.S. Census count of "Russian foreign born" and "Russian foreign stock," and counting "distinctive Jewish names" (DJN) in the phone directory. Currently DJN is the most popular method for estimating the local Jewish population. In its most sophisticated application the DJN method uses a list of distinctive names and counts their occurrence in the local phone directory. This number is multiplied by a numerical constant based on the relative proportion of these names among all Jews. The result is an estimate of Jewish households which is then multiplied by the average family size to produce the population estimate itself.

The great attraction of this method is its relative economy. However, there are a number of methodological issues which have not been adequately addressed. First, the numerical constant used for multiplication, demands, but has never received, ongoing revision to include the effect of factors such as intermarriage or new groups in the Jewish population without distinctive East European names, such as Iranian or Israeli Jews. Second, the same numerical constant is not necessarily valid in all parts of the city. In Los Angeles, for example, the older Beverly-Fairfax neighborhood is overrepresented with older, first-generation Jews more likely to have distinctive names. To this overrepresentation is added the influx of recent Russian immigrants most of whom have distinctively Jewish names. Third, the DJN method assumes that each surname has equal prevalence, while there may be important differences. Finally, the rate of unlisted phone numbers, which varies in different parts of the city, is not taken into account.

When communal surveys are done the most generally used sample frame is the federation list itself. Of the over twenty community surveys cited earlier only two used a sample frame other than the federation list. The Los Angeles survey was entirely based on a random sample, and the Boston survey was partly based on a random sample and partly on a list sample.[9] The problem with list sampling is that it includes only affiliated Jews. This not only biases the sample but makes it impossible to compare affiliated with unaffiliated Jews. In only one study where list sampling was used did the researchers make any attempt to test the completeness of the federation list.[10] Other studies either assume that the federation list covers the majority of Jews in the community or fall back on one or both of two rationales.

The first rationale is that community studies are intended for planning services and unaffiliated Jews do not use federation services. An example of this argument is found in the recently completed survey of the San Diego Jewish community where the researchers assert that "the first priority of this initial analysis was the identification of needs within the existing 'up front' community. These are the individuals who *are* found on the U.J.F. mailing list, who fund the Federation and the JCC, and who comprise the community which utilizes most of these services."[11]

This reasoning is correct in terms of the Jewish Community Center. However, if there is a sizable number of poor and elderly Jews (as in Los

Angeles), it is doubtful that these persons, who are in need of services, will be sampled from the federation list. A second rationale, rarely put in writing but asserted with some frequency, is that Jewish households which do not contribute to the local campaign have forfeited their right to be considered a part of the community. All but the most hard-nosed campaign leadership would find this statement philosophically objectionable. Yet it gains sudden credence when a local community ponders the cost of obtaining a sample at random from the community at large. Ironically, it is usually the same professionals and lay people who balk at sampling the unaffiliated who will elsewhere emphasize the importance of "reaching out" to this group.

In Los Angeles we experimented with a methodology that was addressed to both the population estimate problem and the problem of sampling. The literature on survey research suggests that locating Jews at random is a special application of "screening to locate rare populations."[12] Using a recently developed technique for telephone sampling called Random Digit Dialing, a sampling of 24,000 phone numbers was generated by computer, yielding 12,000 residential phone numbers of which over 900 were Jewish households. Using the 12,000 residential households as one sample, we were able to estimate the number of Los Angeles Jewish households within a few percents.[13] The 900 plus Jewish households yielded 823 interviews which formed the sample used for analyzing characteristics of the Los Angeles Jewish population.

Despite the Los Angeles success in demonstrating the feasibility of exploring new sampling techniques, the individual local community does not have the resources, institutional commitment, or personnel needed for a serious effort at upgrading community survey methodology. Were the proposed center to take on this commitment, four methodological issues should be addressed immediately. First, it may not be economically feasible for all communities to undertake a random sample from the population at large. However, it is imperative that the biases introduced by list sampling be more carefully assessed. How do the age, size, and regional location of a community affect the validity of list sampling? Who tends to be excluded when list sampling is employed? In an effort to address this question, the Los Angeles federation undertook a small experiment that can serve to exemplify the kind of fruitful work the center might undertake on a larger scale. Using federation lists for the Jewishly sparse San Gabriel Valley, a sample of fifty households was interviewed. These will be compared with fifty households sampled at random from the population at large.

Second, there are two ways to screen from the population at large: directly and indirectly. In direct screening, the nature of the survey is explained to the sampled household and the respondent is asked whether there are any Jewish persons living there. Indirect screening involves a preliminary questionnaire (which could form part of a larger study) in which religion is included as a question. If the respondent would otherwise be reluctant to identify himself/herself as Jewish in a direct question, indirect screening should include this respondent in the survey. In theory the indirect approach should be more inclusive of marginal Jews, but more expensive given the time taken for the preliminary questionnaire. Conversely, the direct approach should be less expensive but less inclusive. Are these assumptions correct, and if so, what are the relative costs in dollars and in the accuracy of the two techniques?

The third issue the center should address is the effectiveness of the telephone survey in Jewish community surveys. In the sociological literature telephone surveys are gaining increasing acceptance.[14] While they are considerably cheaper than house-to-house surveys, the effectiveness of telephone surveys in the Jewish community has yet to be studied. If shown to be effective, the general introduction of this method might make the random screening sample an economically viable option for many communities that could not consider it at present.

Finally, there is the effect of sponsorship. Some communities conduct surveys directly, while others employ a university-connected researcher who can downplay the sponsor and add credibility to the study. Do respondents react differently to a university-conducted study than to one conducted directly by the Jewish community?

The focus of community surveys tends to be largely on the immediate provision of services rather than on more long-range planning issues. Historically the federation movement has been oriented toward alleviation of social distress rather than of social change. The academic training of most communal professionals is in community organization rather than in disciplines such as urban planning, health planning, or public administration. In the absence of established Jewish communal planning models, community surveys tend to be cautious and unambitious even in terms of applied research. While most community surveys are described as "demographic" studies, they do not tend to treat demographic issues seriously, settling instead for a market research approach to "demographic variables." This represents a loss not only to the serious scholar but to the user of applied information as well. The federation planner does not have access to the kind of information which will project the kind of community that lies ahead. The treatment of occupation is a good case in point. Questions about intergeneration mobility, occupational choice, and career are notably absent from community surveys. To the majority of federation personnel and lay people such questions are considered too "scientific." Occupational identity may well be competitive with Jewish identity, and the changing occupational structure clearly has implications for the fund-raising apparatus.

The family is another demographic issue that receives only superficial treatment. Community surveys usually identify target family groups such as single-parent families or families with school-age children, but ignore the family per se. There is no sociology of the Jewish family. Community surveys measure intermarriage rates by inquiring about the religious identification of respondent and spouse, but are hesitant about exploring such related factors as where and how respondent and spouse met, parental attitudes toward intermarriage, or the intermarrieds' perception of themselves in relation to the Jewish community. These are all applied questions in the sense that they have the potential to impact programs. If, for example, the organized community wishes to find ways to include intermarrieds in its midst, knowing their perception of the Jewish community would be useful information.

The treatment of Jewish identity by community surveys is particularly problematic. The inclusion of identity is limited to items on objective behavior and in some studies, to a number of social-distance questions. Jewish identity and the future of Jewish survival are generally considered crucial issues facing the community today. If the federations are serious in their intention to strengthen Jewish identity, research in this area must be regarded as applied. If Jewish social research could identify the relative effects on Jewish identity of such factors as generation, Jewish education, Jewish camping, exposure to Israel, and growing up in a Jewish neighborhood — the organized community would have a more conceptually concrete set of theoretical materials from which to build programs.

A Center for Modern Jewish Studies could be a moving force in helping federations bridge the gap between what surveys inquire about now and what they might more fruitfully investigate. It could do so first by moving beyond research into the development of conceptual planning models adapted to the local Jewish community. This would involve the center in policy and planning disciplines as well as in research. However, it is the lack of such perspectives in the organized Jewish community that is at least partly responsible for the unambitious standards current today. With or without this first focus, the center should strive to be a methodological resource for local communities who now turn either to a local social scientist or to a market research company. The former is usually not familiar with the Jewish community, while the latter is generally not committed to rigorous methodology or to a potential contribution of the research. Finally, the center should be encouraged to conduct its own research which could serve both as a model and a stimulus to the local community in broadening its research horizons.

Local Jewish communities tend to underanalyze their findings. Once the report to the federation is prepared the research effort ends — precisely at the time when (assuming the research is valuable) it should just be beginning. The 1975 Boston community survey and the National Jewish Population Survey respectively represent models to be emulated and avoided in encouraging the secondary analysis of Jewish survey data. The 1975 Boston survey is well documented and available on magnetic tape. It has been the basis of an article published in 1979 on Jewish giving.[15]

The outcomes of the NJPS have been disappointing. Although it was the basis of an excellent dissertation,[16] little in the way of scholarly analysis has resulted from the NJPS over the past decade. I suspect this situation results less from a lack of interest than a lack of access to the data.

The general availability of computing facilities and statistical packages has greatly encouraged secondary data analysis and the distribution of data sets. The U.S. Census has a data users division to facilitate the use of its materials. Similarly, the Roper Poll sells its survey tapes to interested researchers. Thus the technical groundwork and administrative structures already exist for the center to adapt in making local community research available to the social scientist. Both communities would profit from the center's active involvement in local communal research. The local community would have access to higher quality and more usable (as well as used) research. The center in turn would have greater confidence in the quality of local materials it would use by virtue of its involvement in their development.

Agency Research

Because of the visibility of the community survey, local research has been identified with these large-scope endeavors. Increasingly important on the local scene will be a research agenda oriented toward service delivery agencies. This agenda has emerged from three related trends. First, the federations are in step with state, local, and federal government in their concern with cost containment. Phrases like "zero-based budgeting," "cost effectiveness," and "accountability," are now a part of the federation vocabulary. Because they depend on the federation for funding, local agencies realize the need to more objectively demonstrate both the need for and effect of their services. Second, professional staffs of local agencies are aware of the evaluation research done in their broader fields such as social work, counseling, and education. They want to keep pace with their own professional fields. Finally, Jewish agencies which have received public monies in the form of grants often find themselves required to produce an evaluation study at the conclusion of their program. The possibilities for agency research are best explored by looking separately at the three generic agency types: casework, groupwork, and Jewish education.

Casework and Counseling. Casework agencies deliver service (usually counseling) to individuals and/or families on a case basis, such as Jewish Family Service or Jewish Vocational Service. The most basic need of these agencies is for administrative data about their clients. Counseling agencies typically need reliable and meaningful data about administrative areas such as the following: (1) a profile of the client population including age, sex, marital status, household composition, source of referral, and focus of service; (2) data on the use of "treatment modalities" such as individual counseling, family counseling, job placement, etc.; (3) case data on length of treatment and patterns of multiple case openings; (4) data on the cost of delivery service to different client populations. Social workers are by training ill-equipped to conduct research and by professional temperament more disposed to helping clients than collecting data about them. Hence Jewish casework and counseling agencies are to varying degrees ignorant about the population they serve. Setting up workable systems for the collection and analysis of service delivery information is an important agency priority over the next decade. While the appropriateness of the center's involvement in the development of information systems is dubious (being primarily a management tool), it illustrates a newly emerging agency orientation toward research and information.

A related trend, more in keeping with the academic nature of the center, is the emergence of evaluation research in the field of social service.[17] In a Jewish setting, evaluation research takes on two dimensions: the clinical aspect of the service and the Jewish impact of the agency. The clinical goals of the agency are articulated as the goals of the social services field in general. The Jewish goals of these agencies tend to be more vague. On the campus, the schools of Jewish communal service address the problem of the Jewish component in social work practice. In the field, this proposition has yet to be tested. The center might contemplate a two-phase program to examine the explicit and implicit goals of Jewish casework agencies and then devise and implement demonstration evaluation projects which would serve as models for the local community. As with the community survey, the demonstration project approach is seen as stimulating similar work in local communities.

Jewish Community Centers. The Jewish community center, like the casework agency, is in need of information about its user and member populations (not always the same). While such studies have been undertaken in the past, they tend to be oriented toward an immediate decision such as program planning or site relocation. The question of the viability of centers and their relationship to issues such as Jewish continuity has gone unasked and unstudied. In this regard evaluation research is relevant to the Jewish community center in two areas. First, to the extent that centers undertake Jewish programming there is the opportunity to evaluate its impact. Second, there is a need to evaluate the basic assumption on which the center movement is based: that by bringing Jews together through informal activities in a nonideological setting the social network and communal ties of its membership are ultimately strengthened. This is a sensitive question, but given the large capital costs of building and maintaining a Jewish community center, it ought to be investigated.

Jewish Education. In terms of agencies of the organized federation community, the Bureau of Jewish Education (BJE) is the topic of concern here rather than Jewish education per se. At the administrative level, the BJE requires accurate administrative data about the "school system." It uses information about school enrollments and financial expenditures to make grant allocations and scholarships available to local schools. To the extent that the BJE functions as a coordinating body and educational resource for local schools it is in an excellent position to undertake and encourage evaluation studies of curricula (old and new), teaching approaches, and alternative learning settings. The last decade has seen the emergence of a new generation of Jewish educators who sponsor their own alternative organizations such as the Conference for Alternatives in Jewish Education. These educators are found in the local Jewish school where theory is put into practice. By developing models for the evaluation of Jewish education, the center could have a dual impact on both the BJE and local schools. First it could conduct evaluation research of its own. Initial efforts would encourage the local community to pursue such directions on their own. Second, it could develop easily applied evaluation models for use in the local community. All this is in addition to, not in place of, other work in Jewish education.

Like the case-worker and group-worker, the Jewish educator is not specifically trained in research. Moreover, the Jewish educator has more pressing responsibilities which preclude involvement in such innovative works as those described above. The center alone could serve as a catalyst to move Jewish education in the direction of evaluation research.

In the first section I have concentrated on one aspect of the organized Jewish community, the federation and its family of agencies. The federation is the only institution primarily concerned with the local community and is the major user and only doer of research there. In discussing the research needs of the federation and agencies I have concentrated on applied research that would directly impact Jewish life as well as federation activities. In discussing the community survey I have stressed the upgrading of its methodological basis and the broadening of its horizons in doing applied research. In discussing agency research I have suggested two areas where the center could contribute: administrative data and evaluation research. In each area the center was portrayed as contributing to the local community in two ways: first as a demonstration research agency which would pioneer new directions, and second as a resource to provide tools and techniques to the local community.

The Local Community as a Research Setting

From one point of view there should be no locally conducted research. Research should be conducted on a nationwide basis to maximize methodological consistency and minimize regional peculiarities. While this is true for subjects such as intermarriage, occupational mobility, and the Jewish family, other issues are best understood in the context of the local community. I have selected three such issues for discussion here: new immigrants, fund-raising, and the elderly. These are not only intimately connected with the dynamics of the local community, but are typical of the kinds of issues with which local communities are increasingly concerned. Finally, I shall argue for the legitimacy of local Jewish community studies in their own right, and not just as a tolerable substitute for nationally conducted studies.

New Immigrants. Israeli and Soviet Jewish immigrants to the United States are the most recent and publicized new American Jewish populations (one might also include Iranians, but this phenomenon is too new to assess). They share the onus of not living in Israel, but the contrasts are more interesting. Soviet Jews are resettled with much attention and publicity. The local news runs footage of arriving immigrants being greeted at the airport, job placements are solicited in the local Jewish press, and the Soviet Jewry movement itself is still very much alive. Israelis arrive individually and unobtrusively. Soviet immigrants have a variety of formal and semiformal institutions they have created or which have been created for them. In Los Angeles these include a Russian-language newspaper, special clubs at the Jewish community center, a separate unit of the Jewish Family Service, and a Russian synagogue set up by Chabad. Israelis, on the other hand, are well known for their lack of specific institutions and organizations. They are organizationally invisible.

Because both groups reside in local communities, these communities share two research questions: How are these groups being integrated into the community (both general and Jewish) and what will their impact be? Because it is difficult to discuss these questions outside of the communal context, and because these two immigrant groups are of such great local concern, the study of new immigrants should be considered as part of local research needs. Treating Israelis and Russians separately, let us detail the kinds of research needed by the local community.

The organized Jewish community has been ambivalent toward immigrants from Israel. On the one hand the organized community desires to include them and provide social services. On the other hand, this might be construed as encouraging immigration and thereby creating problems in and with Israel. As a result, there have been no organized efforts to "resettle" Israelis and include them in the community. Only recently has the Los

Angeles federation created a division of the campaign for wealthy Israelis who have lived in the city for as long as twenty years or more.

Thus from the point of view of the local community the place of Israelis in it is the major research question. First, how have Israelis gone about becoming integrated? What (if any) informal networks have they set up to facilitate housing location, job finding, and so on? In other words, how have Israelis done for themselves what the community does for Soviet Jews? What are the predominant patterns of occupational and residential mobility? What sorts of social networks have been developed, and are they based on cultural-ethnic differences or on class differences? Most important, how do Israeli-Americans view themselves in relation to the rest of the Jewish community?

Given the organized nature of Soviet Jewish resettlement, there is an evaluation aspect involved here as well as a sociological one. The local community is as interested in the work of its agencies as in the situation of immigrants. The following research questions were developed in Los Angeles as part of a pilot evaluation study. They indicate the kinds of concerns felt by the local community with respect to the Soviet immigrant: (1) How successful is the integration of the Soviet Jewish immigrant into American life? What are the patterns of occupational and residential mobility in the United States? What background factors are most associated with successful job placement, for example? (2) How is their integration into the Jewish community proceeding? What practices, if any, appear in the home? What are their Jewish aspirations for their children? How do they see themselves in relation to the rest of the Jewish community? (3) To what extent do they participate in the resettlement of future Soviet immigrants? Will they, like the members of the earlier Russian immigration, assist in their own acculturation? Will they share the economic burden? If so, will this be organized institutionally or simply on the basis of family?

Fund-Raising. While the future of Jewish giving is a national issue (some say a national crisis), it is at the local community level that fund-raising is typically conducted. For many Jews fund-raising and Jewish giving are their principal communal activities. Earlier I made reference to the implications of community survey content for fund-raising. Here I would like to propose that fund-raising itself is an appropriate and necessary field of inquiry.

In a sociology of Jewish giving there are a number of research questions significant to the local community: (1) What is the background of givers both in terms of Jewish exposure and class structure? (2) What is the social process of solicitation? To what extent is it predicated on generation-specific assumptions of lifestyle, identity, and locus in the economic structure? (3) What are the motivations behind Jewish giving? What are its operational psychic rewards? (4) What is the effect of "the book" on

Jewish giving? (5) What research tools might be developed to locate potential new givers? (6) How is leadership developed, and what is the potential for the "young leadership" movements in the community?

To some these issues may sound more like the agenda of a UJA meeting than a research center. They are, however, representative of the kinds of questions asked in the local community. To the extent that giving is a Jewish behavior, such questions are appropriate areas of sociological inquiry.

The Aged. The aging of the American Jewish community is a national trend confronted by the local community. In deciding how to care for the elderly, the local community must begin with the reality that homes for the aged are full and that other alternatives must be found. In this respect, most research questions relevant to the Jewish elderly are topics in public health and gerontology. The Jewish aged share the problems of all American elderly: inadequate health care, inadequate housing, and inadequate alternatives once the private home or apartment is no longer a viable living arrangement.

The organized Jewish community has responded to the crisis with governmental and sectarian supported services and programs. Still, it is overwhelmed with the immensity of the tasks. As a research institution the center might investigate such public health and gerontological questions as the following: (1) Alternatives to board and care and nursing homes which could be developed in the Jewish community. For example, shared housing and case management have been tried as ways to keep older persons in their homes. (2) Researching the level of physical, economic, and emotional impairment among the Jewish elderly. This type of agenda moves far afield from a strictly academic agenda. On the other hand, the care of elders is a core Jewish value as well as a central problem in the local Jewish community.

There are more sociological issues to be investigated as well. For example, these same elderly who are the subjects of care are also the carriers of traditions and values. We have yet to give serious attention to the question of their effect on Jewish identity, and what will be the effect of their eventual absence from the community.

The Local Community as an Object of Analysis. In addition to doing research for and in the local community, the dynamics of the Jewish community itself should be an integral part of the center's research agenda. Without working out the details of specific studies, there are two research items which would form the basis for a Jewish community sociology: the community as a variable and as a system.

Whatever national research might be undertaken by the center will inevitably be conducted on a community basis. In the analysis of the data, the effect of region, community size, and age of the individual communities sampled would be intermediate variables. Beyond its implicit scientific merit, this sort of analysis would also be valuable to the local community. All communities have an interest in what makes them unique and what they share in common. Since communities operate on the assumptions they have of themselves, accurate data comparing communities would make a difference in how those communities carry out their organizational life.

In general sociology the study of the community is a venerable tradition. In Jewish sociology the study of the community as a system of institutions and values has not been given serious attention. The center could rectify this shortcoming by developing a sociology of the Jewish community to study the fundamental dynamics of the Jewish community. How do informal social networks affect formal institutions? Do Jewish communities have a life cycle, and if so, what are its parameters? What functions do older inner-city neighborhoods play with regard to the Jewish identity and stability of suburbs? The list of potential questions is as intriguing as it is beyond the scope of discussion here.

In addition to its obvious academic merits, the study of community dynamics is important to the local community itself. Community organization and development are social work modalities taught and used in Jewish communal service. An understanding of the dynamics of the Jewish community as a community would contribute toward the development of new models both for keeping older areas viable and for encouraging Jewish communal life in new areas and environments.

In the first section I dealt with research specific to the local community: community surveys and agency research. In this section I have isolated certain issues of national scope but best studied in the local context and having specific implications for the local community.

If the implicit model in the first section was a kind of Jewish survey research center, in the second section it is the urban laboratory. Understanding the dynamics of the community is a legitimate sociological concern and an area of inquiry which would benefit the local community.

Concluding Remarks: Structure of the Center

I have attempted to outline the research needs of the local community. Some issues may be deemed appropriate for the center while others will not. I have spoken as a researcher in a local community in arguing for the latter's importance in the center's research formulation. Such a focus may or may not come about. In concluding, I would like to extend further the point of view of the local Jewish community in proposing some structural considerations for the center which evolve from the previous discussion.

In the first section it was proposed that the center be a kind of survey research center through demonstration projects, original research, and the development of resource materials. In the second section an additional model of the urban laboratory was offered. In this model the center would undertake a program of aggressive research at the local community level. The impetus for both models is that they could significantly impact the organized Jewish community as well as the community in its sociogeographic aspect. I would like to conclude by exploring the implications of these two models for the center itself.

Action Orientation

The perspectives and programs outlined in the foregoing discussion imply an action commitment on the part of the center; a commitment to engage in research oriented toward social change. This does not mean that the research will bring about social change; rather, it is research which can form the basis of social change. Most of the research projects proposed here have been related to social change in some form or another. Evaluation studies are action-oriented research. So too are some of the more mundane possibilities described, such as information systems or impairment studies of the elderly. These are action research because they are related to action agencies. I have argued for the inclusion of applied research with more and better applications.

Working Relationships

If the center pursues a research direction related to the local communities, it will have to establish a working relationship with those communities. This will not always be easy. There is both awe and fear of the academy in the organized Jewish community. There is respect for the scholar and even hope that "the professors" may have the answers. But there is also a lack of understanding and empathy with academic thinking and concerns. There is a fear that the academic community cannot identify with the decision-making structure and action orientation of both the lay and professional leadership. If the center seeks to encourage more meaningful research and more consistent methodologies in the local community, it will have to engage in some sort of educational process. With the entrance into a new decade the community is open to new ways of thinking and doing, and thus open to working with a Center for Modern Jewish Studies.

Administrative Structures

Some of the projects proposed here will require special administrative structures. For example, if the center adopts the survey research center model it will need access to adequate computing and personnel to facilitate the distribution of data sets in such a way that they can be set up on a variety of computers. Similarly, if the center adopts the urban laboratory approach, it must be prepared to set up an administrative structure that can supervise and coordinate field work in geographically distant locations.

Linkages will have to be created with methodological specialists who have Jewish concerns, and I include non-Jews as well as Jews in this category. The center should explore relationships with established survey research centers, as these centers are both a potential model and a source of data. Los Angeles, for example, conducts the LAMAS (Los Angeles Metropolitan Area Study) and the University of Michigan conducts its Detroit Area Studies.

New Methodologies

The center should give serious consideration to moving beyond survey research alone. Participant observation has initiated much important work in sociology, and would be particularly useful in researching issues such as the organization of the Israeli or Soviet sectors of the community. Similarly, social history (including oral history) could be a valuable tool in studying the dynamics of the Jewish community. An openness to methodological stances is an extension of what I would like to see as a broader perspective: an openness to exploring new relationships between the academic Jewish community and the larger Jewish community of which it is a part.

Notes

1. Bureau of Social Research, *Jewish Communal Survey of Greater New York* (New York, 1928); Ben Seligman, "Some Aspects of Jewish Demography." In Marshall Sklare (ed.), *The Jews: Social Patterns of an American Group* (New York: Free Press, 1958).
2. Charles Bernheimer, *The Russian Jew in the United States: Studies of Social Conditions in New York, Philadelphia, and Chicago* (Philadelphia: John C. Winston, 1905).
3. Louis Wirth, *The Ghetto* (Chicago: University of Chicago Press, 1928).
4. Marshall Sklare and Joseph Greenblum, *Jewish Identity on the Suburban Frontier* (New York: Basic Books, 1967). See also 2nd ed. (Chicago, University of Chicago Press, 1979).
5. See Erich Rosenthal, "Studies of Jewish Intermarriage in the United States," *American Jewish Year Book* (1963).
6. Union of American Hebrew Congregations, "Forming Your Congregation's Future Planning Committee" (New York, 1980).
7. Charles Liebman and Saul Shapiro, "A Survey of the Conservative Movement and Some of Its Religious Attitudes" (New York: Jewish Theological Seminary and the United Synagogue of America, 1979).
8. Daniel J. Elazar, "What We Know and What We Need to Know about the Status of Jewish Social Research," *The Journal of Jewish Communal Service* (Spring 1978).

9. Floyd J. Fowler, *A Study of the Jewish Population of Greater Boston* (Combined Jewish Philanthropies of Greater Boston, 1975).
10. Sidney Goldstein and Calvin Goldscheider, *Jewish Americans: Three Generations in a Jewish Community* (Englewood Cliffs, N.J.: Prentice-Hall, 1968).
11. D.B. Rosen et al., *Studies of the Jewish Communities in San Diego County* (San Diego, 1980).
12. Seymour Sudman, *Applied Sampling* (New York: Academic Press, 1976).
13. See William G. Cohcran, *Sampling Techniques* (New York: Wiley, 1963); Raymond J. Jessen, *Statistical Survey Techniques* (New York: Wiley, 1978).
14. Don A. Dillman, *Mail and Telephone Surveys* (New York: Wiley, 1978).
15. Paul Ritterband and Steven M. Cohen, "Will the Well Run Dry? The Future of Jewish Giving in America" (National Jewish Conference Center, January 1979).
16. Geoffrey Bock, "The Jewish Schooling of American Jews: A Study of Non-Cognitive Educational Effects" (Harvard University, Ed.D. diss., 1976).
17. See Michael Quinn Patton, *Utilization-Focused Evaluation* (Beverly Hills: Sage, 1978); Clark C. Abt, *The Evaluation of Social Programs* (Beverly Hills: Sage, 1976); Carol H. Weiss, *Evaluating Action Programs* (Boston: Allyn & Bacon, 1972).

11.

On the Preparation of a Sociology of American Jewry

Marshall Sklare

I.

Ordinarily centers do not get involved in the sponsorship of works of synthesis and interpretation such as a sociology of American Jewry. A Center for Modern Jewish Studies cannot afford to neglect such a project. In many areas of scholarship works of synthesis and interpretation take care of themselves inasmuch as they are produced in the ordinary course of the growth of the discipline. Centers devote themselves to other concerns such as projects too large to be handled by a single investigator or too complex for a single discipline. Centers also specialize in projects which involve the collection of large amounts of new data. They may emphasize the implementation of long-range, basic research programs that would be difficult to organize outside of an institutional framework.

As a result of these emphases what generally emanates from a center is articles that appear in scientific journals, books published by specialized houses, and research reports sometimes issued by the center itself. Such publications generally reach only a narrow circle of specialists. But important findings will gradually become known to broader circles. One way in which they are diffused is by being utilized by authors who prepare works of synthesis and interpretation.

The impetus for the preparation of a work of synthesis and interpretation may come from a variety of sources. Instead of pursuing ever more specialized research, investigators may feel the need to develop an overview of their own work and that of their colleagues. There are also members of the discipline who regularly devote a portion of their time to the task of synthesis and interpretation — they are drawn to the effort of piecing together the findings of hundreds, perhaps thousands, of existing investigations. They see possibilities in interpreting the significance of existing data which they feel have been disregarded by those who collected them.

261

The way in which research is organized works in the direction of encouraging narrow research reports and discouraging efforts at synthesis and interpretation. An investigator must prepare a funding proposal when he is in the early stages of a prior project. Once awarded a new grant he is obliged to finish his prior investigation and submit his report to the funding agency whether or not he has fully reflected on the significance of his project. Furthermore, the investigator must rush into print, in part because of his competitors who are working along similar lines. The life of an active investigator is a constant stream of funded projects. Such projects are necessary if only because the investigator must keep his research team together — it would have to be disbanded without a constant stream of new money. The result is that little time exists for reflection and for the preparation of works of synthesis and interpretation.

Whatever the conditions under which a particular investigator may work, sooner or later someone of standing will proceed to prepare a work of synthesis and interpretation. The preparation of the first such book is a crucial event. Such a book may become a landmark volume. Of even greater significance, it may stimulate the preparation of new volumes of synthesis and interpretation. Inevitably other scholars will feel that the first volume has weaknesses and deficiencies and become convinced that they can improve upon it.

Ideology is another potent impetus to the preparation of volumes which follow the pioneer effort in the field. Given the diversity of views which characterize all areas of the humanities and social sciences (and the biological and physical sciences as well), it is inevitable that a single work cannot satisfy everyone. Radicals, liberals, and conservatives all want their say; adherents of different schools of thought are motivated to prepare their own works of synthesis and interpretation. Outside observers may recoil at such diversity — they may feel that disorder or anarchy characterize the discipline and that confusion reigns supreme. Ordinarily, however, the effect of diversity is enrichment rather than chaos.

One important influence in the preparation of works of synthesis and interpretation originates outside of the academy. The publication of the first volume of synthesis and interpretation will catch the eye of alert publishers. It is inevitable that such publishers will be receptive to similar works and will even solicit them. Such solicitation is commonplace at small, highbrow publishing houses. When works of synthesis and interpretation can serve as texts for courses offered at universities to which substantial numbers of students are attracted, the larger, middlebrow publishing houses begin to solicit works of synthesis and interpretation.

The influence of publishers is a potent stimulant. Witness the spectacular rise of books in the field of women's studies in recent years. It is hard to find a well-known house which has not issued several books in the field. A number of houses have built a substantial list in the field of women's studies and do not confine themselves to issuing unrelated volumes. Competition among publishers may result in the multiplication of volumes irrespective of the state of the market, though before long commercial realities intrude. The danger in a trendy field is that the plethora of activity may amount to overkill — that excessive energy will be invested in the preparation of works of synthesis and interpretation to the detriment of the slow, painful, and expensive task of accumulating new data. Although the danger is always present, the expansion of knowledge in new fields generally involves the simultaneous production of monographs and the accumulation of new data together with the creation of works of synthesis and interpretation.

There need be no conflict between "accumulation of data" and the preparation of works of "synthesis and interpretation." The two types of efforts may be mutually reinforcing and fructifying. For example, works of synthesis and interpretation on the Holocaust could not have been written without the work of those who specialized in the accumulation of data and the preparation of journal articles and monographs, as well as the activity of research centers which specialized in the collection of source materials. However, the field of Holocaust studies became a field — or at least took on new significance and importance — as a result of the publication of works of synthesis and interpretation.[1]

Such works have encouraged the introduction of college-level courses on the Holocaust, which in turn have raised the level of existing courses. Furthermore, if only because works of synthesis and interpretation inevitably present divergent views, they have the effect of stimulating the accumulation of additional data and increasing the preparation of specialized articles as well as monographic-type volumes.

Every first-class work of synthesis and interpretation stimulates the growth of the field of which it is a part. It suggests new problems and leads to new works of synthesis and interpretation if only because others interpret the same data differently or place emphasis on different data. The publication of works of synthesis and interpretation provides a spur to projects aimed at accumulating new data. By establishing the importance of the field, such works create interest on the part of scholars — which in due course is communicated to students. Finally, these works help to create public interest in a field and thus provide a stimulus to agencies whose area of service is the support of research.

II.

Why has there not been a substantial work of synthesis and interpretation in the sociology of American Jewry? Why should the Center for Modern Jewish Studies support work which in other fields of study is accomplished outside of the framework of centers? One important reason is that contemporary Jewish studies in general, and the sociology of American Jewry specifically, have not been included in the classical fields of Jewish scholarship. Works of synthesis and interpretation are common in the classical fields of Jewish studies — especially those fields which became classical as a result of the development of *Wissenschaft des Judenthums* in the nineteenth century. The field of Jewish history is a good example. In the nineteenth century not only were monographs published but single and multivolume histories of the Jews began to appear. Such works of synthesis and interpretation continue to appear in our day and vary from modest efforts to projects of staggering magnitude. Salo W. Baron is at work on the eighteenth volume of his *Social and Religious History of the Jews.*[2] A collaborative work of scholars at the Hebrew University entitled *A History of the Jewish People*, edited by the late H.H. Ben-Sasson, appeared recently in English translation.[3] Robert M. Seltzer's more modest volume entitled *Jewish People, Jewish Thought* is an even newer work of synthesis and interpretation.[4]

All these works are devoted to the analysis of Jewish history in its entirety. Similar works of synthesis and interpretation have appeared on ancient Jewry, medieval Jewry, and modern Jewry. There have also been volumes devoted to the history of Jews in individual nations. The history of Polish Jewry has been enriched by a large number of works of synthesis and interpretation. The example is a sad one since the history of Polish Jewry is not a continuing saga. Only a handful of Jews live in contemporary Poland and their number shrinks with each passing year.

Despite the fact that the American Jewish community is very much alive and constitutes the largest Jewish community in the world (indeed the largest in the millennial history of the Jewish people), there is no first-rate and comprehensive history of American Jewry. Perhaps the reason for this surprising situation is that Jewish scholarship is still so classical in outlook that American Jewish history has yet to be fully integrated into the *Wissenschaft des Judenthums* tradition. But in any case the inaction of American Jewish historical societies and of foundations devoted to the cultivation of Jewish scholarship is hard to understand. My own feeling is that once the first authoritative history appears other such volumes will soon follow.

If we do not have an authoritative history of American Jewry it is understandable that we do not possess an authoritative sociology of American Jewry. History ordinarily precedes sociology. Despite its contemporary emphasis, it would be legitimate for a Center for Modern Jewish Studies to stimulate the creation of a volume of synthesis and interpretation in the field of American Jewish history as well as in sociology.

Thus far it has been assumed that works of synthesis and interpretation originate from inside the group. This is not always the case. When a group is seen as a problem by society the initiative may come from the outside. Gunnar Myrdal's *An American Dilemma* is the best-known example.[5] This volume was part of a multilayered project sponsored by the Carnegie Corporation. It did not originate at a Black university, or by Black scholars connected with a White university, or by a Black historical or sociological society. It originated with White officials of a White foundation. The Corporation chose as the director of the study someone who was not American, but as a Swede came from a country "of high intellectual and scholarly standards but with no background or traditions of imperialism which might lessen the confidence of the Negroes in the United States as to the complete impartiality of the study and the validity of its findings."[6] Gunnar Myrdal was chosen not only because as a foreigner he would be more acceptable to Blacks. He was also chosen because as a Swedish White he could be trusted by American Whites. It was felt that the Black problem so preoccupied those reared in American culture that no native White could bring a fresh and unbiased eye to the problem.

Groups which pose problems to society inevitably become the subject of inquiry. Jews have not posed a problem to American society — Abraham Cahan remarked that the problem of Jews in the United States was how to prevent a Jewish problem from emerging. Since a Jewish problem has not emerged, contemporary Jewish studies have been left to the Jews. Productivity has been limited because despite considerable interest in contemporary Jewry (including American Jewry), and despite new and encouraging developments, Jewish scholarship has remained heavily classical.

In lieu of scholarly input the work of synthesis and interpretation has been left to the popular writer. The popular writer may know how to write well. Yet however serious his intentions, he finds it difficult to create what is needed. Works designed to catch popular attention must be somewhat sensational. The popular writer frequently does not know how to discipline himself; he may not know how to control his prejudices, his ambivalences, and how to evaluate his own experience as a Jew. A popular work may have an impact for a time but its staying power is very short. It is in the nature of popular books that they are superseded in due course.[7]

III.

A brief review of the scholarly literature will place the problem of what is needed in sharper perspective. Two small books of synthesis and interpretation have been written by academicians. They are *Jewish Americans* by Sidney Goldstein and Calvin Goldscheider and my volume *America's Jews*.[8] These books are quite dissimilar in approach. The Goldstein and

Goldscheider volume is based on the findings of a local Jewish community study, while data for my own study are drawn from a wide variety of sources. An interesting fact about these books is that they were both written in response to the interest of competing publishers each of whom were producing a series of volumes covering ethnic groups. The idea of each series was to afford the student taking a general course in racial and ethnic groups the opportunity not only to learn general principles but to gain special knowledge of at least one ethnic group. But since they were designed as an enrichment for undergraduates, these two volumes are limited both in size and depth of analysis.

Something must be said about two additional kinds of books: readers, and what for want of a better term I will call "symposium volumes." Readers can serve as a kind of holding action pending the appearance of works of synthesis and interpretation. The preparation of a reader is not an insuperable obstacle as long as enough quality material is available. The problem is that a reader will tend to be misused in the absence of an authoritative work of synthesis and interpretation. Instead of a supplementary volume it will be employed as a primary volume. This is unfortunate since a reader necessarily consists of a series of discrete articles and does not pretend to offer an integrated view.

My own experience with readers has underlined the advantages and limitations of such volumes. My first experience in preparing a reader made a deep impression on me because I felt a responsibility to produce a work which would compare favorably with other volumes in the same series. The series was the set of readers published by The Free Press. My own volume was entitled *The Jews: Social Patterns of an American Group.*[9]

As I sought to put this work together, I realized what a challenge I had accepted. There was a paucity of published material which could be used in its original state. Literature was available but it was in the form of dissertations which needed to be summarized or research reports which had to be rewritten. Some very helpful raw data were available, but it had to be written up in usable form. The end of the matter was that less than half of the material utilized in *The Jews: Social Patterns of an American Group* had been previously published in the form in which it appeared.

Since I felt that quality was all-important, I decided not to treat a subject unless I could locate material which had the potential for acceptability once it had been suitably reworked. Thus certain subjects were not treated in *The Jews: Social Patterns of an American Group* despite their significance. Jewish education was one such subject — despite the importance I attached to this subject I could not discover appropriate material.

The growth of the field is indicated by my subsequent experience in editing two additional volumes of readings: *The Jew in American Society* and *The Jewish Community in America.*[10] These volumes were published by

Behrman House in 1974 and, with the exception of one unpublished article, I relied entirely upon material which had already appeared. Furthermore, suitable articles were available on Jewish education as well as on other subjects not treated in *The Jews: Social Patterns of an American Group*.

The Behrman House volumes have a number of distinguishing features. Both begin with lengthy introductions designed to orient the reader to the subject matter. Rather elaborate introductory remarks were also supplied for each contribution. These, I thought, would be helpful to the general reader and would provide the student with a framework for reading and evaluating the article. Both volumes included sizable bibliographies designed to allow the student to pursue the subject further.

I have no doubt that more readers are in the offing. This is a welcome development although it is regrettable that there is not more consensus among the editors of already published volumes. Thus, *The Ghetto and Beyond* edited by Peter I. Rose, and *The Sociology of American Jews: A Critical Anthology* edited by Jack N. Porter, are quite different in approach from my own work.[11] There is little overlap with the material in the readers I have prepared. Apparently the field is not yet mature enough to have developed a series of "classical" articles which tend to appear in each book of readings whatever the personal proclivities of the editor.

In addition to readers there are the symposium volumes mentioned earlier. An early symposium volume is *Jews in a Gentile World* edited by Graeber and Britt.[12] A recent volume is Bernard Martin's *Movements and Issues in American Judaism*.[13] These two books differ sharply in approach. The tone of *Jews in a Gentile World* is defensive. It was prepared at a time when anti-Semitism was rife. The need of the hour seemed to be one of sympathetically explaining the Jews to anyone who cared to listen. Martin's volume is concerned much more with Jewish self-understanding and with the problem of Jewish survival in a more friendly world.

Symposium volumes have their advantages. They can be designed with an overarching conception and they are not bound by the constraints of what already exists in the literature. On the other hand they are no substitute for a work written by a single author or by the collaboration of two authors. Furthermore the introduction of quality control is most difficult. To reject a commissioned article is difficult. Not only are interpersonal relations at stake, but seldom is there sufficient time or money available to start over again with a new contributor.

IV.

What are some of the problems faced when an original work of synthesis and interpretation is embarked upon? One of the first questions is whether to direct the work outward or inward. That is, should the focus be on the impact of Jews on society or vice versa? Should the focus be on the Jewish impact on American culture or vice versa? Should one emphasize matters such as Jewish religion, which are "inner," despite the fact that they may be deeply influenced by outside forces, or should one emphasize matters such as Jewish political behavior, which are "outer," despite the fact that they may be influenced by Jewish cultural traditions and by the particular place occupied by the Jew in the larger society?

It is difficult to decide such questions in advance — sometimes one may choose to be led by the material rather than begin with a conscious choice. Yet the material rarely speaks for itself; it is the direction in which the analyst takes the material which is determinative. In recent years social scientists interested in the Jewish community have tended to direct themselves to "inner" matters, for these are centrally addressed to the question of the quality of Jewish life and its survival.

Another question which must be faced by the analyst is whether to place Jewish life in a unique or special framework, or whether to place it in some larger framework — to view Jewish life as an instance of minority group behavior and measure the extent to which it parallels the behavior of other groups. The natural inclination of the social scientist is to use a general yardstick rather than a Jewish one. Using a general yardstick has the advantage of making one's work relevant to all social science. Using a Jewish yardstick has the disadvantage that one's work may interest primarily those concerned with Jewish studies.

My view is that while one should be comparative and have all the scholarly equipment, it is frequently more profitable scientifically, if not personally, to use a Jewish yardstick. Let us take an admittedly extreme example — the study of yeshivot. If one uses a general yardstick the investigator will tend to give short shrift to institutions which have as much uniqueness as does the yeshivah. And if the investigator should come to realize the importance of American yeshivot his analysis may be found wanting. Looking for parallels in other groups he may compare yeshivot to inappropriate institutions. In his search for comparability he may analyze yeshivot in such a way as to do violence to their essential characteristics.

In this particular case the analyst will probably be better off if he adopts an inner framework. Doing so will enable him to understand yeshivot more fully and insightfully. Furthermore, while an inner framework does not encourage comparability, it does offer more than adequate room for its own type of comparability. Such comparability can be along a variety of lines: (1) comparisons between contemporary yeshivot in the United States; (2) comparisons between contemporary U.S. yeshivot and those which existed in the United States at an earlier period; (3) comparisons between contemporary U.S. yeshivot and those in European countries in earlier centuries as well as in the twentieth century; and (4) comparisons between contemporary U.S. yeshivot and those in other countries, most notably in Israel.

Another issue is that of scale. Should one attempt a large work on the scale of a Myrdal or — utilizing the Black example again — should one attempt a more modest effort such as E. Franklin Frazier's *The Negro in the United States?*[14] Sometimes this question is decided for the investigator. If funds are not forthcoming to hire collaborators and commission monographs on topics of special interest, one cannot attempt a large-scale project. In any case it is self-defeating to decry the lack of abundant resources. The strategic approach is to settle for a more modest project if that be necessary, but one which goes far beyond what we now have.

There is another issue which confronts the investigator and shapes his product in many subtle ways. It is the issue of Jewish survival. This has at least two dimensions. One is whether the investigator thinks the Jewish group in America will survive in anything like its present numbers and form. The other is whether the investigator *wants* the Jewish group to survive. The relationship between thinking and wanting is very subtle, but whatever one's direction the choice inevitably leads to a selection of emphasis and material. The answer cannot be the one adopted by the Carnegie Corporation regarding Blacks — choosing an outsider who is presumably above the battle. There is no way around the fact that the sociology of Jews will be written by Jews. This being the fact, the investigator should be as self-conscious as possible about his own stance toward the Jewish present and especially the Jewish future.

Another issue is that of Israel. There is no problem here of being anti-Israel.The question is understanding the connection between Israel and American Jewry — a connection which takes many forms and exists on many levels. To apply the usual categories such as assessing what parts of the homeland culture are still retained is to confound the question. American Jewry does not stem from Israeli Jewry, and looking for cultural parallelisms may be counterproductive. The analyst who does not seek to plumb the connections between these two Jewries, or who sees American Jewry as relatively self-contained, will fall wide of the mark.

The final problem in the preparation of a sociology of American Jewry is that of self-censorship, or, to use a more neutral term, self-discipline. We think of this as a problem of social scientists, but we should remember that just a few decades ago this was a problem for physical scientists. Today it is those in the biological sciences who face the problem of the ethics of pursuing certain lines of investigation and the wisdom of making certain discoveries.

At an earlier period in my own scholarly development I felt there was too much sensitivity on this issue — that too many presumed to know what would be good or bad for Jews, and that many fears about what would be bad were unfounded. While I am still unwilling to be bound by certain Jewish sensitivities, I feel that certain subjects need not be completely researched or fully explicated. The Jewish effort to win support for Israel inside the U.S. Congress and in the executive branch of government may be one such issue. There would be a problem here if one considered the entire story vital to a full-scale understanding of American Jewry. I am not convinced that it is vital.

The Center for Modern Jewish Studies can concentrate solely on investigations in one or more of the areas analyzed in this volume such as demography, religion, Jewish education, family, identity, or intergroup relations. Or in addition to such support it may stimulate the preparation of works of synthesis and interpretation. Such a combination may not conform to the model of the "classical" center. There are so many different models of centers that it is difficult to specify what constitutes a "classical" center. In any case, it is not incumbent upon this new institution to replicate old models. The center has a responsibility both to the lay community (general and Jewish) and to the scholarly community (both those who specialize in Jewish studies and those in other disciplines). That responsibility includes encouraging the preparation of works of synthesis and interpretation in the sociology of American Jewry and, if necessary, in ancillary fields such as American Jewish history.

Notes

1. Two standard (and contrasting) works of synthesis and interpretation are Raul Hilberg, *The Destruction of the European Jews* (Chicago: Quadrangle Books, 1961) and Lucy S. Dawidowicz, *The War Against the Jews, 1933–1945* (New York: Holt, Rinehart, & Winston, 1975).
2. For volume 17 see Salo Wittmayer Baron, *A Social and Religious History of the Jews: Late Middle Ages and Era of European Expansion, 1200–1650* (Philadelphia: Jewish Publication Society of America, 1980).
3. Haim Hillel Ben-Sasson (ed.), *A History of the Jewish People* (Cambridge, Mass.: Harvard University Press, 1976).
4. Robert M. Seltzer, *Jewish People, Jewish Thought* (New York: Macmillan, 1980).
5. Gunnar Myrdal, *An American Dilemma: The Negro Problem and Modern Democracy* (New York: Harper & Bros., 1944).
6. Ibid., p. vi.
7. See my review of Roger Kahn's *The Passionate People: What It Means to Be a Jew in America* in *Commentary* 46, no. 4 (October 1968), pp. 82–87.
8. Sidney Goldstein and Calvin Goldscheider, *Jewish Americans* (Englewood Cliffs, N.J.: Prentice-Hall, 1968); Marshall Sklare, *America's Jews* (New York: Random House, 1971).
9. Marshall Sklare (ed.), *The Jews: Social Patterns of an American Group* (Glencoe: Free Press, 1958). This volume is available in a reprint edition published by Greenwood Press in 1977.

10. Marshall Sklare (ed.), *The Jew in American Society* (New York: Behrman House, 1974); id., *The Jewish Community in America* (New York: Behrman House, 1974).
11. Peter I. Rose (ed.), *The Ghetto and Beyond* (New York: Random House, 1969); Jack Nusan Porter (ed.), *The Sociology of American Jews: A Critical Anthology*, 2nd ed. (Washington: University Press of America, 1980). Recently special purpose readers have appeared. They include Marc Lee Raphael (ed.), *Understanding Jewish Philanthropy* (New York: Ktav, 1979); Abraham Lavender (ed.), *A Coat of Many Colors: Jewish Subcommunities in the United States* (Westport, Conn.: Greenwood, 1977).
12. Isacque Graeber and Steuart H. Britt, *Jews in a Gentile World: The Problem of Anti-Semitism* (New York: Macmillan, 1942). This volume is available in a reprint edition published by Greenwood Press in 1979.
13. Bernard Martin, *Movements and Issues in American Judaism* (Westport, Conn.: Greenwood, 1978).
14. E. Franklin Frazier, *The Negro in the United States* (New York: Macmillan, 1949).

12.

Jewish Immigration to the United States from 1967 to the Present: Israelis and Others

Drora Kass and Seymour Martin Lipset

Migration remains a Jewish characteristic from the days of Abraham, Isaac, and Jacob. A people of outsiders, Jews have always shown greater readiness to move in search of a better way of life even when anti-Semitism was not a significant factor. Between 1880 and 1952, nearly five million Jews left their country of origin. Close to three million came to the United States, more than half a million migrated to Western Europe, and one and a quarter million, or one out of every five Jews, made aliya to Eretz Yisrael. Although most of the movement to the United States occurred prior to 1924 before restrictive legislation cut off mass immigration, it is estimated that close to half a million Jews reached these shores between 1924 and 1959 — roughly a quarter of a million before World War II, and another 200,000 during 1945–59.

Mass immigration to this country, thought of not long ago as predominantly a pre–World War I phenomenon, is once more gaining increased attention from policymakers and the public at large. During the past ten years, the number of immigrants to this country has been close to the highest in any decade in American history (Teitelbaum, 1980). The United States is still by far the world's largest receiver of refugees and other immigrants. America's barriers to entry are less stringent than in other developed countries. It also continues to be its own draw. As one commentator has noted: "It is inherently seductive . . . with all its problems, it remains a country of uncommon freedom and uncommon opportunity."

The recent upswing in immigration to this country has also included a renewed Jewish influx, particularly from 1973 onward — a phenomenon whose numbers appear to be underestimated in official community records. Since U.S. government agencies do not inquire into the religious background of immigrants, the major direct source of information is the Hebrew Immigrant Aid Society (HIAS). According to HIAS reports, between 1967 and 1980 the agency assisted in settling over 125,000 Jews in the United States. The bulk of those aided originated from the Soviet Union and other East European countries, with the remainder from the Middle East and Latin America. HIAS records do not include most of the more affluent contemporary Jewish immigrants to the United States from Argentina, Canada, Chile, Colombia, Cuba, Nicaragua, South Africa, and Iran. Nor do they list the several hundred thousand Israelis who have come here from the land established to put an end to the phenomenon of the wandering Jew.

"Pull" Rather Than "Push"

Unlike past waves of Jewish movement to America which resulted from persecution or severe economic deprivation, contemporary immigration reflects the desire to improve status, widen knowledge and horizons, and exploit greater economic opportunities. "Pull" rather than "push" factors motivate a large number to opt for the United States even when persecution or fear of it affects the decision to emigrate. Many are well educated, highly skilled, and often able to bring economic resources with them or find a well-paid job shortly after their arrival. No strangers to Coca-Cola, rock, Kojak, jeans, and hamburgers, these are individuals with a familiarity, and more often than not prior exposure to American ways through the media, personal contacts, and tourism.

With the exception of Jews who have fled dictatorial or anti-Jewish regimes, emigration no longer implies a sharp break with one's roots. The new arrivals can exercise their nostalgia by going back to their homeland for a visit or by entertaining compatriots in their new homes. The numbers involved are not small. One out of every 10 to 12 Jews in the United States is a recent arrival who has been here less than ten years. Of the 350,000 Israelis living here, the majority have left their poor, more demanding, homeland in search of greater educational and economic opportunities. Over 75,000 Soviet Jews have come to these shores since 1972 to escape discrimination and enjoy the benefits of a more affluent society. The other groups of newcomers, though smaller in number, add much to the kaleidoscope of American Jewry.

Although they do not share cultural backgrounds, Jewish immigrants from South Africa, Latin America, and Canada have similar attributes. Almost all speak English well. They have left their native lands not because of direct persecution but because of survival fears shared by the larger group they were affiliated with — Whites in South Africa, the middle class in Latin America, and the English-speaking community in Quebec — or simply because they saw greater opportunity in the United States. They are more widely traveled than the average Israeli or Russian, and generally more affluent. The choice of location for many is determined by climatic conditions and the presence of a significant Jewish community. Miami, Los Angeles, and Houston seem to answer these requirements more than adequately.

Latin American Jews have always been coming here. Some have bought homes and invested in businesses as a hedge against an uncertain future. "There is no future for the middle class in Latin America, no prospect of a stable democracy," commented one new arrival. "There is a general feeling of malaise, a feeling that we cannot do much to change the inevitable process." A steady stream of young Latin American Jews who come to study in this country have remained here because of a sense of greater social, cultural, scientific, or economic opportunities. Their choice often proves to be an added incentive for their parents' emigration. One recent arrival describes the typical pattern: "Education in Latin America is not too good. People prefer to send their kids to an American university and often they don't come back, so the parents follow. First they visit. Then they buy a house. Then they commute for a period. And then they come to settle permanently."

Miami has been the major recipient of Jews from South of the border: the bulk of the Cuban community who fled Castro and the elimination of private business, Chileans who feared that the Allende regime would prove to be another Cuba, Nicaraguans wary of the pro-PLO politics of the regime which replaced Somoza in July 1979, Colombians disturbed by continuing violence, and Argentinians who have reacted both to fears of anti-Semitism and social and political instability in that country. People are rarely persecuted in Argentina because they are Jewish. But if a Jew is caught in, or suspected of radical politics, as some young Jews are, he or she will be treated more brutally by police, army, or rightist thugs than will a non-Jew.

Canadian migration south in search of a warmer climate and a chance to get a bigger slice from a larger pie is not a new phenomenon. English-speaking North America has come close at times to forming one labor market. Millions of Canadians and hundreds of thousands of Americans have moved across the border in the past century. A disproportionate number of them have been Jews. During the 1920s and for a period following World War II, it was easier for immigrants to get into Canada than into the United States. Hence many Jews who would have preferred to settle in the larger, more affluent society went to Canada (or Latin America), hoping to move to the United States at a later stage.

Most recently, the political triumph of the *Parti Québecois*, the French Canadian separatists, followed by the passage of legislation requiring the use of French in diverse activities, the occasional expression of anti-Jewish sentiments by extremists among the nationalists, and anxiety over that province's economic future, have led some Jews to leave. A survey of Quebec's predominantly Anglophone Jewish community of 115,000, taken before the recent referendum, found that if the province were to become independent, 70 percent of those age 40 and under said they would "probably" or "definitely" leave. Furthermore, over 15 percent of the older respondents reported at least one child who had already moved to another part of Canada, and the offspring of over 10 percent of those questioned had chosen to go south rather than west. A 1978 study conducted by the Allied Jewish Community Services of Montreal showed that 40 percent of its respondents did not expect to remain in Quebec upon completion of their studies.

Ruth Wisse and Irwin Cotler of McGill University have described the dilemma facing Quebec's Jews, among whom Holocaust survivors figure prominently: "Quebec's Jews find themselves beset by a *crise de conscience*. On the one hand, they understand, even empathize with the aspirations for self-renewal of the French Canadians. At the same time . . . they wonder at what point their own pluralism . . . will stick in the craw of a nationalist bid for domination." Many feel that while prior to 1976 they were a tolerated and accepted minority, now they share in the antagonism directed against Anglophones in general. Such anxiety is evident in the self-humor of jokes such as: "How does a smart Montreal Jew speak to a dumb one?" "Long distance." With the immediate threat of independence diminished as a result of the 1980 referendum vote against separatism, pressure for emigration may decline.

Another affluent society whose political, ethnic, and racial conflicts have resulted in increased emigration, particularly by Jews, is South Africa. Although in the past South Africans made aliya to Israel or migrated to Britain, many of those who left following the violent race riots of 1976 in the township of Soweto — a Black ghetto on the outskirts of Johannesburg — headed for the United States.

Together with other religious minorities, close to 20,000 Iranian Jews have fled to the United States since the establishment of the Ayatollah Khomeini's fundamentalist Islamic regime. More than any other group of recent arrivals, Iranians still hope eventually to return home, where, under the Shah, they enjoyed equal rights and economic prosperity. Not wanting to foreclose that possibility, very few have sought political asylum in this country.

A Diversity of Jewish Values

All belong to the People of the Book, yet the claim of Jewish newcomers to a common ancestry seems confounded by disparate cultural patterns, a broad range of problems of adjustment to their new home, and varying conceptions of what it means to be Jewish. The Russians are the least Jewish — generally irreligious, with little knowledge of Yiddish or of other aspects of Jewish secular culture. Coming from a country in which any form of religious affiliation is considered backward and deviant, and in which Jewish cultural activities have been virtually nonexistent, only a small minority who come to the United States have Jewish interests or strong Jewish identification. On the whole, they do not relate to institutions except to seek help, or sometimes to participate in community programs run by Soviet Jews and tailored to their needs and interests.

To the average Soviet Jew, emigration is simply a struggle for a better personal future. Research conducted in the United States and in Israel (Elizur and Elizur, 1976; Gitelman, 1978) has shown that motives for emigration are general rather than specifically Jewish. These include aspirations for greater vocational and economic opportunities, the wish to join family, the desire for greater freedom, or simply being caught up in a wave of emigration. Yet ethnic proximity and the desire for educational opportunity for their children may eventually establish links, beyond that of patron and client, between newly arrived Soviet Jews and the larger Jewish community.

While almost all Israeli emigrants speak Hebrew fluently and have varying levels of knowlege of Jewish history, culture, and Bible, the large majority are secular. Coming from a Jewish state they have not had to think about being Jewish. Latin American Jews, largely of East European origin and living on the margins of Hispanic-Portuguese-Catholic societies, have maintained a secular Yiddish culture. Their Jewish commitment facilitates their shift from one diaspora community to another. "In Latin America, Jewishness penetrates all spheres of your life," explains Rabbi Gunther Friedlander, who recently settled in Miami, after having held pulpits for twenty-nine years in a number of Latin American countries. "Going to temple is not a weekly affair, but reading the Jewish newspaper is. And then there are frequent visits to Israel. Here Jewishness is mostly a social affair." The largest and most visible group of Hispanic Jews in the United States, the Cubans, have fitted into their new home as an organized ethnic community whose institutions are an affiliated part of the larger American Jewish society.

Canadian Jews, who have been part of North American English-speaking society, rarely form a distinctive group. They are regarded by American Jews as "in-migrants" rather than foreigners. A greater focus on ethnicity and religion in Canada, which does not separate church and state, has intensified Jewish identity. This background may explain the disproportionate number of ex-Canadians holding American Jewish leadership positions: Edgar M. Bronfman, president of the World Jewish Congress; Bertram H. Gold, executive vice-president of the American Jewish Committee; Norman E. Frimer, former national director of the B'nai B'rith Hillel Foundations and currently executive director of the Memorial Foundation for Jewish Culture; Philip Bernstein, recently retired executive vice-president of the Council of Jewish Federations and Welfare Funds; and Rabbi Wolfe Kelman, executive vice-president of the Rabbinical Assembly (Conservative).

South Africa's 118,000 Jews, living in a society in which people, including Whites, are identified in ethnic terms such as Afrikaaners or English, have always stood out in the diaspora for the intensity of their commitment to and involvement in Jewish activities. They are traditional in their religious orientation. The majority attend Orthodox (equivalent approximately to the American Conservative) synagogues at least a few times a year. Of all diaspora communities they have the highest percentage of children receiving a Jewish education and the largest proportion of Jews affiliated with Zionist organizations. They contribute more to Israel on a per capita basis than any other major community and have sustained the largest rate of aliya from any country which permits free migration.

South Africans continue most of these patterns in their new home. Their strong Jewish identity leads them to settle close to coreligionists and to become rapidly involved in communal activities. They are perceived as a welcome and unproblematic addition to American Jewry. "They're pleasant people whose interpersonal style is familiar," says Sol Brownstein, executive director of the Houston Jewish Federation's Family and Children Service. "And what's more, their Jewish commitment is unquestionable . . . . The Houston Jewish Community is going to be enriched and grow as a result of their presence. They are refined. They are business people. They're the kind of people whom Houstonians can relate to and get along with. The sympathy of the community here has been greater for the South Africans, in terms of their plight certainly, than it's been for the Israelis and in some instances more so than for the Russians."

The Iranians who have come to this country in the last three years, mostly to Los Angeles, are strongly Jewish in religious terms and proud of their ancient heritage. But they are culturally Iranian; they have no secular Jewish language and they lack the tradition of self-help that characterizes European Jews. American Jewish groups who have tried to assist them often feel frustrated, not knowing how to deal with people who, even when well-to-do as many are, do not contribute to local Jewish federations. Iranians, in turn, resent the stereotype of them as a group which is uniformly wealthy. "Like most middle-class people in Iran, we had very few liquid assets," explains a recent arrival to Los Angeles. "We were forced to leave property behind, and what's more, our finances have suffered from the freeze on Iranian banks in this country. We live in constant fear and uncertainty about our future."

If they shy away from participation in the vast network of secular Jewish activities, Iranians do have a role in the more traditional religious community. There are hundreds of Iranian young people studying in various secondary Hebrew day schools and in yeshivoth in Baltimore, Los Angeles, and New York. Rabbi Marc D. Angel of New York's Spanish and Portuguese Synagogue comments: "Iranians have a very strong sense of spirituality when it comes to prayer. They pray with tremendous enthusiasm and devotion." The diverse cultural backgrounds of newly arrived Iranian Jews makes for a wide range of habits, customs, and attitudes which must be adapted to American ways. These vary from basics such as language and adjustment to a value system inherently different from that of the old country, to the loss of luxuries such as servants.

The transition of Soviet Jews is by far the most traumatic. They come to the United States often after a lengthy period of "nonperson" status following their application for an exit visa to Israel (a request for any other destination stands little chance of success). In the words of one Soviet Jew, they "have come from another planet." Of all the recent immigrant groups they are the least familiar with American ways. Though rejecting communist society, Russian Jews have unwittingly accepted much of it as conventional and are startled to find how different things are here. They are accustomed to living in a rigidly regulated, totally statist society, where authorities take responsibility for much that is left here to the individual, such as health care, job placement, and housing. Adaptation to the constant decision making that our system requires is therefore very difficult.

Although native English speakers have the least trouble adjusting, South Africans and Canadians, like transplanted Americans, experience "the typical problems that result from complete separation from the extended family support system," says Sol Brownstein. "Frequently, the sense of isolation they experience as a result of needing to deal with everything within the context and resources of a nuclear family blows their minds . . . and marital problems that might have been kept under control if relatives were around, erupt."

Israelis in Exile

While we have no precise figures, it seems evident that the bulk of Jewish immigration since the mid-1960s has been from Israel.[1] In December 1980 Israel's Central Bureau of Statistics reported 338,000 Israelis living abroad, the large majority in the United States. Based on discussions with Jewish communal leaders throughout the country, as well as with American immigration officials, we estimate that there are over 350,000 Israelis residing in the United States alone.[2]

Sojourners

Israelis are self-defined sojourners. They are the first group of Jewish immigrants, other than some German refugees in the 1930s, who have come to America in the belief that they will return home. German Jewish émigrés felt that their native culture was superior to anything American, and that once Hitler fell they would return home — sentiments which kept them from assimilating well and participating in local Jewish affairs until World War II.

During the period of mass immigration, i.e. before 1924, Jewish newcomers differed from many other Europeans in that they planned to stay in America permanently. Non-Jews, on the other hand, frequently arrived as sojourners for a limited period. They came to make money or gain a worthwhile skill, and then return to their native land. Of the Jews who came to the United States between 1908 and 1924, only 5 percent left compared to 34 percent of the total immigrant population. Unlike members of other ethnic groups, most could not consider leaving the pluralistic *goldene medineh* tolerant of diversity and free. Some did not have the choice of going back to their country of birth.

Students of the immigrant experience have distinguished between the behavior of "sojourners" and "settlers." Those who come to settle are more likely than sojourner ethnic groups to form communal institutions, get involved in local affairs, claim rights, and seek to advance their own position as a group. For example, the lesser participation in unions or communal institutions by Italians than by Jews before World War I has been explained in part as reflecting the sojourner identity of the Italian working class (Liebman, 1978).

Like other non-Jewish sojourners before them, Israelis cling to their culture and are unwilling to organize as permanent residents in America. Even after many years in this country most never fully assimilate. They face a perpetual dilemma: they do not want to return to Israel until they have accomplished the tasks they set out for themselves — higher education, professional training, and the accumulation of material assets. But as this situation is seldom achieved before developing an extensive personal network of connections and involvements, plans for returning become increasingly complex and vague. Yet Israelis continue to associate almost exclusively with people from their own group. Although they may remain abroad their entire lives, they rarely sever their ties with the homeland. They often go back home for visits, only to return to the country in which, more often than not, they still view themselves as foreigners.

Part of the Israelis' reluctance to admit they have chosen a new home or might be in the process of doing so, results from the stigma attached to anyone viewed as an emigrant from Israel. If aliya, or immigration to Israel, is considered the ultimate Zionist injunction, emigration or *yerida* is looked upon as the ultimate betrayal of the Zionist cause. Furthermore it constitutes desertion at a time when Israel is still struggling for a secure and peaceful existence. This long-standing attitude both on the part of Israeli officialdom and the Israeli public at large, leaves Israelis abroad with an ever-gnawing feeling of guilt and a constant need to justify or rationalize their decision, or else to deny the intention of remaining abroad.

Relations with the American Jewish Community

The sojourner outlook of the Israeli immigrants, accompanied by a disdainful attitude toward American culture though admiring of its material achievements, is reinforced by the negative attitude displayed toward them by American Jews. Israeli emigrants' relations with the American Jewish community are at best ambivalent. The two groups have little understanding or tolerance of each other. Israelis living in the United States retain the condescending perception, shared by their compatriots back home, of American Jews as people who have committed their pocket rather than their person to the Jewish state, people who deserve little respect for their monetary contributions to the United Jewish Appeal (UJA) or other Israel-oriented philanthropic agencies. Culturally, there is considerable distance between the two communities. The *Yiddishkeit* of American Jews is foreign to Israelis who eat *hummus* and *felafel* and not bagels and lox. They have grown up in a country to which people come not so much to be a Jew as to cease being "the" Jew.

American Jews join those in Israel in the condemnation of the *yored*, whose very presence here threatens their often excessively idealized view of the Jewish homeland. Most American Jewish organizations have, until recently, regarded Israelis in their midst as neither Jewish immigrants to be helped and guided nor as persons whose knowledge of Hebrew and Israeli culture could contribute to raising the community's Jewish consciousness. The Jewish leadership does not wish to do anything that might encourage Israelis to remain here. HIAS, to take one example, does not provide assistance to Israeli émigrés to this country. As a result, some Israelis have turned to non-Jewish, primarily Catholic agencies dealing with immigrants for assistance.

The treatment of Israeli expatriates as nonpersons is most evident in demographic and other communal analysis and projections. While American Jewry is very concerned about its prospective numerical decline resultant from intermarriage, assimilation, a very low birth rate, and an aging population (the median age of American Jews is 35 compared to 27 for all Americans), mention is rarely made of the fact that 5 percent, or one in twenty Jews in the country, are recent settlers from Israel. One explanation is that Israelis rarely surface in the financial or political structure of the community. Save for some prominent and wealthy individuals, few contribute to fund-raising efforts, perhaps out of a feeling that as Israelis they continue to be part of the receiving rather than the giving sector of Jewry, but also because they have been isolated from the Jewish community. Since most are aliens and cannot vote, they are not useful to the community politically. Even more significant in determining the community's lack of interest is the perception, reinforced by Israelis themselves, that they are or should be sojourners — Jews who belong elsewhere.

This reaction may be contrasted with the Jewish leadership's attitude toward Russian émigrés. In opting for the United States over Israel, Soviet Jews open themselves up to severe criticism from Israeli authorities as well as from ardent Zionist groups in this country. Those who settle in the diaspora are pejoratively labeled *noshrim* ("dropouts") by Israelis. The rejection of Israel by the second largest diaspora community is perhaps an even greater blow to the Zionist dream of the in-gathering of exiles and the conception of Israel as a home and refuge for Jews, than is emigration from the Jewish state.

The proclivity of Soviet Jews to settle in the United States rather than in Israel has stirred up a major controversy as to whether American Jewish resettlement agencies should continue assisting the Russians. Leon Dulzin, chairman of the Jewish Agency, has called for an end to such aid on the grounds that assistance lures potential settlers away from Israel. Yet despite Israeli authorities' vociferous opposition to and resentment of help given to Soviet Jews in their efforts to emigrate to the United States, American Jews have taken a firm stand on the issue. Jewish resettlement agencies and local federations continue to extend aid to the Russians whom they view as refugees from persecution — people like their parents and grandparents who fled czarist oppression. They are not viewed primarily as rejectors of Israel. For American Jews this is an encounter with history, an opportunity to save some remnant of the Jewish people. Soviet Jews, they feel, should be allowed to live where they wish, even if they left the Soviet Union with Israeli visas.

Soviet Jews follow in the tradition of earlier waves of East European immigration. They stand a pole apart from the sojourner orientation. They have come to America to stay. Unlike Israelis, they leave a homeland to which they are not free to return (although should their integration into American society be less than satisfactory, they are always free to go to Israel). Everything in their situation drives them to identify with America.

Given Soviet anti-Semitism — particularly limits on educational and economic opportunities for young Jews — the emigration of Soviet Jews should be considered another example of the effect of "push" factors. But that does not explain the decline in the proportion who opt for Israel. When large-scale emigration began in 1971 less than 1 percent of those living in the Soviet Union proceeded to a country other than Israel. This pattern continued in the following year, but in 1973, 4.5 percent of the emigrants "dropped out" in Vienna and did not arrive in Israel. This percentage grew to 37 percent the following year and increased to 49 percent in 1976. In 1980 it reached 65 percent.

The reasons for the growth in the proportion of Soviet emigrants who opt for the United States or other Western nations is a subject which requires considerable research. Some factors are fairly obvious, including difficulties faced by Russian immigrants to Israel in finding jobs commensurate with the highly specialized education they had in the Soviet Union, Israel's economic problems, its tenuous security situation, and negative reports which reach the Soviet Union from disgruntled Soviet émigrés. The seemingly selective character of Soviet Jewish emigration is also a factor to be considered. Soviet authorities have granted a disproportionately large number of visas to Jews from major urban centers where secular and assimilationist tendencies are stronger, while denying them to persons from smaller, geographically isolated regions. Individuals from the latter regions are more prone to go to Israel as they come from areas where Jewish religious and cultural life has been preserved to some extent.

Factors Influencing Emigration from Israel

The phenomenon of emigration from Israel, disturbing as it is to most Jews both in Israel and the diaspora, is on the upswing. Immigration to Israel by American Jews is at a low annual rate of 2,000-3,000.[3]

The problem is not new. At various times in the past, when conditions deteriorated, many — including dedicated Zionists — left. But whereas in prestatehood days and up to the Six-Day war those departing were mainly immigrants who for one reason or another had not adjusted to that country, from 1967 on native-born Israelis between the ages of 21 and 35 have accounted for a growing percentage of departures.

The phenomena of *yerida* and *yordim* came to the forefront of people's minds at the very moment Israel was in an exalted, happy mood and when the economy appeared to be taking off. The period of relative prosperity following the Six-Day war enabled Israelis to travel and learn about a world they had not known before, or one they thought was out of their reach. Seemingly, the belief that the country was militarily and politically more secure than it had ever been led to a relaxation of some of the psychological barriers to emigration imposed by the notion that to leave involved deserting a beleaguered community.

The days of *chalutzim* and *chalutziut* have long since given way to the conventional model of a modern, materialistic, highly competitive consumer society. Even the Israeli army, once envisioned by Ben-Gurion as the great social equalizer, has unwittingly evolved an ethnic-related social pecking order. Years of foreign aid and cultural exchange with the West have elevated the average Israeli's status expectations far beyond those of the original settlers who dreamed of a free, democratic Jewish state where all forms of labor had dignity and where income differentials were minimal. With the loosening of ideological frameworks accelerated by increasing urbanization, personal fulfillment — whether through financial success or educational or professional achievement — has become the primary target of many a war-weary Israeli.

The shift in emphasis from community to self has played a major role in leading over 15 percent of that country's population to go abroad in search of greener fields. This trend reached a peak following the 1973 Yom Kippur war, as cumulative effects of four wars were beginning to take their toll. Public morale was at a new low. As long as Israelis had perceived their sacrifices as vital to the achievement of the greater cause for which all were struggling, they were ready to accept the constraints imposed upon them by a prolonged situation of no-war-no-peace. But as economic gaps became more blatant and cases of corruption among the country's upper echelons came to light, people began to question whether constant belt-tightening was essential; resentment of those who seemed to get ahead because of personal influence grew and discontent increased.

It is highly probable that most of those who leave sincerely believe they will return. The reasons they give for going are often their conscious motives. Social science research by a number of Israeli scholars has focused on these factors (Elizur, 1974, 1979; Fein, 1978; Toren, 1976). On the "pull" side, Israeli emigrants mention the perception of America as a country with a greater and more mobile opportunity structure, where the able can enjoy a higher income and standard of living. Second on the list is a set of reasons involving the availability of superior educational and professional training in certain fields. Some, of course, mention curiosity to get to know a land which sounds interesting, or simply a thirst for new experiences.

On the "push" side, Israelis cite various features of Israeli society which they find disagreeable: skyrocketing inflation, heavy taxation, severe housing shortages, a bloated bureaucracy, excessive government intervention in one's life, lack of sufficient incentives and opportunities for private initiative, and the like. They particularly stress various aspects of Israeli life such as *protectzia* (connections). It is connections some say, rather than merit, which enable one to get ahead. Linked to this are complaints of discrimination against people who do not belong to the upper-status ethnic groups, comprised disproportionately of Jews of East European origin. Rarely do such reasons as lengthy military reserve duty, physical danger, or other security considerations get mentioned. Seemingly, social pressure to uphold the stereotype of the Sabra as the indefatigable fighter is so considerable as to inhibit expression of such feelings.

Jewish Commitment to Education

Growing emigration from Israel should also be considered within the context of two traits Jews have carried with them for hundreds of years: a stress on learning and high achievement values, and a lack of commitment to place. Given the high achievement values Jews brought with them from the Western diaspora, Israel has always had many more persons seriously aspiring to professional status in areas such as medicine, academia, engineering, and other professions than it requires.[4]

Ironically, opportunity for upward mobility, higher education, professional status, is necessarily much more limited for Jews in Israel than it is for their brethren in North America, in Europe, or in Australasia, where the small minority of Jews can realistically hope to be located in the privileged sectors of their societies. In America, over three-quarters of Jewish youth attend colleges or universities. In Israel, less than one-quarter do. The six million Jews in the United States include 60,000 professors. Israel has less than 5,000 people in academic positions. Competition for the limited number of high-status positions is very harsh. Israel's high school system, modeled on the German, limits access to higher education and the professions to those who can do well in an extremely demanding curriculum. Second-chance institutions, prevalent in America, are virtually nonexistent in Israel.

The socialist intellectuals who founded the kibbutzim and the Histadrut envisioned a Jewish state with a social structure that would not only include Jewish intellectuals, physicians, engineers, bankers, and business people, but also taxi drivers, laborers, factory workers, cargo handlers and the myriad of other working-class occupations. They were, however, not able to invert the stratification values characteristic of all complex societies, which esteem occupations linked to learning and/or making money. Jews everywhere in the Western diaspora, including Eastern Europe, have been disproportionately successful in such pursuits. Unfortunately perhaps for Israel, most of those who moved to the Jewish state retained high aspirations. And strikingly, the dominant European Ashkenazi population which shaped the basic culture of the society, succeeded in transmitting its achievement values to many of those who came from Middle Eastern countries where Jews had been less able to aspire upwards in large numbers. That success, paradoxically, is manifest in the growing number of Israeli-born Sephardim among immigrants to the United States.

The Wandering Jew

The propensity of Israelis for migration must also be placed in the context of the limited Jewish commitment to place. Geographic mobility remains a distinct Jewish characteristic reflecting the fact that for over two millennia most Jews lived as pariahs or second-class citizens. American Jews have not been as mobile in emigrating as others, perhaps because no other country offers them greater opportunity, but also because America is a populous society spanning a large continent around which they can freely migrate. As Americans, they have given particular bent to their geographic restlessness through tourism. Holding income level constant, Jews are much more likely to travel long distances and go abroad for vacations than other Americans.

The Jews of Israel are still Jews, even though they have come "home." For many, life in a tiny Middle Eastern state sealed off from its neighbors is claustrophobic. For others, particularly the well educated, it is provincial, isolated from cosmopolitan centers. Zionist ideology and the experience of living in a Jewish society have not eliminated the urge to move around.

Life in America

Whatever the reasons for leaving, the great majority of Israelis believe they are only departing temporarily. But like many others who have gone abroad, what is planned as a limited stay often turns into permanent residence. A study of returning Israelis (Toren, 1976) has shown that the minority who go back are drawn almost exclusively from Israelis who have been in the United States for less than five years. Hence, efforts to bring Israelis back home must necessarily concentrate on more recent arrivals. In the words of Avner Michaeli, director of the Israeli Ministry of Labor's New York-based Bureau for Israeli Professionals in the United States and Canada: "We must catch the *yored* at the right moment . . . the moment he has reached the conclusion that the U.S. will not greatly change his economic situation, when he is disillusioned, and before he has struck roots and gotten used to the American standard of living."

The desire to return to Israel is strongly associated with emotional sentiments rather than material and practical considerations. The most important motives voiced for going back are generally of a nonmaterialistic character. They include national allegiance and a sense of belonging to the nation of Israel, the wish to rejoin the family, the children's education and future, and the desire to protect offspring from the American counterculture. Other reasons include avoidance of high tuition for children's schooling and fear of intermarriage.

Nonemployed family members are often decisive in determining attitudes toward returning. If the wife wants to remain or the children object to going back to what has become for them a foreign land, there is little likelihood of reemigration. The reluctant role of the spouse is particularly relevant. Although a little more than half of those sampled in Elizur's surveys were single on emigration, after five years or more in America the great majority had found a mate, usually American-born. (Eight percent of the 1977 sample reported a non-Jewish spouse, a fact which suggests that close to one-fifth of the single immigrants had intermarried. See Elizur, 1979.) A large majority (70 percent) of Elizur's respondents reported continued strong emotional ties with Israel. Their spouses and children were less disposed to feel this way. Most of the Israeli emigrants polled (81 percent) felt more Israeli than American, but this attitude held true for only about half the mates, a third of whom had never lived in Israel, while a majority (61 percent) of their children identified more with America than with Israel.

The ties of Israeli emigrants to their homeland are not simply of nostalgic longing. The overwhelming majority (85 percent) questioned by Elizur have visited Israel at least once since leaving, while more than half of them (59 percent) have been there a number of times. Over three-quarters (79 percent) correspond regularly with friends and relatives back home. Almost all (85 percent) read Israeli newspapers with some frequency, while close to three-fifths (58 percent) listen to Hebrew broadcasts. Half report speaking Hebrew at home.

This commitment to Israel may explain the data which suggest that, unlike most American Jews, Israelis who had become American citizens followed the recommendation of Israeli officialdom that Nixon be supported in 1972 because of his strong commitment to Israel. A study by Esther Smith (1975) indicates that 54 percent voted for Nixon, 28 percent for McGovern, while 12 percent abstained. Estimates of the votes of all American Jews indicate that two-thirds supported McGovern.

The great majority of Israelis in the United States cannot vote since they are not citizens. Most have come on nonimmigrant visas as tourists, students, businessmen, or investors. Some secure residency status by marrying Americans, although a number of marriages are in name only. Others are able to obtain resident status by finding an employer willing to sponsor them. Like the Mexicans, many of the undocumented aliens provide a source of cheap labor, often for fellow Israelis who own factories here and exploit their inability to acquire work permits.

Professionally, Israelis form a broad occupational cross-section, including doctors, engineers, architects, entertainers, cab drivers, small businessmen, diamond merchants, students, and academics. A few have become part of the recently publicized Los Angeles "Israeli Mafia," specializing in insurance frauds through arson, as well as drug peddling and smuggling. Some have risen to fame and fortune: the Nakash brothers, who have made a multimillion dollar enterprise of Jordache jeans; Meshulam Riklis, who controls the Rapid American Corporation; violinists Yitzhak Perlman and Pinchas Zuckerman; former presidential advisor Amitai Etzioni; Universal Studios vice-president Raphi Etkes; singer Theodore Bikel; Harvard's Middle East expert Nadav Safran; and Stanford's Amos Twersky, the world's leading authority on mathematical models in psychology. Others, once well known, have faded into obscurity: Dalia Lavi, Israel's Brigitte Bardot of the early 1960s, has become just another rich Jewish lady living in Miami, as have several of Israel's former beauty queens who married wealthy Americans.

Well educated or not, most new arrivals are forced initially to take lower-status positions at inadequate salaries. To function at such levels in Israel would be unthinkable, or would constitute one of the factors pressing them to emigrate. But in America these jobs are perceived as the first rung on a ladder to that much desired commodity, the "green card" (resident alien permit) and success.

A report on the occupations of new American citizens indicates that Israelis attain a higher socioeconomic status than those from other countries. According to various academic surveys, Israelis are also more likely to report larger incomes and express greater satisfaction with their jobs here than with the positions they held back home. Perception of a more equitable meritocratic reward system here has pressed many to work much harder in the United States than they did at home, to rely more on themselves and less on the system. Israelis come from a country which, although democratic, is highly centralized, so much so that job mobility is often dependent either on someone's retirement or death, or on *proteczia*.

While America seems to have largely lived up to their material expectations, personal relations in this atomized society are distressing to these newcomers who hail from a very intimate, closely knit community. Most Israelis complain that life in America lacks the camaraderie of Israeli society, that Americans are friendly and polite on the surface but hard to get close to.

Changing Attitudes

Until recently Israeli officials have followed an implicit policy of nonrecognition of their expatriates. There is growing recognition, however, that Israeli citizens residing abroad represent a sizable potential population source. Efforts to encourage the remigration of Israelis seem especially worthwhile, as the returnees know the country and its language, so that their consequent reabsorption is inherently easier than the adjustment of new immigrants. Those in authority, however, experience great difficulties in trying to overcome their mixed feelings toward expatriates. While wanting to maintain close ties with the emigrants' children, viewed as potential returnees, officials feel that by extending help to émigrés or establishing special schools for their offspring, they might encourage or facilitate their stay abroad, legitimize their emigration, and thus reduce the guilt feelings of their expatriates — thereby making them less prone to return.

To reduce the rate of emigration and encourage the return of large numbers of those now abroad will require major changes in Israel's economy and culture, reforms which are not likely to occur in the near future even if the peace process proceeds at a more rapid pace than at present. Regardless of what Israel does in the short run, the proportion of emigrants in the United States who fail to go back, will increase. Yael Dayan, daughter of the Israeli foreign minister, emphasizes the doubt of "many of us that they will return home. They were not driven away by war, and peace may not attract them back."

In tandem with a partial shift in the attitude of Israeli authorities, several groups in the American Jewish community have begun to change their views and reach out to Israelis. As one Jewish journalist writes: "There is certainly nothing to be gained by criticizing these people. They made their choice, much as the bulk of American Jewry decided to remain in America." The Los Angeles federation has moved more rapidly than others in establishing a division to organize and raise funds among the estimated 70-100,000 Israelis in the region. A report of a study conducted for the Community Planning Committee of the Federation of Jewish Philanthropies of New York, issued in December 1978, concludes that "the needs of Jews from Israel . . . must be acknowledged. It is . . . to our advantage to attempt to absorb these Jews into the Jewish community, while strengthening their Jewish identity . . . rather than continue on the periphery where they may be isolated and allowed to assimilate."

Following up on this study the New York federation has established an ongoing committee that includes representatives from various Israeli groups in New York, and one staff person to generate ways of involving Israelis in Jewish communal life and putting them in touch with federation agencies. Donald Feldstein, the federation's director of community services, has elaborated sympathetically on the need for a comprehensive program in terms which constitute a sharp reversal of past attitudes of communal leaders:

> I think that in any society there will be a percentage who will emigrate . . . I don't have the hang up that it [emigration from Israel] is treachery. But I think that unfortunately many of the Israelis who come here do, and it's a serious mental health problem, not unlike the problem of Puerto Ricans here

whose kids go back every so often to see their grandparents and still don't know where "home" is . . . . I see a group identified as Jews but equally clearly not identified as religious people, who want some way of maintaining their Jewish identity and connections without being locked into religious schools. . . . We are ready to lend our support in helping them to establish credit unions, and other self-help and advice groups. . . . I don't think we can afford to lose any Jews.

By sheer weight of numbers Israelis in America appear to be breaking down some of the barriers to their acceptance by their fellow Jews in the United States. Hopefully, they will not fall between two stools, but will find their way either into the American Jewish community or they will return to Israel. Until now they have been almost a pariah people, suspended between two worlds, "managing to live with their own guilt and our fair share of resentment," as Yael Dayan put it. If Jews have been the proverbial marginal people, Israeli emigrants are the marginal Jews.

The Need for Research

In spite of the significant role recent Jewish immigrants may be expected to play in the future of the American Jewish community, there has been surprisingly little research in this area. There is considerable journalistic literature on Israelis in America. The few serious studies conducted have focused on the reasons for which Israelis leave, or on factors relevant to the return to Israel by the small minority who do. There has been no systematic research on the life of this group here: its culture, problems, and the extent of its adaptation and integration.

The growing list of publications on Russian Jews is also limited to journalistic descriptions or to analyses of some of their adjustment problems in the social work literature. There are few, if any, analytic sources for other groups including Latin Americans, Canadians, South Africans, and Iranians. We have no precise estimates of how many persons are involved and what their social characteristics are. It appears that many have entered the United States at a fairly high level — as professionals, managers, and business people. To some extent they may be disproportionately represented among those who have contributed intellectual skills to America. Increased international student mobility, which has played a significant role in the brain drain from the less-developed poorer countries to the more affluent, has brought a disproportionate number of Jews to these shores. The available data have not been analyzed with this issue in mind.

The extremely useful detailed ethnographic and statistical analyses of immigrant communities conducted in the decade or so before World War I, were not repeated for the postwar immigration, Jewish or other. Yet new immigrants who may constitute over one-tenth of the Jewish community by the next decade, will necessarily affect the nature of the community, particularly since they are generally much younger than the average American-born Jew, and hence form a much larger proportion of Jews under 35 years of age.

Research Topics

Ethnography

Detailed ethnographic studies of various immigrant groups, insofar as they constitute communities with geographic centers, would give us a benchmark of the values and organization of these ethnic groups in the first generation. Seemingly, Israelis in New York and Los Angeles; Russians in New York, Boston, Los Angeles, and elsewhere; Cubans in Miami; South Africans in Houston and San Diego; and Iranians in Los Angeles, already constitute distinct communities. Ethnographic-oriented scholars should analyze the culture of these groups through participant observation and in-depth interviews. These should focus initially on describing the aspects of national and Jewish culture the immigrants bring with them. It will be interesting to examine how these groups develop here and how they compare with non-Jewish groups from similar national backgrounds.

Demography

Given the unavoidable implications of the low birth rate of native American Jews, it would be particularly important to study the demographic behavior of new immigrants to see to what extent and how quickly they accommodate to American patterns.

Jewish Identity

Jewish identity, knowledge of Judaism, and degree of Jewish commitment vary greatly among the different national groupings. Jews from many parts of Latin America, Canada, and South Africa have been reared in communities in which secular *Yiddishkeit* remains much stronger than in the United States. Israelis come with considerable knowledge of Jewish culture, a strong commitment to Israel, but often also with a disdain for diaspora Jewry and its institutions, including what appears to them as watered-down religion. Systematic data should be gathered on the attitudes of samples of these groups toward Jewish matters. The establishment of benchmarks will enable systematic comparisons at regular intervals.

The study of Jewish identity should also relate to practice, to information concerning the extent and nature of participation in organized Jewish life and of involvement in Jewish affairs, both before and after the immigrants' arrival in the United States. Does the immigrant experience press people to look to the Jewish community for aid and identification? What aspects of their Jewish identity do immigrants choose to pass on to their children? What are the avenues through which they transmit these values? Which communities and what types of new immigrants are more likely to assimilate into the larger society. Will they fully integrate eventually into the larger American Jewish community, or will some, like the Israelis, form separate groups? What adjustment is required of the Jewish community in order to absorb these newcomers? Is there need for new structures, or perhaps a new way of thinking that will take into account the vast differences in forms of Jewish expression these immigrants have brought with them?

Attitudes toward Israel

While clearly part of the Jewish identity issue, attitudes toward Israel ought to be considered separately in light of their importance. We know a fair amount about the orientations of Israelis but little has been written about the others. In some ways the migration of diverse groups of Jews to the United States constitutes a greater challenge to Israel than the emigration of its own citizens. It was to be expected that Israel, like other immigrant-receiving societies, would inevitably lose many people who could not adjust to its special conditions. But a basic assumption of Zionism has been that Israel would continue to attract diaspora Jewry and that it would be a refuge for those suffering from persecution or political insecurity. The fact that a majority of Russian, South African, Iranian, Argentinian, and other Jews who choose to leave their native lands have decided to go to the United States and other disapora communities, would seem to refute this Zionist premise.

By rejecting Israel, are these people also rejecting Judaism? Do they begin or continue a process which can only lead them or their offspring to total assimilation? It is important to get a sense of how they view Israel, to find out whether they considered going there, and what connection they perceive between their Jewish identity or commitment and their emotional and practical ties to Israel. Having rejected Israel, do they feel psychologically pressed to justify that decision by a negative evaluation of the Jewish state and by a positive response to adverse information about it? Israeli emigrants have dealt with the problem by asserting that they are sojourners, that they will eventually return. The rejectees, to coin a term, cannot maintain such a belief. On the other hand, the combination of past Zionist values, the desire to have a place of refuge, and personal and family relations with Israelis may keep them actively aligned.

Social Mobility

The record of Jewish accomplishment in economic and educational spheres is phenomenal, surpassing all other ethnic communities. Nathan Glazer pointed out years ago, when he reviewed the pre–World War I studies of immigrant Jews, that, although poor and living in slums, they were able to maintain work and study habits characteristic of the middle class — traits which presumably help explain their subsequent success. While the current waves include a large number who come here with a high level of education, some skills, and some money, many still arrive who are less well-off, particularly among Russian Jews and Israelis.

We should seek to obtain knowledge as to the achievement orientation of the various new Jewish immigrant groups as well as their behavior. Such information may shed considerable light on the sources of past Jewish achievement. A close look at these groups will extend our knowledge of the immigrant experience. First-hand observations will yield insights about the nature of the absorption experience unavailable in works based on retrospective materials.

Finally, we would reiterate our recommendation that a detailed ethnography of a number of new immigrant groups be undertaken, one which relies on diverse methods drawn from all the social sciences. American Jewry missed a major opportunity when it ignored a large number of immigrants who came here between the two wars and immediately following. We should not do so again.

Notes

1. Since emigration is a highly emotional and politicized issue, Israeli authorities seek to minimize the numbers involved. The most commonly employed official definition considers an emigrant one who has been out of the country for at least four years without returning for a visit. Hence the many Israeli emigrants who visit their homeland at regular intervals are not counted as such.
2. American official statistics also do not yield reliable estimates, partly because many Israelis come on the passports of other countries or on nonimmigrant visas — as tourists, students, businessmen, and then remain here illegally. American classification of immigrants by country of birth and not by citizenship further complicates the count. Three years ago a high-placed U.S. government official estimated that there were 300,000 Israelis living permanently in the United States. The 1970 U.S. Census reported 100,000 people in families in which Hebrew is the main language spoken at home.
3. There are vast differences in the characteristics of those who move in each direction. Those who move to Israel from the United States are drawn heavily from the more religious, Orthodox, more Jewishly-active sector. Conversely, those who leave Israel come disproportionately from the least religious, most secularized elements. Lest it be concluded that the interchange must undercut the Jewishness of the diaspora, it should be noted that the Israelis, though secu-

larized, are obviously much more steeped in Hebrew and Israeli-Jewish culture than Western Jews. They are necessarily fluent in the Hebrew language. Furthermore, living abroad seems to have intensified their continual identification with Israel as their homeland, much as it has done for emigrants from various European nations. The selective character of emigration from and immigration to Israel suggests changes in the composition of its population which may have long-range effects on Israeli culture and politics in the direction of stronger nationalism and an increase in orthodoxy.

4. In 1948, the Jewish population of the new state had a higher proportion of university graduates than any other country in the world, including the United States.

References

Elizur, D., *Israelis in the U.S.: Motives, Attitudes, and Intentions* (Bar Ilan University and the Israel Institute of Applied Social Research, Jerusalem, 1979, monograph).

Elizur, D., and Elizur, M., *Stay or Leave? The Tendency to Emigrate among Soviet Immigrants* (Israel Institute of Applied Social Research, Jerusalem, 1976, monograph).

Elizur, D., and Elizur, M., "The Long Way Back: Attitudes of Israelis Residing in the U.S. and in France toward Returning to Israel," *Israel Yearbook* (1974).

Fein, A., "The Process of Migration: Israeli Emigration to the U.S." (Ph.D. thesis, Case Western Reserve University, 1978).

Gidwitz, B., "Problems of Adjustment of Soviet Jewish Emigres," *Soviet Jewish Affairs* 6, no. 1 (1976).

Gitelman, Z., "Soviet Immigration and American Absorption Efforts: A Case Study in Detroit," *Journal of Jewish Communal Service* 55 (Fall 1978).

Gitelman, Z., "Soviet Jewish Emigrants: Why Are They Choosing America?" *Soviet Jewish Affairs* 7, no. 1 (1977).

Glaser, W., and Haber, C., "Migration and Return of Professionals," *International Migration Review* 8, no. 6 (Summer 1974).

Halevy, Z., "Were the Jewish Immigrants to the U.S. Representative of Russian Jews?" *International Migration* 16, no. 2 (1978).

Jacobson, G.I., "The International Migration Factor," *Journal of Jewish Communal Service* 53, no. 4 (Summer 1977).

Johnson, G.E., "Which Promised Land? The Realities of the American Absorption of Soviet Jews," *Analysis* (Synagogue Council of America) 47 (November 1974).

Kass, D., and Lipset, S.M., "America's New Wave of Jewish Immigrants," *New York Times Magazine* (December 7, 1980).

Kass, D., and Lipset, S.M., "Israelis in Exile," *Commentary* 68, no. 5 (November 1979).

Levenfeld, B., "Recent Soviet Immigration to the U.S.," *Contemporary Jewry* 3, no. 2 (Spring-Summer 1977).

Levin, D.P., "Israelis in America: Profiles from the New Promised Land" (M.A. thesis, Columbia University, 1975).

Liebman, A., *Jews and the Left* (New York: Wiley, 1978).

Nahshon, G., "Israelis in America: Moral Lepers," *Midstream* 22, no. 8 (October 1976).

Peterson, W., "International Migration," *Annual Review of Sociology* 4 (1978).

Ritterband, P., "The Determinants of Motives of Israeli Students Studying in the U.S.," *Sociology of Education* 42, no. 4 (Fall 1969).

Samuel, T.J., "Migration of Canadians to the U.S.A.: The Causes," *International Migration* 7, no. 3–4 (1969).

Smith, E., "A Comparative Assessment of the Relative Adjustment of Two Basic Ethnic Groups Concerning their Resettlements in the U.S." (Ph.D. thesis, University of Illinois, Urbana, 1975).

Taft, E., "Absorption of Soviet Jewish Immigrants," *Journal of Jewish Communal Service* 54, no. 2 (Winter 1977).

Teitelbaum, M.S., "Right versus Right: Immigration and Refugee Policy in the United States," *Foreign Affairs* 59, no. 1 (Fall 1980).

Teller, H., "The American Welcome to the Russian Immigrants," *Jewish Observer* 13, no. 6 (October 1978).

Toren, N., "Return to Zion," *Social Forces* 54, no. 3 (March 1976).

Waller, H.M., "Montreal Jews Face the Challenge of Quebec Nationalism," *Analysis* 65 (September 1978).

Weinberg, A.A., *Migration and Belonging* (The Hague: Martinus Nijhoff, 1961).

Weiss, D., "Is There a Future for the Montreal Jewish Community?" *Journal of Jewish Communal Service* 56, no. 1 (Fall 1979).

Wisse, R.R., and Cotler, I., "Quebec Jews: Caught in the Middle," *Commentary* 64, no. 3 (September 1977).

Index